U0465279

阿 甘 正 传

·中英双语版·

[美]温斯顿·葛鲁姆 著

赵文伟 译

FORREST
GUMP

WINSTON
GROOM

重庆出版集团 重庆出版社

果麦文化 出品

献给金博·米多尔和乔治·拉德克利夫——
他们一直善待阿甘和他的朋友们。

第一章

这么说吧：当白痴可不像一盒巧克力。别人会笑话你，对你不耐烦，态度恶劣。现在人们说，要善待受苦之人，但我跟你说，事实上可不总是这样。即便如此，我也没什么怨言，因为，可以这么说，我觉得我的生活过得相当有趣。

我生下来就是白痴。我的智商接近七十，他们说，这个数字挺适合我的。不过，我大概更接近低能儿，甚至傻瓜，但就我个人而言，我宁愿认为自己是个笨蛋什么的——绝对不是白痴——因为，人们一想到白痴，就会想到唐氏综合征——那种两只眼睛离得很近、老流哈喇子、自己跟自己玩的人。

我这个人比较迟钝——我承认这一点，但我可能比人们以为的要聪明得多，因为我脑子里想的东西和人们看到的不太一样。比方说，我能把事情想得挺好，但一说出来，或写下来，就会变成一团糨糊。我给你举个例子，你就明白我的意思了。

一天，我走在街上，有个男人在他家的院子里干活儿。他有一大堆灌木要栽种，他问我："阿甘，你想不想赚点钱？"我说："嗯哼。"于是，他让我运土。大热天的，我用独轮车装了十一二车土，运到各处。我干完活儿，他从口袋里掏出一块钱。他给这么低的工资，我本该跟他大闹一场，但是我没有，而是接过那该死的一块钱,说了句"谢谢"之类的傻话,然后沿着那条街继续往前走,手里攥着那张钞票,揉成一团,再展开,感觉自己像个白痴。

你明白我的意思了吗?

哦,我对白痴有所了解。这大概是我唯一了解的东西了,但我确实读过关于白痴的书——从那个叫陀思妥耶夫斯基的家伙笔下的傻瓜,到李尔王里的傻瓜,再到福克纳笔下的白痴班吉,甚至《杀死一只知更鸟》里的老布·拉德利——哦,他是个真正的白痴。不过,我最喜欢的是《人鼠之间》里的老莱尼。大多数作家说得很清楚,因为他们笔下的白痴总比人们以为的要聪明。啊呀,我同意这个观点。任何一个白痴都会同意。嘻嘻。

我出生后,妈妈给我取名叫福瑞斯特,因为内战时期有个将军叫内森·贝德福德·福瑞斯特。妈妈总说,我们和福瑞斯特将军有点儿亲戚关系。而且她说,他是个了不起的人,只是内战结束后,他创立了三K党,连我奶奶都说那是一群坏蛋。我倒是同意这个说法,因为在我们这儿,那个自称"尊贵的废话"还是什么的家伙在镇上经营一家枪店,有一次,我大概十二岁吧,路过那里,我朝窗户里面看,里面挂着一根很大的绞索。他发现我在看,就把绞索套在自己脖子上,像被绞死那样,把绳子往上一拉,舌头伸出来,他这么做完全是为了吓唬我。我跑开了,躲在停车场的汽车后面,直到有人报警,警察来把我送回家,交给我妈妈。所以说,不管老福瑞斯特将军做过什么,成立那个三K党就不是个好主意——任何一个白痴都会这么告诉你。总之,我的名字就是这么来的。

我妈妈是个大好人。大家都这么说。我出生后不久,我爸爸就死了,所以,我根本不认识他。他在码头当装卸工,一天,一台起重机从联合水果公司的一艘船上吊起很多香蕉,然后,什么东西断了,香蕉砸在我爸爸身上,把他压扁了。有一次,我听到有人谈论那次事故——说惨不忍睹,半吨香蕉把我爸爸压扁在底下。我不太喜欢吃香蕉,除了香蕉布丁。这个我还是很喜欢的。

我妈妈从联合水果公司领到一点儿抚恤金,此外,她把我们家空余的房间租出去了,所以,我们的日子还算过得去。我小时候,她经常把我关在家里,这样,其他孩子就不会打扰到我。夏天的下午,天特别热的时候,她经常把我放在客厅,拉上窗帘,这样,屋里又暗又凉,她给我倒上一壶酸橙汁。然后,她坐下来跟我聊天,一直聊啊,聊啊,没什么特别的话题,就像一个人和小猫小狗说话那样,不过,我习惯了,而且很喜欢,因为她的声音很舒服,让我有安全感。

在我成长的过程中,一开始,她让我出去跟大家玩,但后来,她发现,他们都戏弄我,有一天,他们在后边追我,一个男孩用棍子打我,打得我后背一片红肿。从那之后,她就不让我跟那些男孩玩了。我开始试着跟女孩玩,但情况也没好到哪儿去,她们都躲着我。

妈妈认为读公立学校对我有好处,因为这可能会帮助我变得和其他人一样,但没过多久,校方就来告诉妈妈,我不该和其他人一起上学。不过，他们还是让我念完了小学一年级。有时候，老师讲课的时候，我就坐在那里，我也不知道我脑子里在想什么，窗外有一棵大橡树，我会看小鸟、松鼠，和其他爬上去并坐在那棵树上的东西，然后，老师就会过来训斥我。有时候，我会突然有一种很奇怪的感觉，于是开始大喊大叫，然后，老师就让我出去，坐在走廊的长椅上。其他孩子从来不跟我玩，除了在后面追我，或者惹得我大喊大叫，这样，他们就可以嘲笑我——除了珍妮·柯伦，至少她不躲着我，有时候放了学，她还让我跟她一起走路回家。

但是第二年，他们把我转到了另一所学校，我跟你说，这所学校很奇怪，他们好像到处搜集滑稽的家伙，把他们放在一起，年龄有跟我差不多的，也有比我小的，甚至还有十六七岁的大男孩。他们是各种弱智和癫痫病患者，甚至还有不会自己吃东西、上厕所的小孩。我大概是这群人中最正常的了。

有个男孩，是个大胖子，怎么也有十四岁了，他得了一种病，像坐在电椅上那样浑身发抖。我们的老师玛格丽特小姐让我陪他上厕所，这样，他就不会做出什么怪事，但是他照做不误。我不知道怎么才能拦住他，所以，我干脆把自己锁在一个隔间里，一直在里面待到他做完，然后把他送回教室。

我在那所学校待了五六年。其实，学校还不错。他们让我们用手指画画，做些小东西，但主要教我们做一些——比如怎么系鞋带，不要对着食物流口水，不要发疯、大喊大叫、到处乱扔东西之类的事。对了，他们不教我们课本知识，只教我们认识路牌，区分男厕所和女厕所什么的。学校里那么多疯疯傻傻的人，即使老师想教点儿别的，也不可能。而且，我认为这也是为了不让我们打扰别人。谁会想让一群弱智到处乱跑？这个道理连我都懂。

等我长到十三岁，一些很不寻常的事开始发生。首先，我开始蹿个儿，六个月长了六英寸，妈妈成天帮我把裤子放长。同时，我开始横着长。十六岁时，我身高六英尺六英寸，体重二百四十二磅。我知道，因为他们带我称了重，说他们简直不敢相信。

接下来发生的事给我的生活带来了真正的改变。一天，我从傻瓜学校回家，正在街上溜达，一辆汽车在我身边停下。车里那个人叫我过去，问我叫什么名字，我告诉了他。接着，他问我在哪个学校读书，怎么没在附近见过我。我把傻瓜学校的事告诉了他，他问我打过橄榄球没有。我摇头。其实，我应该告诉他，我见其他孩子打过，但他们从来不让我玩。不过就像我说过的，我不太擅长跟人长谈，所以我只是摇了摇头。那是开学后大概两周的事。

大约过了三天，他们过来把我从傻瓜学校接走了。当时，我妈妈在场，车里那个人和另外两个看上去像打手的人也在场——我猜，他们在场是为了防止我惹事。他们把我书桌里的东西全都掏出来，装进一个牛皮纸袋，然后让我和玛格丽特小姐说再见，突然，她哭了，紧紧抱住我。然后，我和其他傻瓜道别，他们流哈喇子、抽搐、用拳头砸桌子。然后，我就走了。

妈妈和那个家伙坐前面，我坐在后座上，夹在两个打手中间，就像电影里警察带你"进城"那样，只不过我们没进城。我们去了那所新建的高中。到了学校，他们把我带到校长办公室，妈妈和我，还有那个家伙进去，两个打手在走廊里等着。校长是一位白发苍苍的老人，领带上有块污渍，裤子松松垮垮，看上去倒像是刚从傻瓜学校里出来的。我们都坐下来，他开始讲解情况，问我问题，我只是点头，但他们想让我打橄榄球。这都是我自己琢磨明白的。

原来车里那个家伙是橄榄球教练，名叫费勒斯。那天，我没去上课，但费勒斯教练把我带回更衣室，一个打手给我找来一套球服，带各种护垫，还有一顶很棒的塑料头盔，头盔前面有个东西，可以防止我的脸被压扁。唯一的问题是，他们找不到我能穿的鞋，所以我只能暂时穿我自己的运动鞋，等订到合适的球鞋再换上。

费勒斯教练和那两个打手帮我穿上球服，然后让我脱下来，然后再从头来一遍，如此反复十几二十次，直到我能自己穿脱球服为止。唯一不太好穿的是那个护裆，因为我不明白有什么必要穿它。哦，他们试着给我解释，然后，一个打手对另一个打手说我是个"笨蛋"什么的，我猜，他以为我听不懂他说的话，但是我听懂了，因为我会特别留意这种屁话。不是因为这种话会令我不悦。见鬼，有的人骂的比这难听多了。但我还是注意到了。

过了一会儿，一群孩子走进更衣室，取出他们的橄榄球用具，穿戴整齐。然后，我们全都走到外面，费勒斯教练把所有人叫到一起，他让我站在他们面前，把我介绍给大家。他说了一堆屁话，我没听太懂，因为我吓坏了，从来没有人当着一群陌生人介绍过我。但后来，有些人走过来跟我握手，说很高兴认识我。然后，费勒斯教练吹了一声哨子，吓得我魂飞魄散，大家开始跳来跳去，进行热身活动。

接下来发生的事说来话长，但总之，我开始打橄榄球了。我不会打球，费勒斯教练和其中一个打手给予了我特别的帮助。我们有个拦截对手的技术动作，他们努力跟我解释，但我们试了好多次，大家似乎都厌烦了，因为我总也记不住该怎么做。

然后，他们尝试了另一种他们称为防守的方法，他们让三个人挡在我面前，我要穿过他们，抓住那个带球的人。第一部分比较容易，因为我可以把他们推倒，但他们对我抓住那个带球的人的方式不满意，最后，他们让我去擒抱一棵大橡树，大概十五到二十次吧，我猜是为了让我找找感觉。过了一阵子，他们觉得我已经从橡树那儿学到了一些东西，就又让我和那三个家伙，还有那个带球的人练习，后来，他们生气了，因为摆脱其他人后，我没有凶狠地扑到带球队员身上。那天下午，我挨了不少骂，但训练结束后，我去见了费勒斯教练，告诉他，我不想扑到那个带球的人身上，我怕伤到他。教练说，伤不到他，因为他穿着橄榄球服，而且还佩戴了护具。其实，我并不是很担心伤到他，而是害怕如果我对大家不太好，他们会生我的气，又开始追着我打。长话短说，我花了一段时间才摸清门路。

打球的同时，我还要上课。在傻瓜学校，我们几乎无事可做，但在这儿，他们对待学业要认真得多。反正，他们给我安排好了课程表，我有三节自习课，你就坐在那儿，想干什么就干什么，还有三节课，一位女士教我识字。只有我们两个人。她长得特别漂亮，我不止一次对她动过邪念。她叫亨德森小姐。

我唯一喜欢的课是午餐，但我估计，午餐不算是一门课。上傻瓜学校的时候，妈妈会给我准备一份三明治、一份曲奇饼干和一份水果——除了香蕉——我会带到学校去吃。但这所学校有一个自助餐厅，有十来种吃的，我总是拿不定主意吃什么。我想，一定是有人说了什么，因为大约一个星期后，费勒斯教练朝我走过来，跟我说，想吃什么就吃什么，都"安排妥当了"。老天，太棒了！

你猜谁来我的自习教室了，除了珍妮·柯伦，还能是谁？她从走廊朝我走来，说她从小学一年级就记得我。她出落成大姑娘了，一头乌黑的秀发，两条大长腿，一张漂亮的脸蛋，还有别的东西，但我不敢讲。

橄榄球队的情况并不完全符合费勒斯教练的心意。他似乎很生气，总对人大喊大叫。他也对我大喊大叫。他们试着想办法让我待在原地不动，不让其他人抓住我方带球的人，但除非他们把球传到中线，否则这个方法不管用。教练对我的阻截也不太满意，我告诉你吧，我在那棵橡树上花了不少时间。但我就是做不到像他们希望的那样扑倒带球的人。我好像有什么顾忌。

后来有一天发生的事，改变了这一切。在自助餐厅，我取了食物，走过去坐在珍妮·柯伦旁边。我不想这么说，但她的确算是我在这个学校唯一的熟人，而且和她坐在一起感觉很好。大多数时候，她并不注意我，而是和别人说话。一开始，我和几个橄榄球运动员坐在一起，但他们好像把我当隐形人。至少珍妮·柯伦当有我这么个人在。但过了一段时间，我注意到另一个家伙也经常在，他开始拿我开涮。说什么"笨蛋怎么样"之类的屁话。这种情况持续了一两个星期，我什么也没说，但最后，我说——我到现在都不敢相信我说过这种话——但我说，"我不是笨蛋"，那个家伙看着我，开始哈哈大笑。珍妮·柯伦让那个家伙闭嘴，但他拿起一盒牛奶，倒在我腿上，我跳起来跑了出去，因为我吓坏了。

大约过了一天，我在走廊上碰到那个家伙，他朝我走过来，说要"打我一顿"。我战战兢兢了一整天，那天下午晚些时候，我离开教室去体育馆的时候，他在那儿，还有他的一群朋友。我想走另一条路，但他来到我跟前，推我的肩膀。他说我各种坏话，叫我"笨蛋"什么的，还照着我的肚子来了一拳。虽然不怎么疼，但我还是哭了，我转身就跑，听到他在我身后，其他人也在后面追我。我以最快的速度朝体育馆飞奔，穿过橄榄球训练场，突然，我看到了费勒斯教练，他正坐在露天看台上看着我。追我的那几个家伙停下来，走开了，费勒斯教练的表情很奇怪，他叫我立刻换上球衣。过了一会儿，他走进更衣室，手上拿着一张纸，上面画着三种战术——三种——

叫我尽量记牢。

那天下午训练的时候，他把大家排成两队，突然，四分卫把球递给我，我应该沿着右边线，跑向球门柱。他们都开始追我的时候，我就拼命跑——我闪过七八个人才被他们扑倒。费勒斯教练高兴极了，上蹦下跳，大喊大叫，拍大家的背。我们之前比过很多次，看我们能跑多快，但我想，有人追我的时候，我跑得快多了。哪个白痴不是这样呢？

总之，从那以后，我受欢迎多了，队里的其他人也比以前对我好了。我们打了第一场比赛，我吓死了，但是，他们把球传给我，我达阵两三次，从那以后，大家对我前所未有地友善。这所高中确实开始改变我的生活，甚至让我喜欢上了带球跑，不过，他们主要是让我绕着边线跑，因为我还是做不到在中间把人撞倒。一个打手说，我是全世界块头最大的高中中卫。我不认为他是在夸我。

此外，我还跟亨德森小姐学识字，进步不小。她给了我一本《汤姆·索亚历险记》，还有另外两本书，我不记得书名了，我把书带回家看，但后来，她给我做了个测试，成绩不怎么样。可我真的很喜欢那几本书。

过了一阵子，我又回到自助餐厅，挨着珍妮·柯伦坐，很长一段时间没有遇到过任何麻烦。但后来，春天的一天，我放学后走在回家的路上，那天那个把牛奶倒在我腿上，又追我的男孩出现了。他手里拿着根棍子，骂我"白痴""笨蛋"什么的。

有人看热闹，然后，珍妮·柯伦来了，我又想逃走，但不知道为什么，我没有这么做。那个家伙拿棍子戳我的肚子，我对自己说，管他呢，我抓住他的胳膊，用另一只手敲他的脑壳，这件事差不多就这样结束了。

那天晚上，妈妈接到那个男孩父母打来的电话，说如果我再碰一下他们的儿子，他们就报警，把我"关起来"。我试着跟妈妈解释，她说她明白，但我感觉她很担心。她告诉我，我现在长得人高马大，做事要小心点儿，因为我可能会伤到别人。我点点头，向她保证，我不会再伤到别人了。那天晚上，我躺在床上，听见她在她的房间里偷偷哭。

不过，敲那个男孩脑壳的事，让我对打橄榄球有了全新的认识。第二天，我要求费勒斯教练让我直接带球往前冲，他说可以，于是我撞翻四五个人，直到摆脱擒抱，他们不得不再次开始追我。那年，我入选了全州橄榄球队。我简直不敢相信。我生日那天，妈妈送我两双袜子和一件新衬衫。她攒了些钱，给我买了一套新西装，我穿着它去领全州橄榄球奖。这是我的第一套西装。妈妈给我系好领带，我就出发了。

第二章

全州橄榄球盛会将在一个叫弗洛马顿的小镇举行，费勒斯教练把它形容为"道岔"。我们这一带有五六个人获奖，我们坐上一辆送我们去那里的巴士。巴士开了一两个小时才到，车上没有厕所，出发前，我还喝了两杯思乐冰，所以等我们到了弗洛马顿，我都快憋坏了。

大会在弗洛马顿高中礼堂举行，进去后，我和其他几个人找到厕所。可是，不知怎的，拉裤子拉链时，拉链夹住了衬衫下摆，拉不下去了。我费了半天劲，后来，对手学校一个好心的小家伙出去找费勒斯教练，他带着那两个打手进来，他们试图把我的裤子脱下来。一个打手说，只有一个方法，干脆扯开。听他这么说，费勒斯教练双手叉腰，说："我猜，你是希望我让这个孩子就这样出去，门襟大开，那个玩意吊在外头——你觉得这会给人留下什么印象？"说完，他转过身对我说："阿甘，你先憋着点儿，等这个事结束后，我们再帮你把裤子弄开，好不好？"我点点头，因为我不知道还能怎么办，但我想，我将在这里度过一个漫长的夜晚。

我们走进礼堂时，成千上万的人围坐桌旁，见我们走出来，大家微笑鼓掌。我们被安排坐在主席台上一张大长桌前，面向大家，我最担心的事发生了，果然，这是一个漫长的夜晚。礼堂里的人似乎都要上台发言，连侍者和门房也不例外。我多么希望妈妈在，因为她会帮我，可是，她得了流感，在家躺着。最后，轮到我们领奖了，奖杯是一个金色的小橄榄球，当叫到我们的名字时，我们应该走到麦克风前领奖，说声"谢谢"，他们还告诉我们，如果有谁还有什么要说的，请尽量简短，因为我们想在新世纪到来之前离开这里。

几乎所有人领完奖，说声"谢谢"就走了，然后，轮到我。有人对着麦克风喊"福瑞斯特·甘"，如果我之前没告诉你的话，甘是我的姓，于是，我站起来，走过去，他们把奖杯递给我。我俯身对着麦克风说"谢谢"，所有人从座位上站起来欢呼鼓掌。我猜，有人事先告诉过他们我是个白痴什么的，所以，他们表现得特别友善。但这一切我十分震惊，我不知如何是好，于是愣在那里。然后，全场安静下来，麦克风前面那个人凑过来问我还有什么要说的。于是，我说："我要尿尿。"

观众席上鸦雀无声，大家一脸滑稽的表情，你看看我，我看看你，接着开始小声嘀咕。费勒斯教练走过来，抓住我的胳膊，把我拉回到座位上。他瞪了我一晚上，但宴会结束后，教练和打手把我带到厕所，撕开我的裤子，我尿了一大桶！

"甘，"我尿完，教练说，"你说话可真有一套。"

第二年没什么大事，只是有人散播消息，说有个白痴进了全州橄榄球队，于是从全国各地寄来一大堆信，妈妈把它们收集起来，开始做剪贴簿。一天，从纽约寄来一个包裹，里面有一只棒球联赛指定用球，上面有纽约洋基队所有队员的签名。这是我遇到的最好的事！我把那只棒球当金砖一样珍惜，直到有一天，我在院子里随便抛球，一只大狗跑过来，一口叼住，把球咬烂了。我总遇到这种事。

一天，费勒斯教练叫我过去，把我带到校长办公室。那里有一个大学来的人，他和我握了手，问我想没想过去大学打橄榄球。他说他们一直在"观察"我。我摇摇头，因为我没想过。

大家似乎都很敬畏这个人，对他点头哈腰，称呼他"布赖恩特先生"。但他让我叫他"大熊"，我觉得这个名字很好玩，不过，他在某些方面确实像熊。费勒斯教练指出，我不是一个很聪明的人，但大熊说，他的大部分球员都这样，他想找人给我补补课。过了一个星期，他们给我做了一次测试，里面有各种我不熟悉的、古怪的问题。过了一会儿，我觉得无聊，就不肯再答题了。

两天后，大熊又来了，我被费勒斯教练拽进校长办公室。大熊愁眉苦脸，但态度依然亲切；他问我那次考试我尽力了没有。我点点头，但校长翻了个白眼，大熊说："哦，那太遗憾了，因为分数似乎表明，这个男孩是个白痴。"

这次，校长点了点头，费勒斯教练站在那里，双手插兜，脸色很难看。我去大学打橄榄球的事好像没戏了。

我笨到不能去大学打橄榄球这个事实似乎对美国陆军没有丝毫影响。那是我上高中的最后一年，春天，其他同学都毕业了。不过，他们也让我坐在台上，甚至给了我一件黑袍子，轮到我的时候，校长宣布，他们将给我颁发一张"特殊"文凭。我站起来，走到麦克风前，两个打手也站起来跟着我走——我猜，这样我就不会说出我在全州橄榄球盛会上说过的那种话。妈妈坐在台下前排，她流着泪，扭绞双手，我的心情好极了，就像真的完成了某个任务似的。

可是，当我们回到家，我才明白她为什么痛哭，而且哭个没完——陆军来了一封信，说我必须去当地的征兵委员会报到。我不知道这是怎么回事，但我妈妈知道——那是一九六八年，即将发生各种鸟事。

妈妈给了我一封校长写的信，让我交给征兵委员会的人，但不知道怎么搞的，去征兵委员会的路上，我把那封信弄丢了。征兵的场景很疯狂。一个身穿陆军军装的大块头黑人冲着大家吼叫，把大家分成几组。我们都站在那儿，他走过来喊道："好了，我要你们一半人去那边，一半人来这边，另一半人留在原地不动！"大家转来转去，一脸困惑，连我都能看出这家伙是个笨蛋。

他们把我带进一个房间，让我们排好队，命令我们脱下衣服。我不太情愿，但其他人都这么做了，我也只好这么做。他们检查了我们身上的每一个地方——眼睛、鼻子、嘴巴、耳朵——甚至我们的私处。某一刻，他们命令我"弯腰"，我弯下腰时，有人把手指塞进我的屁眼。

够了！

我转过身，抓住那个浑蛋，照着他的脑袋就是一拳。突然，一阵骚动，一群人跑过来，扑到我身上。不过，我已经习惯别人这么对待我了。我把他们甩开，跑出门去。我回到家，把事情的经过告诉了妈妈，她很心烦，但她说："别担心，阿甘，一切都会好起来的。"

结果没有。下个星期，一辆面包车停在我家门口，一群身穿陆军军装、头戴闪亮黑头盔的人敲门找我。我躲在我的房间，但妈妈走过来说，他们只是想开车送我回征兵委员会。一路上，他们紧盯着我，好像我是个疯子。

他们有一扇门通向一间大办公室，办公室里坐着一位老人，身穿笔挺的军装，他上上下下仔细打量了我一番。他们让我坐下来，又把一张考卷推到我面前，虽然比大学橄榄球队考试简单得多，但仍旧不是很容易。

做完测试，他们带我去另一个房间，那里有四五个人坐在一张长桌旁，他们开始问我问题，还传看好像是我的考卷的东西。然后，他们凑在一起，商量了一下，商量完，其中一人签署了一份文件，然后把文件递给我。我把那份文件带回家，妈妈读后，扯头发，流眼泪，赞美上帝，因为纸上写的是"暂缓征召"，因为我是个傻瓜。

那个星期还发生了一件事——我生命中的一件大事。和我们住在一起的一位女房客在电话公司上班，是个接线员。她叫弗伦奇小姐。她是一位非常和善的淑女，大部分时间不与人来往，但是，一天晚上，天特别热，外面打着雷，下着雨，我从她门前经过时，她探出头来，对我说："阿甘，今天下午我刚买了一盒很好吃的奶油蛋白软糖——你想吃一块吗？"

我说"想"，然后，她把我领进她的房间，软糖放在梳妆台上。她给了我一块，接着，她又问我要不要再来一块，然后，她指着床，让我坐下。我吃了十来块软糖，外面电闪雷鸣，窗帘被风吹起，弗兰奇小姐推了我一把，让我躺在床上。她开始用一种很私密的方式抚摸我。"你把眼睛闭上就行，"她说，"没事的。"接下来，你知道吗，发生了一件从没发生过的事。我也说不清那是什么，因为我一直闭着眼睛，也因为，万一妈妈知道了，她肯定会宰了我，不过，我跟你说——它让我对未来有了全新的看法。

问题是，尽管弗兰奇小姐是一位和蔼可亲的淑女，但她那天晚上对我做的事，我更希望是珍妮·柯伦对我做的。可是，对我来说，这是根本不可能的，想都别想，就我这副德行，向任何女生提出邀约都不是一件容易的事。这还是委婉的说法。

但有了这个新的经历，我鼓起勇气问妈妈该怎么约珍妮出来，当然，我对我和弗兰奇小姐的事只字未提。妈妈说把这事交给她办，她打电话给珍妮·柯伦的妈妈，跟她解释了一下情况，第二天晚上，你瞧，珍妮·柯伦居然出现在我们家门口！

她打扮得很漂亮，穿了一条白色的连衣裙，头上插着一朵粉红色的花，我做梦都没想到她会这么美。她进门了，妈妈把她带到客厅，给了她一杯冰淇淋饮料，妈妈叫我下楼，我一看到珍妮·柯伦沿着小路走过来，就跑回我的房间去了。我宁愿五千个人在后面追我，也不愿意这个时候走出房间，但是妈妈上楼来，拉着我的手，把我领下楼，也给了我一杯冰淇淋饮料。这样我就没那么紧张了。

妈妈说，我们可以去看场电影，我们走出门时，她给了珍妮三块钱。珍妮从没对我这么好过，有说有笑，我则不停地点头，咧着嘴笑，像个白痴。电影院离我们家只有四五个街区，珍妮买了两张电影票，我们走进电影院，坐了下来。她问我要不要吃爆米花，等她买完爆米花回来时，电影已经开演了。

这是一部关于两个人，一男一女，"邦尼与克莱德"，抢劫银行的电影，电影里还有其他几个有趣的人物，但也有很多开枪杀人的鬼东西。我觉得人们这样开枪互杀挺滑稽的，所以每当出现这种场景，我都会哈哈大笑，可是我一笑，珍妮·柯伦似乎总是蜷缩在座位里。电影看到一半时，她几乎蜷缩在地上。我突然看到这一幕，以为她从座位上掉下去了，于是伸手抓她的肩膀，想把她拉起来。

我这么一拉，就听见什么东西撕裂的声音，我低头一看，珍妮·柯伦的裙子被整个撕开了，所有东西都露在外面。我伸出另一只手，想帮她遮一遮，但她叫起来，胡乱踢打，我试图抓住她，这样她就不会再次摔倒，或者衣服掉下来，周围有人回头看，想知道这么热闹到底出了什么事。突然，一个家伙沿着过道走过来，拿刺眼的手电筒照我和珍妮，由于暴露在众人面前，珍妮开始尖叫、痛哭，然后跳起来，一溜烟儿跑出了电影院。

接下来，我只知道两个男人过来叫我站起来，我跟着他们进了一间办公室。几分钟后，四个警察到了，叫我跟他们走。

他们把我带上一辆警车，两个人坐前面，两个人和我一起坐在后面，就像和费勒斯教练的那两个打手一样，不过，这次我们确实进了城。他们押着我进了一个房间，录指纹，拍照，然后把我投入监狱。这是一次可怕的经历。我一直很担心珍妮，但过了一会儿，我妈妈出现了，她走进来，用手帕擦眼泪，扭绞着手指，我知道我又有麻烦了。

几天后，法院举行了某种仪式。妈妈给我穿上西装，带我去那里，我们遇到一个留着小胡子、拎着一个大提包、面容亲切的男人，他跟法官说了一大堆话，然后其他人——包括我妈妈——也说了一些屁话，最后轮到我。

留小胡子的男人拉着我的胳膊，让我站起来，法官问我这一切是怎么发生的？我想不出该说什么，所以只是耸了耸肩，然后，他问我还有什么要补充的吗，我就说："我要尿尿。"因为我们已经在那儿坐了快半天了，我的尿泡都快憋爆了！法官从他那张大桌子后面探出身子，盯着我看，好像我是火星人似的。然后，那个留小胡子的家伙说话了，他说完，法官让他带我去厕所，他带我去了。我们离开房间时，我回头看，正好看到可怜的妈妈抱着头，用手帕揩眼泪。

总之，我回来时，法官挠着下巴，说整件事"非常奇怪"，但他认为我应该去参军什么的，或许可以矫正我的毛病。我妈妈告诉他，美国陆军不要我，因为我是个白痴，但就在那天上午，大学寄来一封信，说如果我愿意为他们打橄榄球，我可以免费去那里上学。

法官说，这件事听起来也有点儿奇怪，但只要我滚出城，他一点儿都不介意。

  第二天早上,我收拾好行李,妈妈带我去汽车站,把我送上巴士。我望向窗外,妈妈一边哭,一边用手帕擦眼泪。这个场景太熟悉了,永久铭刻在我的记忆中。总之,巴士启动,我上路了。

第三章

我们到了大学，布赖恩特教练来到体育馆，我们穿着短裤和运动衫坐在那里，听他讲话。他和费勒斯教练说的内容类似，不过，连我这样的傻瓜都看得出来，他是个说到做到的人！他的讲话简短而又温柔，最后，他说，最后一个上巴士去训练场的人将不会坐巴士，而是坐布赖恩特教练的鞋子去。是，教练。我们丝毫不怀疑他的话，于是像烙饼一样，一个摞着一个挤上了巴士。

这一切都发生在八月，亚拉巴马州比其他地方热一些。也就是说，如果你把鸡蛋放在你的橄榄球头盔上，大约十秒钟就能煎熟。当然，从来没有人这么试过，因为这样可能会惹怒布赖恩特教练。没有人愿意这么做，因为事实上，日子已经快令人无法忍受了。

布赖恩特教练让他的打手们带我四处参观一下。他们把我带到我要住的地方，那是校园里一栋漂亮的砖楼，有人说它叫"人猿宿舍"。打手们开车送我到那里，把我带到楼上我的房间。可惜，外面看着很漂亮的东西，里面看就不一定了。首先，这栋楼好像很久没有人住过似的，到处脏兮兮的，大部分房门被砸烂了，合页被扯掉了，大部分窗户也被砸碎了。

几个人躺在里面的行军床上，几乎没穿衣服，因为屋里的温度有一百一十华氏度，苍蝇等蚊虫嗡嗡直叫。走廊里放着一大摞报纸，一开始，我担心他们让我们读报，这里毕竟是大学，但很快我就得知，他们把报纸铺在地上，这样走路的时候就不会踩到脏东西。

打手们把我带到我的房间，说希望我能在那里见到我的室友，他叫柯蒂斯什么的，但是我没见到他。所以，他们帮我打开行李，告诉我厕所在哪儿，那间厕所看上去比单泵加油站的厕所还要糟糕，然后，他们就走了。但走之前，一个打手说，我和柯蒂斯应该合得来，因为我们俩都呆头呆脑的。我死死盯着说这话的打手，因为我已经听腻了这些屁话，但他让我趴下，做五十个俯卧撑。从那之后，我就乖乖听话了。

我在床上铺了张床单，盖住灰尘，然后躺下来睡着了，我梦见我和妈妈坐在客厅里，像过去天热的时候那样，她给我倒了一杯酸橙汁，跟我聊了好几个小时——突然，房门被撞开了，把我吓个半死！一个男的站在门口，表情狂野，瞪着眼珠，没牙少口的，鼻子像个黄色的南瓜，头发根根竖立，好像他把他那玩意儿插进了插座似的。我猜，这就是柯蒂斯。

他走进房间，好像以为有人会朝他扑过去似的，左瞧瞧，右看看，然后踩着刚被他撞坏的门走了进来。柯蒂斯的个子不是很高，看上去像一台冰箱。他上来就问我是哪里人。听我说是莫比尔，他说那是个无聊的地方，他告诉我他来自奥普，那里生产花生酱，如果我不喜欢，他会亲手打开一罐，把花生酱抹在我屁股上！这就是我们认识一两天的谈话内容。

那天下午训练的时候，球场上的温度大概有一万度，布赖恩特教练的所有打手都在周围跑来跑去，对我们怒吼，逼我们练习。我的舌头像领带一样耷拉下来，但我正尽力做对的事。最后，他们给我们分了组，把我和后卫分在一起，我们开始练习各种跑位传球的技术。

我来大学之前，他们寄给我一个包裹，里面装着大约一百万场不同橄榄球比赛的资料，我问过费勒斯教练，我该怎么处理这个包裹，他只是悲哀地摇摇头，说什么也不用做，等我进了大学，让他们自己想办法。

我真希望当时没听费勒斯教练的话，因为我跑出去第一次传球的时候就转错了方向，头号打手冲过来，对着我大喊大叫，吼了一大通后，他问我难道我没研究过他们寄给我的比赛资料吗？听到我说呃呃，他上蹿下跳，挥动胳膊，好像黄蜂落在了他身上似的。他冷静下来后，命令我绕球场跑五圈，同时他去找布赖恩特教练商量拿我怎么办。

布赖恩特教练坐在一座巨大的塔楼里，大神一样俯视着我们，我一边跑圈，一边看着那个打手爬上去。他爬到最高处后，表明自己的想法，布赖恩特教练伸长脖子，我感觉他灼热的目光盯着我又大又蠢的屁股。突然，扩音器里传来一个声音："阿甘，到教练塔报到。"我看见布赖恩特教练和那个打手爬下来。我一直往那边跑，但我多么希望自己正在朝相反的方向跑。

不过，你可以想象一下，当我看到布赖恩特教练面带笑容时，我心里会有多么惊讶。他示意我去看台，我们坐下，他又问我研究过他们寄给我的比赛资料没有。我开始解释费勒斯教练跟我说过的话，但布赖恩特教练打断我的话，让我回到队伍中接球，然后，我给他讲了一件我猜他不太想听的事，那就是我在高中时从来没接过传球，因为他们觉得，让我记住我们自己的端线（goal line）在哪儿已经够难的了，更何况跑来跑去，还要从半空中接住球。

听到这个情况，布赖恩特教练眯起眼睛，露出一种非常奇怪的目光，他看向远方，好像望着月亮什么的。然后，他让那个打手去拿一个橄榄球，球取来后，布赖恩特教练让我稍微跑出去一点，然后转身，我转身时，他把橄榄球扔给我。我看到球几乎像慢动作一样飞过来，但它从我的手指上弹开，掉在地上。布赖恩特教练上下点头，好像早就料到了似的，但不知怎的，我感觉他不高兴了。

从小，我一做错事，妈妈就会说："阿甘，你要小心，因为他们会把你关起来。"我很害怕被关起来，所以一直尽力做得更好，但无论他们把我关在哪儿，都不可能比我现在住的这个"人猿宿舍"更糟糕。

这里的人干的那些鸟事连傻瓜学校都容忍不了，比如把马桶拆掉，所以你上厕所的时候只能找到地板上的一个坑，你就朝那个坑里拉屎；他们会举起马桶，丢到窗外，有人正好开车经过，就砸在那个人的车顶上。一天晚上，一个打边卫的大块头的傻瓜拿出一支步枪，把街对面兄弟会会所的窗玻璃全都打碎了。校警赶来，但那个家伙把不知道从哪儿找到的一台外置发动机扔出窗外，砸在警车车顶上。布赖恩特教练为此让他多跑了好几圈。

我和柯蒂斯不是很合得来，我从来没感觉如此孤独过。我想妈妈，我想回家。和柯蒂斯相处的麻烦在于，我听不懂他说的话。他说的每一句话都带很多脏字，好不容易弄懂那些脏字是什么，却错过了他说的重点。大多数时候，我猜，他的重点是他对某件事不满意。

柯蒂斯有辆车，他经常开车送我去训练场，但有一天，我去跟他碰头时，他正弯着腰，对着街上一个很大的下水道盖子咒骂怒吼。他的轮胎好像爆了，换轮胎的时候，他把轮毂螺母放在轮毂盖上，结果不小心碰了一下，螺母掉到下水道里去了。我们肯定要迟到了，这可不是什么好事，所以，我对柯蒂斯说："你干吗不从另外三个轮胎上各取下一个轮毂螺母，这样，每个轮胎上就会有三个螺母，撑到训练场应该不成问题吧？"

柯蒂斯不再骂街，他抬起头，看着我说："你应该是个白痴吧，你是怎么想出来的？"我说："也许我是个白痴，但至少我不笨。"听我这么说，柯蒂斯一下子跳了起来，拿着装胎工具追我，用他能想到的最难听的话骂我，这件事几乎毁了我们的关系。

从那之后，我决定另找一个地方住，练完球，我去了"人猿宿舍"的地下室，并在那里度过余下的夜晚。地下室并不比楼上的房间脏，而且有一个电灯泡。第二天，我把我的小床搬到那儿，从那时起，我就开始住地下室。

与此同时，学校已经开学了，他们得想办法安置我。体育系有个家伙，他好像什么都不干，只是想办法安排笨蛋上能通过考试的课。有些课应该很简单，比如体育，他们给我选了这门课。但我还要选一门英文课和一门科学或数学课，这是没有办法的事，怎么都绕不过去。后来我得知，有些老师会放橄榄球运动员一马，这意味着，他们理解他全身心扑在橄榄球运动上，没有太多时间学习。科学系有这样一位老师，可惜的是，他只教一门课，叫"中级光学"，显然，这是为物理还是什么专业的研究生开设的课程。但他们还是让我去修了这门课，尽管我分不清物理（physics）和体育（phys-ed）。

英文课就没这么幸运了。显然，这个系没有什么富有同情心的人，所以，他们告诉我尽管去上课，不及格的话，他们会想别的办法。

修"中级光学"这门课时，他们给了我一本五磅重的教科书，看起来像是中国佬写的。每天晚上，我都会把这本书带到地下室，坐在我的小床上，在那个灯泡下面看，没过多久，出于某种奇怪的原因，我开始看懂了。当初我们为什么要学这门课，这不合理，不过，算出那些方程式对我来说易如反掌。我的老师是胡克斯教授，第一次测验后，他让我下课去他办公室。他说："阿甘，我希望你跟我说实话，是不是有人把答案给你了？"我摇头，于是他递给我一张纸，上面写着一道题，他让我坐下来解出这道题。我做完题，胡克斯教授看着我的解答，摇着头说："伟大全能的主啊！"

英文课则完全是另外一回事。老师是布恩先生，他是一个非常严厉的人，话很多。第一天下课前，他让我们当天晚上坐下来写一篇简短的自传交给他。这大概是我这辈子做过的最难的事，但我熬了大半宿，想一会儿，写一会儿，想到什么就写什么，反正他们跟我说，这门课不及格也无所谓。

过了几天，布恩先生把我们的作业连同他的评语一同发还给我们，还嘲笑每个人写的自传。接着，轮到我的作业，我想，我肯定要丢人了。但是他举起我的作业，念给大家听，他哈哈大笑，其他人也跟着一起笑。我讲了我在傻瓜学校的事，跟着费勒斯教练打橄榄球的事，参加全州橄榄球盛会的事，征兵委员会的事，还有和珍妮·柯伦看电影的事。布恩先生念完我的自传后，说："这才是创造力！这才是我想要的东西。"大家扭过头来看着我，他说："甘先生，你应该考虑进创意写作系——你是怎么想出来的？"我说："我要尿尿。"

布恩先生愣了一下，然后放声大笑，其他人也笑了，他说："甘先生，你真是一个有趣的家伙。"

我再次感到惊讶。

第一场橄榄球比赛定在几周后的一个星期六。训练情况多半很糟糕，直到布赖恩特教练想出拿我怎么办，和费勒斯教练在高中时用过的办法差不多。他们干脆把球交给我，让我跑。那天，我跑得很好，四次达阵得分，我们以大比分——三十五比三——击败佐治亚大学队，所有人拍我的背，把我的背都拍疼了。洗完澡，我打电话给妈妈，她通过收音机收听了比赛，她高兴得快爆炸了！那天晚上，所有人都去参加派对什么的，但没有人邀请我，于是，我回到地下室。我在地下室待了一会儿，后来听到楼上传来音乐声，非常优美，我也不知道为什么，总之，我决定上楼去看看到底是怎么回事。

有一个叫布巴的家伙，坐在他的房间里吹口琴。他训练时脚受伤了，不能上场，也无处可去。他让我坐在一张小床上听他吹口琴，我们没有说话，他坐在一张小床上，我坐在另一张小床上，他吹他的口琴。大约过了一个小时，我问他我可不可以试一下，他说："好的。"我不知道吹口琴这件事将会永远改变我的生活。

我摆弄了一会儿口琴，渐渐地，就吹得相当不错了，布巴兴奋到发疯，说从来没听过这么好听的音乐。天色已晚，布巴让我把口琴带走，我把口琴带回地下室，又吹了很久，直到困了，上床睡觉。

第二天，星期天，我想把口琴还给布巴，但他让我留着，因为他还有一只，我很高兴，然后去散步，坐在树下，吹了一整天，直到没有曲子可吹了。

天色已晚，太阳快落山了，我朝"人猿宿舍"走去。我正穿过四方院子，突然听到一个女孩喊："阿甘！"

我转身一看，我身后竟然站着珍妮·柯伦。

她面带灿烂的笑容，走上前拉住我的手，说她昨天看见我打球了，说我打得真棒。原来她并没有因为那天电影院的事生我的气，她说那不是我的错，那只是件小事。她问我要不要和她一起喝杯可乐。

我竟然和珍妮·柯伦坐在一起,这太美好了,简直令人难以置信。她说她选修了音乐和戏剧课,将来打算做演员或者歌手。她还加入了一个创作民谣音乐的小乐队,她告诉我,他们明天晚上在学生会大楼演出,让我过去看。这么说吧,我已经迫不及待了。

第四章

布赖恩特教练他们想出一个妙招，不能透露给任何人，哪怕是我们自己人。他们一直在教我接球。每天训练结束后，我和那两个打手，还有一个四分卫留下来继续训练，我不停地跑出去接传球，跑出去接传球，直到筋疲力尽，舌头都快耷拉到肚脐眼上了。但渐渐地，我能接住球了，布赖恩特教练说，这将是我们的"秘密武器"——就像"原子弹"之类的，因为过不了多久，其他球队就会发现，队友不把球传给我，他们也就不再提防。

"然后，"布赖恩特教练说，"我们会让你撒开腿跑——六英尺六英寸高，两百四十磅重——跑一百码九秒五。那场面一定非常壮观！"

这会儿，布巴和我已经成了真正的好朋友，他用口琴教会我几支新曲子。有时候，他会来地下室找我，我们坐在一起吹口琴，但布巴说，我吹得比他强多了，他这辈子也吹不了我这么好。我告诉你吧，要不是因为口琴音乐，我可能早就卷铺盖回家了，但口琴让我感觉好极了，这种感觉难以形容，好像我的整个身体是口琴，吹口琴时，音乐使我浑身起鸡皮疙瘩。吹口琴的诀窍主要在于舌头、嘴唇、手指，以及你如何移动脖子。我想，不停跑动接球，让我的舌头伸出来的时间更长，这可以说是个很糟糕的事。

接下来的星期五，我打扮得干净利落，布巴把他的护发素和剃须水借给我用了，然后，我去了学生会大楼。那里有一大群人，果然，珍妮·柯伦和三四个人在台上。珍妮穿长裙，弹吉他，有一个人弹班卓琴，还有一个人拨弄着低音提琴。

他们演奏得很好，珍妮看见我在人群后面，微笑着用眼神示意我坐到前面来。坐在地上看着珍妮·柯伦并听她弹琴，这种感觉太美好了。我心想，过一会儿，我去买点儿软糖，看她是不是也想吃。

他们表演了大约一个小时，所有人看起来都很开心，感觉很好。他们唱了琼·贝兹的歌、鲍勃·迪伦的歌，还有彼得、保罗和玛丽三重唱的歌。我向后靠着，闭着眼睛听，突然，不知怎的，我掏出口琴，跟着他们一起吹了起来。

这事太奇怪了。当时珍妮正在唱《答案在风中飘荡》，我开始吹口琴后，她停下来，班卓琴手也停下来，他们露出讶异的表情，接着，珍妮咧开嘴笑了，继续唱下去，班卓琴手则停下来，让我来一段口琴独奏，我吹完后，所有人鼓掌欢呼。

唱完这首歌，乐队休息了一会儿，珍妮从台上下来，说："阿甘，怎么回事？你在哪儿学的那玩意儿？"总之，从那之后，珍妮让我和他们的乐队一起演出。每周五演出，只要没有在外地的比赛，我一个晚上赚二十五块钱。这简直就是天堂般的生活，直到我发现珍妮·柯伦和班卓琴手睡觉。

可惜，英文课上得不是很顺利。布恩先生在给全班读了我的自传大约一个星期后，把我叫到他的办公室，说："甘先生，我认为你应该停止搞笑，开始认真起来了。"他把我写的关于诗人华兹华斯的作业还给了我。

"浪漫主义时期，"他说，"并非遵循一堆'经典的废话'。诗人蒲伯和德莱顿也不是两坨'臭狗屎'"。

他让我把作业重写一遍，我开始意识到，布恩先生并不知道我是个白痴，但很快他就会发现的。

与此同时，肯定有人对某人说了些什么，因为有一天，我在体育系的辅导员把我叫过去，告诉我不用上课了，第二天早上去大学医学中心的米尔斯医生那里报到。我一大早就去了，米尔斯医生正在翻阅摆在他面前的一大摞文件，他让我坐下，开始问我问题。他问完问题，让我脱衣服——只保留内裤，听他这么说，我松了一口气，因为上次和陆军军医之间发生的事——他开始仔细研究我，直视我的眼睛，还用一把小橡胶锤轻敲我的膝盖骨。

接着，米尔斯医生问我是否介意下午再来一趟，问我能不能带上口琴，因为他听说我会吹口琴，还问我是否介意在他的医学课上演奏一支曲子。我说我愿意，尽管连我这样的傻瓜都会觉得这件事很奇怪。

医学课上有一百来个学生，都系着绿围裙，做着笔记。米尔斯医生让我坐在讲台上的一把椅子上，面前放着一个水罐和一杯水。

他说了一大堆我听不懂的废话，但过了一会儿，我感觉他在说我。

"白痴天才（Idiot savant）。"他大声说，所有人都盯着我看。

"一个人，不会系领带，几乎不会系鞋带，智力只相当于一个六到十岁的孩子水平，在这种情况下，他有一副阿多尼斯的身体。"米尔斯医生对我微笑，我不喜欢他的表情，但我猜，我被困在这里了。

"但是头脑，"他说，"白痴天才的头脑里装着各种罕见的才能，所以这个阿甘能解出把你们所有人都难倒的高级数学方程式，他可以像李斯特或贝多芬那样，轻而易举地掌握复杂的音乐主题。白痴天才。"他又说了一遍，同时朝我这边摆了一下手。

我不知道该做什么，但他之前说让我吹首曲子，于是我掏出口琴，吹起了《神龙帕夫》。大家都坐在那儿看着我，好像我是只虫子什么的，这首歌吹完了，他们还坐在那儿看着我，也不给鼓个掌什么的。我猜，他们不喜欢，所以，我站起来说了声"谢谢"就走了。去他们的。

那个学期剩下的时间，只有两件事还算比较重要。第一件事是我们赢得了全美大学橄榄球锦标赛（the National College Football Championship），并参加了橘子碗。第二件事是我发现珍妮·柯伦和班卓琴手睡觉。

那天晚上，我们本来要在大学的兄弟会派对上表演。下午，我们训练得很辛苦，我渴极了，简直可以像狗一样喝马桶里的水。离"人猿宿舍"五六个街区的地方仅有个小商店，训练结束后，我走过去买酸橙和糖，想给自己做一杯以前妈妈给我做的那种酸橙汁。柜台后面有一个长着斗鸡眼的老女人，她看我的眼神，好像我是个抢劫犯似的。我在找酸橙，过了一会儿，她问："需要我帮忙吗？"我说："我想买几个酸橙。"她告诉我店里没有酸橙。于是，我问她有没有柠檬，因为我觉得柠檬汁也可以，但店里连一个柠檬都没有，也没橙子什么的。这家店不卖那种水果。我大概找了一个多小时，那个女人紧张起来，最后，她说："你什么都不买吗？"于是，我从架子上拿了一罐桃子和一袋白糖，心想，如果买不到别的东西，也可以做个桃汁什么的，我快渴死了。回到地下室，我用刀打开罐头，把桃子塞进我的一只袜子里挤碎，然后把桃汁过滤到一个罐子里，再加入一些水和糖，搅拌了一下，不过，我跟你说——那味道一点也不像酸橙汁——说实在的，那味道像极了热袜子。

总之，我应该七点到兄弟会，我到的时候，几个家伙正在安装设备，珍妮和班卓琴手却不见人影。我四处打听了一下，然后出去到停车场透口气。我看见了珍妮的车，以为她刚到。

所有车窗都蒙着一层水汽，看不见车里的情形。突然，我想她可能在车里，出不来了，可能尾气中毒了什么的，于是我打开车门，往里看。我打开车门时，灯亮了。

她在这儿，躺在后座上，裙子的上半身拉下来，下半身拉上去。班卓琴手也在，在她身上。珍妮看到我，尖叫起来，挥舞胳膊，就像那天她在电影院里所做的那样，我突然想到她可能被猥亵了,所以我抓住班卓琴手的衬衫,反正他身上就这一件衣服,把他从她身上拽下来。

傻瓜都能看出来我又做错事了。天哪,你想象不出我怎么会做出这种蠢事。他骂我,她也骂我,还上下拉扯自己的裙子,最后,珍妮说:"哦,阿甘——你怎么能这样!"说完,她就走了。班卓琴手拿起他的班卓琴,也走了。

总之,从那以后,显然,他们不欢迎我再参加小乐队的演出了,于是,我又回到地下室。我还是不明白到底发生了什么事,但那天晚上,布巴看见我的灯亮着,于是,下来找我,我把这件事告诉了他,他说:"哎呀,阿甘,他们在做爱!"好吧,我想我可能已经想到这一点了,但坦白地说,我并不想知道。可是,有时候,男人必须面对事实。

一直忙着打球也许是好事,因为意识到珍妮和班卓琴手干那种事,而且,她可能对我完全没有这方面的想法,我心里挺难受的。但到目前为止,我们整个赛季保持不败,并将在橘子碗比赛中与内布拉斯加大学剥玉米人队争夺全国冠军。每次和北方球队比赛都是大事,因为他们那边肯定有黑人球员,有些人会因此惊慌失措——比方说,我的前室友柯蒂斯——我自己就从来没有担心过,因为我遇到的大部分黑人都比白人对我好。

总之,我们去迈阿密参加橘子碗比赛,快开赛了,我们有点激动。布赖恩特教练走进更衣室,他没多说什么,只是说,要想赢,就要拼命打之类的话,然后,我们上场,对方开球。球直接传给我,我接住球,径直冲进一群来自内布拉斯加州的剥玉米的黑鬼和又壮又笨的白人男孩中间,他们个个都有五百磅重。

整个下午都是这样。中场休息时,他们以二十八比七领先,而我们是一群绝望可怜的家伙。布赖恩特教练走进更衣室,摇着头,好像早就料到我们会让他失望似的。接着,他开始在黑板上写写画画,跟四分卫"毒蛇"和其他几个人说话,然后,他叫我的名字,让我跟他到走廊上去。

"阿甘,"他说,"太糟糕了,这种状况必须到此为止。"他的脸几乎贴到我脸上,我的脸颊感觉到他口中呼出的热气。"阿甘,"他说,"整整一年了,我们一直在秘密训练你跑动传球,你表现得很棒。下半场,我们要用这种战术对付内布拉斯加大学剥玉米人队,给他们来个下马威,吓得他们护裆掉到脚脖子上。不过,这一切都取决于你,小伙子——所以,等会儿上场,你要像有野兽在后面追你一样拼命跑。"

我点点头,该回到场上去了。所有人呐喊欢呼,但这副重担压在我肩上,我觉得有点不公平。可是,管他呢,有时候就是这样。

我们第一次拿球发起进攻前,四分卫"毒蛇"在聚商时说:"好了,我们现在要开始阿甘打法了。"接着,他对我说:"你跑出二十码,然后回头看,球就会到你手里。"果然,球到我手里了。比分突然变成了二十八比十四。

从那以后,我们打得很棒,只是那些内布拉斯加州剥玉米的黑鬼和又壮又笨的白人男孩不只是坐在那儿旁观。他们有自己的花招——主要是所有人都跑过来,把我们撞倒,好像我们是纸板或什么东西做的。

但他们还是有点儿惊讶我能接住球,我又接了四五次球后,比分变成了二十八比二十一,他们开始派两个家伙盯着我。可是,这样一来,就没有人盯着端锋格温了,他接住"毒蛇"的传球,把球带到十五码线。踢定位球的"黄鼠狼"射门得分,现在,比分是二十八比二十四。

场边的布赖恩特教练走到我面前,对我说:"阿甘,你也许是个笨蛋,但你必须帮我们渡过这个难关。只要你再次持球越过对方端线,我一定保证让你当上美国总统,你想要什么都行。"说完,他拍了拍我的头,好像我是条狗,然后,我又回到比赛中。

第一次进攻,"毒蛇"就在得分线之外被拖住了,时间很快就到了。第二次进攻,他骗他们,没有长传,而是把球传给了我,但约有两吨重的内布拉斯加州剥玉米人,有黑有白,马上扑到我身上。我躺在那儿,仰面朝天,我想那一大捆香蕉砸在我爸爸身上就是这样的吧,然后,我又跟大家抱团商讨策略。

"阿甘,""毒蛇"说,"我会假装传球给格温,但我会把球扔给你,所以,我要你跑到那边的角卫那里,然后向右转,球就在那里。""毒蛇"的眼神如老虎般狂野。我点点头,照他的吩咐去做。

果然,"毒蛇"把球传到我手上,我奔向球场中央,门柱就在正前方。但突然,一个巨人扑过来,我的速度被迫慢了下来,接着,这世界上所有内布拉斯加州剥玉米的黑鬼和又壮又笨的白人男孩开始抓我、挠我、踩我，我摔倒在地。该死！我们离赢得比赛只差几码远了。当我爬起来时，我看到"毒蛇"已经让大家排好队，准备最后一次进攻，因为我们已经没有暂停的机会了。我刚回到我的位置，他就叫我开球，我跑了出去，但他突然把球从我头顶上方二十英尺的地方扔了出去，故意扔出界——我猜是为了暂停计时，时间还剩下两三秒。

可惜，"毒蛇"自己糊涂了，我想，他以为这是第三次进攻机会，我们还有一次机会，但实际上，这是第四次进攻机会，所以我们输了这个球，当然也就因此输掉了这场比赛。这更像我会干出来的事。

总之，我特别难过，因为我觉得珍妮·柯伦会看比赛，如果我拿到那个球，并赢得比赛，她也许会原谅我对她做过的事。但这是不可能的。布赖恩特教练对这个结果非常不满，但他强忍着不悦，说："好了，小伙子们，明年还会有机会的。"

是的，除了我。我和他们都没有这个机会了。

第五章

橘子碗比赛结束后,体育系拿到了我第一学期的成绩,没过多久,布赖恩特教练就叫我去他的办公室。我走进去,发现他情绪低落。

"阿甘,"他说,"你的英文不及格,我能理解,但我怎么也想不明白,那个什么'中级光学'考试,你居然得了个A,体育课却只拿了个F——你刚刚被提名为东南区最有价值的大学后卫!"

说来话长,我不想让布赖恩特教练听得厌烦,可是,我为什么要知道足球场上两根门柱之间的距离是多少呢?哦,布赖恩特教练看着我,面带可怕的悲伤表情。"阿甘,"他说,"很遗憾,我不得不告诉你,你已经被学校开除了,我也无能为力。"

我傻愣在那儿,扭绞着双手,直到我突然明白他说的是什么意思——我再也不能打橄榄球了。我必须离开这所大学。也许我再也见不到其他人了。也许我再也见不到珍妮·柯伦了。我必须搬出地下室,下学期,我不能像胡克斯教授说的那样,修"高级光学"课了。泪水不知不觉地盈满了我的眼眶。我一声没吭,只是站在那儿,耷拉着脑袋。

这时,教练也站了起来,他走到我身边,伸出胳膊搂着我。

他说:"阿甘,没关系,孩子。你刚来的时候,我就料到会发生这种情况。但我当时告诉他们,我说,把这个孩子交给我一个赛季——我只有这一个要求。好吧,阿甘,我们这个赛季打得非常出色。这是肯定的。当然,'毒蛇'在第四次进攻时把球抛出界外不是你的错……"

这时,我抬起头,教练正紧紧地盯着我,眼中闪烁着泪光。

"阿甘,"他说,"这个学校从来没有过你这样的球员,以后也不会有了。你非常棒。"

说完,教练走到窗前,站在那儿,望着窗外说:"祝你好运,孩子——现在滚出去吧!"

就这样,我不得不离开了大学。

我回去收拾我放在地下室的东西。布巴下楼来找我,他拿来两瓶啤酒,给了我一瓶。我从来没喝过啤酒,但我明白男人为什么会爱上喝啤酒。

布巴和我一起走出"人猿宿舍",哎呀,整个橄榄球队的人都站在那里。

他们非常安静,"毒蛇"走过来,跟我握手,他说:"阿甘,真对不起,那次传球是我的错。"我说:"没关系,毒蛇。"他们一个接着一个上来跟我握手,连柯蒂斯也跟我握了手,他脖子往下戴着护架,因为他在"人猿宿舍"撞倒了太多扇门。

布巴想帮我把行李拎到长途汽车站,我说我想一个人去。

"保持联络。"他说。总之,在去车站的路上,我经过学生会商店，但那天不是星期五，珍妮·柯伦的乐队也没有演出，所以我说，去他的，然后坐上巴士回家了。

巴士到莫比尔时已经是深夜。我没告诉妈妈发生了什么事，我知道她会很难过，所以，我继续往家走，但楼上她的房间亮着灯，我走进家门时，她果然像我记忆中那样号啕大哭。她告诉我，美国陆军已经听说我的成绩不及格，当天就下来一份通知，要我去美国陆军征兵中心报到。早知如此，我绝不会让自己被学校开除。

几天后，妈妈带我去了征兵中心。她给我准备了一盒午餐，免得我路上饿。大约有一百个人闲站在那里，还有四五辆巴士等着。一个大块头的中士冲着大家喊叫，妈妈走过去，对他说："我不明白你们怎么能带走我的儿子，他是个白痴。"但那个中士只是看着她说："好啦，女士，你认为其他人是什么？爱因斯坦吗？"说完，他继续喊叫。很快，他冲着我喊叫，我上了车，我们就这样离开了。

自从我离开傻瓜学校，人们就一直对我大吼大叫，费勒斯教练、布赖恩特教练和他的打手们，现在是陆军的人。不过，这么说吧：军队里的人比任何人吼的时间更长、更大声，说的话也更脏。他们从来没快乐过。此外，他们不会像教练那样抱怨你傻、抱怨你笨，他们更感兴趣的是你的私处或者排便，所以，他们总是在喊叫前说些"龟头""屁眼"之类的话。有时候，我忍不住怀疑柯蒂斯打橄榄球之前是不是当过兵。

总之，在巴士上坐了大约一百个小时后，我们到了佐治亚州的本宁堡，我满脑子都是三十五比三——我们大败佐治亚大学斗牛犬队时的比分。实际上，营房的居住条件比"人猿宿舍"稍好一点儿，但吃的不行——种类丰富，但很难吃。

除此之外，在接下来的几个月，他们让我们干什么，我们就干什么，还有就是被他们大声呵斥。他们教我们射击、扔手榴弹、匍匐前进。不训练的时候，我们就跑腿，或者打扫厕所什么的。本宁堡让我记忆犹新的一点是，似乎没有什么人比我聪明多少，我确实因此松了一口气。

我到那儿没多久，他们就让我下伙房帮厨，因为在步枪靶场，我不小心把水塔射穿了一个洞。我到了厨房，厨师好像病了，有人指着我说："甘，今天你来当厨师。"

"我做什么呢？"我问，"我从来没做过饭。"

"管他呢，"有人说，"你知道，这里又不是无忧宫（Sans Souci）。"

"要不你炖一锅菜吧？"另一个人说，"做起来更容易。"

"炖什么呢？"我问。

"你去看看冰箱和食品储藏室，"那个人说，"把你看到的东西全都丢进锅里，煮熟就行了。"

"不好吃怎么办？"我问。

"谁在乎好不好吃，你在这儿吃过好吃的东西吗？"

这一点，他说对了。

于是，我把冰箱和食品储藏室里能拿的东西全都拿出来了。有一罐罐的番茄、豆子、桃子，还有培根和大米，一袋袋的面粉、一麻袋一麻袋的土豆,还有一大堆我不认识的东西。我把这些食物全都聚拢到一块,然后问其中一个人:"我用什么锅来炖?"

"壁橱里有几口锅。"他说。可是,我往壁橱里瞅了一眼,发现全是小锅,根本装不下为全连两百号人做的炖菜。

"你干吗不问一下中尉?"有人说。

"他在野外演习呢。"有人回答。

"我不知道,"一个人说,"不过,今天他们回来,肯定特别饿,所以你最好想想办法。"

"这个怎么样?"我问。角落里有一个大家伙,铁的,大约有六英尺高,周长五英尺。

"那个?那就是个该死的蒸汽锅炉。不能用那个玩意儿煮东西。"

"为什么?"我说。

"哦,我不知道。我反正不会这么做。"

"锅炉是热的。里面有水。"我说。

"随你便吧,"有人说,"我们还有别的事要做。"

于是,我用了蒸汽锅炉。我打开所有罐头,把所有土豆都削了皮,把我能找到的各种肉统统扔进去,还有洋葱和胡萝卜,再倒上十几二十瓶番茄酱和芥末什么的。大约过了一个小时,你就能闻到炖菜的香味了。

"晚饭准备得怎么样了?"过了一会儿,有人问。

"我去尝尝。"我说。

我把锅盖打开,看到里面的东西冒泡、沸腾,不时有个洋葱或土豆浮到表面，漂来漂去。

"我来尝一口。"一个家伙说。他拿起一个锡杯，舀了一些炖菜。

"哎呀，这玩意儿还没熟呢，"他说，"你最好加加压。那些家伙随时会到。"

于是，我给锅炉加了压，果然，那个连的士兵陆续从野地回来了。你能听见他们在营房里洗澡、更衣，准备吃晚饭，没过多久，他们陆续来到食堂。

可是，炖菜还没做好。我又尝了一下，有些东西还是夹生的。他们开始在外面的食堂闹情绪，嘴里嘟嘟囔囔，很快，他们就齐声高喊，于是我又给锅炉加了压。

大约半个小时后，他们开始用刀叉敲桌子，就像监狱里发生了暴动，我知道，得赶紧做点什么了，于是我把锅炉的压力开到最大。

我坐在那儿看着锅炉，紧张得不知所措，突然，军士长破门而入。

"到底是怎么回事？"他问，"兄弟们的晚饭呢？"

"快好了，军士长。"我说，就在这时，锅炉开始隆隆作响，摇晃起来。蒸汽从两边冒出来，锅炉的一只脚掉了。

"那是什么？"军士长问，"你在用那个锅炉煮什么东西吗？"

"那是晚饭。"我说，军士长一脸诧异，一秒钟后，他又一脸惊恐——车祸前那种表情，接着，锅炉爆炸了。

我不太确定接下来发生了什么。我只记得食堂的屋顶被掀开了,所有门窗都被炸飞了。

洗碗的人穿墙而出,摞盘子的人飞到空中,有点儿像火箭人。

我和军士长,奇迹般幸免于难,就像人们说的,离手榴弹很近,反倒不会被炸伤。但不知怎的,我们俩的衣服都被炸掉了,只剩下我当时戴的那顶大厨师帽。炖菜溅了我们一身,所以,我们俩看起来——哦,我也不知道我们看起来像什么——总之,样子很奇怪。

不可思议的是,那些坐在食堂里的人也毫发无损。他们坐在桌前,进了一身炖菜,像患了炮弹休克症似的,但他们确实因此闭上了他们的臭嘴,不再问他们的晚饭什么时候准备好了。

突然,连长跑进大楼。

"什么声音!"他喊道,"出了什么事?"他看着我们俩,然后喊道:"克兰兹军士长,是你吗?"

"甘——锅炉——炖菜!"军士长说,接着,他似乎镇定下来,从墙上抓了一把切肉刀。

"甘——锅炉——炖菜!"他尖叫着,攥着切肉刀追我。我跑出门去,他绕着整个练兵场追我,甚至穿过军官俱乐部和车辆调度中心。不过,我跑得比他快,因为这是我的专长,但我这么跟你说吧:我心里很清楚,这次,我肯定有麻烦了。

秋天的一个晚上,军营的电话响了,是布巴打来的。他说他们不给他发体育奖学金了,因为他的脚伤比他们想象的要严重，所以，他也要离开学校。但他问我能不能到伯明翰来看校队和密西西比极客队的比赛。可那个周六我不能离开营房，自从炖菜爆炸后，每周末都这样，已经快一年了。总之，我去不了，所以，我一边刷洗公共厕所，一边听收音机里的比赛。

第三节结束时，比分非常接近，这对"毒蛇"来说是个重要的日子。我们三十八比三十七领先，但密西西比极客队在离比赛结束还剩一分钟的时候达阵得分。突然，第四次进攻开始了，我们没有暂停时间了。我默默祈祷"毒蛇"不要再做那次橘子碗比赛中做过的事，也就是在第四次进攻时将球扔出界，然后再次输掉比赛，但他就是这么做的。

我的心一沉，但突然，欢声雷动，你根本听不见播音员在说什么，当一切安静下来以后，你才明白是怎么回事："毒蛇"在第四节假装传球出界，想暂停计时，但实际上，他把球传给了柯蒂斯，柯蒂斯带球触地得分，取得了比赛的胜利。这样你就大概知道布赖恩特教练有多么老奸巨猾了。他已经料到密西西比极客队的球员很笨，他们以为我们会蠢到重蹈覆辙。

比赛赢了，我真的很高兴，但我想知道珍妮·柯伦是不是在看比赛，她有没有想我。

结果，想不想我都无所谓了，因为一个月后，我们就出发去国外执行任务了。在将近一年的时间里，我们像机器人一样接受训练，并将奔赴万里之外的某个地方，这并不是夸大其词。我们要去越南，但据说在那里受的苦还没有我们过去一年的经历糟糕。不过，结果证明，这确实是夸大其词。

我们是二月份到越南的，然后坐牛车从南海沿岸的归仁到高原上的波来古。这是一段不错的旅程，沿途风光秀丽、有趣，有香蕉树和棕榈树，还有小个子越南佬在稻田里犁地。站在我们这边的越南人都很友好，朝我们挥手。

由于一大团红色的尘雾笼罩波来古上空，我们几乎在半天车程之外就能看到它。郊区有一些简陋的小棚屋，比我在亚拉巴马看到的任何房子都糟糕，人们挤在单坡顶的简易房里，大人没有牙齿，孩子没有衣服，基本上算是乞丐。等我们到达旅总部和消防基地时，情况看起来并不是太糟糕，除了漫天的红色尘雾。我们感觉没有什么大事，营区干净整洁，入眼是一排排的帐篷，周围的沙土耙得整整齐齐。一点儿也不像打仗的样子。我们仿佛回到了本宁堡。

总之，他们说，这么安静是因为现在是越南佬的新年——春节（Tet）之类的——伊始，双方正在休战。所有人长舒了一口气，因为我们已经够害怕的了。然而，这种祥和宁静并没有持续太久。

我们收拾好营房后，他们让我们去旅部淋浴处洗澡。旅部淋浴处就是地上一个浅坑，旁边停着三四辆大水罐车，我们奉命把军装叠好，放在坑边，然后下到坑里，他们往我们身上喷水。

即便如此，也不算太糟，因为我们已经快一个星期没洗澡了，身上闻起来开始有一股臭味。我们在坑里，他们拿水管浇我们，天快黑了，突然，空中传来一种奇怪的声音，有个正用水管朝我们喷水的家伙喊道："来了！"然后，坑边的人全都消失得无影无踪。我们光着屁股站在那里，你看看我，我看看你，接着，附近传来巨大的爆炸声，接着，又是一声巨响，所有人喊叫、咒骂，试图找到自己的衣服。我们周围不停传来爆炸声，有人大喊："趴下！"这话有点儿可笑，因为我们全都趴在坑底，现在，我们更像是虫子，而不是人。

一次爆炸后，炸弹的碎片飞进我们的澡坑，远侧的几个男孩被炮弹击中，他们喊叫，流血，抓住伤口。很明显，这个坑并不是一个安全的藏身之处。克兰兹军士长突然出现在坑边，大声叫我们所有人离开这里，跟他走。两次爆炸间有一小段休息时间，我们赶紧离开。我爬到坑顶往下看，天哪！四五个拿着管子朝我们喷水的家伙躺在那里——几乎看不出人样了，炸得血肉模糊，像被塞进捆棉花机似的。这之前，我从没见过死人，这是我经历过的最可怕的事，不论之前，还是之后！

克兰兹军士长示意我们跟着他爬，我们照做。从上面往下看我们，场面一定非常壮观！一百五十来个大男人全身赤裸，排成一长串，在地上蠕动。

那里挖出一排散兵坑，克兰兹军士长让三四个人挤一个坑。但一进散兵坑，我就意识到，还不如待在刚才那个澡坑里。散兵坑里积满了雨水，齐腰深，黏糊糊的，臭气熏天，各种各样的青蛙、蛇和虫子在坑里爬行，跳跃，扭动。

轰炸持续了一整夜，我们不得不待在散兵坑里，没有吃晚饭。天亮前，炮火减弱，我们奉命赶紧离开散兵坑，穿上衣服，拿起武器，准备进攻。

由于我们还算是新兵，真的没有什么事可做——他们甚至不知道该把我们安置在哪里，所以，他们派我们去守卫南边的边界，那里是军官厕所所在地。但那个地方比散兵坑还要糟糕，一枚炸弹击中厕所，将整个地区大约五百磅军官粪便炸得到处都是。

我们在那里待了一整天，没有早饭，也没有午饭；太阳落山时，他们又开始轰炸，我们只好躺在粪便上。哎呀，哎呀，太恶心了。

终于有人想起来我们可能饿了，于是运来很多箱C口粮。我拿到冷火腿和蛋，罐头上的日期是1951年。各种谣言满天飞。有人说，越南佬攻占了波来古。还有人说，越南佬有原子弹，只用迫击炮轰我们是为了削弱我们的防御力量。还有人说，炮轰我们的根本不是越南佬，而是澳大利亚人、荷兰人，或者挪威人。我觉得到底是谁干的并不重要。该死的谣言。

总之，第一天过后，我们开始在南边给自己建一个适合居住的地方。我们挖了散兵坑，用军官厕所里的木板和马口铁搭起小茅屋。对方还没有打到这里，我们也从没见过一个可以让我们开枪打的越南佬。我想他们也许足够聪明，不会轰炸厕所。有三四天的时间，他们每天晚上都炮轰我们。终于有一天早上，炮击停止了，副营长鲍尔斯少校爬到我们连长跟前，说我们必须北上，去援助在丛林里遭难的另一个旅。

过了一会儿，胡珀中尉叫我们"上马"，所有人尽量把更多的C口粮和手榴弹往口袋里塞——这其实造成了一种两难的困境，因为手榴弹不能吃，但没准儿什么时候能用上。总之，他们把我们送上直升机，我们飞走了。

直升机还没降落，你就能看到第三旅的情况有多惨。丛林里烟雾缭绕，地面被炸得一块一块的。我们还没着陆，他们就开始朝我们射击。他们炸毁了我们在空中的一架直升机，那个场景非常可怕，人身上都着火了，我们却无能为力。

我负责携带机关枪弹药，因为他们认为我这个体格可以扛很多东西。我们离开前，又有两个家伙问我是否介意帮他们带几颗手榴弹，这样，他们就可以多带些口粮，我同意了。这对我来说并没有什么害处。此外，克兰兹军士长还让我背一个重约五十磅的十加仑水桶。就在我们离开前，负责携带机关枪三脚架的丹尼尔斯拉肚子，去不了了，所以，三脚架也由我来拿。所有东西加一块儿，我相当于扛了一个内布拉斯加大学剥玉米人队。但是这可不是橄榄球比赛。

快到黄昏时，我们奉命爬上一个山脊，解救查理连，他们要么被越南佬困住了，要么就是困住了越南佬，这要看你从哪里得到的消息，《星条旗报》，还是你环顾四周看到的惨状。

总之，我们爬上去以后发现炮弹齐飞，有十几个人受了重伤，呻吟、哭泣，四面八方传来各种噪声，几乎谁也听不清什么。我蹲得很低，想把扛在身上的所有弹药、水桶、三脚架，还有我自己的东西送到查理连所在的地方，我正吃力地爬过一个狭长的散兵坑时，坑里有个家伙突然对另一个家伙大声说："看那个大块头的笨蛋——简直像个科学怪人什么的。"我刚要回他一句，因为即使没有人取笑你，情况似乎也已经够糟糕的了。但就在这时，我简直不敢想象！散兵坑里的另一个人突然跳起来喊道："阿甘——福瑞斯特·甘！"

天哪，是布巴。

简言之，事情是这样的，尽管布巴的脚伤得很重，没办法打橄榄球了，但仍没能阻止他奉命代表美国陆军绕过半个地球来越南打仗。总之，我拖着我可怜的屁股和其他东西到了我该去的地方，过了一会儿，布巴也上来了，于是，我们趁着炮击的间歇（每次我们的飞机出现时都会停止），我和布巴叙了叙旧。

他告诉我，他听说珍妮·柯伦辍学了，跟一群反战人士走了。他还说，有一天，柯蒂斯把一个校警痛揍了一顿，因为人家给他开了一张停车罚单，正当他踢得校警满校园打滚的时候，警察来了，用一张大网扣住他，把他拖走了。布巴说，布赖恩特教练罚柯蒂斯在训练后多跑五十圈。

柯蒂斯还是老样子。

第六章

那个晚上漫长且难受。我们不能坐飞机走,所以他们尽情轰炸了大半夜。两个山脊间有一个小小的鞍部,他们在一个山脊上,我们在另一个山脊上,下面的鞍部就是激战的地方——不过,我不知道谁想要那块烂泥地。然而,克兰兹军士长一再对我们说,我们被带到这里来不是为了了解正在发生什么事,而是为了奉命行事。

很快,克兰兹军士长出现,告诉我们该怎么做。他说,我们必须把机关枪移动大约五十米,在鞍部中央耸立的那棵大树左边找个安全的地方架起来,这样我们就不会被炮弹炸飞。据我所闻所见,任何地方——包括我们目前所在的地方——都不安全,但下到鞍部去,则是他娘的荒谬至极。但我尽力做对的事。

我和机关枪手伯恩斯,以及另一个携带弹药的多伊尔,还有两个人从散兵坑里爬出来,沿着小斜坡走。走到一半,越南佬就发现了我们,并开始用机关枪朝我们射击。不过,在发生任何不测之前,我们已经慌忙爬下斜坡,进入丛林中。我不记得一米究竟有多长——和一码差不多吧,所以,当我们靠近那棵大树时,我对多伊尔说:"也许我们最好向左走。"他死死地盯着我，怒吼道："闭上你的臭嘴，阿甘，这里有越南佬。"还真是，六七个越南佬蹲在大树底下吃午饭。多伊尔拿起一枚手榴弹，拉开保险栓，朝那棵树扔去。手榴弹还没落地就爆炸了，越南佬那边传来一阵嘈杂声，接着，伯恩斯用机关枪扫射他们，我和另外两个家伙又投出几枚手榴弹。这一切发生在短短一分钟之内，当周遭再次安静下来时，我们已经上路了。

我们找了个地方架设机关枪，然后，一直在那儿待到天黑——待了一整夜，但什么事情也没发生。我们听到其他地方闹哄哄的，但这里只有我们几个。太阳升起来了，我们又累又饿，但强撑着。这时，克兰兹军士长那边来了一个送信的，他说，等我们的飞机把鞍部的越南佬消灭干净，查理连就会立刻进入鞍部，也就几分钟的时间。果然，飞机来了，丢下了炸弹，一切都被炸毁了，消灭了所有的越南佬。

我们看到查理连离开山脊线，下到鞍部，但他们刚刚翻越山脊边缘，开始沿斜坡奋力赶来，所有的武器都开始向查理连射击，发射迫击炮弹什么的，乱成一团。从我们所在的位置看不到任何越南佬，因为丛林茂密得像搭筑篝火的柴枝，但那里肯定有人朝查理连开枪。也许是荷兰人，甚至是挪威人，谁知道呢？

这期间，机关枪手伯恩斯看上去非常紧张，因为他已经想到，炮弹是从我们前方飞来的，这意味着，越南佬在我军和我们所在的位置之间。换句话说，这里只有我们几个人。他说，如果越南佬不干掉查理连，他们迟早会回到我们这边来，如果他们在这里发现我们，他们肯定不乐意。关键是，我们必须赶快离开这里。

我们收拾好东西，朝山脊走去，但就在这时，多伊尔突然看向我们右下方的鞍部，他看到一整车前来增援的越南佬，他们全副武装，向查理连所在的山上爬。我们当时最好试着跟他们交朋友，把其余的事全忘掉，但这种事是不可能发生的。于是，我们只是蹲在一大片灌木丛中，等他们爬上山顶。然后，伯恩斯用机关枪扫射他们，他立刻就干掉了十多个越南佬。我、多伊尔和另外两个家伙投掷手榴弹，情况开始对我们有利，直到伯恩斯的弹药用完，需要换上一条新的弹药带。我递给他一条新的弹药带，但就在他准备扣动扳机时，一颗越南佬的子弹正中他的头部，将它炸开了花。他躺在地上，手仍拼命握着枪，但他已经命丧黄泉。

哦，上帝，这太可怕了——而且越来越糟糕。万一越南佬抓住我们，不知道会怎么处置我们。我喊多伊尔到我这边来，但没有人回应。我一把将机关枪从可怜的伯恩斯手中夺过来，匍匐着朝多伊尔爬去，但他和另外两个家伙也中弹了，躺在那里。他们死了，但多伊尔还在喘气，所以，我抓住他，像扛面口袋一样把他扛在肩上，穿过灌木丛，朝查理连跑去，因为我已经吓傻了。我跑了大约二十码，子弹从我身后呼啸而过，我想，我的屁股肯定会中弹。但后来，我穿过一片竹林，来到一片矮草区，令人惊讶的是，那里到处都是越南佬，他们趴在那儿，朝另一边看，朝查理连开枪——我猜。

现在我该怎么办？我身后有越南佬，前面有越南佬，脚下还有越南佬。我不知道怎么办才好，所以，我全速冲锋，开始大吼大叫。我想，我有点失去理智，因为我不记得接下来发生了什么，除了我仍然一面扯着嗓子咆哮，一面拼命奔跑。一切乱成一团，然后，突然间，我来到查理连，所有人都在拍我的背，就像我达阵得分了一样。

那些越南佬好像被我吓跑了，迅速逃回到他们原来住的地方。我把多伊尔放在地上，医务人员过来给他包扎，很快，查理连的连长走到我身边，摇晃我的手，告诉我我是个好人。然后，他问："你到底是怎么做到的，甘？"他在等我的回答，但我也不知道我是怎么做到的，所以，我说："我要尿尿。"——我真的很想撒尿。连长用很奇怪的眼神看我，然后，看着也走上前来的克兰兹军士长，克兰兹军士长说："哦，老天爷，跟我来。"说完，他把我带到一棵树后面。

那天晚上，我和布巴碰面，共用一个散兵坑，晚饭吃的是C口粮。然后，我拿出布巴送给我的口琴，我们吹了几支曲子。在丛林里吹《哦，苏珊娜》和《牧场之家》，听起来真的很怪异。布巴掏出一小盒他妈妈寄来的糖果——果仁糖和奶油蛋白软糖——我们俩都吃了几块。这么跟你说吧——那个软糖确实勾起了我的一些回忆。

稍后，克兰兹军士长过来问我，那个十加仑饮用水桶放哪儿了。我告诉他，我过来的时候要扛着多伊尔，还要背着机关枪，我就把水桶丢在丛林里了。有那么一刻，我以为他会让我回去拿，但他没有。他只是点了点头，然后说，既然多伊尔受伤了，伯恩斯牺牲了，现在我必须担任机关枪手。我问他谁扛三脚架、弹药什么的,他说也得我来扛,因为没有其他可以做这件事的人了。这时,布巴说,他可以做这个,如果能把他调到我们连。克兰兹军士长想了一会儿,然后说,也许可以安排一下,因为查理连剩下的人都不够扫厕所的了。就这样,布巴和我又在一起了。

那几个星期过得太慢了,我几乎感觉时间在倒流。上一座山,下另一座山。有时,山上会有越南佬;有时,没有。不过,克兰兹军士长说,一切都好,因为实际上,我们要齐步走回美国了。他说,我们要从越南出发,穿过老挝,接着,穿过中国和俄罗斯,到达北极,然后穿过冰层,到达阿拉斯加,我们的妈妈可以在那里接我们回家。布巴说,别理他,因为他是个白痴。

丛林里的生活非常原始——没地方拉屎,像动物一样睡在地上,吃罐头食品,没地方洗澡什么的,衣服也都腐烂了。每个星期我都会收到妈妈写来的信。她说家里一切都好,但自从我离开后,那所高中再也没有拿过冠军。只要有空,我就会给她回信,但我要跟她说什么才不会让她再次放声大哭呢?所以,我只是说,我们在这里过得很愉快,每个人都对我们很好。我做了一件事,我写了封信给珍妮·柯伦,让妈妈转交给她,问可否让珍妮的家人把信寄给她——无论她在哪儿。可是,没有任何回音。

与此同时,布巴和我,我们已经订好了退役后的计划。我们要返回家乡,弄一艘捕虾船,做养虾生意。布巴来自拜尤拉巴特里，他从小就在捕虾船上干活儿。他说，也许我们可以弄到一笔贷款，我们可以轮流当船长什么的，我们可以住在船上，我们会有事情可做。布巴把一切都想好了。多少磅虾用来还清买船的贷款，我们要付多少油费，多少伙食费，等等，剩下的钱，我们就可以随便花了。我的脑海中浮现出这样的画面：站在捕虾船的船舵前——如果能坐在船尾吃虾就更好了！但是，当我把这件事告诉布巴时，他说："啊呀，阿甘，你这么大的块头，会把我们吃得倾家荡产的。还没赚钱的时候，我们一只虾也不能吃。"好吧，这话说得有道理。我不介意。

有一天，下起雨来，一下就是两个月，没停。大概除了雨夹雪和冰雹，我们经历过各种各样的雨，有时下毛毛细雨，有时下倾盆大雨。有时斜着下，有时直着下，有时雨甚至像从地上冒出来的。尽管如此，我们还是要做我们自己的事，主要是上山下山，寻找越南佬。

有一天，我们发现了他们。他们肯定是在召开越南佬大会什么的，因为感觉就像踩到了一个蚁丘，所有蚂蚁一拥而上。我们的飞机也不能在这种情况下飞行，所以在两分钟左右的时间里，我们又遇到了麻烦。

这次，他们给我们来了一个出其不意。我们正在穿过一片稻田，突然，他们从四面八方向我们开枪。人们呼喊，叫嚷，中弹，有人喊："撤退！"好吧，我拿起机关枪，和其他人并肩朝几棵棕榈树跑去，至少那边看起来可以躲雨。我们已经围成一个圆，准备迎接又一个漫长的夜晚，这时，我四下看了看，发现布巴不见了。

有人说，布巴在稻田里，受伤了，我说："该死。"克兰兹军士长听见我的话，说："阿甘，你不能去。"可是，去他的——我丢掉机关枪——毕竟带着它只会增加重量——向我最后见到布巴的地方飞奔。可是，跑到半道，我差点儿踩到二排一个家伙，他受了重伤，他伸出手，抬眼看着我，所以我想，我能怎么办？所以，我把他拉起来，尽快和他一起跑回去。子弹满天飞。这是我根本无法理解的事——我们为什么要这么干？打橄榄球是一回事。但是这个，我不明白为什么。该死。

我把那个男孩送回去，又跑出来，见鬼，路上又遇到一个家伙。于是，我弯下腰，打算把他抱起来，但就在我这么做时，他的脑子掉到稻田里了，因为他的后脑勺被炸掉了。该死。

于是，我把他放下来，继续往前走，果然，布巴在那儿，胸部中了两枪，我说："布巴，没事的，你听见我说话了吗，因为我们要弄到那艘捕虾船。"说完，我把他抱回营地，我把他放在地上。停下来喘气时，我低头一看，我的衬衫上沾满了从布巴的伤口里流出来的鲜血和青黄色的黏液，布巴抬头看着我，说："该死的，阿甘，为什么会这样？"唉，我能说什么呢？

接着，布巴问我："阿甘，你能用口琴给我吹首歌吗？"于是，我拿出口琴，随便吹了起来，我都不知道我吹的是什么，布巴又说："阿甘，你能吹《沿着斯旺尼河走》吗？"我说："当然可以，布巴。"我擦了擦吹口，吹了起来，周围依旧枪声不断，我知道我应该带着机关枪，管他呢，我吹起那首歌。

我没注意，雨已经停了，天空变成一种可怕的粉红色，把每个人的脸都衬托得像死人的脸，出于某种原因，越南佬暂时停火了，我们也停火了。我跪在布巴身旁，一遍遍吹着《沿着斯旺尼河走》，医生给他打了一针，尽全力照顾他。布巴抓着我的腿，他的眼睛变得混浊起来，可怕的粉红色的天空似乎吸干了他脸上的血色。

他想说点儿什么，于是，我俯下身，凑得很近，想听他在说什么。但我听不清他说的是什么。于是，我问医生："你听见他说什么了吗？"

军医说："回家。他说，回家。"

布巴，他死了，关于这件事，这就是我要说的。

那是我经历过的最糟糕的一夜。暴风雨又来了，我们得不到任何援助。越南佬离我们很近，我们甚至能听到他们交谈，一排的士兵甚至跟他们肉搏过。黎明时，他们叫来一架携带凝固汽油弹的飞机，飞机差点儿把那些该死的玩意儿扔在我们头顶上。我们自己都被熏黑了，跑到空旷的地方，瞪大眼睛，所有人骂骂咧咧，战战兢兢，树林着起火来，该死的，火差点儿把雨烧灭了！

这期间，我挨了一枪，幸好是屁股中弹。我不记得当时是怎么回事。我们的状态都很糟糕。我不知道发生了什么。一切都搞砸了。我索性丢下机关枪。我什么也不在乎了。我走到一棵树后面，蜷缩成一团，哭了起来。布巴走了，捕虾船也没了；他是我唯一的朋友——也许除了珍妮·柯伦，我把那段感情也搞砸了。要不是为了我妈妈,我还不如死在那儿——老死,或者怎么死,随便怎么个死法——我都无所谓。

过了一会儿,他们用直升机运来增援部队,我猜,凝固汽油弹把越南佬吓跑了。他们肯定想,我们对自己人下手都这么狠,天知道会怎么对付他们。

他们把伤员运走了,这时,克兰兹军士长走过来,他的头发烧焦了,衣服烧破了,好像刚从大炮里被发射出来似的。他说:"阿甘,你昨天表现得很棒,孩子。"接着,他问我要不要来根烟。

我说我不抽烟,他点点头。"阿甘,"他说,"你可能不是我见过的最聪明的人,但你是一个了不起的士兵。我希望我手下有一百个你这样的士兵。"

他问我疼不疼,我说不疼,但这不是实话。"阿甘,"他说,"你要回家了,我猜你已经知道了。"

我问他布巴在哪儿,克兰兹军士长用有点儿滑稽的眼神看着我。"他会被直接送回去。"他说。我问,我能不能和布巴坐同一架直升机回去,克兰兹军士长说,不行,布巴必须最后回去,因为他牺牲了。

他们用那种很粗的针管给我打了一针,针管里装满某种会让我感觉舒服点儿的狗屁药水,但我记得,我抬起手,抓住克兰兹军士长的胳膊,我说:"我这辈子从来没求过人,可是,你能不能亲自把布巴送上直升机,确保他顺利到家?"

"当然可以,阿甘,"他说,"哎呀——我们甚至会给他安排头等舱。"

第七章

我在岘港的医院住了将近两个月。就医院本身而言,其实不怎么样,但我们睡在带蚊帐的床铺上,地上铺的是木地板,每天打扫两次房间,这和我已经习惯了的生活相比,已经好得没话说了。

这么跟你说吧,这家医院里有些人的伤势比我严重得多。可怜的男孩们缺胳膊少腿,断手断脚,谁知道还缺点儿什么。有些男孩则腹部、胸部和脸上中弹。一到晚上,这个地方就像个审讯室——这些家伙鬼哭狼嚎,喊着要妈妈。

我隔壁床躺着一个叫丹的家伙,他是在坦克里被炸伤的。他全身烧伤,身上插满管子,但我从没听他抱怨过一句。他说起话来轻声细语,大约一天后,我们就成了朋友。丹来自康涅狄格,他们拉他去参军的时候,他是一名历史老师。因为他很聪明,被送进军官学校,成了一名中尉。我认识的大多数中尉都和我一样头脑简单,但丹不同。对于我们为什么会在那里,他有一套自己的理念,那就是,我们可能出于对的原因做了错的事,或者反过来,但无论如何,我们做得不对。他是一名坦克军官,他说,我们在一个几乎不能使用坦克的地方发动战争是荒谬的,因为这里的土地大多是沼泽或山脉。我把布巴的事告诉了他，他很难过地点点头，说这场战争结束以前，还会有更多的布巴丧命。

差不多一个星期后，他们把我转到普通病人休养身体的病房，但每天，我还是会回到加护病房，陪丹坐一会儿。有时候，我用口琴给丹吹小曲听，他非常喜欢。妈妈给我寄的一包"好时"牌巧克力棒终于辗转送到了医院，我想和丹一起吃，但他什么都不能吃，除了通过管子输入他身体里的东西。

我认为坐在那儿和丹聊天对我的人生产生了很大的影响。我知道，我是个白痴，不该有属于自己的人生观，但也许这只是因为，从来没有人花时间跟我谈论过这种事。丹认为，发生在我们身上的一切，其实，发生在任何地方的任何事，都会受到掌管宇宙的自然法则支配。他对这个问题的看法非常复杂，但他说的大意开始改变了我对事物的整体看法。

我一辈子都搞不懂周围在发生什么事。一件事发生了，接着发生了别的事，接着又发生了别的事，依此类推，有一半时间，一切没有任何意义。但丹说，这都是某种计划的一部分，想要配合这个计划，我们最好搞清楚如何融入其中，然后坚守自己的岗位。不知道为什么，明白这个道理后，周围的一切变得清楚起来了。

总之，接下来的几个星期，我的病情大有好转，屁股愈合得特别好。医生说，我有一张"犀牛"皮。医院有一间娱乐室，因为没有太多其他事情可做，有一天，我闲逛到那儿，有两个人在那儿打乒乓球。过了一会儿，我问，我能不能玩一会儿，他们同意了。我输掉了前几分，但过了一会儿，我就把他们俩打败了。"你这么大块头,动作可真够快的。"其中一个人说。我只是点点头。我争取每天都打会儿球,球技练得相当不错,信不信由你。

下午,我去看望丹,早上,我一个人待着。如果我愿意,他们允许我离开医院,还有一辆巴士可以带我这样的病人去岘港,去城里转转,或者去越南佬的商店买些小玩意儿。但我不需要那些东西,所以,我只是随便走走,欣赏风景。

海边有个小市场,卖鱼虾什么的,一天,我去那里买了些虾,医院的一个厨子把虾煮熟,当然味道很好。我多么希望可怜的丹能吃几口。他说,如果我把虾肉压烂,也许他们就可以把虾肉放进管子里喂给他吃。他说,得问一下护士,但我知道,他是在开玩笑。

那天晚上,我躺在病床上,想着布巴,想他可能也喜欢吃这些虾,想着我们的虾船什么的。可怜的布巴。所以,第二天我问丹,布巴怎么会死,什么狗屁自然法则允许这种事情发生。他想了一下,然后说:"好吧,我告诉你,阿甘,所有法则都不能令我们满意,但它们仍然是法则。就像一只老虎在丛林里扑向一只猴子——这对猴子不利,但对老虎有好处。事情就是这样。"

几天后,我又回到那个鱼市,一个小个子越南佬正在那里卖一大袋子虾。我问他从哪里弄来的虾,他对我叽里呱啦说起来,因为他不懂英语。总之,我像印度人那样打手语,过了一会儿,他就明白了,示意我跟他走。起初,我有点儿疑心,但他面带笑容,我就跟他去了。

我们走了至少一英里路，经过海滩上所有的船，但他没有带我上船。那是水边沼泽地里的一个小地方，有点像池塘什么的，他在南海涨潮时潮水进来的地方放了一张铁丝网。那个婊子养的在那儿养虾！他拿了个小网子，舀了一些水，果然，网子里有十几只虾。他给了我一个小袋子，里面装着几只虾，我给了他一条好时巧克力棒。他高兴坏了。

那天晚上，野战军总部附近放露天电影，我过去看，但前排有几个家伙因为什么事大打出手，有个人被举起来，扔到银幕上，银幕破了个洞，电影就这样结束了。所以，后来，我躺在病床上想事情，突然，我有了个主意。我知道退伍以后干什么了！我回到家乡，在海湾附近找个小池塘，养虾！布巴死了，也许我搞不到捕虾船，但我肯定可以去沼泽地，弄到一些铁丝网，这就是我要做的事。布巴肯定会很高兴。

接下来的几个星期，每天早上我都会去那个小越南佬养虾的地方。芝（Chi）先生是他的名字。我只是坐在那儿看着他，过了一阵子，他教我怎么养虾。他用小抄网在沼泽地周围抓几只虾苗，扔进他的池塘里。然后，当潮水进来的时候，他把各种各样的东西丢进去——残羹剩饭之类的东西，这些东西会长出很小的、黏糊糊的东西，虾吃了它们，会长得又大又肥。这活儿太简单了——低能儿都会干。

过了几天，野战军总部几个有权势的人来到医院，兴奋地说："列兵甘，为了表彰你英勇无畏的精神，你将被授予国会荣誉勋章，后天，你将乘坐飞机回国，接受美国总统亲自授予的勋章。"当时是清晨，我躺在那里，想去洗手间，但是，他们来了,期待我说点儿什么,我猜,我都快尿裤子了。但这次,我只说了句"谢谢",就闭上了我的大嘴巴。也许这也是自然计划的一部分。

总之,他们走后,我又去加护病房看望丹,可是,到了那儿,我发现他的病床空了,床垫都叠起来了——他走了。我很担心他出什么事,跑去找护理员,但他也不在。我看到一个护士在走廊上,于是问她:"丹怎么了?"她说:"他走了。"我问:"他去哪儿了?"她说:"不知道,当时不是我当班。"于是,我找到护士长,问她,她说,丹已经被送回美国了,他在那里能得到更好的照顾。我问她他还好吗,她说:"他两个肺有刺伤,肠子切掉一截,脊椎分离,少了一只脚,一条腿截肢,大半个身子三度烧伤,如果你认为这样算还好,那么,他就还好。"我向她道了谢,继续往前走。

那天下午,我没打乒乓球,我很担心丹。我忽然想到,他可能死了,只是没有人愿意这么说,因为要先通知最近的亲属什么的。谁知道呢?但我垂头丧气,一个人四处溜达,踢着石头、锡罐什么的。

我终于回到病房时,床上放着几封信,是辗转寄到医院来的。妈妈写来一封信,说家里失火了,房子被烧毁了,没上保险什么的,她只好搬到济贫院去住。她说,当时,弗兰奇小姐正在给她的猫洗澡,用吹风机给它吹毛,结果着起火来,不是猫着火了,就是吹风机着火了,就是这么回事。她说,从今以后,我给她写的信要寄到"安贫小姊妹会"转交。我想,未来的岁月里，她还会流很多泪。

还有一封写给我的信，上面写着："亲爱的甘先生：只要您寄回随信所附的那张卡片，并承诺购买一套精美的百科全书，并在您的有生之年，每年以七十五美元的价格购买一本最新的年鉴，您就将获得一辆全新的庞蒂亚克GTO。"我把这封信丢进了垃圾桶。我这样的白痴要什么百科全书，况且，我又不会开车。

但第三封信是亲笔写给我的，信封背面写着："存局候领邮件，马萨诸塞州，剑桥市，珍妮·柯伦。"我的手抖得厉害——几乎拆不开信封。

"亲爱的阿甘，"信上写道，"我妈妈把你妈妈给她的信转交给我了，听说你不得不参加这场可怕的、不道德的战争，我很遗憾。"她说，她知道，看到身边一直有人伤亡，一定很可怕。"卷入其中必定使你良心难安，尽管我知道你是被迫的，他们违背了你的意愿。"她写道，没有干净的衣服、没有新鲜的食物什么的，一定很糟糕，但我有一句话，她没看懂是什么意思，那就是："我不得不在军官的粪便里趴了两天。"

"简直令人难以相信，"她说，"连他们都会逼你做这么粗俗的事。"我想，那个部分我可以解释得更清楚一点。

总之，珍妮说："我们正在组织反对法西斯分子的大规模示威活动，阻止这场可怕的、不道德的战争，表达人民的心声。"这方面的内容她写了一页左右，意思都差不多，但我还是非常认真地读了，因为光是看到她的笔迹就足以让我心里小鹿乱撞。

"至少,"最后,她说,"你见到布巴了,我知道,痛苦的时候身边有朋友陪伴,你一定很高兴。"她让我向布巴问好,还在附言里补充道,她赚了点儿钱,现在她每周和一个小乐队在哈佛大学附近的一家咖啡馆里演出两个晚上,如果将来我去那边,可以去找她。她说,乐队的名字叫"裂蛋"。从那时起,我一直找借口去哈佛大学。

那天晚上,我收拾东西,准备回家,领取荣誉勋章,并觐见美国总统。可是,除了医院给的睡衣、牙刷和剃须刀,我没什么可收拾的,因为我的衣物都在波来古的炮兵基地。不过,野战部队派来一位和蔼可亲的中校,他说:"别去管那些破玩意儿了,阿甘——今天晚上,我们让西贡的二十几个越南佬专门为你赶制一套崭新的军服,你总不能穿着睡衣去见总统吧。"中校说他会一直陪我到华盛顿,确保我有地方住,有饭吃,有车去我们要去的地方,他还会教我在那个场合如何举止得体,等等。

古奇中校是他的名字。

那天晚上,我和野战军总部的一个人进行了最后一场乒乓球比赛,他应该是陆军最好的乒乓球运动员。他身材矮小精瘦,不肯直视我的眼睛,而且,他自带球拍,装在皮套里。我很轻松就能打败他,但他停下来说乒乓球不好,天气太潮,把球都毁了。说完,他收拾好球拍走了,我觉得没什么,因为他把他带来的乒乓球留下了,医院的娱乐室可以用这些球。

我要离开的那天早上,一个护士进来,留下一个写着我名字的信封。我拆开信封,是丹写来的,还好,他没事,信上写道：

亲爱的阿甘：

很抱歉，我离开前，我们没有时间见面，这是医生们临时做的决定，我不知道是怎么回事就被带走了，不过，我问他们可不可以给我点时间写这封短信，因为我在这儿的时候，你对我很好。

我感觉到，阿甘，你生活中即将发生非常重要的事，某种变化或事件，将你朝不同的方向推，你必须抓住这个机会，不要让它从你身边溜走。如今回想起来，你眼中有某种东西，不时闪烁的微弱的火花，通常在你微笑的时候出现，而且，在那些罕见的时刻，我相信，我所看到的东西，几乎就是我们作为人类思考、创造和存在的能力起源。

这场战争不适合你，老朋友，也不适合我，我很幸运，摆脱了它，我相信你也会及时逃离战场。关键问题是，你将来做什么？我根本不认为你是白痴。也许根据某些测试或对愚人的判断，你属于某种类型，但内心深处，阿甘，我看到好奇的火花在你的内心深处燃烧。顺势而为，我的朋友，当你被时代的潮流裹挟时，也要让它为你所用，跟浅滩和阻碍做斗争吧，永不屈服，永不放弃。你是个好人，阿甘，你胸怀宽广。

——你的朋友

丹

我把丹这封信反复看了十几遍，里面有些东西我看不懂。我的意思是，我想我明白他在说什么，但有些词句我不知道是什么意思。第二天早上，古奇中校进来，说我们要立刻动身，先去西贡拿昨晚二十个越南佬为我赶制的新军装，然后马上回美国什么的。我给他看了丹的信，请他告诉我这封信到底是什么意思，古奇中校仔细读了一遍，然后把信还给我，说："哦，阿甘，我觉得他说得很清楚，他的意思是，当总统把勋章别在你身上时，你可千万别搞砸咯。"

第八章

我们飞越太平洋,古奇中校告诉我,回到美国后,我将是一个多么伟大的英雄。他说,人们会出来游行什么的,我根本不用自己买酒喝,买饭吃,因为其他人会争着为我付账。他还说,陆军想让我全国巡回演讲,做征募新兵、销售债券之类的事,他还说,我会享受"王室待遇"。这一点,他说得对。

飞机降落在旧金山机场时,一大群人等着我们下飞机。他们举着标语和横幅。古奇中校望向窗外,说很奇怪,竟然没有看到铜管乐队来迎接我们。事实证明,那群人已经够多的了。

我们下飞机后发生的第一件事是那群人开始对着我们齐声高呼口号,然后有人扔了一个大番茄,正好砸在古奇中校的脸上。那之后,天塌地陷,乱作一团。机场有几个警察,但是人群冲破警察的防线,朝我们跑过来,大声嚷嚷着各种难听的话,他们大概有两千人,留着大胡子什么的,这是自我在稻田里见到布巴战死以来最可怕的事。

古奇中校拼命擦掉脸上的番茄,做出一副很有尊严的样子,但我想,管他呢,因为对方人数是我们的一千倍,而且我们手无寸铁,所以我拔腿就跑。

那群人肯定也在找可以追赶的人,因为所有人都开始追赶我，就像我小时候那样，大喊大叫，挥舞着标语。我几乎跑遍机场的跑道，然后跑回航站楼，这比当时内布拉斯加大学剥玉米人队绕着橘子碗追我的情形还要可怕。最后，我跑进厕所，坐在马桶上，关上门，一直到我觉得他们放弃了，回家了。我肯定在厕所里躲了一个来钟头。

我从厕所出来后，朝大厅走去，古奇中校被一群宪兵和警察包围着，愁眉苦脸，直到看见我。"快来，阿甘！"他说，"他们给我们准备了一架飞机，送我们去华盛顿。"

我们上了飞往华盛顿的飞机，发现飞机上还有一群平民百姓，古奇中校和我坐在前面的座位上。飞机还没起飞，我们周围的人就都站起来，坐到后面去了。我问古奇中校怎么回事，他说，可能我们身上有怪味什么的。他说，不用担心。他说，到了华盛顿，情况就会好转。但愿如此，因为，连我这样的白痴都能明白，到目前为止，情况并不像中校说的那样。

飞机抵达华盛顿时，我简直兴奋得快要爆炸了！我们可以看见华盛顿纪念碑和国会大厦，都是从窗口看见的，以前我只见过照片，但现在，它们就在那儿，实实在在矗立眼前。陆军派了一辆车来接我们，我们被带到一个很不错的酒店，有电梯，还有人帮着拎行李什么的。我从来没坐过电梯。

我们把东西放好后，古奇中校过来，说我们要去一个小酒吧喝一杯，他记得那地方有很多漂亮姑娘，他说这儿和加州很不一样，因为东部人很文明什么的。这次，他又错了。

我们在一张桌旁坐下，古奇中校给我点了一杯啤酒，也给自己点了一杯喝的，他开始交代明天总统向我颁授勋章时，我该如何在仪式上表现。

他说到一半时，一个漂亮姑娘走到桌前，古奇中校抬头看她，让她再给我们拿两杯酒来，因为我猜他以为她是服务员。但她低下头说："我连一杯热唾沫都不会给你拿，你这个肮脏的浑蛋。"说完，她转过身对我说："你今天杀死了多少婴儿，你这只大猩猩？"

那之后，我们回到酒店，叫了客房服务，点了几瓶啤酒，古奇中校必须把明天我该做的事交代完。

第二天，我们一大早就起床，步行到总统住的白宫。这是一栋非常漂亮的房子，有一个大草坪，看起来几乎和莫比尔的市政厅一般大。很多军人在那儿跟我握手，说我是个多么优秀的人，然后就到了领取勋章的时候。

总统是一位身材高大的老人，听口音像是从得克萨斯，还是什么地方来的，他们召集了一大群人，其中有些看起来像女仆和清洁工之类的，但他们都生活在这座美丽的玫瑰园里，站在明媚的阳光下。

一名陆军军官开始朗读一篇废话，大家都听得很认真，除了我，因为我饿了，我们还没吃早饭呢。终于，那个陆军军官念完了，然后，总统走到我面前，从盒子里取出勋章，别在我胸前。然后，他和我握手，所有人都开始拍照、鼓掌什么的。

我以为仪式结束了，我们可以离开这儿了，但总统还站在那儿，用有点儿滑稽的表情看着我。最后，他说："孩子，是你的肚子在咕咕叫吗？"

我瞟了一眼古奇中校,但他只是翻了个白眼,于是,我点了点头,说:"嗯哼。"总统说:"好啦,来吧,小伙子,我们去弄点儿吃的!"

我跟着他进了白宫,我们走进一个圆形的小房间,总统让一个侍者模样的人给我送一份早餐过来。房间里只有我们两个人,趁我们等早餐的工夫,他开始问我问题,比如说,知道我们为什么要和越南佬打仗吗,他们在军队里对我们好不好?我只是点头,过了一会儿,他就不问我问题了,两个人都沉默了。然后,他问:"你想一边看电视,一边等早餐吗?"

我又点了点头,总统打开办公桌后面的电视机,我们一起看《贝弗利山乡巴佬》(*The Beverly Hillbillies*)。总统看得很开心,说他每天都会看这个节目,而且我让他想到了杰思罗。吃完早餐,总统问我要不要他带我参观一下白宫,我说"好的",我们就出去了。我们来到外面,所有摄影师跟着我们转,接着,总统决定坐在一张小椅子上,他对我说:"孩子,你受伤了,是不是?"我点点头,然后他说:"哦,你看这个。"说着,他拉起衬衫,给我看他肚子上一个手术后留下的大疤。他问:"你伤在哪儿了?"于是,我脱掉裤子给他看。所有摄影师冲上来拍照,几个人跑过来,急忙把我架到古奇中校等着的地方。

那天下午,回到酒店,古奇中校突然拿着几张报纸闯进我的房间,天哪,他气疯了。他吼我、骂我,把报纸摔在我床上,我上了报纸头版,露出我的大屁股,总统也在展示他的伤疤。有一张报纸在我的眼睛上画了一个小小的黑眼罩,这样读者就认不出我来了，就像对待黄色图片那样。

照片下面写道："约翰逊总统和战斗英雄在玫瑰园中小憩。"

"阿甘，你这个白痴！"古奇中校说，"你怎么能这样对我？我完了。我的职业生涯可能就这样结束了！"

"我不知道，"我说，"我只是尽力做对的事。"

总之，从那之后，我又陷入了麻烦，但他们还没有放弃我。陆军决定让我去巡回征兵，鼓动小伙子们报名参战，古奇中校找人给我写了一篇演讲稿。那篇稿子很长，净是"危机时刻，参军报国是最光荣、爱国的行为"之类的屁话。麻烦的是，这篇稿子我绝对不可能背下来。哦，那些词我记得清清楚楚，但一到说的时候，就成了一团糨糊。

古奇中校丧失了理智。为了让我把演讲稿记牢，他让我每天熬到将近半夜，但最后，他放弃了，说："看来这么做行不通。"

接着，他有了个主意。"阿甘，"他说，"这么办吧。我把这个演讲稿删短点儿，你说几句话就行。我们试试看。"哦，他越删越短，越删越短，直到他终于满意我能记住演讲稿，看起来不像个白痴了。到最后，我只需要说："参军吧，为你的自由而战！"

我们巡回征兵的第一站是一所规模不大的学院，他们找来几个记者和摄影师，我们坐在大礼堂的主席台上。古奇中校起身发表本该由我发表的演讲。讲完，他说："现在，我们有请刚刚获得国会荣誉勋章的陆军一等兵福瑞斯特·甘讲几句话。"他示意我上前。一些人在鼓掌，等他们停下来后，我俯身，说："参军吧，为你的自由而战。"

我想，观众以为我会多说几句，但他们就让我说这么多，所以，我站在那里，大家看着我，我看着大家。突然，前排有人喊道："你怎么看这场战争？"我想到什么就说了什么，也就是："一坨狗屎。"

古奇中校走过来，一把抢过话筒，让我坐下，但所有记者飞快记下我说的话，摄影师们咔咔拍照，观众全都变得疯狂起来，他们欢呼雀跃。古奇中校马上把我带出礼堂，我们坐上车，汽车飞速驶出城，一路上，中校什么都没跟我说，他只是喃喃自语，发出疯癫古怪的笑声。

第二天早上，我们在一家酒店准备此行的第二场演讲，这时，电话铃响了，找古奇中校的。电话那头的人，无论他是谁，似乎一直在讲话，中校只是听着，连声应着"是，长官"，还不时瞪我一眼。他终于放下了电话，他盯着自己的鞋子说："好了，阿甘，这下你做到了。巡回演讲取消了，我被调到冰岛的一个气象站，我不知道，也不在乎你这浑蛋会有怎样的下场。"我问古奇中校，我们能不能要一瓶可口可乐，他只是看了我一会儿，接着又开始喃喃自语，发出那种疯癫古怪的笑声。

那之后，他们把我打发到迪克斯堡，并把我分配到蒸汽供热连。整整一天加半个晚上，我不停地往锅炉里铲煤，让营房保持暖和。连长是个什么都不在乎的家伙,他说我到了那儿以后,还有两年就退伍了,只要别惹是生非,就万事大吉。我就是这么打算的。我时常想起妈妈,想起布巴和养虾生意,想起哈佛大学的珍妮·柯伦,偶尔还打打乒乓球。

第二年春天的某一天,有通知说即将举行一场乒乓球比赛,获胜者将前往华盛顿参加全军锦标赛。我报了名,结果赢得很轻松,因为唯一一个打得还不错的家伙在战争中被炸掉了手指,不停地掉球拍。

下个星期,我被派往华盛顿,比赛在沃尔特·里德医院举行,所有伤员都可以坐在一旁观看比赛。第一轮,我赢得很轻松,第二轮也赢了,但第三轮,我抽到一个小个子,他会给球加各种旋转,打他很费劲,搞得我狼狈不堪。就在他四比二领先,眼看着我就要输了的时候,我突然看向人群,有个人坐在轮椅上,原来是岘港医院那个丹中尉。

局与局之间有短暂的休息时间,我走到丹跟前,低头看着他,他的两条腿没了。

"他们不得不把它们锯掉,阿甘,"他说,"不过,除此之外,我很好。"

他们还取下了他脸上的绷带,坦克着火,他被严重烧伤,浑身都是疤。此外,他的轮椅上竖着一根竿子,竿子上挂着个瓶子,瓶子上插着根管子,液体通过管子进入他体内。

"他们说就这样了,"丹说,"他们觉得管子插在我身上挺好看的。"

然后,他凑过来,直视着我的眼睛,说:"阿甘,我相信你想做什么都能做成。我一直在看你打球,你能打败那个小个子,因为你的乒乓球打得棒极了,你注定会成为顶尖高手。"

我点点头,该回到场上去了,那之后,我一分没丢,打进决赛,并夺得了冠军。

我在那儿待了大约三天,和丹共度了一些时光。我推着他的轮椅,带他到处走,有时在花园里,他可以晒晒太阳,晚上,我给他吹口琴,就像我给布巴吹口琴一样。大多数情况下,他喜欢谈论事情——各种各样的东西——比如历史和哲学,有一天,他谈到爱因斯坦的相对论,以及它在宇宙间的意义。我拿来一张纸,给他画了出来,整个公式,因为这是我们在大学的中级光学课上必须做的事。他看着我画的方程式,说:"阿甘,你总能给我带来惊喜。"

一天,我正在迪克斯堡的蒸汽供热连铲煤,五角大楼的一个家伙突然出现,胸前挂着一大堆勋章,面带灿烂的笑容。他对我说:"陆军一等兵甘,我很高兴地通知你,你入选了美国乒乓球队,将前往红色中国与中国佬打乒乓球。这是一项殊荣,因为这是近二十五年来,我们国家第一次和中国佬打交道,而且这件事比任何该死的乒乓球赛都要重要得多。这是外交,人类的未来可能在此一举。你明白我的意思吗?"

我耸了耸肩,点了点头,但心里猛地一沉。我只是一个可怜的白痴,如今却要关照全人类。

第九章

我来了,又绕了半个地球,这次是在中国,北京。

在乒乓球队打球的其他人,人都很好,来自各行各业,他们对我特别好。中国佬也很友善,他们和我在越南见到的亚洲佬很不一样。首先,他们干净整洁,而且很有礼貌;其次,他们不想杀了我。

美国国务院派了一个人和我们一起去,他教我们如何在中国佬面前举止得体,在我认识的所有人当中,他是唯一一个不太友善的。事实上,他简直就是一坨臭狗屎。他叫威尔金斯先生,留着稀疏的小胡子,成天夹着个公文包,时刻担心自己的鞋子是否锃亮,裤子是否板正,衬衫是否干净。我敢打赌,他早上起床后一定会吐口唾沫,擦亮自己的屁眼。

威尔金斯先生总是盯着我。"阿甘,"他说,"中国佬给你鞠躬的时候,你也要给人家鞠躬。阿甘,不要再在公共场合整理衣服。阿甘,你裤子上是什么污渍?阿甘,你像猪一样不懂餐桌礼仪。"

最后这一点,也许他说得对。中国人用两根小棍子吃饭,几乎不可能把任何食物送进嘴里,结果很多食物掉到我身上。难怪在中国见不到几个胖子。

总之，我们要跟中国佬打很多场比赛，他们有几个特别出色的球员，但我们也会展现自己的能力。几乎每天晚上，他们都会给我们安排活动，比如出去吃饭，或者听音乐会。一天晚上，我们要去一家叫北京烤鸭的餐馆，我下楼到酒店大堂时，威尔金斯先生说："阿甘，你回去换一件衬衫吧，你看上去就像跟谁互丢过食物。"他把我带到酒店前台，找了个会说英语的中国佬给我写了张纸条，上面用中文写道："我要去北京烤鸭店"，让我把这张纸条交给出租车司机。

"我们先去，"威尔金斯先生说，"你把纸条交给司机，他会把你送到那儿。"于是，我回房间，换了一件衬衫。

总之，我在酒店门口找到一辆出租车，我上了车，司机就把车开走了。我一直在找那张给司机的纸条，等我意识到我把纸条落在脏衬衫里的时候，我们早就到了市中心。司机不停回头跟我说话，我猜他是问我要去哪儿，我一直说："北京烤鸭，北京烤鸭。"但最后，他放弃了，带我参观了这座城市。

这种状况持续了一个来小时，我跟你说吧，我还真的看了不少地方。最后，我拍了拍他的肩膀，他转过身来，我说，"北京烤鸭"，然后我像鸭子拍打翅膀那样，挥动两只胳膊。突然，司机露出灿烂的笑容，点点头，开车离开。他不时回头看我，我就拍打翅膀。大约过了一个钟头，他停了车，我看向窗外，该死，他竟然把我拉到了机场！

哦，这时候，天已经黑了，我还没吃晚饭呢，我都快饿死了，所以，经过一家餐馆时，我让司机停车，让我下去。我递给他一沓他们给我们的中国钱，他找给我一些钱，然后开车走了。

我走进餐厅,坐下来,感觉像是到了月球上。一位女士走过来,用很滑稽的眼神看我,她递给我一份菜单,但菜单上写的是中文,所以,过了一会儿,我指了四五个菜,心想,总有一个菜可以吃吧——实际上,那几个菜都挺好吃的。吃完饭,结了账,我来到大街上,想办法找回酒店的路,但他们接到我的时候,我猜,我已经走了好几个小时了。

接下来,我只知道我被送进了警察局。一个会说英语的高大的中国佬在问我各种问题,他还像老电影里演的那样,给我敬烟。直到第二天下午,他们才把我放出去。威尔金斯先生来到监狱,他跟他们谈判了大约一个小时,后来,他们就放我走了。

威尔金斯先生暴跳如雷。"阿甘,你知道他们以为你是间谍吗?"他说,"你知道这会给我们付出的所有努力造成怎样的影响吗?你疯了吗?"

我本想对他说:"我不知道,我只是个白痴。"但想想算了。总之,从那以后,威尔金斯先生从街头小贩那儿买了一个大气球,系在我的衬衫纽扣上,这样他就可以"随时"知道我在哪儿。而且,从此以后,他在我西装的翻领上别了一张纸条,上面写着我是谁,我住在哪儿。这让我觉得自己像个傻瓜。

回国后,他们把我送回了迪克斯堡,但并没有让我回蒸汽供热连,我听说他们让我提前退伍了。也就用了一天左右的时间，我就走了。他们给了我一些钱买回家的车票，我自己还有几块钱。现在我必须决定接下来做什么。

我知道我应该回家看望妈妈，因为她住在济贫院。我想，也许我该做养虾生意了，开始做出一番事业，但我心里一直惦记着哈佛大学的珍妮·柯伦。我坐上一辆巴士去火车站，一路上，我都在考虑怎么做才是对的。但到了买票的时候，我告诉售票员，我要去波士顿。有时候，不能让对的事挡住你的去路。

第十章

我没有珍妮·柯伦的住址，只有她的一个邮政信箱，但我收到过她写来的一封信，她说她和她的乐队"裂蛋"在一个很小的地方演出，信上写了那个地方的名字——丑八怪俱乐部（Hodaddy Club）。我从火车站往那儿走，但总是迷路，最后只好叫了辆出租车。当时是下午，俱乐部里空荡荡的，只有几个喝醉的家伙和昨晚留在地板上大约半英寸深的啤酒。但吧台后面有个家伙说，珍妮他们大概九点钟到。我问我可不可以在那里等他们，那个家伙说："当然可以。"于是，我坐了五六个小时，让我的两只脚好好休息一下。

很快，那个地方就满员了。大多是大学生模样的孩子，但打扮得像杂耍表演里的怪人（geek）。所有人都穿着脏兮兮的蓝色牛仔裤和T恤衫，所有男人都留着胡子，戴着眼镜，所有女孩的头发都像随时会有一只鸟飞出去。这时，乐队上了台，开始鼓捣乐器。有三四个人，都拿着巨大的电家伙，到处插电。这当然和我们在大学学生会大楼玩的那一套有很大的区别。另外，我连珍妮·柯伦的影子都没看见。

他们安装好电器后，开始演奏，这么跟你说吧：这几个人很吵！很多彩灯闪烁起来，他们弹奏的音乐听起来有点像喷气式飞机起飞时的声音。但他们唱完一首歌后，观众喜欢，而且所有人欢呼尖叫。接着，一束光打在舞台一侧，她在那儿——珍妮！

她变了，和我认识的那个她不一样了。首先，她的头发垂到屁股，在屋子里还戴墨镜，而且是大晚上！她穿着蓝色牛仔裤，衬衫上贴了很多亮片，活像个电话总机。乐队再次开始演奏，珍妮开始唱歌。她手握麦克风，绕着整个舞台跳舞，上蹿下跳，挥舞胳膊，狂甩头发。我试图理解歌词的含义，但乐队的伴奏声太大，不停击鼓，猛敲钢琴，狠拨电吉他，屋顶都快被震塌了。我心想，这是什么破玩意儿？

后来，他们要休息一会儿，于是，我站起来，想穿过通往后台的一扇门。但有个家伙站在那儿，说我不能进去。当我走回座位时，我发现所有人都盯着我的军装。有人说："你这身行头不错。"还有人说："棒极了！"另一个人说："他是认真的吗？"

我又开始觉得自己像个白痴，于是，我走到外面，心想，也许我可以四处转转，把事情想清楚。我大概走了半个小时，等我回到那个地方时，等着进去的人在外面排起了长队。我走到队伍最前面，跟那个人解释，说我的东西都在里面，但他让我去队尾等。我想，我在那儿站了一个来小时，听着里面传出来的音乐声，说实话，离远了听，还稍微好听点儿。

总之，过了一会儿，我觉得很无聊，就沿着一条小巷，绕到俱乐部后面。那里有几个小台阶，我坐在台阶上，看老鼠在垃圾堆里互相追逐。我口袋里揣着口琴，所以为了打发时间，我掏出口琴，吹了起来。我仍听得见珍妮的乐队演奏的音乐，过了一会儿，我发现我可以跟着他们一起吹了，比如用半音音栓（chromatic stop）降半调，这样就能和他们的演奏融为一体。不知道过了多久，应该没过多久，我就能用 C 大调自己发挥了，奇怪的是，自己吹起来就不觉得那么难听了，只要你不去听它。

突然，我身后的门开了，珍妮站在那里。我猜，他们又休息了，但我没在意，继续吹。

"谁在那儿？"她问。

"是我。"我说。但巷子里很黑，她把头探出来，说："谁在那儿吹口琴？"

我站起来，因为这身衣服，我有点儿尴尬，但我还是说："是我。阿甘。"

"谁？"她说。

"阿甘。"

"阿甘？福瑞斯特·甘！"突然，她冲出门，扑进我怀里。

我和珍妮坐在后台叙旧，直到她要去唱下一组歌。其实，她并不是辍学，而是被学校开除了，因为一天晚上，他们发现她在一个男生的房间留宿。那个年代，有这种违规行为是会被学校开除的。班卓琴手不想参军，逃到加拿大去了，小乐队从此解散。珍妮去加州待了一阵子，头上戴花，但她说，那是一群怪胎，成天吸毒吸得精神恍惚，后来，她遇到一个男人，于是跟着他来到波士顿，他们搞了几次和平示威活动，但后来，她发现他是个同性恋，就跟他分手了，开始和一个真正的和平示威者交往，那人还制造炸弹，炸毁建筑物什么的。这次恋爱也没谈成，后来，她遇到了一个在哈佛大学教书的男人，结果他已经结婚了。接下来，她和一个看上去还不错的男人好上了，但有一天，他因为在商店偷东西搞得他俩双双被捕，这时，她才觉得是时候振作起来了。

她和"裂蛋"乐队一起演出，表演一种新的音乐，渐渐地，他们在波士顿附近相当受欢迎，下个星期，他们甚至要去纽约录制唱片。她说，她现在交往的男朋友在哈佛读书，是哲学系的学生，但今晚演出结束后，我可以去她家，跟他们一起住。我很失望她找了男朋友，但我没有别的地方可去，于是就去了她家。

她男朋友叫鲁道夫，身材瘦小，也就一百来磅重，头发像拖把一样，脖子上戴了很多珠子，我们到他们家时，他正坐在地板上，像印度古鲁一样冥想。

"鲁道夫，"珍妮说，"这是阿甘。我老家的朋友，他要跟我们住一阵子。"

鲁道夫没吭声，只是像赐福的教皇那样挥了挥手。

珍妮只有一张床，但她给我打了个地铺，那就是我睡觉的地方。这并不比我在军中睡过的很多地方差，甚至比某些地方还要好得多。

第二天早上我起床时，看见鲁道夫还坐在屋子中央冥想。珍妮给我做了早餐，然后，我们留下鲁道夫坐在那儿，她带我去游览剑桥。她说的第一件事是，我必须买套新衣服，因为这儿的人不明白，还以为我想戏弄他们。于是我们去了一家军用品二手店（surplus store），我买了一条连体工装裤和一件短夹克，立刻换上，把我的军服装在纸袋里。

我们在哈佛大学校园里转，珍妮碰巧遇到了她约会过的那个已婚教授。她仍然是他的朋友，尽管私底下她喜欢叫他"堕落的杂碎"。奎肯布什博士是他的名字。

总之，他很兴奋，因为下周他要开一门新课，这个课程完全是他自己设计的，名字是"世界文学中的白痴角色"。

我鼓起勇气说，我觉得这门课听起来很有趣，他说："好啊，阿甘，你干吗不来旁听？没准儿你会喜欢。"

珍妮看着我们俩，表情有点滑稽，但什么也没说。我们回到家，鲁道夫仍一个人蹲在地上。我们进了厨房，我小声问她，鲁道夫会不会说话，她说，会，迟早会的。

那天下午，珍妮带我去认识乐队里的其他人，她告诉他们，我吹的口琴声犹如天籁，今晚何不让我和他们一起在俱乐部演出。其中一个人问我最喜欢吹什么曲子，我说："迪克西——"他说他没听见我说什么，珍妮立刻插嘴道："没关系，一旦他能听懂我们的东西就不会有问题的。"

于是当晚，我和乐队一起演出，所有人都认为我的贡献很大，而且，坐在那儿看珍妮唱歌，满场飞，我的心情很愉快。

下个星期一，我决定去旁听奎肯布什博士的课——"世界文学中的白痴角色"。光是这个课程的名字就足以让我觉得自己很重要了。

奎肯布什博士对着全班同学说:"今天,我们有位客人,他会偶尔来旁听这门课。让我们欢迎福瑞斯特·甘先生。"大家转过身看我,我挥了挥手,然后开始上课。

奎肯布什博士说:"多年来,白痴一直在历史和文学中发挥着重要的作用。我想,大家都听说过村庄白痴(village idiot),他通常是一个住在某个村庄、智力迟钝的家伙。他时常是被蔑视、嘲笑的对象。后来,贵族们习惯把弄臣放在身边,这种人会做各种取悦皇亲贵族的事。在许多情况下,这个人确实是个白痴或傻瓜,在其他情况下,他只是一个小丑,或滑稽人物……"

他这样讲了一会儿,我渐渐明白,白痴不只是无用之人,上帝把他们带到这个世界上来是有目的的,有点儿像丹说的那样,目的是让大家笑。至少这是有意义的。

"对于大多数作家而言,在书中安排一个傻瓜的目的是,"奎肯布什博士说,"采用双关语(double entendre)的手法,允许他们让傻瓜出丑,同时也让读者发现愚蠢更大的意义。偶尔,莎士比亚这么伟大的作家也会让傻瓜使一个主角犯傻出丑,从而提供一个转折,让读者恍然大悟。"

听到这儿,我有点儿糊涂了。不过,这也很正常。总之,奎肯布什先生说,为了证明他一直所表达的观点,我们要演《李尔王》中的一场戏,戏里有一个傻瓜、一个装疯卖傻的人和已经发疯的国王。他让那个叫埃尔默·哈灵顿三世的家伙扮演发疯的汤姆·白德兰这个角色,让一个叫露西尔的女孩扮演弄人(傻瓜),让另一个叫贺拉斯还是什么的人扮演疯狂的李尔王。然后,他说:"阿甘,你何不扮演葛罗斯特伯爵这个角色?"

与此同时,我们的乐队——裂蛋乐队——发生了一些事。一个家伙从纽约飞过来,听了我们的音乐后,说他想让我们进录音棚,把我们的音乐做成磁带。大家都很兴奋,当然也包括珍妮·柯伦和我。那个从纽约来的家伙叫费布尔斯坦先生。他说,如果一切顺利,我们乐队可能是自夜间棒球发明以来最炙手可热的东西。费布尔斯坦先生说,我们要做的就是在一张纸上签字,然后开始发财。

乔治,那个为我们弹键盘的家伙,一直在教我弹键盘,有时候,鼓手摩斯也让我敲敲他的鼓。学习演奏这些乐器挺好玩的,也包括我的口琴。每天,我都会练习吹口琴,每天晚上,乐队都会在丑八怪俱乐部演出。

后来,有一天下午,我下课回家,珍妮一个人坐在沙发上。我问她鲁道夫去哪儿了,她说他跟她"掰"了。我问她为什么,她说:"因为他和其他人一样,是个一无是处的浑蛋。"我说,"我们干吗不出去吃晚饭,边吃边聊?"

当然,聊天的时候主要是她说话,实际上就是一连串对男人的抱怨。她说,我们男人是"懒惰、不负责任、自私、卑鄙、说谎的狗屎"。她就这样埋怨了一会儿,然后哭了起来。我说:"呃,珍妮,不要这样。这不算什么。那个鲁道夫看着就不适合你,成天坐在地板上。"她说:"是啊,阿甘,也许你说得对。我现在想回家了。"于是,我们回了家。

回到家,珍妮开始脱衣服,脱到只剩内裤,我只是坐在沙发上，尽量不去注意她，可是，她走过来，站在我面前，说："阿甘，我要你。"

我大吃一惊！我只是坐在那儿，抬起头，呆呆地看着她。接着，她挨着我坐下，开始玩弄我的裤子，接下来我只知道，她脱掉我的衬衣，搂我、亲我什么的。最初，她做这一切，我只感觉怪怪的。当然，我一直梦想有这么一天，但没想到会是这样。但后来，哦，我大概是被什么东西冲昏了头脑，我以为会怎样并不重要，因为我们已经在滚沙发了，衣服也几乎脱光，然后，珍妮扯下我的内裤，突然，她瞪大眼睛，说，"哇——瞧你那玩意儿！"她抓住我，就像那天弗兰奇小姐一样，不过，珍妮始终没让我闭上眼睛，我也就没闭眼睛。

哦，那天下午，我们做了各种各样的事，都是我做梦都想不到的事。珍妮教我各种我自己根本搞不懂的鬼玩意儿，我们在客厅滚完，滚进厨房——压坏家具，打翻东西，扯下窗帘，弄乱地毯，甚至不小心打开了电视机。最后，我们到水槽里，不过，别问我是怎么回事。终于完事后，珍妮躺了一会儿，然后，看着我说："该死，阿甘，这么长时间你都去哪儿了？"

"一直在你身边。"我说。

当然，从那以后，我和珍妮的关系就有点儿不一样了。我们开始睡同一张床，一开始，我觉得有点儿别扭，后来就慢慢习惯了。在丑八怪俱乐部演出时，珍妮经常从我身边走过，随手拨乱我的头发，或者用手指划我的脖颈。突然间，对我来说，世界变了——仿佛我的整个生活才刚刚开始。我是全世界最幸福的男人。

第十一章

我们要在哈佛大学奎肯布什教授的课堂上演戏的日子到了。我们要演的那场戏是，李尔王和他的弄人来到荒野——类似老家的沼泽或田野的地方——暴风雨袭来，所有人跑进一个叫"茅屋"的棚屋。

茅屋里有一个叫汤姆·白德兰的人，其实，他是一个叫爱德伽的人乔装成的疯子，因为他被他的浑蛋哥哥害得很惨。此时，国王也完全疯掉了，爱德伽也在装疯，当然，弄人也表现得像个疯子。我扮演的角色是葛罗斯特伯爵，他是爱德伽的父亲，相比于其他丑角，他算是一个"直人"。

奎肯布什教授已经用一条毯子还是什么，搭起了一个类似茅屋的东西，他还搞到一台造风机，制造暴风雨的音效——一台大风扇，用晾衣夹将一张张纸夹在扇叶上。总之，扮演李尔王的埃尔默·哈灵顿三世出场了，他身上披着一条麻袋，头上扣着一个沥水篮。那个演弄人的女孩不知道从哪儿找来一件傻瓜的戏服，她头戴一顶系着铃铛的小帽子，脚蹬一双阿拉伯人穿的那种鞋尖翘起来的鞋子。扮演汤姆·白德兰的家伙从垃圾堆里捡到一顶假发和几件衣服，还抓了把泥抹在脸上。他们都非常认真地对待这场演出。

不过，我可能是这群人里最好看的了，因为珍妮坐下来，认认真真地用床单和枕套给我缝了一套戏服，穿在我身上像尿布似的，她还用桌布给我做了一件斗篷，超人穿的那种。

总之，奎肯布什教授开动他的造风机，让我们从第十二页开始演，疯狂的汤姆正在给我们讲他的悲惨故事。

"做做好事，救救那给恶魔害得好苦的可怜的汤姆吧！"汤姆说。

李尔王说："什么！他的女儿害得他变成这个样子了？你不能留下一些什么来吗？你都给她们了吗？"

弄人说："不，他还留着一方毡毯，否则我们大家都要不好意思了。"

这番屁话持续了一会儿，然后，弄人说："这寒冷的夜晚将使我们大家都变成傻瓜和疯子。"

这一点，弄人说得对。

就在这时，我应该手持火炬走进茅屋，火炬是奎肯布什教授从戏剧系借来的。傻瓜喊道："瞧！一团火走来了。"奎肯布什教授点燃我的火炬，我穿过房间，走进茅屋。

"这就是那个叫作'弗力勃铁捷贝特'的恶魔。"汤姆·白德兰说。

"他是谁？"国王问。

我说："那边是什么人？你找谁？"

疯狂的汤姆说他只是"可怜的汤姆，他吃的是泅水的青蛙、蛤蟆、蝌蚪、壁虎和水蜥……"还有一堆其他的屁话，然后我应该突然认出国王，说："什么！陛下竟会跟这种人做起伴来了吗?"

疯狂的汤姆回答说:"地狱里的魔王是一个绅士;他的名字叫作摩陀,又叫作玛呼。"

这时,造风机吹得很猛,我估计奎肯布什教授在搭建这座茅屋时没有考虑到我身高六英尺六英寸,因为火炬顶部碰到了天花板。

这时,疯狂的汤姆应该说:"可怜的汤姆冷着呢。"但他说:"小心火炬!"

我低头看我的剧本,想看看这句话是从哪儿来的,埃尔默·哈灵顿三世对我说:"小心火炬,你这个白痴!"我回了他一句:"我这辈子就这么一次不是白痴——你才是白痴!"突然间,茅屋的屋顶着火了,火星落在疯狂的汤姆的假发上,假发也被点燃了。

"关掉那台该死的造风机!"有人喊道,可是,为时已晚。所有东西都烧起来了!

疯狂的汤姆大喊大叫,李尔王摘下沥水篮,扣在他头上,把火扑灭。人们跳来跳去,又呛又咳又骂,扮演弄人的女孩变得歇斯底里,高声尖叫道:"我们都会被烧死在这里!"有那么一两分钟,情况看起来确实是这样的。

我转过身,该死,我的斗篷居然着火了,于是,我一把推开窗户,拦腰抱起弄人,我们俩跳了出去。那是二楼的窗户,地上的灌木丛起到了缓冲作用,但当时是午饭时间,几百个人在院子里溜达。而我们,全都着着火,冒着烟。

黑烟从教室敞开的窗户涌出来,突然间,奎肯布什教授探出身子，环顾四周，握着拳头，脸上沾满烟灰。

"阿甘，你这个该死的白痴——你这个愚蠢的浑蛋！你会为此付出代价的！"他喊道。

弄人在地上匍匐，痛哭着，扭绞着双手，但她没事——只是脸熏黑了——于是，我拔腿就跑——以最快的速度跑过院子，斗篷还在燃烧，身后拖着一道烟。我一直跑到家才停下来，进了家门，珍妮说："哦，阿甘，怎么样？我敢打赌你一定演得很棒！"说着，她的脸上露出奇怪的表情。"哎呀，你身上怎么有一股烧焦了的味道？"她问。

"说来话长。"我说。

总之，从那以后，我再也没有旁听过"世界文学中的白痴角色"这门课，我见过的白痴已经够多的了。但每天晚上，我和珍妮都和裂蛋乐队一起演出，我们白天做爱、散步，在查尔斯河畔野餐，这简直是天堂般的生活。珍妮写了一首很温柔、很好听的歌，叫《尽情爱我》，在这首歌中，我有大约五分钟的口琴独奏。多么美好的春夏。我们还去了纽约，为费布尔斯坦先生录制磁带，几个星期后，他打电话说我们要录制一张唱片。那之后不久，很多人打电话，让我们去他们的城市演出，我们拿着从费布尔斯坦先生那里赚到的钱，买了一辆巴士，车上有床什么的，然后我们就上路了。

那段时间，还有一样东西在我的生活中扮演了非常重要的角色。一天晚上，我们在丑八怪俱乐部演完第一场，裂蛋乐队的鼓手摩斯把我拉到一旁说："阿甘，你是个整洁的帅小伙儿,但有样东西,我想让你试试,我认为它会让你的口琴吹得更好。"

我问他是什么,摩斯说:"给。"说着,他递给我一根很细的烟。我告诉他我不抽烟,谢谢,摩斯说:"这不是普通的烟,阿甘,里面有种东西可以拓宽你的眼界。"

我告诉摩斯,我不确定我是否需要拓宽眼界,但他坚持让我抽烟。"至少试试看。"他说。我想了一下,不过是根烟,不会有什么害处的,于是,我就抽了。

嗯,这么说吧:我的眼界确实拓宽了。

一切似乎慢了下来,前景变得很乐观。那天晚上的第二场演出是我有生以来最棒的演出,我吹奏曲子时,所有音符我好像都听过一百遍似的,后来,摩斯走过来,对我说:"阿甘,你以为这样就挺好——做爱的时候用一下,你就知道什么是好了。"

我用了,这次,他说的也是对的。我花了点儿钱买这种东西,不知不觉间,我已经天天吸这种烟了。唯一的问题是,过了一阵子,它好像让我变笨了。早上一起床,我就点上一根大麻烟(他们管这玩意叫大麻烟),然后,躺一整天,直到该去演出了。一开始,珍妮什么都没说,因为大家都知道,她自己也抽两口,但有一天,她问我:"阿甘,你不觉得那破玩意儿你抽得太多了吗?"

"我不知道,"我说,"多少是太多啊?"

珍妮说:"你现在抽的这个量就是太多。"

但我不想戒掉它。不知怎么的,它让我摆脱了一切烦恼,尽管当时我也没有太多烦恼。晚上，在丑八怪俱乐部演出间隙，我会出去，坐在小巷里，仰望星空。如果天上没有星星，我还是会抬头看，一天晚上，珍妮出来，发现我在抬头看雨。

"阿甘，你必须把这个东西戒掉，"她说，"我很担心你，除了演出，你整天躺着，什么都不干。这样生活很不健康。我认为你需要离开一阵子。从明天开始，我们在普罗温斯敦就没有演唱会了，我想，也许我们应该找个地方度假，去山里玩玩。"

我只是点点头。我甚至不确定她说的话我听全了没有。

呃，第二天晚上在普罗温斯敦，我找到后台出口，去外面点上一根大麻烟。我一个人坐在那儿，自顾自地抽，这时，两个女孩走过来。其中一个说："嘿，你不就是裂蛋乐队的口琴手吗？"

我点点头，结果，她一屁股坐在我腿上。另一个女孩咧嘴笑着、叫着，突然脱掉自己的上衣。腿上那个女孩则试图拉开我的裤子拉链，还把她的裙子拉起来，而惊呆的我，只是坐在那里。突然，舞台的门开了，珍妮喊道："阿甘，该……"她停了一秒，然后说："哦，该死！"然后，她摔上门。

我一下子跳起来，坐在我腿上的女孩摔在地上，另一个女孩骂骂咧咧，但进去以后，我发现珍妮靠在墙上哭。我走到她面前，但她说："离我远点儿，你这个浑蛋！你们男人都一个德行，像狗一样——你们不尊重任何人！"

我从来没这么愧疚过。我记不太清最后一场演出的情况了。回去的路上，珍妮坐到巴士前头，根本不想和我说话。那天晚上，她睡在沙发上，第二天早上，她说，也许我该出去找

95

个地方住了。于是，我收拾好东西就走了。我的头垂得很低。没法跟她解释清楚。我又被抛弃了。

那之后，珍妮去了别的地方。我四处打听，没有人知道她的下落。摩斯说，我在找到住处之前可以跟他住一起，但那段时间，我很孤独。我们暂时没有任何演出，所以没有什么事情可做，我想，也许该回家看看妈妈了，也许去可怜的布巴的老家做点养虾生意。也许我根本不是一块做摇滚明星的料。我想，也许，我只是一个笨手笨脚的白痴。

但后来有一天，摩斯回到家，说他在街角的一家酒吧看电视新闻，结果看见珍妮·柯伦了。

他说，她在华盛顿，参加一场反对越战的大型示威活动，摩斯说，他搞不懂她为什么要费心干那种鸟事，她本该在这里和我们一起赚钱。

我说我要去看她，摩斯说："好吧，看看你能不能把她带回来。"他说，他知道她大概会住哪儿，因为有一群波士顿人去华盛顿参加反战游行，在那里租了一间公寓。

我收拾好行李——我的一切家当——对摩斯表示感谢后就上路了。我是否会回来，我不知道。

我到华盛顿时，那里的情况简直一团糟。到处是警察，人们在街上呐喊，像发生暴乱一样乱扔东西。警察用警棍哐哐敲那些扔东西的人的头，看来局势快要失控了。

我找到珍妮可能住的地方的地址，走过去，但家里没人。

我在台阶上等了大半天，然后，大约晚上九点钟的时候，一辆车停下来，几个人下了车，里面有她！

我从台阶上站起来，朝她走去，但她转过身，跑回车里。其他人，两个男孩和一个女孩，他们不知道怎么办才好，也不知道我是谁，但后来，其中一个人说："听我说，如果我是你，我现在可不敢招惹她——她非常难过。"我问为什么，那家伙把我拉到一边，告诉我：

珍妮刚出狱。前一天，她被捕了，在女子监狱过了一夜，今天早上，他们还没来得及把她保释出去，监狱里的人说她头上可能有虱子什么的，因为她的头发太长，然后把她的头发剃光了。珍妮现在是个秃头。

哦，我猜，她不想让我看到她秃头的样子，因为她钻进汽车后座，躺下了。于是，我手脚并用爬过去，这样我就看不见车窗内的情形，我说："珍妮——是我，阿甘。"

她一声不吭，于是，我告诉她，对于之前发生的事，我有多么懊悔。我告诉她，我再也不吸大麻烟了，再也不跟乐队一起演出了，因为有太多不好的诱惑。我说，我为她的头发感到难过。然后，我爬回台阶上，我的行李放在那儿，我从我的帆布包里翻出一顶当兵时发的针织冬帽，然后爬回汽车那儿，把帽子顶在一根棍子上，从车窗伸进去。她接过帽子，戴上，然后，下了车，说："呃，快来，你这个大笨蛋，进屋吧。"

我们坐下来聊了一会儿，其他人吸大麻、喝啤酒，我什么都没碰。他们在讨论明天干什么，国会大厦门口将举行一场大规模的示威活动，一群越战老兵将摘下他们的勋章，扔到国会大厦的台阶上。

珍妮突然说:"你们知道吗,阿甘获得过国会荣誉勋章。"现场立刻鸦雀无声,然后看看我,又看看彼此,其中一个人说:"耶稣基督刚刚赐给我们一份礼物!"

第二天早上,珍妮走进客厅,我睡在沙发上,她说:"阿甘,我想让你今天和我们一起去,我还要你穿上你的军装。"我问为什么,她说:"因为你要做点儿什么,阻止越南那边的一切苦难。"于是,我穿上军装,过了一会儿,珍妮拿着她在五金店买的一串铁链回来了。她说:"阿甘,把这条铁链缠在身上。"

我又问为什么,但她说:"按我说的去做就行了,过一会儿你就明白了。你希望我开心,不是吗?"

我们就这样出发了,我穿着军装,身上缠着铁链,跟着珍妮他们。那是一个晴朗的日子,到了国会大厦,我看见那里有一群人扛着摄像机,还有乌泱乌泱的警察。所有人高声呼喊,并向警察竖中指。过了一会儿,我看到其他几个穿陆军军装的人,他们聚在一起,然后,一个接一个地,尽可能靠近国会大厦的台阶,他们摘下勋章,扔了出去。有些人坐在轮椅上,有些人瘸了腿,有些人缺胳膊少腿。一些人只是把勋章扔到台阶上,另一些人则真的用力扔。有人拍了拍我的肩,说轮到我了。我回头看了一眼珍妮,她点点头,于是,我独自继续朝那边走。

四周稍微安静了一些,接着有人用大喇叭宣布我的名字,说我要丢掉国会荣誉勋章,表示对结束越战的支持。所有人欢呼鼓掌,我看见其他勋章躺在台阶上。在这之上,在国会大厦的门廊上，一小群人站在那里，两三个警察和几个西装革履的人。好吧，我想，我必须尽力而为，于是，我摘下勋章，看了一会儿，我想起了布巴他们，还有丹，反正，我被某种感觉攫住了，但我必须扔掉它，所以我扬起胳膊，使出浑身力气把那枚勋章扔了出去。几秒钟后，门廊上一个穿西装的家伙突然倒了下去。很不幸，我把勋章扔得太远，砸中了他的脑袋。

这下全乱套了。警察冲入人群，人们大喊大叫，警察发射催泪弹，突然，五六个警察朝我扑过来，开始用警棍打我。又有一群警察跑过来，接下来，我只知道，我被戴上了手铐，扔进警车，送进了监狱。

我在监狱待了一整夜，早上，他们带我去见法官。我上过法庭。

有人告诉法官，我被指控"持凶器——一枚勋章——伤人，以及拒捕"，等等，并递给他一张纸。"甘先生，"法官说，"你知道你用你的勋章砸中了参议院书记员的头吗？"

我什么也没说，但看来这次有大麻烦了。

"甘先生，"法官说，"我不明白，你这么有名望的人，精忠报国的人，怎么会和一群扔掉勋章的傻瓜混在一起，不过，我要告诉你，我命令你接受三十天精神病观察，看他们能否搞清楚你为什么会做出如此白痴的行为。"

这之后，他们把我送回牢房，过了一会儿，他们又把我送上一辆巴士，巴士把我拉到圣伊丽莎白精神病院。

我终于被"关起来"了。

第十二章

这地方是个真正的疯人院。他们把我和一个叫弗雷德的家伙关在一个房间,他在这儿已经待了将近一年。他一见面就告诉我要对付怎样的疯子。有一个家伙毒死了六个人,另一个人用切肉刀砍自己的亲妈。这里的人做过各种各样的鸟事——谋杀、强奸、自称西班牙国王,或者拿破仑。最后,我问弗雷德他为什么会在这里,他说因为他用斧头砍死过人,不过,再过一个星期左右,他们就放他出去了。

我到那儿的第二天,他们让我去我的精神科医生沃尔顿医生的办公室报到。结果,沃尔顿医生是个女的。她说,首先,她要给我做一个小测试,然后给我体检。她让我在一张桌子旁边坐下,开始给我看一些上面有墨渍的卡片,问我觉得它们是什么。我一直说"墨渍",后来,她生气了,让我说点儿别的,于是我开始瞎编。接着,她递给我一张很长的试卷让我做。我做完后,她说:"把衣服脱下来。"

哦,除了一两次例外,每次我脱衣服,都会有不好的事情发生,所以,我说,还是别脱了,她记下这个情况,然后对我说,要么我自己脱,要么她让护理员来帮我脱。看来非脱不可了。

我开始脱衣服,当我把屁股露出来时,她走进房间,上下打量我,说:"哎呀,哎呀——你真是男性的典范!"

总之,她开始用一把小橡胶锤敲我的膝盖,就像在大学里他们对我做的那样,然后,她捅捅这儿,戳戳那儿,但始终没让我"弯腰",为此我非常感激。然后,她说我可以穿好衣服,回我的房间了。回去的路上,我路过一个有玻璃门的房间,里面有一群矮小的家伙,坐着,或躺着,流口水,痉挛,用拳头捶打地板。我站在那儿好一会儿,往里面看,我真为他们感到难过——这让我回想起我在傻瓜学校的那段日子。

几天后,他们又让我去沃尔顿医生的办公室报到。到了她的办公室,我发现她和另外两个医生模样的人在一起,她说他们是公爵医生和伯爵医生——他们都来自国家心理卫生研究所。她说,他们对我的情况很感兴趣。

公爵医生和伯爵医生让我坐下来,开始问我问题——各种各样的问题——他们俩轮流用橡胶锤敲我的膝盖。公爵医生说:"听我说,阿甘,我们已经拿到了你的测试成绩,你在数学方面表现得非常出色。所以,我们想让你做一些其他的测试。"他们拿出试卷让我做,这次比第一次复杂得多,但我觉得我做得还不错。如果我知道接下来会发生什么,我一定会故意考砸。

"阿甘,"伯爵医生说,"这太惊人了。你的大脑像电脑一样。我不知道你的推理能力如何——这可能就是你当初来这里的原因——我反正从来没遇见过这种情况。"

"你知道,乔治,"公爵医生说,"这个人真的非同寻常。前一阵子,我为宇航局做过一些工作,我认为我们应该把他送到休斯敦的航空航天中心去,让他们给他检查一下。他们一直在找这种人。"

所有医生盯着我,点头,然后他们又用锤子敲我的膝盖,看样子我又要离开这里了。

他们用一架大飞机把我送到得克萨斯州的休斯敦,飞机上除了我和公爵医生,没有别人,不过,这是一次愉快的旅行——除了他们把我的手脚拴在座位上。

"听我说,阿甘,"公爵医生说,"这笔交易是这样的。你用勋章砸中参议院书记员惹了大祸。你可能会因此入狱十年。但如果你和宇航局的这些人合作,我会确保你获释——你觉得怎么样?"

我点了点头。我知道我必须出狱,我要见到珍妮。我太想她了。

我在位于休斯敦的宇航局待了大约一个月。他们检查我、测试我,还问了我很多问题,我感觉我要上约翰尼·卡森的节目似的。

当然不是。

一天,他们把我拖到一个大房间,告诉我他们的打算。

"阿甘,"他们说,"我们想让你参加一次外太空之旅。就像公爵医生说的那样,你的头脑就像一台电脑,甚至比电脑更强。如果我们能给它设计正确的程序，你将对美国的太空计划十分有用。你觉得怎么样？"

我想了一会儿，然后说，我最好先问一下我妈妈，但他们提出了一个更强有力的论据——比如接下来的十年我在监狱里度过。

于是，我说"好"，通常，这个"好"字每次都会给我惹麻烦。

他们想出的主意是把我放到一艘宇宙飞船上，发射到太空，绕着地球转上大约一百万英里。他们把人送上过月球，但没在那儿发现任何有价值的东西，所以，接下来，他们打算访问火星。幸好，他们目前并不打算去火星——相反，这次算是一项训练任务，他们想弄清楚哪种人最适合火星之旅。

除了我，他们还挑选了一个女人和一只猿猴同行。

这个女人是珍妮特·弗里奇少校，看上去脾气很坏，她应该是美国第一位女宇航员，只是没有人知道她，因为这一切都是最高机密。她个子很矮，发型好像是头上扣了只碗剪出来的，她似乎对我和那只猿猴都没有多大用处。

说实在的，那只猿猴不错。那是一只个头很大、名叫苏的母猩猩，是他们从苏门答腊岛还是什么地方的丛林里抓来的。其实，他们这里有一大群猿猴，而且早就被送上过太空，但他们说，苏最适合这次旅行，因为她是母猴，母猴比公猴友善，而且，这将是她的第三次太空之旅。当我了解这一情况后，我不禁纳闷儿，他们要把我们送上太空，为什么唯一有经验的成员是一只猿猴。这一点确实引人思考，不是吗？

总之，在太空旅行前，我们必须接受各种训练。他们把我们放在回旋加速器里，让我们旋转，还把我们放在没有重力的小房间里等等。他们整天把他们想让我记住的狗屁东西往我的脑子里塞，比如计算我们所在的地方与他们想让我们去的地方之间的距离，以及如何再次返回地球的方程式；还有各种比如同轴坐标、余弦计算、球面三角学、布尔代数、反对数、傅里叶分析、象限和矩阵数学等狗屁东西。他们说，我要成为备用计算机的"备用机"。

我给珍妮·柯伦写了一大堆信，但所有信都被退回来了，"查无此人"。我还给我妈妈写了信，她给我回了一封长信，大意是："你可怜的妈妈住在济贫院，你是她在世上唯一的亲人，你怎么能这样对待她？"

我不敢告诉她，我不这么做的话，将有牢狱之灾，所以，我只是给她回信，说不用担心，因为有一个组员经验丰富。

好了，那个重要的日子终于到了，这么跟你说吧：我不只是有点紧张——我简直吓得半死！即使这是最高机密，消息还是泄露给了媒体，现在我们要上电视了。那天早上，有人给我们带来了报纸，让我们看我们有多么出名。下面是一些新闻标题：

"女人、猿猴和白痴，下次美国太空探索的主角。"

"美国向外星球发射奇怪信使。"

"女子、呆子和猴子，今日升空。"

《纽约邮报》甚至有个标题是："他们飞上太空——但谁说

了算?"

唯一一个听起来还算客气的是《纽约时报》的标题——"新太空探测器成员多样。"

好吧,像往常一样,我们一起床就乱成一团。我们去吃早饭,有人说:"出发当天,他们不应该吃早饭。"接着,又有人说:"不,应该吃。"接着,有人说:"不,不应该吃。"他们就这样争论了好一会儿,直到最后谁都不饿了。

他们让我们穿上宇航服,然后用一辆小巴士把我们送到发射台,苏坐在车后面的笼子里。这艘宇宙飞船大约有一百层楼高,起泡沫、嘶嘶响、冒热气,看样子像要把我们活活吃掉!电梯把我们带到我们要去的太空舱,他们给我们系上安全带,把苏放在后面它的座位上。然后我们等待。

我们又等了一会儿。

我们又等了一会儿。

我们又等了一会儿。

这期间,宇宙飞船一直在沸腾、嘶嘶响、咆哮、冒热气。有人说,有一亿人在电视机前看着我们。我想,他们也在等待。

总之,快到中午的时候,有人过来敲宇宙飞船的门,说,这次任务暂时取消,直到他们把宇宙飞船修好。

所以,我们——我、苏和弗里奇少校只好再次坐电梯下去。她是唯一一个有怨言的人,因为苏和我都大大地松了一口气。

然而,轻松的感觉并没有持续太久。一个小时后,我们正要坐下来吃午饭,有人跑进我们的房间,说:"快穿上你们的宇航服！他们准备送你们去太空了！"

所有人大喊大叫，跑来跑去。我估计很多电视观众打电话来抱怨什么的，所以，他们决定，无论如何也要点燃我们屁股底下那团火。不管出于什么原因，现在都不重要了。

总之，我们坐上巴士，前往宇宙飞船，电梯坐到一半时，突然有人说："天哪，我们忘了那只该死的猿猴！"他开始对地上的人大喊，让他们回去把苏带来。

我们再次系上安全带，当他们把苏带进舱门后，有人从一百开始倒数。我们都靠在座位上，倒数到大约"十"的时候，我听到身后苏的座位上传来奇怪的咆哮声。我回头一看，天哪，坐在那里的根本不是苏，而是一只巨大的公猿猴，他龇牙咧嘴，抓着安全带，好像随时要挣脱！

我告诉弗里奇少校，她转过身，说："哦，我的上帝！"然后打开无线电，对地面塔台的人说："听着，你们犯了一个错误，和我们在一起的是一只公猿猴，所以，最好取消这次计划，等问题解决了再说。"但突然间，宇宙飞船隆隆作响，颤抖起来，塔台里的家伙通过无线电说："大姐，现在这是你的问题了，我们要按时完成任务。"

然后，我们就升空了。

第十三章

我的第一感觉是被什么东西压扁了,就像香蕉砸在我爸爸身上时那样。动弹不得,叫不出声,什么都不能说,什么也不能做——我们在这里完全是为了这次太空之旅。外面,透过窗户,我只能看到蓝天。飞船正冲向太空。

过了一小会儿,速度似乎慢了些,我的心情也随之放松下来。弗里奇少校说,我们现在可以解开安全带,继续做我们自己的事了。她说,现在我们正以一万五千英里的时速行驶。我回头一看,果然,地球在我们身后只是一个小球,就像所有在外太空拍的照片一样。我环顾四周,发现那只大公猴表情木讷、闷闷不乐,瞪着弗里奇少校和我。她说,也许他想吃午饭什么的,让我去后面给他拿根香蕉,免得他发脾气,干出什么坏事。

他们给猿猴包了一小袋食物,里面有香蕉、麦片、干浆果、树叶之类的东西。我打开那个袋子,在里面翻找能让猿猴开心的东西,与此同时,弗里奇少校正用无线电和休斯敦地面控制中心的人通话。

"现在,你们听我说,"她说,"关于这只猴子,我们必须想办法做点儿什么。他不是苏,他是一只公猴,他看上去一点儿都不高兴。他甚至可能会动粗。"

她的话好一会儿才传到地面，再从地面传来回复，但地面有个人说："呃，一只猴子和另一只猴子会有什么不一样。"

"才不是呢，"弗里奇少校说，"如果你和那个大家伙挤在这个小太空舱里，你就不会这么说了。"

过了一两分钟，一阵噼里啪啦的声音从无线电那边传过来，说："听着，上面命令，你不得向任何人透露此事，否则，我们都将沦为笑柄。对你和其他任何人来说，那只猴子就是苏——不管它的两腿间有什么。"

弗里奇少校看着我，摇了摇头。"是，是，长官，"她说，"可是，只要我和那个畜生在一起，我就会用安全带把他拴在座位上——你明白吗？"

地面控制台只传回来一个词：

"收到。"

其实，习惯了以后，在外太空待着挺好玩的。我们没有重力，所以可以到处飘，风景非常壮观——月亮和太阳，地球和星星。我想知道珍妮·柯伦在下面什么地方，在做什么。

我们绕着地球转了一圈又一圈。白天和黑夜每隔一小时左右变换一次，这会让你改变看问题的角度。我的意思是，现在，我在太空，等我回去了——或者，我应该说，如果我回去——然后呢？做我的养虾生意？再去找珍妮？跟裂蛋乐队一起演出？为住济贫院的妈妈做点儿什么？这一切都很奇怪。

弗里奇少校一有空就打个盹儿，但不睡觉的时候，她就一直抱怨。埋怨那只猴子，埋怨地面控制台那帮浑蛋，埋怨她没有地方化妆，埋怨我在非晚餐或午餐时间吃东西。见鬼，我们只能吃格兰诺拉麦片棒。我不想牢骚满腹，但他们本可以挑一个好看的女人，至少别这么没完没了地抱怨。

此外，我跟你说：那只猴子也不是什么理想的同伴。

我先是给了他一根香蕉——不是吗？他抓住香蕉，开始剥皮，但接着，他放下了香蕉。那只香蕉开始在太空舱里飘浮。我不得不抓住它。我把香蕉递给猴子，他把香蕉捣烂，然后把糊糊扔得到处都是，我还得去清理干净。他时刻想要关注。只要你不理它，他就大声喧哗，开始上下磕牙，像给牙上发条似的。没过一会儿，你就会被他逼疯。

最后，我拿出口琴，开始吹曲子——好像是《牧场之家》。猿猴不那么激动了。于是，我又吹了几支曲子，比如《德州黄玫瑰》和《我梦见浅棕色头发的珍妮》。猿猴躺在那儿，看着我，安静得像个婴儿。我忘了宇宙飞船里有一台电视摄像机，地面控制台能接收到这一切。第二天早上我醒来时，看见有人在休斯敦的摄像机前举着一张报纸给我们看。标题是："白痴吹奏太空音乐安抚猿猴。"我还要应付这种屁话。

总之，事情进展得很顺利，但我注意到，苏正用一种奇怪的眼神看弗里奇少校。每次她靠近他，苏都会变得更活跃，伸出手，好像要抓住她似的，她骂他："离我远点儿，你这个讨厌的家伙。别碰我！"但苏心里有主意。这一点我还是能看出来的。

没过多久，我就知道他在想什么了。我曾悄悄跑到那块小隔板后面，在罐子里撒尿，突然，一阵骚动。我把头探出隔板，看见苏抓住了弗里奇少校，手伸进她的宇航服里。她扯着嗓子喊，还用无线电麦克风啪啪打苏的头。

我忽然明白问题出在哪儿了。尽管我们才在太空中待了将近两天，但苏一直被绑在座位上，没有机会撒尿！我当然记得那是什么感觉。他的尿泡一定快憋爆了！总之，我走过去，把他从弗里奇少校身边带走，她仍然大喊大叫，称他是"肮脏的畜生"什么的。弗里奇少校脱身后，走到驾驶舱前部，低下头，抽泣起来。我解开苏身上的安全带，把他带到隔板后面。

我找了个空瓶子，让他把尿撒在里面，但他尿完尿，拿起瓶子扔到一个彩灯板上，瓶子碎了，尿液在宇宙飞船里飘浮。我说，见鬼，我刚要带苏回他的座位，这时，我看到一大团尿液直奔弗里奇少校去了，看样子会打到她的后脑勺，于是，我放开苏，试图用他们给我们用来捕捉飘浮物的网抄子抄起尿团。但就在我准备抄起那团尿时，弗里奇少校坐起来，转过身，那个尿团正中她的面门。

她又开始喊叫、痛哭，而这时，苏已经走开，并伸手扯下控制面板上的电线。弗里奇少校尖叫着："拦住他！拦住他！"但很快，火花什么的就在宇宙飞船里到处飞，苏上蹦下跳，胡乱撕扯。无线电里传来一个声音，想知道"上面到底出了什么事"，然而，为时已晚。

宇宙飞船摇晃、翻滚，我、苏和弗里奇少校像软木浮子一样被抛来掷去。什么都抓不住，什么都关不掉，站不起来，也坐不下去。地面控制中心的声音再次从无线电里传来："我们注意到你们的飞船的稳定性出了点问题。阿甘,你能手动把 D-6 程序插入右舷电脑吗?"

狗屁——他开玩笑呢吧!我像陀螺一样转圈,此外,我这儿还有一只野猴在胡闹!弗里奇少校大吼大叫,我什么也听不见,更没办法思考,她说的大意好像是,宇宙飞船即将坠毁。我瞥了一眼窗外,情况确实不太妙。地球正飞快地靠近我们。

我总算挪到右舷电脑那儿了,我一只手抓着控制面板,另一只手将 D-6 插入机器。这个程序旨在将宇宙飞船降落在印度洋上,以防我们遇到麻烦,眼下我们确实遇到了麻烦。

弗里奇少校和苏拼命抓住东西,但弗里奇少校喊道:"你在那边干什么?"我告诉她,她说:"算了吧,你这个笨蛋——已经过了印度洋了。等我们再转一圈,你看能不能降落在南太平洋。"

信不信由你,坐宇宙飞船环游世界,并不需要太多时间,弗里奇少校抓住无线电麦克风,对着地面控制中心的人喊叫,说宇宙飞船要么即将在南太平洋溅落,要么坠毁,让他们尽快来接我们。我发疯似的按按钮,巨大的地球逐渐向我们逼近。我们飞越了一块陆地,弗里奇少校觉得那好像是南美洲,接着是一大片水域,南极在我们左边,澳大利亚在前方。

然后,一切变得炽热起来,船舱外还传来奇怪的声音,船身开始震动,并咝咝作响,地球赫然出现在我们眼前。弗里奇少校朝我吼叫:"拉降落伞操纵杆!"可是,我被卡在座位上。她的身体则紧贴着船舱的天花板,所以,看样子我们要完蛋了，因为我们正在以一万英里的时速，直奔海洋中的一大片绿地。以如此快的速度撞向陆地，我们大概连个骨头渣都不会剩。

但是突然，什么东西"砰"的一声，飞船的速度慢了下来。我一看，原来是苏拉了降落伞操纵杆，救了我们一命。此时此地，我想，等这一切结束后，我会喂他一根香蕉。

总之，飞船在降落伞下面来回摆动，看样子我们就要撞到那一大片绿地了——显然，情况不太妙，因为我们应该落入水中，然后会有船来接我们。但自从我们踏上这个奇妙的装置，凡事都没顺利过，所以，为什么现在还会抱有这种奢望？

弗里奇少校正用无线电对地面控制中心说："我们即将降落在澳大利亚北部海洋中的某个地方，但我不确定我们的具体位置。"

几秒钟后，一个声音传回来："如果你不知道你们在哪儿，为什么不看看窗外，你这个笨娘儿？"于是，弗里奇少校放下无线电，往窗外看了看，她说："天哪，这里好像是婆罗洲还是什么地方。"可是，当她想告诉地面控制中心的时候，无线电通信竟然出故障了。

这时，我们离地球越来越近了，飞船还在降落伞下面摇摆。我们脚下，除了一个看上去是褐色的小湖，只有丛林和山脉。我们几乎看不清下面湖边正在发生什么。我们仨——我、苏和弗里奇少校——都把脸贴在窗户上往下看，弗里奇少校突然喊道："天哪！这不是婆罗洲，这是该死的新几内亚，地上那些鬼东西一定是货物崇拜（Cargo Cult）之类的！"

我和苏拼命往下看，湖岸上有大约一千个土著人回头望着我们，全都朝我们高举双臂。他们穿着小草裙，头发乱蓬蓬的，有些人还手持盾牌和长矛。

"该死，"我说，"你说这是什么？"

"货物崇拜，"弗里奇少校说，"二战期间，我们曾经把一包包糖果之类的东西扔给这些黑鬼，让他们站在我们这边，他们永远不会忘记这一点。他们以为这是神，还是什么人干的，从那以后，他们就一直等我们回来，甚至为此建造了粗糙的跑道，你看见下面那些东西了吗？他们用又大又圆的黑色的桩子标出了降落区。"

"那些东西怎么看着像大炖锅。"我说。

"是啊，确实有点儿像。"弗里奇少校好奇地说。

"食人族就是这儿的吧？"我问。

"我想，我们很快就会知道的。"她说。

宇宙飞船轻轻地朝湖边荡去，就在我们落水前，他们开始敲鼓，嘴巴一张一合。我们在太空舱里，什么也听不见，但我们的想象力还是很丰富的。

第十四章

我们在小湖上着陆的情况还不错。先是溅落,接着反弹,然后又回到陆地上。周围悄然无声,我和苏,还有弗里奇少校偷偷往窗外看。

大约十英尺开外的岸上,站着一整支部落的土著人,他们正看着我们,他们有着你能想象得到的最凶狠的面容——他们皱着眉头,凑过来,想看我们是什么东西。弗里奇少校说,也许他们不高兴,因为我们没从飞船上给他们扔东西。总之,她说,她要坐下来想想现在该怎么办,因为我们已经走到这一步了,还算顺利,她可不想在这些黑鬼身上出岔子。七八个大块头的家伙跳进水里,把我们往岸上推。

弗里奇少校还坐在那儿盘算,这时,有人砰砰敲飞船的门。我们面面相觑,弗里奇少校说:"谁都别动。"

我说:"我们不让他们进来,他们可能会生气的。"

"别出声,"她说,"也许他们以为这里没人,就走了。"

于是,我们等着,果然,过了一会儿,又有人来敲宇宙飞船的门。

我说:"不应门是不礼貌的。"

弗里奇少校对我发出嘘声:"闭上你的笨嘴——你看不出这

些人很危险吗?"

突然,苏走过去,把门打开了。站在外面的是一个自从我们在橘子碗和内布拉斯加大学剥玉米人队对抗以来,我见过的最高大的黑人。

他的鼻子上插了一根骨头,穿着草裙,手拿长矛,脖子上挂着很多珠子,他的头发有点像莎士比亚戏剧里汤姆·白德兰戴的那种假发。

发现苏在舱门口盯着他看,他好像吓了一大跳。事实上,他吓得突然昏倒在地。我和弗里奇少校又往窗外偷看,其他土著人看到这个家伙突然倒地,立刻跑到灌木丛里躲了起来——我猜是等着看接下来会发生什么。

弗里奇少校说:"别动——一动也不许动。"可是,苏随手抓起一个瓶子,跳到地上,把瓶子里的液体全都倒在那个家伙脸上,让他苏醒过来。突然,那个家伙坐了起来,开始叽里呱啦、噼噼啪啪、吐口水、咳嗽,还不停地摇头。他确实醒过来了,但苏抓起来的是我尿尿用的瓶子。这时,那个家伙又认出了苏,他举起双手,跪在地上,像阿拉伯人那样磕头。

这时,其余的人从灌木丛里走出来,动作缓慢,满脸惊恐,眼珠瞪得溜圆,准备掷出手中的长矛。地上那个家伙不再叩头,他抬起头,看到其他人来了,他喊了一句什么,他们放下长矛,走过来,聚集在飞船周围。

"这会儿他们看起来挺友善的,"弗里奇少校说,"我想,我们还是出去亮明身份吧。航天局的人过几分钟就会来接我们。"结果,这是我这辈子听过的最扯淡的话——空前绝后。

总之，我和弗里奇少校，我们走出宇宙飞船，所有土著人发出"哦""啊"的声音。那个躺在地上的家伙看着我们，表情十分困惑，但他站起来说："你好，我，好人。你们是谁？"说着，他伸出手。

我和他握了手，但随后，弗里奇少校试图告诉他我们是谁，她说我们是"美国宇航局多轨道前行星亚重力球间太空飞行训练任务的参与者"。

那个家伙只是站在那儿，目瞪口呆地看着我们，好像我们是太空人似的，于是，我说："我们是美国人。"突然，他的眼睛亮了，他说："看出来了！美国人！啊呀，多么精彩的演出！"

"你会说英语？"弗里奇少校问道。

"哎呀，是的，"他说，"我去过美国。打仗的时候。我被战略情报局招募学习英语，然后被派回到这里，组织我们的族人进行抗日游击战。"听到这话，苏的眼睛变得又大又亮。

不过，我觉得这事挺蹊跷的——这么偏僻的地方，这么一个大老黑居然说一口流利的美国话，于是，我问："你念的是什么学校？"

"哎，我念的是耶鲁大学，老弟，"他说，"布拉——布拉，什么的。"他说"布拉——布拉"时，其他黑人也跟着齐声高喊"布拉——布拉"，鼓声再次响起，直到这个大块头的家伙摆手让他们安静下来。

"我叫萨姆，"他说，"至少在耶鲁他们是这样叫我的。我的真名很拗口。欢迎光临。你们想喝茶吗？"

我和弗里奇少校对视了一下。她几乎说不出话来，于是我说："好啊，那太好了。"这时，弗里奇少校能说话了，她尖着嗓子说："你们有电话可以让我们用一下吗？"她说。

大山姆微微皱眉，挥了挥手，鼓声再次响起，在一片"布拉——布拉"的高呼声中，我们被护送进丛林中。

他们在丛林中搭建了一个小村庄，有点像电影里看到的草屋什么的，大山姆的草屋是其中最宏伟的一座。屋前摆着一把看起来像王座的椅子，四五个光着上身的女人听凭他吩咐，他叫她们给我们弄点茶水来，然后，他指着两块大石头，让弗里奇少校和我坐下。苏一直拉着我的手，跟在我们身后，大山姆示意他坐在地上。

"你们这只猴子挺棒的，"山姆说，"从哪儿弄来的？"

"他为美国宇航局工作。"弗里奇少校说。她似乎对我们的处境不太满意。

"真的吗？"大山姆说，"他有工资吗？"

"他可能想吃根香蕉。"我说。大山姆说了句什么，其中一个土著女人给苏拿来一根香蕉。

"真不好意思，"大山姆说，"我好像还没问过你们的名字。"

"珍妮特·弗里奇少校，美国空军。编号04534573。我只能告诉你这么多。"

"噢，亲爱的女士，"大山姆说，"你不是这里的囚犯。我们只是可怜的落后部落的成员。有人说，自石器时代以来，我们就没有多大进步。我们不会伤害你们的。"

"在我能使用电话之前，我没有别的话可说。"弗里奇少校说。

"好吧，"大山姆说，"那你呢，年轻人？"

"我叫福瑞斯特。"我告诉他。

"是吗，"他说，"这个名字是不是取自你们著名的内战将军内森·贝德福德·福瑞斯特？"

"是的。"我说。

"太有趣了。啊呀，阿甘，你在哪儿念的书？"

我本想说我在亚拉巴马大学念过一段时间，但后来我决定谨慎行事，所以我告诉他我念的是哈佛大学，这并不完全是谎话。

"啊，哈佛啊——深红色，"大山姆说，"哦，我太了解哈佛了。一群可爱的家伙——即使他们上不了耶鲁。"说完，他放声大笑："说实话，从这一点上来讲，你确实有点儿像哈佛人。"他说。不知道为什么，我感觉有祸事临头。

傍晚，大山姆让两个土著女人带我们去我们的住处。那是一间草屋，泥土地面，入口很小，让我想起李尔王去过的茅屋。两个手持长矛的大块头的家伙走过来，在我们门外站岗。

土著人整夜敲鼓，高呼"布拉—布拉"，我们从门口看到他们架起一口巨大的锅，锅下还生起了火。我和弗里奇少校不知道这一切到底是怎么回事，但我猜苏知道，因为他独自坐在角落里，一副闷闷不乐的样子。

到了九点、十点钟，他们还没给我们送饭来，弗里奇少校说，也许我应该去找大山姆打听一下晚饭的事。我刚要往门外走，两个土著人将长矛交叉，挡在我面前，我明白他们的意思，于是退回屋内。我忽然明白为什么我们没有被邀请吃晚饭了——因为我们就是晚饭。前景不容乐观。这时，鼓声停了，人们不再高呼"布拉——布拉"。我们听到有人在外面高声大气地讲话，另一个人则高声大气地回答，听着像大山姆的声音。一来一去，持续了好一会儿，争论得越来越激烈。就在他们似乎不能喊得更大声时，我们听到"咚"的一声巨响，听起来像是有人头上挨了一板子。周围顿时安静下来，接着，鼓声再次响起，所有人再次高呼"布拉——布拉"。

第二天早上，我们坐在草屋里，大山姆进门，说："你们好，昨晚睡得好吗？"

"一点儿都不好，"弗里奇少校说，"外面那么吵，我们怎么可能睡得着？"

大山姆露出痛苦的神情，说："哦，我很抱歉。不过，你们知道，我的族人，啊，他们看见你们的飞船从天而降，还以为会收到什么礼物。自打一九四五年以来，我们就一直盼着你们美国人带礼物回来。他们看到你们没带礼物，自然认为你们就是礼物，他们本来打算把你们煮了吃掉，直到我说服他们别这么做。"

"你骗我，小子。"弗里奇少校说。

"正相反，"大山姆说，"你看，我的族人可算不上你们所谓的文明人——至少按照你们的标准来说——因为他们特别爱吃人肉。尤其是白人的肉。"

"你是想告诉我你们这些人是食人族吗?"弗里奇少校说。

大山姆耸了耸肩:"差不多吧。"

"真恶心,"弗里奇少校说,"听着,你必须确保我们不会受到任何伤害,让我们离开这里,回到文明世界中去。宇航局的搜索队可能随时会到。我要求你像对待盟国那样尊重我们。"

"啊,"大山姆说,"昨天晚上他们正是这么想的。"

"现在你听好咯!"弗里奇少校说,"我要求你立刻释放我们,并允许我们前往离这儿最近的有电话的城市。"

"恐怕,"大山姆说,"这是不可能的。即使我们真把你们放了,俾格米人也会在你们刚进入丛林时就抓住你们。"

"俾格米人?"弗里奇少校问。

"我们和俾格米人世代交战。有人曾经偷了一头猪,我想——没有人记得是谁偷的,以及在哪儿偷的——失传了。但实际上,我们被俾格米人包围了,而且从所有人记事以来就是这样的。"

"好吧,"弗里奇少校说,"我宁愿去俾格米人那儿碰碰运气,也不愿意留在一群该死的食人族身边——俾格米人不是食人族吧?"

"不是,夫人,"大山姆说,"他们是猎头族。"

"太棒了。"弗里奇少校没好气地说。

"昨天晚上,"大山姆说,"我把你们从大炖锅里救出来,但我不确定我还能阻挡我的族人多久。他们决心要把你们的到来变成某种好处。"

"是这样吗?"弗里奇少校说,"比如?"

"嗯,首先,你们的猿猴。我想,他们至少希望能吃掉他。"

"那只猿猴是美利坚合众国独有的财产。"弗里奇少校说。

"尽管如此,"大山姆说,"我认为你们总要展现出一种外交姿态。"

苏皱着眉,缓缓点头,忧愁地望着门外。

"其次,"大山姆继续说,"我想,既然你们已经在这儿了,也许可以为我们干点活儿。"

"哪类活儿?"弗里奇少校狐疑地问。

"哦,"大山姆说,"农活儿。农业。你们知道吗,多年来,我一直努力改善族人耻辱的命运。不久前,我无意中有了以下想法。如果我们能将这里肥沃的土地变成我们的优势,并引进一些现代农学技术,我们就可以慢慢摆脱部落的困境,并在世界市场上发挥作用。简言之,让我们远离这种落后陈旧的经济,变成一个有生存能力的、有文化教养的民族。"

"什么样的农活儿?"弗里奇少校问。

"棉花,我亲爱的女士,棉花!经济作物之王!多年前,贵国曾建立过一个棉花帝国。"

"你指望我们种棉花!"弗里奇少校尖叫道。

"没错,大姐。"大山姆说。

第十五章

于是，我们在这儿种起了棉花。一亩，一亩，又一亩的棉花。上上下下，满眼都是棉花田。如果说我这辈子有什么东西是确定的，那就是，如果有朝一日我们能离开这个地方，我绝不想成为一名棉农。

从在丛林中遇到大山姆和食人族的第一天起，确实发生了一些事。首先，弗里奇少校和我说服了大山姆，不要让我们把可怜的苏交给他的部落吃掉。我们还说服他，让苏帮我们种棉花，这比只是让他成为一顿饭有用得多。于是，苏每天都和我们在一起，戴着一顶大草帽，背着一个麻袋，种棉花。

另外，在我们到这儿的第三个星期，还是第四个星期，大山姆走进我们的小屋说："听我说，阿甘，你会下棋吗？"

我说："不会。"

他说："哦，你可是哈佛人，你没准儿喜欢学下棋呢。"

我点点头，我就是这样学会下棋的。

每天晚上，我们在棉花田里干完活儿，大山姆就会拿出他的棋盘，我们围坐在火堆旁，玩到深夜。他给我演示各种下法，头几天，他还教我各种策略。后来，他就不教了，因为我赢了他一两盘。

没过多久，下棋的时间就变长了。有时候会持续好几天，因为大山姆决定不了下一步该怎么走。他坐在那儿，研究半天才走一步，但我总能打败他。有时，他很生自己的气，用棍子敲自己的脚，或者拿脑袋往石头上撞什么的。

"对于一个哈佛人来说，你是一个相当不错的棋手，"他会说，或者，"听我说，阿甘——你为什么要走最后那步棋？"我什么都不会说，或者只是耸耸肩，这会搞得大山姆暴跳如雷。

有一天，他说："你知道吗，阿甘，你来这儿，我很高兴，这样就有人陪我下棋了，我也很高兴把你从炖锅里救出来。唯一的问题是，我真的很想赢你一盘。"

说完，大山姆舔了舔嘴唇，傻子都能明白，我只要让他赢一盘，他就会心满意足，然后立刻把我当晚餐吃掉。我必须保持警惕，如果你明白我的意思。

与此同时，弗里奇少校遇到一件很奇怪的事。

一天，她和苏，还有我一起从棉花田往回走，这时，一只大黑胳膊从灌木丛里伸出来，向她招手。我和苏停了下来，弗里奇少校走到灌木丛前说："谁在里面？"突然，那只大胳膊伸出来，抓住弗里奇少校，把她拽进了灌木丛。我和苏你看看我，我看看你，接着往她那边跑去。苏先到的，我正要跳进灌木丛，苏拦住了我。他摇头，摆手让我走开，我们走到一边等着。里面传出各种声音，灌木丛发疯般地摇晃。我终于明白是怎么回事了，但从弗里奇少校发出的动静判断，她似乎没有什么危险，所以，我和苏继续走回村子。

大约一个小时后，弗里奇少校和那个大块头的家伙来了，他笑得合不拢嘴。她牵着他的手走。她把他领进小屋，对我说："阿甘，我想让你认识一下格鲁克。"说完，她领着他往前走。

"嗨。"我说。我以前在村子里见过这家伙。格鲁克咧嘴笑着点头，我也对他点头。苏则在一旁挠蛋蛋。

"格鲁克让我搬过去和他一起住，"她说，"我想我会搬过去的，咱们三个住在这儿有点儿挤，你说是不是？"

我点点头。

"阿甘，你不会把这件事说出去吧？"弗里奇少校问道。

她觉得我能告诉谁，我倒是很想知道。但我只是摇摇头，弗里奇少校收拾好东西，和格鲁克一起去了他的住处。事情就是这样。

日子一天天，一月月，最后一年年过去，我、苏和弗里奇少校每天在棉花田里干活，我感觉自己就像雷姆斯大叔。晚上，我下棋大败大山姆后，和苏一起走进小屋，我们闲坐了一会儿。我和苏已经到了可以通过嘴里叽里咕噜、做鬼脸和摆手互相交谈的程度。过了很长时间，我把他的经历拼凑出来了，结果差不多和我的一样悲惨。

当他还是一只小猿猴时，有一天，他的爸爸妈妈在丛林里散步，几个家伙走过来，用一张网罩住他们，把他们拖走了。苏尽力和叔叔阿姨处好关系，直到他们嫌弃他吃得太多，把他撵走了，从此，他就自食其力了。

他过得不错，成天在树上荡秋千，吃香蕉，直到有一天，他开始好奇外面的世界，他荡过一棵又一棵树，来到丛林边缘的一个村庄。他口渴了，下来坐在溪边喝水，这时，一个家伙划着独木舟经过。苏从没见过独木舟，所以坐在那儿看着它，那个家伙朝他划过来。他以为那个家伙想送他一程，但相反，那个家伙用桨打了苏的脑袋，还把他四马攒蹄地捆了起来，接下来，他只知道，他被卖给了某个人，把他送到巴黎的展览会上展示。

展览会上还有一只猩猩，名叫多丽丝，她是他见过的最漂亮的猿猴之一，没过多久，他们就坠入了爱河。举办展览的家伙带他们环游世界，他每去一个地方，最大的卖点就是把多丽丝和苏关在一个笼子里，这样，所有人都可以看他做爱——就是这种展览。总之，苏觉得很难堪，但这是他们活下去的唯一机会。

后来，有一次，他们在日本展出，有个人走到主办者跟前，出价并买下了多丽丝。她走了，苏不知道她去哪儿了，他又孤零零的了。

这件事导致苏的态度发生了明显的变化。他的脾气变得很糟糕，他们展示他时，他经常咆哮、号叫，最后，他甚至拉屎，还把屎扔到笼子外面花大价钱来看猩猩的人身上。

这样过了一段时间，主办展览的家伙受够了，把苏卖给了宇航局，所以最终他来到这里。我多少了解他的感受，因为寂寞的他想念多丽丝，就像寂寞的我依然想念珍妮·柯伦，我没有一天不惦记她现在过得怎么样。但现在，我们俩都在这里，困在这个偏僻的地方。

大山姆的棉花种植生意好得超乎所有人想象。我们播下种子，收获一捆捆棉花，然后把它们存放在离地搭建的大草棚里。终于有一天，大山姆说，他们打算造一艘大船，驳船，把棉花装上船，穿过俾格米人部落进城，卖掉棉花，赚一大笔钱。

"我都搞清楚了，"大山姆说，"我们先把棉花拍卖掉，拿到钱，然后用这笔钱购置一些我的族人需要的物品。"

我问他买什么，他说："哦，你知道，老弟，珠子、小饰品什么的，也许买一两面镜子、一台便携式收音机、一盒上好的古巴雪茄，还有一两箱酒。"

这就是我们的交易方式。

总之，几个月过去了，我们收获了当季最后一批棉花。大山姆那艘带我们穿过俾格米人部落进城的内河驳船快造好了，就在我们动身的前一晚，他们举办了一场盛大的土风舞会，庆祝这一切，并驱除邪灵。

整个部落围坐在篝火旁，一边敲鼓，一边高呼"布拉——布拉"。他们还把那口大锅拖出来，架在火上煮，但大山姆说，这只是一种"象征性的姿态"。

我们坐在那儿下棋，这么跟你说吧——我兴奋得都快爆炸了！只要让我们靠近一个村镇或城市，我们就可以逃走。苏也知道这个计划，因为他坐在那边，一边挠着腋下，一边咧着大嘴笑。

我们下了一两盘棋，快下完另一盘棋时，我突然低头一看，该死，大山姆快把我将死了。他笑得很灿烂，黑暗中，我只看到他的牙齿，我想我最好尽快摆脱这种局面。

唯一的问题是，我摆脱不了。我的如意算盘打得太早，让自己陷入了一个极其困难的境地。我无路可走了。

我研究了半天棋局，火光照在大山姆微笑的牙齿上，牙面上清楚地映出我紧锁的眉头，然后，我说："啊，你听我说——我去撒个尿。"大山姆点点头，仍然咧嘴笑着，我跟你说，在我的印象中，这是我头一次说这种话没让我陷入困境，而是摆脱了困境。

我去小屋后面尿尿，但尿完尿，我并没有回去下棋，而是进屋找苏，跟他解释了一下情况。然后，我偷偷溜进格鲁克的小屋，低声叫弗里奇少校出来。她出来了，我把我的想法也告诉了她，说我们最好在他们把我们煮熟之前赶紧离开这里。

哦，我们一致决定尽快逃走。格鲁克说，他要跟我们一起走，因为他爱上了弗里奇少校——不管他是怎么说的，大概意思是这样的。总之，我们四个偷偷溜出村子，来到河边，我们正要登上一条本地人的独木舟，突然，我抬头一看，大山姆和一千来个土著人正站在我面前，表情邪恶而又失望。

"拜托，老弟，"他说，"你真以为你比我这个老家伙精明吗？"我告诉他："哦，我们只是想在月光下划划船——你明白我的意思吗？"

"明白。"他说，他明白我的意思，接着，他的手下抓住我们，把我们押回村里。大炖锅冒着气泡和热气，他们把我们绑在地上的木桩上，前景不太乐观。

"哦，老弟，"大山姆说，"发生这种变故确实令人遗憾。不过，你可以从这个角度看，你起码可以这样安慰自己，你喂饱了一两张饥饿的嘴。而且，我必须告诉你，毫无疑问，你是我遇到过的最棒的棋手，我在耶鲁四年，拿了三年国际象棋冠军。"

"至于你嘛，女士，"大山姆对弗里奇少校说，"我很抱歉，不得不让你和格鲁克的风流韵事到此为止了，不过，你知道我为什么会这么做。"

"不，我不知道是怎么回事，你这个卑鄙的野蛮人，"弗里奇少校说，"你怎么敢这样？你应该为自己感到羞耻！"

"也许我们可以把你和格鲁克放在一个盘子里端上桌，"大山姆咯咯笑着说，"一点白肉配黑肉——我自己嘛，我要吃一条大腿，也可能吃一个乳房——这个主意不错。"

"你这个无耻的、坏透了的浑蛋！"弗里奇少校说。

"随你怎么说，"大山姆说，"现在，宴会开始！"

他们给我们松绑，一群黑人把我们往大锅那边拖。他们先把可怜的苏举起来，因为大山姆说，拿他炖汤，味道肯定不错，他们把他举起来，正要往大锅里丢，突然，不知道从哪儿冒出来一支箭，射中了一个举起苏的家伙。那个家伙倒下，苏落在他身上。然后，更多的箭从丛林边，如雨点般朝我们射过来，所有人惊慌失措。

"俾格米人！"大山姆喊道，"拿起你们的武器！"所有人跑去拿他们的长矛和刀。

我们没有长矛，也没有刀，弗里奇少校、我、苏和格鲁克只好又朝河边跑，但我们沿着小路跑了还不到十英尺，突然，我们被树丛中设下的罗网倒吊在半空。

我们吊在那里，像蝙蝠一样倒挂着，血液涌向头部，这时，一个小家伙从灌木丛里走出来，对着被捆起来的我们嘻嘻哈哈笑。村里传来各种野蛮的声音，但过了一会儿，周遭安静了下来。然后，一群俾格米人过来，割开网子，把我们放下来，接着，他们又捆住我们的手脚，把我们带回村子。

当时的场景实在壮观！他们抓住了大山姆和所有土著人，也捆住了他们的手脚。看来，他们要把土著人统统扔进沸腾的大锅里。

"哦，老弟，"大山姆说，"看来你们是在最后一刻得救的，是吗？"

我点点头，但我不确定我们是不是刚出油锅，又入火坑。

"我跟你说，"大山姆说，"看样子，我和我的同伴们都要完蛋了，但也许你还有机会。如果你能拿到你的口琴，吹一两首小曲，或许能挽救你的性命。俾格米人的酋长特别喜欢美国音乐。"

"谢谢。"我说。

"别客气，老弟。"大山姆说。他们把他高高举到沸腾的大锅上，突然，他对我喊道："马落在象三——然后，车十落在王七，我就是这样打败你的！"

"扑通"一声，水花四溅，然后，被捆住手脚的大山姆族人们开始齐声高呼"布拉——布拉"。所有人的情况似乎都不妙。

第十六章

俾格米人煮完大山姆的族人,并将他们的人头缩水后,把我们倒挂在长竿上,像抬猪一样抬进丛林。

"你认为他们打算拿我们怎么办?"弗里奇少校大声问我。

"我不知道,我也不在乎。"我吼道,但这是真话。我受够了这些烂事。这是我能忍受的极限。

总之,大约一天后,我们来到俾格米人的村庄,你大概已经想到了,丛林中的空地上有很多小屋。他们把我们抬到空地中央一间小屋前,那里站着一群俾格米人,还有一个没牙老头,留着长长的白胡子,像个婴儿似的,坐在高脚椅上。我猜,他就是俾格米人的酋长。

他们把我们扔在地上,给我们松了绑,我们站起来,拍拍身上的土,俾格米人的酋长含混不清、叽里咕噜地说起话来,说完,他从椅子上下来,径直走到苏面前,照着他的裆部踹了一脚。

"他干吗要踹他?"我问格鲁克,他和弗里奇少校同居期间学了点儿英语。

"他想知道这只猿猴是公的,还是母的。"格鲁克说。

我想一定有更好的方法找出答案,但我什么也没说。

接着，酋长走到我面前，叽里咕噜跟我说话——俾格米语，管它是什么话——我也准备裆部挨一脚，但格鲁克说："他想知道你为什么和他们，这些可怕的食人族，一起生活。"

"告诉他，可不是我们想跟他们住在一起的。"弗里奇少校说。

"我有个主意，"我说，"告诉他，我们是美国乐手。"

格鲁克把这话转达给酋长，酋长死死地盯着我们，然后问了格鲁克一句什么。

"他说什么？"弗里奇少校想知道。

"他问猿猴弹什么乐器。"格鲁克说。

"告诉他，猿猴会弹长矛。"我说，格鲁克转述给他，然后，俾格米人的酋长宣布他想听我们演奏。

我拿出口琴，吹了一支曲子——《康城赛马歌》。俾格米人的酋长听了一会儿，然后开始拍手，跳起了一种类似木屐舞的舞蹈。

我吹完曲子，他说他想知道弗里奇少校和格鲁克弹什么乐器，我告诉格鲁克，说弗里奇少校弹奏刀子，格鲁克什么乐器都不会——他是经纪人。

俾格米人的酋长露出疑惑的表情，他说，他从没听说过有人会弹奏刀子或者长矛，但他吩咐手下给苏拿来几根长矛，给弗里奇少校拿来几把刀，想看看我们能奏出怎样的音乐。

我们一拿到长矛和刀，我就说："好了——动手！"苏用长矛狠狠地敲俾格米人的酋长的脑袋，弗里奇少校则用刀吓唬几个俾格米人，我们趁机跑进<u>丛林</u>，俾格米人在后面紧追不舍。

131

俾格米人从后面朝我们扔各种石头,还朝我们射箭、吹箭,投掷飞镖什么的。突然,我们来到河岸上,无处可去,俾格米人迅速追上来。我们正要跳进河里,往对岸游,突然,河那边传来一声来复枪声。

俾格米人已经朝我们扑过来了,但又一声枪响,他们掉头跑回丛林。我们望向河对岸,瞧啊,那边有两个穿丛林夹克的家伙,头上戴着白色的木髓头盔,你在电影《丛林中的拉马尔》(*Ramar of the Jungle*)里看到的那种帽子。他们登上独木舟,朝我们这边划过来,他们靠近时,我看到其中一人的木髓头盔上印着"美国宇航局"的字样。我们终于得救了。

独木舟划到我们这边的岸边后,头盔上印有"美国宇航局"字样的家伙下了船,朝我们走过来。他径直走到苏跟前,伸出手说:"我猜,您是甘先生吧?"

"你们这帮浑蛋死哪儿去了?"弗里奇少校大吼道,"我们被困在这个该死的丛林里将近四年了!"

"很抱歉,夫人,"那个家伙说,"不过,我们也有要优先处理的事情,你知道。"

总之,我们终于逃脱了比死亡更可怕的命运,他们让我们登上独木舟,朝下游划去。其中一个人说:"哦,伙计们,文明世界就在前方。你们可以把你们的经历卖给杂志社,赚一大笔钱。"

"停船!"弗里奇少校突然喊道。

那两个人对视了一眼,但还是把独木舟划回岸边。

"我做了一个决定,"弗里奇少校说,"我这辈子头一次找到一个真正理解我的男人，我不会放他走的。近四年来，我和格鲁克幸福地生活在这片土地上，我决定和他留在这里。我们要到丛林里去，开始属于我们自己的新生活，组建一个家庭，从此过上幸福的日子。"

"可是，这个男人吃人肉。"其中一个人说。

"比你强多了，小家伙儿。"弗里奇少校说完，和格鲁克下了独木舟，手牵手，回到丛林中。就在他们消失前，弗里奇少校转过身，朝我和苏挥了挥手，然后，他们转身离去。

我回头看船尾，苏正坐在那儿扭绞手指。

"等一下。"我对那两个家伙说。我回去，坐到苏旁边，问他："你在想什么？"

苏什么也没说，但眼里有一滴泪，我知道接下来会发生什么了。他搂住我的肩膀，给了我一个热烈的拥抱，然后跳下船，爬上岸边的一棵树。我们看到他的最后一幕是，他抓着一根藤条，在丛林中越荡越远。

宇航局的家伙摇了摇头。"哎，你呢，傻瓜？你也要跟着你的朋友们去那个野蛮的地方生活吗？"

我目送了他们一分钟，然后说："呃，不。"说完，我坐回独木舟里。他们划桨远离时，我确实有过留下来的念头。可是，我做不到。我想，我还有更重要的事情要做。

他们用飞机把我送回美国，路上告诉我，他们将为我举办一场盛大的欢迎会，不过，这话我好像在哪儿听过。

果然，飞机在华盛顿机场一降落，就有上百万人在那里欢呼鼓掌,表现得好像很高兴见到我似的。我坐在一辆黑色大轿车的后座上进了城,他们说要带我去白宫觐见总统。没错,我也去过白宫。

哦,当我们到了白宫,我以为会见到那个请我吃早饭、让我看《贝弗利山乡巴佬》的总统,可是现在有了新总统——头发整齐地梳到脑后,腮帮子鼓鼓的,长了一个匹诺曹式的鼻子。

"跟我讲讲,"这位总统说,"这次旅行是不是很刺激?"

一个穿西装的家伙站在总统旁边,他俯身对总统说了句什么,突然,总统说:"哦,啊,其实,我的意思是说,你在丛林中受尽了磨难,能从那里逃出来实在了不起。"

穿西装的家伙又对总统耳语了几句,于是,总统对我说:"呃,你的同伴呢?"

"苏?"我说。

"她叫这个名字吗?"他看着手中的一张小卡片,"这里写的是珍妮特·弗里奇少校,就在你们获救时,她被一个食人族拖进了丛林。"

"在哪儿写的?"我问。

"就这儿。"总统说。

"事实不是这样的。"我说。

"你是在暗示我撒谎吗?"总统问。

"我只是说不是这样的。"我说。

"你听我说,"总统说,"我是你们的三军总司令。我不是骗子。我不撒谎!"

"我很抱歉，"我说，"但弗里奇少校的真实情况不是这样的。你只是照着卡片说（You just take that off a card），但是——"

"录音带（tape）！"总统喊道。

"什么？"我说。

"不，不，"穿西装的家伙说，"他说的是'卡片'，不是'录音带'，总统先生。"

"录音带！"总统尖叫道，"我告诉过你，永远不要在我面前提这个词！你们都是一群不忠的蠢猪。"总统用拳头捶打自己的膝盖。

"你们都不明白。我什么都不知道！我什么都没听说过！即使我听说过，我也忘了，要么就是最高机密！"

"可是，总统先生，"穿西装的家伙说，"他没说那个词。他只是说——"

"你竟然说我是骗子！"他说，"你被解雇了！"

"可是，您不能解雇我，"那个家伙说，"我是副总统。"

"好吧，请原谅我这么说，"总统说，"如果你到处说你的三军总司令是骗子，你永远也当不上总统。"

"哦，我想您说得对，"副总统说，"请原谅。"

"不，我请你原谅。"总统说。

"随便吧，"副总统说，他看上去有点坐立不安，"恕我失陪，我得去尿尿。"

"这是一天来我听到的第一个合理的想法。"总统说。说完，他转向我，问道："哎呀，你不就是那个打乒乓球的人吗？"

我说："是的，"然后，总统说："你为什么要那么做？"

我说："因为当时他快淹死了。"总统说："你应该把他压在下面，而不是救他。反正都过去了，因为你在丛林里的时候，那个婊子养的死了。"

"你有电视机吗？"我问。

总统看着我，表情有点滑稽："有，我有一台电视机，但我最近没怎么看。坏消息太多了。"

"你看过《贝弗利山乡巴佬》吗？"我说。

"电视上没播。"他说。

"现在电视上在播什么？"我问。

"《说出真相》——但你肯定不想看——全是一派胡言。"接着，他说，"听我说，现在我要去开个会，我送你到门口吧？"我们走到外面的门廊上，总统压低声音说："喂，你想不想买块手表？"

我说："什么？"他走到我身边，拉起西服袖子，哎呀，他的胳膊上戴了起码二三十块手表。

"我没钱。"我说。

总统放下袖子，拍拍我的后背，说："好吧，等你有钱了再来，我们会想出办法的，嗯？"

他和我握了手，一群摄影师走过来给我们拍照，然后，我就走了。不过，我要说的是，这个总统看起来倒像个好人。

总之，我不知道他们打算怎么处置我，不过，我不用琢磨太久。

大约过了一天，事态才算平息下来，他们把我安置在一家旅馆，但一天下午，两个家伙走进我的房间，说："听着，阿甘，不劳而获的日子结束了。政府不再买单了——从现在起，你只能靠你自己了。"

"哦，好吧，"我说，"但你们总得给我点儿回家的路费吧。我现在有点儿缺钱。"

"想都别想，阿甘，"他们说，"你用勋章砸参议院书记员的头没坐牢已经够幸运的了。我们帮你洗脱了罪名——但从现在开始，我们不想再管你的破事了。"

于是，我不得不离开旅馆。我没有什么东西可收拾，所以并不难，我只是走到大街上。我走了一会儿，路过总统住的白宫，出乎我意料的是，白宫前有一大群人戴着总统模样的橡胶面具，手里还举着标语。我想，他一定很高兴自己如此受人爱戴。

第十七章

虽然他们说不会给我钱,但在我离开旅馆前,其中一个家伙还是借给了我一块钱。我一见到公共电话,就打电话到我妈妈住的济贫院,告诉她我没事。但一位修女说:"甘太太已经不住我们这儿了。"

我问她去哪儿了,修女说:"不知道——她跟一个新教徒跑了。"我向她道谢,挂了电话。在某种程度上,我松了一口气。至少妈妈跟人跑了,不住在那个济贫院了。我想,我必须找到她,但说实话,我并不是很着急,因为就像天一定会下雨,她会因为我离开家这件事对我又哭又叫又闹。

天还真下雨了,倾盆大雨,我找到一个雨篷,站在下面,直到有个家伙出来,把我赶走。我很冷,浑身被雨淋透了,经过华盛顿的一栋政府大楼时,我看见人行道中间有一个很大的塑料垃圾袋。就在我靠近时,那个袋子动了一下,里面好像有东西!

我停下来,走到塑料袋前,用脚轻轻推了一下。突然,袋子向后跳了大约四英尺,一个声音从袋子下面传出来:"你给我滚远点!"

"谁在里面?"我问。那个声音回答说:"这是我的窨井盖——你去找你自己的。"

"你在说什么？"我说。

"我的窨井盖，"那个声音说，"从我的窨井盖上下去！"

"什么窨井盖？"我问。

突然，袋子抬起来了一点儿，一个家伙探出头来，他眯着眼睛看我，好像我是个白痴似的。

"你是新来的吧？"那个家伙问。

"差不多吧，"我回答，"我只是想躲雨。"

塑料袋下面那个家伙样子很可怜，头发半秃，几个月没刮胡子，眼睛通红，布满血丝，大部分牙齿都掉了。

"好吧，"他说，"既然是这样，让你待一会儿也无妨——拿去。"他伸出手，递给我一个叠好的垃圾袋。

"这个东西怎么用？"我问。

"打开，钻进去，你这个该死的傻瓜——你说你想躲雨。"说完，他把袋子拉回来，盖在自己身上。

好吧，我照着他说的做了，说实话，还真不赖。窨井盖里冒出热气，使袋子里变得温暖舒适，而且挡住了雨。我们把垃圾袋盖在身上，并排坐在窨井盖上，过了一会儿，那个家伙问我："你叫什么名字？"

"福瑞斯特。"我说。

"是吗？我曾经认识一个叫福瑞斯特的人。那是很久以前的事了。"

"你叫什么名字？"我问。

"丹。"他说。

"丹？丹？——嘿，等一下。"我说。我掀开我的垃圾袋，然后过去掀开那个家伙身上的垃圾袋，果然是他！他没有腿，坐在一辆底下带滚轮的小木车上。他看上去老了二十岁，我几乎认不出他来了。但就是他，没错。丹中尉！

从陆军医院出院后，丹回到康涅狄格，他想继续干老本行，教历史。但历史老师的职位没有空缺，他们让他教数学。他讨厌数学，而且，数学教室在学校的二楼，没腿的他费很大力气才能爬上楼。还有，他老婆和一个住在纽约的电视制片人跑了，并且以"感情破裂"为由起诉离婚。

他开始酗酒，丢了工作，游手好闲了一阵子。小偷把他家搬空了，退伍军人医院给他做的义肢尺寸不对。他说，几年后，他索性"破罐子破摔"，过起了流浪汉的生活。每个月，他会领到一点伤残抚恤金，但大多数时候，他会把钱送给其他流浪汉。

"我不知道，阿甘，"他说，"我想，我只是在等死。"

丹给了我几块钱，让我去街角买两瓶红匕首葡萄酒。我只买了一瓶，剩下的钱给我自己买了一个三明治，因为我一整天没吃东西了。

"好吧，老弟，"丹咕咚咚咚喝下半瓶酒后说，"说说吧，自从我上次见到你，你都在忙些什么。"

我讲给他听。我告诉他，我去中国打过乒乓球，我又见到了珍妮·柯伦，我和裂蛋乐队一起演出过，参加过和平示威活动，我把勋章扔了，还因此被关进了监狱。

"嗯,这个事我记得。当时,我还在医院。我想过去华盛顿参加游行,但我大概不会扔掉我的勋章。你看——"说着,他解开夹克的扣子,衬衫上挂满了勋章——紫心勋章、银星勋章——肯定有十一二枚。

"它们会让我想起一些东西,"他说,"我不太确定是什么——当然有战争,但只是其中一部分。我遭受了损失,阿甘,比失去两条腿更大的损失。可以说,我失去的是我的精神、我的灵魂。现在,那里只剩一片空白——原先我的灵魂所在之处,现在是勋章。"

"可是掌管一切的'自然法则'呢?"我问他,"我们所有人都必须融入其中的'万物计划'呢?"

"都滚蛋吧,"他说,"净是一堆哲学屁话。"

"可是,自从你告诉我之后,我就一直遵循这些屁话。我一直顺势而为,努力做到最好。做对的事。"

"好吧,也许对你有用,阿甘。我曾经以为对我也有用——可是,你看看我。你看看我,"他说,"我还有什么用?我是个该死的没有腿的怪物。一个乞丐。一个酒鬼。一个三十五岁的流浪汉。"

"可能会更糟。"我说。

"哦,是吗?怎么个糟糕法?"他说,我想他把我难住了,所以我继续把我的经历讲完——被关进疯人院,然后坐着火箭上太空,掉到食人族部落,我还讲了苏、弗里奇少校和俾格米人的事。

"哎呀,我的上帝,阿甘,我的朋友,你的冒险经历可真够刺激的,"丹说,"那你怎么会落得跟我一起盖着垃圾袋,坐在窨井盖上?"

"我不知道,"我说,"但我不打算在这儿待太久。"

"你有什么想法吗?"

"雨一停,"我说,"我就去找珍妮·柯伦。"

"她在哪儿?"

"我不知道,"我说,"不过,我会知道的。"

"听起来你可能需要帮助。"他说。

我看向丹,他的眼睛在胡子后面闪闪发光。我感觉他才是那个需要帮助的人,不过,我没意见。

那晚,雨下个不停,我和丹住进一家廉价的教会旅馆,丹付了每人五十美分的晚餐费和二十五美分的床费。只要你坐下来听布道之类的东西,就可以得到免费的晚餐,但丹说,他宁可睡在雨地里,也不愿意浪费宝贵时间听一个狂热的《圣经》宣讲者告诉我们他对这个世界的看法。

第二天早上,丹借给我一块钱,我找到一部公用电话,打电话给在波士顿的摩斯,他曾是裂蛋乐队的鼓手。果然,他还住在老地方,他完全没想到会接到我的电话。

"阿甘——我简直不敢相信!"摩斯说,"我们还以为你回不来了!"

他说,裂蛋乐队已经解散了。费布尔斯坦先生答应给他们的钱全被开支什么的耗尽了,第二张唱片之后,他们没有得到任何合同。摩斯说,人们现在听一种新的音乐——滚石、老鹰什么的——裂蛋乐队的大部分成员离开了，找到了正经工作。

摩斯说，很久没有珍妮的消息了。她去华盛顿参加和平示威活动，我在那儿被捕后，她回来过，和裂蛋乐队一起演出了几个月，但摩斯说，她好像和从前不太一样了。他说，有一次，她在台上突然哭了起来，他们只好靠器乐演奏完成整场演出。后来，她开始喝伏特加酒，演出迟到，他们正要找她谈谈这个事，她自己干脆不干了。

摩斯说，他个人觉得她的行为和我有关，但她从来没聊过这事。过了两个星期，她就离开了波士顿，说要去芝加哥，这是他近五年来最后一次见到她。

我问他是否知道有什么办法可以联系到她，他说也许他还留着她离开前给他的一个旧号码。他放下电话，几分钟后，他回来了，把那个电话号码告诉了我。除此之外，他说："我一点儿头绪都没有。"

我跟他说保重，还说，如果什么时候去波士顿，我会去找他。

"你还吹口琴吗？"摩斯问。

"嗯，有时候吹。"我说。

我又跟丹借了一块钱，然后拨了那个芝加哥的电话号码。

"珍妮·柯伦——珍妮？"一个男人的声音说，"哦，对——我记得她。那是个小美人。我已经很久没见过她了。"

"你知道现在她在哪儿吗？"

"她临走的时候说要去印第安纳波利斯。谁知道呢？她在天波禄找到了一份工作。"

"在哪儿?"

"天波禄——轮胎厂。你知道,做轮胎的——汽车轮胎。"

我对那个家伙表示了感谢,然后回去告诉丹。

"好吧,"他说,"我还没去过印第安纳波利斯呢。听说那个地方秋天很美。"

一开始我们想搭便车离开华盛顿,但运气不好。一个家伙让我们坐在一辆运砖头的卡车后面,送我们到城郊,但那之后,没有人肯让我们搭车。也许是我们的样子太滑稽了——丹坐在他那台小滑轮车上,大块头的我站在他旁边。总之,丹说,我们干吗不坐巴士走,他的钱够买车票。说实在的,花他的钱,我心里有点儿过意不去,但既然他想走,让他离开华盛顿也是好事。

于是我们坐上了一辆开往印第安纳波利斯的巴士,我把丹放在我旁边的座位上,把他的小滑轮车塞到上面的架子上。一路上,他都在慢悠悠地喝红匕首葡萄酒,说世界是个多么狗屎的地方。也许他说得对。我不知道。反正,我只是个白痴。

巴士停在印第安纳波利斯市中心,我和丹站在大街上,正想着下一步怎么办,这时,一个警察走过来,说,"不准在街上逗留",于是,我们往前走。丹问一个人天波禄轮胎公司在哪里,结果在远郊,于是我们朝那个方向走。走着走着,人行道没了,丹不能推着他的小滑轮车往前走了,于是,我一只胳膊夹着他，另一只胳膊夹着小滑轮车，我们就这样继续往前走。

大概中午的时候，我们看见一块大牌子，上面写着"天波禄轮胎"，我们猜这就是那个地方。丹说他在外面等，我走进去，桌子后面有个女人，我问能不能见一下珍妮·柯伦。那个女人看了一下名单，说珍妮在"轮胎翻新"车间上班，不过，除了在这个工厂上班的人，任何人不准入内。好吧，我只好站在那儿，琢磨怎么办好，那个女人说："听我说，亲爱的，过一会儿，他们就午休了，你何不绕到大楼旁边去等。也许她会出来。"我照办了。

过了一会儿，果然出来很多人，我看见珍妮独自穿过一扇门，走到一棵树下，她从纸袋里掏出一个三明治。我走过去，悄悄来到她身后，她坐在地上，我说："这个三明治看上去很好吃。"她头也没抬，眼睛一直盯着前方，说："阿甘，一定是你。"

第十八章

哦，我这么跟你说吧——这是我这辈子最快乐的重逢。珍妮哭着，拥抱我，我也哭着，拥抱她，"轮胎翻新"车间的其他人全都立在那儿，不知道发生了什么事。珍妮说她大约三个小时后下班，她让我和丹去街对面那家小酒馆喝杯啤酒什么的，在那里等她，然后她会带我们去她住的地方。

我们去了那家小酒馆，丹点了瑞波葡萄酒，因为没有红匕首，但他说，总之，瑞波酒更好，因为这种酒香气更浓。

酒馆里还有一群人，玩飞镖，喝酒，在一张桌子上掰手腕。一个大块头好像是这个酒馆最厉害的掰手腕选手，不时有人过去跟他较量，但都掰不过他。他们还押注，一次五块十块的。

过了一会儿，丹低声对我说："阿甘，你觉得你能掰过那边那个大块头吗？"我说，我不知道，丹说："这样吧，这是五块钱，我打赌你会赢。"

于是，我走上前，对那个家伙说："你介意我坐下来和你掰手腕吗？"

他抬头看看我，微笑道："只要你有钱，欢迎试一试。"

于是我坐下来，我们握住对方的手，有人说了声："开始！"然后，掰手腕比赛就开始了。那个家伙嘴里咕哝着，像狗拉屎一样费劲，但大约十秒钟后，我就把他的胳膊扳倒在桌子上了，在掰手腕比赛中战胜了他。所有人过来，围住桌子，嘴里发出"哦""啊"声，我听见丹大声欢呼。

好吧，那个家伙不太开心，但他给了我五块钱，然后从桌边站起来。

"我的胳膊肘滑了一下，"他说，"不过，下次你来这儿，我还想跟你比试比试，听见了吗？"我点点头，回到丹那桌，把钱给了他。

"阿甘，"丹说，"我们可能找到了一种轻轻松松就能赚钱糊口的方法。"我问丹能不能给我二十五美分，我想从柜台上的罐子里拿一个腌鸡蛋，他给了我一块钱，说："想吃什么就拿什么，阿甘。我们现在有办法谋生了。"

下班后，珍妮来到小酒馆，带我们去她的住处。她住的是一间小公寓，离天波禄轮胎公司不远，房子用毛绒玩具什么的装饰得很漂亮，卧室门上还挂着彩色珠帘。我们去杂货店买了点儿鸡肉，珍妮为丹和我做了晚餐，我把最后一次见到她以来发生的事一五一十告诉了她。

她主要对弗里奇少校好奇，不过，当我说她跟一个食人族跑了以后，珍妮似乎更放心了。她说，这几年，她过得也不是很如意。

离开裂蛋乐队后，珍妮和她在和平运动中认识的一个女孩一起去了芝加哥。她们上街示威游行，并多次被关进监狱，珍妮说，她终于厌倦了出庭，此外，她还担心自己有多次犯罪记录。

总之，她和大约十五个人住在一栋房子里，她说，他们跟她不是一类人。他们不穿内衣，或者干脆什么都不穿，也没有人冲马桶。她和这个男的决定合租一套公寓，因为他也不喜欢他们住的地方，但结果并不顺利。

"你知道吗，阿甘，"她说，"我甚至试着让自己爱上他，但我怎么都做不到，因为我心里一直想着你。"

她曾写信给她妈妈，让她妈妈联系我妈妈，想知道我被关在哪儿了，但她妈妈给她回信说，我们的房子被烧毁了，我妈妈住在济贫院，但珍妮收到信的时候，我妈妈已经和那个新教徒跑了。

总之，珍妮说她没钱，所以，听说轮胎公司招人，她就来到印第安纳波利斯，并得到了这份工作。大约就在那个时候，她在电视上看到我即将被发射到太空，但她没时间去休斯敦。她说她"惊恐地看着"我的宇宙飞船坠毁，她还以为我死了。从那以后，她就把时间全都花在翻新轮胎上。

我把她抱在怀里，我们就这样待了一会儿。丹自己转着小车去了厕所，说他想尿尿。他进去以后，珍妮问他怎么尿，不需要帮助吗？我说："不用，我见过他尿尿。他能行。"

她摇摇头，说："这就是越战带给我们的后果。"

这一点也没有什么争议。一个没腿的人不得不把尿撒在帽子里，然后把尿倒进马桶，这是一个多么令人伤心难过的场景。

从那以后，我们仨一起住在了珍妮的小公寓。珍妮在客厅一角给丹打了个地铺，还在浴室地上放了个罐子，这样他就不用尿在帽子里了。每天早上她去轮胎公司上班，我和丹会坐在家里聊会儿天，然后去珍妮公司附近的小酒馆等她下班。

我们这么做的第一个星期，掰手腕输给我的那个人想有机会拿回他那五块钱，我给了他这个机会。他又试了两三次，最后损失了大概二十五块钱，此后，他再也没有回来过。但总有人想碰碰运气，一两个月后，来自全镇和其他小镇的男人，都来找我较量。我和丹，我们俩每星期大约能赚一百五十到两百块钱，这样的收入真不赖，我跟你说。酒馆老板说，他要举办一场全国性的比赛，还让电视台转播什么的。但在这之前，发生了另一件事，并彻底改变了我的生活。

一天，一个家伙走进酒馆，他穿着白色西装、夏威夷衬衫，脖子上挂着很多金首饰。他在吧台前坐下，看我打败一个跟我掰手腕的家伙后，他走过来，坐到我们这桌。

"我叫迈克，"他说，"我听说过你。"

丹问他听说过什么，迈克说："这个家伙是全世界最强壮的人。"

"那又怎样？"丹说，那个人说："我有个主意，能让你们赚很多钱，而不是像在这儿赚个仨瓜俩枣的。"

"怎么赚？"丹说。

"摔跤，"迈克说，"不是这种小打小闹——我指的是真正的比赛。在擂台上，有很多付费观众。"

"跟谁摔跤？"丹问道。

"谁都行，"迈克说，"有一个职业摔跤巡回赛——蒙面侠、无敌浩克、华丽的乔治、肮脏的麦克猪——凡是你能叫出名字来的人都会来。顶尖选手一年能赚十到二十万美元。我们让这个孩子慢慢起步。先教他一些技巧，传授给他一些诀窍。哎呀，我敢打赌，用不了多久，他就会成为大明星——让大家都能赚到一大笔钱。"

丹看着我，说："你觉得呢，阿甘？"

"我不知道，"我说，"我有点儿想回老家，做点儿养虾的小生意。"

"养虾！"迈克说，"哎呀，小伙子，干这个赚的钱比养虾多五十倍！你不用一辈子都干这个——只要干几年，赚点儿钱存到银行做储备金，以备不时之需。"

"也许我应该先征求一下珍妮的意见。"我说。

"听我说，"迈克说，"我来这儿，可是为了给你一个千载难逢的机会。你不想干就直说，我马上走人。"

"不，不，"丹说，然后转向我，"听我说，阿甘，这个人说的话还是有点道理的。我的意思是，你干什么能赚到足够的钱去做养虾生意？"

"这样吧，"迈克说，"你可以和你的朋友一起干。他可以做你的经纪人。什么时候想退出都行。你觉得怎么样？"

我想了一下，听起来不错，但通常有诈。尽管如此，我还是张开我的大嘴，说出了那个致命的词："好。"

就这样，我成了一名职业摔跤手。迈克的办公室设在印第安纳波利斯市中心一个健身房里,每天,我和丹都会坐公交车去那儿,学习摔跤的正确方法。

简言之,是这样的:应该不会有人受伤,但看起来像是要受伤的样子。

他们教给我各种招式——单臂扼颈、顶旋摔、波士顿蟹式固定、打桩机、锁臂,等等。

此外,他们还教丹如何对裁判大吼大叫,把场面搞得越混乱越好。

珍妮不太热衷摔跤这件事,因为她说我可能会受伤,我说,没有人会受伤,因为都是演出来的,她说:"那这么做有什么意义?"这是个好问题,我不知如何作答,但我还是期望能为我们赚点钱。

一天,他们教给我一种叫"肚皮跳水"的招式,我要飞起来,落到对方身上,但最后一刻,他会滚到一旁。不知道为什么,我总是搞砸,有两三次,那个家伙还没来得及轱辘到一边,我就落到他身上了。最后,迈克走到场中说:"天哪,阿甘——你是个白痴吗!你这样会伤到别人的,你就像一头大驼鹿!"

我说:"对呀,我就是白痴。"迈克说:"你什么意思?"丹把迈克叫过去,跟他解释了一下。迈克说:"我的天哪!你不会跟我开玩笑吧?"丹摇头。迈克看着我,耸了耸肩,说:"好吧,世界之大,无奇不有。"

总之,大约一个小时后,迈克从他的办公室跑出来,跑到丹和我所在的场地。

"我想出来了！"他喊道。

"想出什么来了？"丹问。

"他的名字！我们必须给阿甘取个绰号。我刚想到叫什么了。"

"叫什么？"丹说。

"呆瓜！"迈克说，"我们给他穿上尿布，再给他戴一顶圆锥形的大呆瓜帽。观众一定会喜欢！"

丹想了一下。"我不知道，"他说，"我不太喜欢。听起来你好像在戏弄他。"

"这个名字是给观众取的，"迈克说，"他必须有绰号。所有大明星都会给自己取绰号。没有比呆瓜更好的绰号了！"

"叫他太空人怎么样？"丹说，"这个名字比较合适。他可以戴一顶塑料头盔，头上再插几根天线。"

"已经有人叫太空人了。"迈克说。

"我还是不喜欢，"丹说，他看着我，问道，"你觉得呢，阿甘？"

"我无所谓。"我说。

嗯，事情就是这样。经过几个月的训练，我终于要以摔跤手的身份初次登台了。大赛前一天，迈克来到健身房，他有一个盒子，里面装着我的尿布和一顶很大的黑色呆瓜帽。他说明天中午还会来健身房，然后开车送我们去曼西，参加我的第一场摔跤比赛。

那天晚上，珍妮回家后，我走进浴室，穿上尿布，戴上呆瓜帽，走进客厅。丹正坐在他的小平板车上看电视，珍妮在看书。我进门时，他们俩都抬起头。

"阿甘，这到底是怎么回事？"珍妮说。

"这是他的服装。"丹说。

"你看起来像个傻瓜。"她说。

"你这么看，"丹说，"你就当他是在演戏。"

"他还是像个傻瓜，"珍妮说，"我简直不敢相信！你竟然让他们把他打扮成这样去公共场所？"

"只是为了赚钱，"丹说，"有个摔跤的家伙叫'蔬菜'，他拿萝卜叶子当护裆，把一个挖空的西瓜顶在头上，再挖两个小洞看外面。还有个家伙自称'仙女'，背着一对翅膀，拿着一根魔法棒。这个家伙大概有三百磅重——你应该去看看他。"

"我不在乎其他人什么样，"珍妮说，"这身打扮我一点儿都不喜欢。阿甘，你去把这身衣服脱掉。"

我回到浴室，脱下这身衣服。也许珍妮说得对，我在想——但男人总要赚钱谋生。不管怎么说，这身打扮比我明天晚上在曼西要对战的那个家伙强得多。他自称"粪球"，穿一件很大的连体紧身衣，衣服画得像一坨屎。天知道他身上什么味。

第十九章

曼西这场比赛的剧本是：我将惨败给"粪球"。

去曼西的路上，迈克告诉我们，原因是，"粪球"比我"资历"深，所以他应该赢，而且，这是我第一次登台，所以我必须输。迈克说，他只是想把丑话说前头，别生气。

"这也太荒唐了，"珍妮说，"居然有人自称'粪球'。"

"他可能就是个粪球。"丹说，他想逗她开心。

"你要记住，阿甘，"迈克说，"这一切都是在作秀。你不能发脾气。没有人会受伤。'粪球'必须赢。"

我们终于到了曼西，那里有一个大礼堂，摔跤比赛将在那里举行。一场比赛正在进行——"蔬菜"和一个自称"野兽"的家伙较量。

"野兽"浑身是毛，像只猿猴，他戴着黑眼罩，一上台就夺下"蔬菜"扣在头上那个挖空的西瓜，然后把它踢到上面的看台上。接下来，他抓住"蔬菜"的头，使劲往角柱上撞。他还咬了"蔬菜"的手。我很同情这个可怜的"蔬菜"，不过，他也会耍花招——那就是把手伸进羽衣甘蓝叶子做的护裆里，抓了一把什么东西，揉在"野兽"眼睛上。

"野兽"低吼，脚步踉跄，满台摇晃，揉眼睛，想把那个东西弄出来,"蔬菜"从他身后上来,踢了他的屁股一脚,接着,把"野兽"扔到绳圈上,拿绳子把他缠住,让他动弹不得,接着,把"野兽"痛揍了一顿。观众嘘"蔬菜",朝他扔纸杯什么的,"蔬菜"对着观众竖中指。我有点好奇这场比赛如何结束,但就在这时,迈克朝我和丹走来,叫我们回更衣室,换好服装,因为接下来,我要对阵"粪球"。

我穿上尿布,戴上呆瓜帽后,有人敲门问:"'呆瓜'在吗?"丹说:"在。"那个人说:"该你上场了,出来吧。"然后,我们就出场了。

丹推着他的小车跟在我身后走上过道时,"粪球"已经在擂台上了。"粪球"在台上跑来跑去,朝人群做鬼脸,他穿着那件紧身连体衣,看着可真像个"粪球"。总之,我爬上擂台,裁判把我们叫到一起,说:"好了,小伙子们,我想看一场干净的比赛——不许刺眼睛,不许击打腰带以下部位,不许有咬人或者挠人等动作。"我点头说:"嗯哼。""粪球"狠狠地瞪着我。

铃响了,我和"粪球"绕着彼此转圈,他伸出脚想绊我,但没绊倒,我抓住他的肩膀,把他扔到绳圈上。这时,我才发现,他往身上抹了一种很滑溜的东西,让人很难抓住他。我试图抱住他的腰,但他像鳗鱼一样从我手中溜走了。我去抓他的胳膊,太滑,又没抓住,他咧着嘴嘲笑我。

接着,他朝我跑过来,用头顶我的肚子,但我闪到一旁,"粪球"穿过绳圈,落在前排的看台上。所有人都嘘他,喝倒彩，但他爬回擂台上，手里拿着一把折叠椅。他拎着椅子追我，我手里没拿任何家伙，只能逃跑，但"粪球"用椅子打到我后背，我跟你说，很疼。我试图把椅子从他手上夺下来，但他用椅子砰砰砸我的脑袋，我在一个角落里，无处可躲。接着，他踢我的小腿，当我弯腰抱住我的小腿时，他又踢我的另一条小腿。

丹坐在台口，对裁判大喊大叫，让"粪球"放下椅子，但没有用。"粪球"用椅子打了我四五次，把我打倒，然后，骑在我身上，抓住我的头发，把我的头往地板上撞。接着，他又抓住我的胳膊，开始掰我的手指。我望着丹，问："这是怎么回事？"丹试图钻到擂台上来，但迈克站起来，薅住丹的衣领，把他拉回去了。突然，铃声响了，我朝我的角落走去。

"听我说，"我说，"这个浑蛋想弄死我，拿椅子打我的头什么的。我必须做点什么。"

"你要做的就是输给他，"迈克说，"他并不是想弄伤你——他只是想让比赛好看。"

"可是我感觉不好。"我说。

"你再多待几分钟，让他把你压制在擂台上，"迈克说，"记住，你来这儿，输了，你就能赚到五百块钱，赢了，你一个子儿都拿不到。"

"他再用那把椅子打我，我不知道该怎么办。"我说。我望着观众席，珍妮坐在那里，既愤怒，又难堪。我开始觉得这么做不对。

总之，铃声再次响起后，我回到场上。"粪球"试图抓住我的头发，但我把他甩开，他像陀螺一样飞到绳圈上。然后，我抱住他的腰，把他举起来，但他从我手中滑落，一屁股坐在地上，他呻吟，抱怨，揉屁股，接下来我只知道，他的经纪人递给他一把撅子，那种末端是橡胶的东西，他开始用撅子打我的头。呃，我把撅子从他手中夺下来，抬起腿，在膝盖上将它掰成两截，然后开始追他，但我看到迈克在那边摇头，所以，我让"粪球"过来，抓住我的胳膊，给我来了一个锁臂。

这个该死的狗娘养的差点把我的胳膊弄断。接着，他把我推倒在地，用胳膊肘击打我的后脑勺。我看到迈克在那边点头，微笑赞许。"粪球"从我身上下来，用脚踢我的肋骨和肚子，接着，他又抄起那把椅子，狠狠地在我头上打了八九下，最后，他用膝盖顶住我的后背，而我无能为力。

我趴在地上，他坐在我头上，裁判数到三，比赛应该结束了。"粪球"站起来，低头看着我，朝我脸上啐了口唾沫。这太糟糕了，我不知道该怎么办，我忍不住哭了起来。

"粪球"神气十足地绕着擂台走，丹推着小车来到我身边，用一块毛巾擦我的脸，接下来我只知道，珍妮来到场上，抱着我哭，观众大喊大叫，往场地里扔东西。

"走吧，我们离开这里。"丹说，我站起来，"粪球"朝我吐舌头，做鬼脸。

"你的名字取得可真贴切，"我们离开擂台时，珍妮对"粪球"说，"丢人现眼。"

这句话适合我们俩。我这辈子都没觉得这么丢脸过。

回印第安纳波利斯的路上，气氛很尴尬。丹和珍妮没说什么话，我坐在后座上，浑身酸痛。

"你今晚的表演太精彩了，阿甘，"迈克说，"尤其是最后哭那段——观众太喜欢了！"

"那根本不是表演。"丹说。

"哦，哎呀，"迈克说，"听我说——总要有人输嘛。这样吧，下次，我一定让阿甘赢。你觉得怎么样？"

"不会有下次了。"珍妮说。

"今天晚上他赚了一大笔钱，不是吗？"迈克说。

"他被人打得屁滚尿流才赚五百块，不怎么样。"珍妮说。

"哦，这才是他的第一场比赛。这样吧——下次，我给他涨到六百。"

"一千二怎么样？"丹问。

"九百。"迈克说。

"让他穿泳衣，不戴呆瓜帽，不穿尿布怎么样？"珍妮说。

"观众喜欢，"迈克说，"这也是他吸引人的地方。"

"你怎么不打扮成那样？"丹说。

"我又不是白痴。"迈克说。

"闭上你的臭嘴。"丹说。

好吧，迈克说到做到。下次我摔跤的对手是一个叫"人蝇"的家伙。他戴着一个苍蝇那种又大又尖的口器似的东西，还戴着一个面具，上面有一双凸出来的大眼睛。我把他在台上扔来扔去，最后一屁股坐在他头上，领到我的九百块钱。此外，所有人疯狂地欢呼呐喊："我们要'呆瓜'！我们要'呆瓜'！"这笔交易不赖。

接下来，我要和"仙女"摔跤，他们甚至让我用他的魔法棒打他的脑袋。从那之后，我和很多人过过招，丹和我为养虾生意攒了大约五千块钱。不过，这么跟你说吧：我变得很受欢迎。女人给我写信，她们甚至开始卖我戴的那种呆瓜帽当纪念品。有时，我上场，看到观众席里有上百人戴呆瓜帽，大家鼓掌、欢呼，喊我的名字。这让我感觉挺好的，你知道吗？

同时，我和珍妮相处得也很融洽，除了在摔跤这件事上有分歧。每天晚上，她回到家，我们就自己做饭吃，然后我、她和丹围坐在客厅里，计划如何着手养虾生意。在我们的想象中，我们会去拜尤拉巴特里，可怜的布巴的家乡，然后在墨西哥湾的某个地方找一块沼泽地。我们还要买一些铁丝网和小网子、一条小船，还有虾饲料。丹说，我们在等待第一笔利润的时候，还要找个地方住，买杂货什么的，还要想办法把这些虾推销出去。他认为，第一年把一切准备就绪总共需要大约五千块钱——那之后，我们就可以自给自足了。

我现在的问题是珍妮。她说，我们已经有五千块钱了，何不立刻收拾行李南下？哦，她说得有道理，但说实话，我还没做好离开的准备。

你知道，自从我们在橘子碗和内布拉斯加大学剥玉米人队比赛以来，我没有过真正的成就感。或许在红色中国打乒乓球赛那些天有过那么一点，但时间很短，只持续了几个星期。而现在，你看，每星期六晚上，我都会去那里，听他们欢呼。他们在为我喝彩——无论我是不是白痴。

"格罗斯波因特磨刀匠"上场时身上粘满百元大钞，你应该听听我打败他时观众的欢呼声。然后是"从阿马里洛来的了不起的艾尔"，我给他来了一个波士顿蟹式固定，并赢得了东部赛区冠军腰带。那之后，我和"巨人朱诺"较量过，他足有四百磅重，穿着一身豹皮衣服，拿着一根纸糊的棍子。

但有一天，珍妮下班回家后对我说："阿甘，我们得好好谈谈。"

我们出门，在一条小溪附近散步，珍妮找了个地方坐下，然后说："阿甘，我觉得摔跤这个事没必要再继续下去了。"

"你什么意思？"我问，虽然我大概知道是怎么回事。

"我的意思是，我们现在有将近一万块钱了，这是丹说的养虾启动资金的两倍多。我很纳闷儿，怎么每个星期六晚上你还要去那儿出洋相呢？"

"我没出洋相，"我说，"我要考虑我的粉丝。我很受欢迎。我不能说走就走。"

"胡说，"珍妮说，"你所谓的'粉丝'是什么，你说的'受欢迎'是什么意思？那些人不过是一群花钱看那些狗屁玩意的怪胎。一帮老爷们穿着护裆上台，假装互相伤害。谁听说过有人自称'蔬菜'或'粪球'什么的——还有你，竟然自称'呆瓜'！"

"那有什么不好？"我说。

"呃，你认为这会让我有什么感觉，我爱的男人是远近闻名的'呆瓜'，每个星期都会出洋相——还上电视！"

"上电视能挣外快。"我说。

"去他的外快,"珍妮说,"我们不需要外快!"

"谁听说过有人不需要外快的?"我说。

"我们并不那么迫切地需要外快,"珍妮说,"我的意思是,我想找一个安静的小地方住下来,你找一份体面的工作,比如养虾——我们也许可以买一栋小房子,有个花园,养条狗什么的——甚至可能有孩子。我在裂蛋乐队的时候也算出过点小名,但没干出什么大名堂。当时,我并不快乐。现在,我都快三十五岁了。我想安定下来……"

"你听我说,"我说,"在我看来,是否继续做下去应该由我来决定。我不会永远干这一行——我要等待合适的时机。"

"好吧,我也不会永远等下去的。"珍妮说,但我不相信她说的是真话。

第二十章

那之后,我又打了两场比赛,当然,两场都赢了。然后,有一天,迈克把丹和我叫进他的办公室,他说:"听我说,这个星期,你要和'教授'较量一下。"

"这人是谁?"丹问。

"他来自加州,"迈克说,"是那边的热门人物,西部赛区亚军。"

"我没问题。"我说。

"不过,还有一件事,"迈克说,"这次,阿甘,你必须输。"

"输?"我说。

"输,"迈克说,"你看,这几个月,你一直赢,每个星期都赢。难道你不觉得你应该偶尔输一场,来保持你的人气吗?"

"你怎么会这么想?"

"很简单。人们喜欢不被看好的那个。这会让你下次看起来更风光。"

"我不喜欢。"我说。

"你打算给多少钱?"丹问道。

"两千。"

"我不喜欢。"我又说。

"两千可是很多钱。"丹说。

"我还是不喜欢。"我说。

但我还是接受了这笔交易。

最近,珍妮的举止有点怪异,但我把这归结为神经质什么的。然后,有一天,她回到家,说:"阿甘,我快受不了了。请不要去那儿摔跤了。"

"我得去,"我说,"反正,这次我要输。"

"输?"她说。我像迈克跟我解释那样,跟她解释了一遍,她说:"呃,阿甘,这太过分了。"

"这就是我的人生。"我说——不管这句话是什么意思。

总之,过了一两天,丹从某个地方回来,说我们俩得谈谈。

"阿甘,我想我找到解决我们的问题的方法了。"

我问什么方法。

"我想,"丹说,"我们最好尽快退出这一行。我知道珍妮不喜欢你干这个,如果我们想做养虾生意,我们最好好好谈谈这件事。不过,我想,我有办法退出,同时又能大赚一笔。"

"怎么做?"我问。

"我一直跟市里的一个人聊天。他经营一家博彩公司,有消息说,这周六,你会输给'教授。'"

"所以呢?"我说。

"如果你赢了呢?"

"赢？"

"揍他一顿。"

"那我会和迈克结下梁子。"我说。

"去他的迈克，"丹说，"你看，是这样的。我们有一万块钱，假设我们把这笔钱押在你身上，赔率是二比一，你觉得怎么样？然后，你揍他一顿，我们就会得到两万块钱。"

"可是，这样我的麻烦就大了。"我说。

"我们拿着两万块钱，赶快离开这里，"丹说，"你知道我们能用两万块钱做什么吗？我们可以大做养虾生意，还能剩很多钱。反正，我在想，也许你该退出摔跤这行了。"

嗯，我在想，丹是经纪人，而且珍妮也说过我该退出摔跤这行，两万块钱也不是个小数目。

"你觉得怎么样？"丹说。

"好，"我说，"好。"

我和"教授"摔跤的日子到了。这场比赛将在韦恩堡举行，迈克过来接我们，他正在外面按喇叭，我问珍妮准备好了没有。

"我不去了，"她说，"我看电视转播。"

"可是，你得去。"我说，然后我让丹解释原因。

丹把我们的计划告诉珍妮，她必须去，因为我打败"教授"以后，我们需要有人开车送我们回印第安纳波利斯。

"我们俩都不会开车，"他说，"比赛结束后，赛场外要有一辆快车，把我们送回这里，从博彩公司拿到那两万块钱，然后迅速离开这个城市。"

"哦,我不想和这种交易有任何瓜葛。"珍妮说。

"那可是两万块钱啊。"我说。

"是,那也是欺诈。"她说。

"呃,这么说,他一直都在欺诈,"丹说,"输赢都是事先安排好的。"

"我不会干这种事的。"珍妮说。迈克又在按喇叭,丹说:"好吧,我们得走了。比赛结束后,我们在这儿碰头——无论结果如何。"

"你们俩应该为自己感到羞耻。"珍妮说。

"等我们口袋里揣着两万块钱回来,你就不会这么傲慢了。"丹说。

总之,我们出发了。

去韦恩堡的路上,我没怎么吭声,因为要对迈克做的事让我觉得有点难为情。他待我不错,但话说回来,就像丹说的那样,我也为他赚了很多钱,所以算是扯平了。

我们到了比赛场地,第一场比赛已经开始了——"巨人朱诺"被"仙女"踢得满地找牙。接下来是女侏儒双打比赛。我们走进更衣室,我穿上尿布,戴上帽子。丹让人给出租车公司打电话,安排一辆出租车在我比赛结束后等在外面,车不能熄火。

有人拍门,该我上场了。我和"教授"这场比赛是当晚的重头戏。

我出来时，他已经在擂台上了。"教授"身材瘦小，留着胡子，戴着眼镜，穿一件黑色长袍，戴着学位帽。他还真像个教授。我当下决定让他吃下那顶帽子。

我爬上擂台，主持人说："女士们，先生们。"听到这话，很多人发出嘘声，接着，他说："今晚，我们很荣幸地邀请到北美职业摔跤协会的两大夺冠热门人物——'教授'和'呆瓜'——为我们献上这场重头戏！"

听到这里，观众发出一片嘘声和欢呼声，搞不清楚观众是高兴，还是愤怒。没关系，因为铃声响了，比赛开始。

"教授"也已经脱掉长袍，摘掉眼镜和学位帽，围着我转，他像责骂我似的，对我摇手指。我想抓住他，但每次，他都跳开，继续摇手指。这种状况持续了一两分钟，然后，他犯了个错。他跑到我身后，想踢我屁股，但我抓住了他的胳膊，把他扔到绳圈上。他像弹球一样，从绳圈上弹回来，当他从我身边经过时，我将他绊倒，当我正要用腹压的招数扑向他时，他急忙爬到他的角落，我抬头看时，他手里拿着一把大戒尺。

他用戒尺啪啪拍手心，好像要拿它打我的屁股。这次我想抓他时，他却用戒尺戳我的眼睛，想把它挖出来。我跟你说——很痛，我跌跌撞撞，努力恢复视力，他则跑到我身后，把什么东西放在我的尿布上。没一会儿，我就知道是什么了——蚂蚁！他从哪儿弄来的蚂蚁，天知道，但蚂蚁开始咬我，这次可糟了。

丹在那儿，大叫着要我干掉他，但裤子里有蚂蚁，干掉他可不是一件容易的事。这时，铃声响了，第一回合结束。我回到我的角落，丹努力把蚂蚁清理干净。

"这招可真够黑的。"我说。

"一定要打败他，"丹说，"千万不能搞砸，我们可承受不起。"

"教授"出战第二回合。他对我做鬼脸。等他离我足够近时，我一把抓住他，举过头顶，开始做顶旋摔。

我把他转了大概四五十圈，直到我确定他头晕目眩，然后用尽全力把他扔到绳圈外的观众席上。他落在看台大约第五排一位正坐在那儿织毛衣的老太太腿上，她拿起雨伞打他。

问题是，顶旋摔也给我带来了不利的影响。我感觉天旋地转，但我觉得没什么，眩晕感很快就会停止，而"教授"，反正也被我打败了。然而，在这一点上，我想错了。

就在我快要从眩晕中恢复过来时，突然有个东西套住了我的脚脖子。我低头一看，"教授"居然爬回擂台上，还带回了那个老太太织毛衣用的线团，现在，他把毛线缠在我脚上。

我扭动身体，极力挣扎，但"教授"拿着线团，绕着我跑，把我缠成了一具木乃伊。很快，我的手脚都被绑住，动弹不了了。"教授"停下来，把毛线打了一个漂亮的结，然后站在我面前鞠了一躬——好像他是个魔术师，刚变了个戏法似的。

然后，他漫步到他的角落，拿了一本大书——好像是一本辞典——然后回来，又鞠了一躬。接着，他拿那本书啪啪打我的头。我束手无策。我倒下之前，他肯定敲了十多下。"教授"坐在我肩上，把我的双肩压制在垫子上，他赢得了这场比赛。我听到观众的欢呼声，那时，我很无助。

迈克和丹来到擂台上，解开我身上的毛线，把我扶起来。

"太棒了！"迈克说，"真是太棒了！我都设计不出这么精彩的比赛！"

"哦，闭嘴！"丹说完，转向我，说，"还不错，被'教授'用计谋打败了。"

我一声没吭。我很痛苦。全输光了，有一件事我确定无疑，那就是，我不会再摔跤了。

比赛结束，我们已经不需要逃跑用的出租车了，所以，我和丹搭迈克的车返回印第安纳波利斯。开车回去的路上，迈克不停地说，这样输给"教授"太棒了，还下次一定让我赢，让大家都赚上几千块钱。

迈克把车停在公寓前，伸出手，递给丹一个信封，里面装着他要付给我的这场比赛的酬劳——两千块钱。

"别拿。"我说。

"什么？"迈克说。

"听着，"我说，"我得跟你说一件事。"

丹插话道："他想说的是，他不会再摔跤了。"

"你开玩笑呢吧？"迈克说。

"没开玩笑。"丹说。

"呃，怎么会这样？"迈克问，"怎么了，阿甘？"

还没等我开口，丹就说："他现在不想谈这事。"

"好吧，"迈克说，"我明白了，我猜。去吧，好好睡一宿觉。明天一早我就来，到时候，我们再谈，好吗？"

"好。"丹说,我们下了车。迈克走后,我说:"你不该拿那个钱。"

"哎呀,我们现在就剩这点儿钱了。"他说。其余的钱全没了。直到几分钟后,我才意识到他这么做有多么正确。

我们进了公寓,哎呀,珍妮也不见了。她的东西全没了,她给我们留了几条干净的床单和毛巾,还有一些锅碗瓢盆类的东西。客厅的桌子上放着一张纸条。丹先发现的,他大声念给我听。

亲爱的阿甘:(纸条上写着)

　　我真的再也无法忍受下去了。我曾试着跟你谈我的感受,但你似乎并不在乎。你今晚要做的事尤其糟糕,因为这是欺诈,恐怕我不能再和你继续走下去了。

　　这也许是我的错,一部分原因是,我已经到了需要安定下来的年纪。我想有个家,有个房子,上教堂什么的。我从小学一年级就认识你,阿甘——快三十年了——我看着你长大,长成高大强壮的好人。当我终于意识到我有多么喜欢你时——你来波士顿的时候——我是世界上最幸福的女孩。

　　后来,你成天吸大麻,你还在普罗温斯敦和那些姑娘胡闹,即使在那之后,我还是很想你,很高兴你在和平示威活动期间来华盛顿看我。

　　可是,当你被宇宙飞船送上太空,在丛林中消失了近四年后,我想,也许我变了。我不像从前那样满怀希望了,我觉得找个地方过简单的生活，我就很满足了。所以，现在我必须去找。

亲爱的阿甘，你也有变化。我认为你身不由己，因为你一直是一个很"特别"的人，但我们的想法似乎不一样了。

写这封信时，我哭了，但现在我们必须分手。请不要再找我。祝福你，亲爱的——再见。

——爱你的

珍妮

丹把那张纸条递给我，但我任凭它飘落在地，我愣在那里，这是我有生以来第一次体会到当白痴的滋味。

第二十二章

这之后，我就是一个心存愧疚的浑蛋。

那天晚上，丹和我住在公寓里，但第二天早上，我们就开始收拾东西，因为没有理由再留在印第安纳波利斯了。丹走过来对我说："给，阿甘，拿着这个钱。"他手里攥着两千块钱，那是迈克给的我和"教授"摔跤的酬劳。

"我不要。"我说。

"哦，你最好拿着，"丹说，"我们就这点儿钱了。"

"你留着吧。"我说。

"你至少要拿一半，"他说，"听着，你必须带点路费。无论你想去哪儿，有钱才能去。"

"你不和我一起去吗？"我问。

"恐怕不行，阿甘，"他说，"我想，我已经把你害得够惨的了。昨晚，我一宿没睡。我在想，是我让你同意赌上所有的钱的，珍妮显然要崩溃了，我却还让你继续摔跤。你被'教授'打败不是你的错。你已经尽力了。我才是那个罪魁祸首。都是我不好。"

"呃，丹，这也不是你的错，"我说，"如果我没有被当'呆瓜'冲昏头脑，而且开始相信他们说我的那些屁话，我从一开始就不会陷入这种困境。"

"总之,"丹说,"我只是觉得不能再跟着你一起走了。你现在有更重要的事要做。去做吧。忘了我吧。都是我不好。"

我和丹聊了很久,还是没能说服他,后来,他拿了自己的东西,我把他抱下楼,最后,我目送他推着小车在街上走,所有衣物堆在他的腿上。

我去了长途汽车站,买了一张去莫比尔的车票。这本来应该是一趟两天两夜的旅程,经过路易斯维尔、纳什维尔、伯明翰,然后到莫比尔。我是个可怜的白痴,长途车向前行驶,我呆坐在车上。

长途车夜里经过路易斯维尔,第二天,在纳什维尔停下来,换另一辆车。大约要等三个小时,于是我决定去城里转转。我在快餐店买了一个三明治和一杯冰茶,走在街上,我看到一家酒店门口立着一块很大的牌子,上面写着:"欢迎光临国际象棋大师邀请赛。"

这块牌子勾起了我的好奇心,因为我在丛林里和大山姆下过很多盘棋,于是,我走进那家酒店。他们正在舞厅里下棋,有一大群人围观,但旁边有块牌子上写着"入场券五元",我一分钱都不想花,但我在门口看了一会儿,然后独自到大堂坐坐。

我对面有一把椅子,椅子上坐着个小老头儿。他浑身皱巴巴的,看上去脾气很暴躁,他穿着黑色的西装和鞋罩,打着领结,面前的桌子上摆着一副棋盘。

我坐下后，他每隔一会儿就会移动一枚棋子，我渐渐明白，他是在跟自己下棋。我想，还有一个来小时才开车，就问他想不想找个人一起玩。他只是看了我一眼，然后低头看他的棋盘，什么也没说。

过了半天，老头儿已经盯着棋盘研究了快半个小时了，这时，他把他的白象移到黑格七，他正要把手从棋盘上拿开时，我说："不好意思。"

老头嗖的一下跳起来，像一屁股坐在了大头钉上，然后瞪着桌子对面的我。

"你要是走这一步，"我说，"你就会门户大开，先丢掉你的马，再丢掉你的后，你会让自己陷入困境。"

他低头看着自己的棋盘，手一直没从象身上拿开，然后，他把它放回原处，对我说："也许你说得对。"

他继续研究棋盘，我想我该回汽车站去了，但就在我准备离开时，那个老头说："不好意思，不过，你刚才的判断非常准确。"

我点了一下头，然后他说："听着，显然，你下过棋，你何不坐下来跟我下完这盘棋？你就用白棋吧。"

"我不能跟你下棋了。"我说，因为我还要坐长途车什么的。他只是点点头，给我敬了个举手礼，我则朝长途汽车站走去。

可是，等我到了那儿，那辆该死的长途车竟然开走了，我只能留下来，明天才有其他车。我什么事都做不好。哦，我有一天时间可以消磨，于是，我走回酒店，那个小老头儿还在跟自己下棋，他好像快赢了。我走到他面前，他抬头看了我一眼，示意我坐下。我这边的情况很惨——我的一半兵没了，也没有车，只剩一个象，我的后接下来要被吃掉。

我花了将近一个小时才将局面扳平，每次我改善我的处境，老头都会咕哝、摇头。最后，我牺牲一子，结果他真上钩了，又走了三步后，我把他将死了。

"见鬼，"他说，"你到底是谁？"

我告诉他我的名字，他说："不，我是说，你在哪儿下过棋？我怎么不认识你。"

我告诉他我在新几内亚学的下棋，他说："天哪！你的意思是，你连地区性的比赛都没参加过？"

我摇头，他说："好吧，不管你知不知道，我是前国际象棋大师，照理说，刚才那个局面，你根本赢不了我，而你却把我彻底打败了！"

我问他怎么没在里面和其他人比赛，他说："哦，我以前参加过比赛。现在我都快八十岁了，而且有一种年长者的比赛。真正的荣耀属于现在的年轻人——他们的思维更敏捷。"

我点点头，感谢他跟我下棋，然后起身要走，但他说："听我说，你吃过晚饭了吗？"

我告诉他，几个小时前我吃了一个三明治，他说："那我请你吃饭怎么样？毕竟，你让我见识了一场精彩的比赛。"

我说好的，然后我们走进这家酒店的餐厅。他是个好人。特里布尔先生是他的名字。

"听我说,"我们吃饭时,特里布尔先生说,"我得再跟你下几盘才能确定,不过,除非今晚你的表现纯属侥幸,否则,你可能是国际象棋界最大的遗珠之一。我想赞助你参加一两场比赛,看看结果如何。"

我告诉他,我打算返乡,从事养虾业什么的,但他说:"呃,这对你来说可能是个千载难逢的机会,阿甘。你知道,你可以靠下棋赚很多钱。"他让我今天晚上考虑一下,明早再告诉他。于是,我和特里布尔先生握了手,然后来到街上。

我闲逛了一会儿,但纳什维尔没什么好看的,最后,我坐在公园的长椅上。我努力思考,这对我来说不是一件容易的事,想清楚接下来做什么。我脑子里想的基本都是珍妮和她在哪儿。她不让我去找她什么的,但我内心深处总有一种感觉,她并没有忘记我。我在印第安纳波利斯确实出了洋相,我知道。我觉得这是因为我没有尽力做对的事。而现在,我不知道什么才是对的。我是说,我在这儿,身无分文,想做养虾生意必须有本钱,特里布尔先生说,我能在国际象棋巡回赛上赢一大笔钱。但好像每次我没回家做养虾生意,而是干了别的事,我都会陷入水深火热——所以,我又不知道怎么办才好了。

我还没琢磨多久,就来了一个警察,问我在干什么。

我说我只是坐在这儿想事情,他说,任何人都不许晚上坐在公园里想事情,他让我赶紧走。我回到街上,那个警察在后面跟着我。我不知道该去哪里,所以,过了一会儿,我看到一条巷子,就走进去,找个地方坐下来歇脚。我坐下还不到一分钟,那个警察刚好经过,看见我在那里。

他说:"好了,出来。"我走出巷子,来到街上,他又说:"你在巷子里做什么?"

我说:"什么都没做。"他说:"我想也是——你因为滞留街头被捕了。"

他把我送进监狱,关了起来,第二天早上,他们说,如果我愿意,可以打个电话。当然,除了特里布尔先生,我不认识任何可以打电话的人,于是,我打电话给他。大约半小时后,他出现在警察局,把我从监狱里救出去了。

他在酒店请我吃了一顿丰盛的早餐,他说:"听着,你何不让我帮你报名参加下周在洛杉矶举行的国际锦标赛?冠军奖金是一万美元。我会支付你的一切费用,你赢得的奖金,无论多少,咱俩平分。我看你需要一笔奖金什么的,而且,说实话,我自己也会很开心。我会做你的教练和顾问。你觉得怎么样?"

我依然有疑虑,但又觉得不妨试一下。于是我说我愿意干一段时间,直到攒够钱从事养虾生意。我和特里布尔先生握了手,成了合作伙伴。

洛杉矶是个五光十色的城市。我们提前一个星期到的,特里布尔先生用一天的大部分时间指导我、磨炼我的棋艺,但过了一阵子,他摇着头说,没有必要再指导我了,我已经将每一步棋牢记在心。所以,我们去城里走走。

特里布尔先生带我去了迪斯尼乐园,让我玩了几个游乐设施,然后又安排我参观了一家影城。影城里正在拍摄各种电影，人们跑来跑去，喊着"第一条""停""开始"之类的屁话。正在拍摄的电影中有一部是西部片，我们看到一个家伙被人扔出一扇玻璃窗，这个动作他做了大概十次才做对。

总之，我们站在那儿看热闹，这时，一个人走过来，问："打搅一下，你是演员吗？"

我说："啊？"特里布尔先生说："不是，我们是国际象棋选手。"

那个人说："啊呀，真可惜，因为这个大块头的家伙看上去很适合我正在拍的一部电影里的一个角色。"说完，他转向我，摸了摸我的胳膊说："天哪，天哪，你可真是个壮汉——你确定你不会表演吗？"

"我还真演过一次。"我说。

"真的吗？"那家伙说，"演过什么？"

"《李尔王》。"

"太棒了，宝贝。"他说，"太好了——你有 SAG 卡吗？"

"我有什么？"

"美国演员工会卡——哦，没关系，"他说，"听我说，宝贝，给你弄到那张卡肯定不成问题。我想知道的是，你一直躲在什么地方？我的意思是，你看看你！一个典型的高大、沉默的硬汉——又一个约翰·韦恩。

"他不是约翰·韦恩，"特里布尔先生没好气地说，"他是一个世界一流的国际象棋选手。"

"哦，那就更好了，"那家伙说，"一个聪明、高大、沉默的壮汉。非常罕见。"

"我并不像看上去那么聪明。"我想说实话,但那家伙说无所谓,因为演员并不需要聪明、诚实什么的——只要能站在那儿说台词就行。

"我叫费尔德,"他说,"我是拍电影的。我想让你试个镜。"

"明天他要参加一个国际象棋比赛,"特里布尔先生说,"他没时间演戏或者试镜。"

"哦,总能挤出点儿时间吧?毕竟,这可能是你一直在寻找的机遇。你干吗不一起来?特里布尔先生,我们也让你试个镜。"

"我们尽量吧,"特里布尔先生说,"走吧,阿甘,我们还有一些工作要做。"

"宝贝,回头见,"费尔德先生说,"千万别忘咯。"

然后,我们就走了。

第二十二章

第二天早上，国际象棋比赛在贝弗利山酒店举行。我和特里布尔先生早早就来了，他给我报了名，参加全天的比赛。

总的来说，没什么大不了的。我大概用了七分钟就战胜了第一个人，他是一名地区性大师，也是某所大学的教授，这令我心中暗喜，毕竟，我打败了一位教授。

接下来是一个大约十七岁的孩子，不到半个小时，我就把他解决了。他大发脾气，又哭又闹，他妈妈不得不把他拖走。

那天和第二天，我和各种各样的人下棋，但很快就打败了他们，这让我松了一口气，因为和大山姆对弈时，我必须一直坐在那儿，不能去厕所什么的，因为，只要我一离开，他就会挪动棋子，企图作弊。

总之，最后我进了决赛。决赛前，我有一天休息时间。我和特里布尔先生一起回到酒店，发现拍电影的费尔德先生给我们留了言，他说"今天下午请打电话到我的办公室，安排明早试镜"，还留了一个电话号码。

"哦，阿甘，"特里布尔先生说，"我不知道该怎么处理这件事。你是怎么想的？"

"我也不知道。"我说，不过，说实话，这事听起来挺刺激的,在电影里面演一个角色,没准儿还能认识拉蔻儿·薇芝呢。"

"噢,去试一下也无妨,"特里布尔先生说,"我打电话,跟他约一下吧。"于是,他打电话到费尔德先生的办公室,搞清楚我们要去的时间地点,突然,他用手捂住话筒,问我:"阿甘,你会游泳吗?"我说:"会。"他对着电话说:"会,他会游泳。"

他挂断电话后,我问他们为什么想知道我会不会游泳,特里布尔先生说他不知道,但他认为我们到了就知道了。

我们去的不是上次那个片场,一个警卫在门口迎接我们,把我们带到试镜的地方。费尔德先生正在那儿和一位女士争吵,而这位女士长得确实有点像拉蔻儿·薇芝。看见我来了,他的脸上立刻堆满笑容。

"啊,阿甘,"他说,"你来了,真是太好了。现在,我要你做的是穿过那扇门,去服化组,他们给你弄完以后会把你送回来的。"

于是,我穿过那扇门,两个女人站在那儿,其中一个女人说:"好了,脱掉你的衣服。"又让我脱衣服,但我照办了。我脱完衣服,另一个女人递给我一大团衣服,看起来像橡胶做的,上面布满鳞片什么的,还带有很滑稽的手蹼和脚蹼。她让我穿上它。我们仨花了大概一个多小时才把我套进这件衣服里。然后,她们指给我化妆组怎么走,到了化妆组,他们让我坐在椅子上,一个女的和一个男的把一张很大的橡胶面具套在我头上，接在服装上，然后遮盖接缝处。弄完以后，他们让我返回片场。

脚上有蹼，我几乎走不了路，手上有蹼，又很难打开门，但最后，我还是做到了，突然，我发现自己置身户外，这里有一大片湖、各种香蕉树和热带风情的破玩意儿。费尔德先生看到我，吃了一惊，说："太棒了，宝贝！你太适合这个角色了！"

"什么角色？"我问他。

他说："哦，我没告诉你吗？我正在翻拍《黑湖妖潭》。"

连我这样的白痴都能猜到他想让我扮演什么角色。

费尔德先生示意刚才跟他争吵的那位女士过来。"阿甘，"他说，"我想让你认识一下拉蔻儿·薇芝。"

呃，我大吃一惊！她就在我眼前，盛装打扮，穿着低胸礼服。"很高兴认识你。"我隔着面具说。可是，拉蔻儿·薇芝转向费尔德先生，暴跳如雷。

"他说什么？他在说我的奶子，是不是？"

"不，宝贝，不是，"费尔德先生说，"他只是说，他很高兴认识你。他戴着那个面具，你听不太清他说的是什么。"

我伸出长蹼的手，想跟她握手，但她向后跳了大约一英尺，说："呃！快把这个该死的事弄完吧。"

总之，费尔德先生说，剧情是这样的：拉蔻儿·薇芝在水中挣扎，然后晕了过去，接着，我从她身下出现，把她托起来，然后抱着她从水里走出来。但她醒来后，抬头看见我，吓得尖叫起来，说"放下我！救命啊！强奸！"等屁话。

但费尔德先生说，不要放下她，因为几个恶棍正在追赶我们；相反，我要把她抱到丛林里去。好吧，我们试拍了这场戏，第一次演完，我觉得效果挺好，真把拉蔻儿·薇芝抱在怀里的感觉挺刺激的，尽管她大叫"放我下来！救命啊，警察！"什么的。

但费尔德先生说还不够好，要我们再来一次。这次还是不行，所以，同一场戏，我们演了十几遍。拍摄间隙，拉蔻儿·薇芝一直在抱怨、咒骂费尔德先生，对他口出恶言，他却只是不停地说"好极了，宝贝，好极了！"诸如此类的话。

我这边也开始遇到一个真正的问题。这身怪兽装我已经穿了快五个小时，衣服上没有拉链，也没有可以尿尿的地方，我的尿泡都快憋爆了。但我不想吭声，因为这是一部真正的电影，我不想惹任何人生气。

但我必须做点儿什么，所以我决定下次下水的时候，我就尿在衣服里，尿会顺着我的腿或者什么的，流到湖里。费尔德先生一喊"开始"，我就走进水里，开始尿尿。拉蔻儿·薇芝拼命挣扎，接着，昏了过去，我潜入水中，抓住她，把她拖到岸上。

她醒来后，不停打我，嘴里大喊着："救命啊！杀人啦！放我下来！"但突然，她不喊了，问道："什么味？"

费尔德先生喊："停！"然后站起来说："宝贝，你说什么？剧本里没有这句话。"

拉蔻儿·薇芝说："去他的剧本！这儿好臭！"接着，她突然看着我说："嘿，你——不管你是谁——你是不是尿尿了？"

我很尴尬，不知所措。我只是呆立在那里，抱着她，然后摇着头说:"没有。"

这是我有生以来说的第一句谎话。

"哼,肯定有人尿尿了,"她说,"我一闻就知道是尿!而且不是我尿的!所以肯定是你干的!你竟敢在我身上撒尿,你这个大笨蛋!"说完,她用拳头捶我,大喊:"放我下来!""离我远点!"什么的,但我只想,这场戏又要开拍了,所以我抱着她往丛林里走。

费尔德先生大喊一声:"开始!"摄影机再次转动起来,拉蔻儿·薇芝对我发疯般又打又挠又喊。费尔德先生大声喊道:"这就对了,宝贝——太棒了!继续!"我看见特里布尔先生也回来了,坐在椅子上,摇着头,看向别处。

我回到丛林里,没走多远,就停下来,转过身,看费尔德先生会不会像之前那样准备大声喊"停",但他野人似的跳来跳去,示意我继续往前走,同时大喊:"太棒了,宝贝!这就是我想要的!把她抱到丛林里去!"

拉蔻儿·薇芝还在对我又踢又挠又抓又打,同时尖叫着"滚开,你这个粗俗的畜生!"之类的话,但我听导演的,继续往前走。

突然,她尖叫起来:"哦,我的上帝!我的裙子!"

之前我一直没注意,这会儿,我低头一看,该死,她的裙子被后面的灌木钩住,整个扯掉了,拉蔻儿·薇芝正一丝不挂地躺在我怀里!

我停下来说:"哦噢。"然后准备转身,想把她抱回去,但她尖叫道:"不,不行!你这个白痴!我不能就这样回去!"

我问她想让我怎么做，她说我们得找个地方躲起来，直到她把这件事想清楚。于是，我继续往丛林深处走，突然，不知道从哪儿冒出来一个大家伙，他拽着一根藤条，穿过树林，朝我们这边荡过来。那个家伙从我们身边荡过去了，我认出是某种猿猴，接着，他又荡回来了，他从藤条上下来，落到我们跟前。我差点儿晕过去——居然是苏！

拉蔻儿·薇芝又大哭大叫起来，苏则搂住我的腿，抱着我。我不知道他怎么还能认出穿一身怪兽装的我，也许是闻到了我身上的气味。总之，拉蔻儿·薇芝终于开口道："你认识这只该死的狒狒？"

"他不是狒狒，"我说，"他是一只猩猩。他的名字是苏。"

她面带有点儿滑稽的表情看着我说："哎呀，如果他是公的，为什么会叫苏这个名字？"

"说来话长。"我说。

总之，拉蔻儿·薇芝试图用手遮住身体，苏知道怎么做，他从一棵香蕉树上扯下两片大叶子递给她，她把自己的部分身体遮盖起来。

后来我才知道，我们穿过了我们的丛林拍摄地，来到了另一个正在拍泰山电影的片场，苏在那里做临时演员。我从新几内亚的俾格米人手中获救后不久，白人猎人就来了，他们抓走了苏，把他运到洛杉矶的某个驯兽师那里。那之后，他们就一直用他拍电影。

总之，我们现在没工夫瞎胡闹，因为拉蔻儿·薇芝又在尖叫、发牢骚："你得带我去个地方，我要弄身衣服穿上！"呃，我不知道丛林里哪儿能找到衣服，即使这里是片场，于是我们继续往前走，希望会发生点什么事。

果然出事了。突然，我们来到一大片围栏前，我想，也许能在围栏那边给她找到衣服。苏在围栏上发现一块松动的木板，他取下那块木板，让我们钻过去，可是，我刚抬脚迈到另一边，脚下却是空的，我和拉蔻儿顺着山坡滚了下去。我们终于一路滚到了山脚，我环顾四周，该死，我们居然滚到一条大马路边上。

"噢，我的上帝！"拉蔻儿·薇芝喊道，"我们在圣莫尼卡高速公路上！"

我抬头一看，苏来了，他脚步轻快地跑下山坡。他终于来到我们身边，我们仨站在那儿。拉蔻儿·薇芝上下移动香蕉叶，极力遮住身体。

"现在我们怎么办？"我问。一辆辆汽车呼啸而过，我们的样子一定很奇怪，但根本没有人注意到我们。

"你得带我去个地方！"她大喊道，"我得找件衣服穿上！"

"去哪儿？"我说。

"随便什么地方！"她尖叫道。于是，我们沿着圣莫尼卡高速公路走。

走了一会儿，我们看到远处山上有一块白色的大牌子，上面写着"好莱坞"。拉蔻儿·薇芝说："我们必须从这条该死的高速公路上下去，走到罗迪欧大道，我可以在那儿买衣服。"她忙着用香蕉叶遮盖身体——每当有车朝我们这边驶来，她就会把香蕉叶放在前面,如果有车从后面驶来,她就把叶子移到后面,盖住屁股。如果车来车往,那场面可就壮观了——就像在跳扇子舞。

于是,我们下了高速公路,穿过一大片田野。"那只该死的猴子非要一直跟着我们吗?"拉蔻儿·薇芝说,"我们的样子已经够可笑的了!"我一声没吭,但回头看了一眼,苏脸上露出痛苦的表情。他以前没见过拉蔻儿·薇芝,我认为他的感情受到了伤害。

总之,我们继续往前走,还是没有人注意我们。最后,我们来到一条繁华的大街上,拉蔻儿·薇芝说:"我的老天,这就是日落大道!我该怎么解释我在光天化日之下光着屁股穿过日落大道!"在这一点上,我理解她的意思,我有点庆幸我穿着怪兽装,所以没有人能认出我——即使我和拉蔻儿·薇芝在一起。

我们来到一个红绿灯前,灯变成绿色后,我们仨穿过马路,拉蔻儿·薇芝起劲跳着扇子舞,对车里的人微笑,就像她在舞台上那样。"太丢人了!"她低声对我表示不满,"我被亵渎了!等这件事过去了,有你好瞧的,你这个该死的白痴!"

有些坐在车里等红绿灯的人开始按喇叭、挥手,他们肯定认出了拉蔻儿·薇芝,我们过马路后,几辆车掉头,跟着我们。等我们到了威尔夏大道时,我们已经吸引了一大群人;人们从自己家和商店里走出来,全都跟着我们——像花衣魔笛手似的——拉蔻儿·薇芝羞得满面通红。

"你甭想再在这个城市工作了!"她对我说,同时朝人群笑了一下，但牙关紧咬。

我们继续往前走了一会儿，她说："啊——终于到了——这就是罗迪欧大道。"我看向街角，果然，这里有一家女装店。我拍了拍她的肩，指了一下那家店，但拉蔻儿·薇芝说："呃——那是波帕加洛。这年头没人会穿波帕加洛家的裙子。"

于是，我们又走了一会儿，她说："你瞧——吉亚尼——他们家有好东西。"于是，我们走了进去。

门口站着一个男店员，留着小胡子，穿着白西装，上衣口袋里露出手帕的一角，我们进门时，他仔细打量了我们一番。

"我可以帮助您吗，夫人？"他问。

"我想买条连衣裙。"拉蔻儿·薇芝说。

"您打算买什么样的？"那家伙说。

"什么样的都行，你这个笨蛋——你看不出是怎么回事吗？！"

男店员指着两个架子的连衣裙说，那里可能有适合她的尺码，于是拉蔻儿·薇芝走过去，开始翻看那些衣服。

"两位先生，有什么可以为你们效劳的吗？"那家伙对我和苏说。

"我们只是陪她来的。"我说。我回头一看，门外聚集了一群人，鼻子贴在玻璃窗上。

拉蔻儿·薇芝拿了八九件衣服去后面试穿。过了一会儿，她出来说："你觉得这个怎么样？"这是一条棕了吧唧的连衣裙，有很多腰褶，领口开得很低。

"噢，我说不好，亲爱的，"店员说，"总感觉不是您的衣服。"于是她回去，换上另一条裙子，店员说："哦，太好了！您看起来美极了！"

"这件我要了。"拉蔻儿·薇芝说。

店员说："好的——您想怎么付账？"

"你什么意思？"她问。

"哦，现金、支票，还是信用卡？"他说。

"听我说，你这个笨蛋，你难道看不出来我身上没带这种东西吗？你觉得我会把它放哪儿？"

"女士，请不要这么粗俗。"店员说。

"我是拉蔻儿·薇芝，"她告诉那个家伙，"待会儿我会派人过来付账。"

"非常抱歉，女士，"他说，"但我们不这样做生意。"

"可我是拉蔻儿·薇芝！"她喊道，"你不认识我吗？"

"听着，女士，"那个家伙说，"来这里的人有一半会说她们是拉蔻儿·薇芝、费拉·福赛特什么的。您有身份证吗？"

"身份证！"她喊道，"你觉得我会把身份证放哪儿？"

"没有身份证，没有信用卡，没有钱，就没有衣服。"店员说。

"我必须证明我是谁，"拉蔻儿·薇芝说着，突然扯下连衣裙，"这种小地方，除了我，谁还会有这种奶子！"她尖叫道。外面，人们拍打窗户，叫喊，欢呼。但店员按下一个小按钮，一个大块头的保安走过来，说："好了，你们几个都被捕了。乖乖跟我走就不会有麻烦。"

第二十三章

于是,我又被关进了监狱。

吉亚尼那个保安把我们逮捕后,两车警察呼啸而至,一个警察走到店员跟前说:"这里出了什么事?"

"这个人说她是拉蔻儿·薇芝,"店员说,"穿着一堆香蕉叶进来,买衣服,不给钱。我不知道另外两个是怎么回事,但看样子,相当可疑。"

"我就是拉蔻儿·薇芝!"她喊道。

"当然,女士,"警察说,"我还是克林特·伊斯特伍德呢。你何不跟这两位老兄走一趟?"他指了指另外两个警察。

"好啦,"警察的头儿看着我和苏说,"说说你们的情况吧?"

"我们在拍电影。"我说。

"所以你穿这身怪兽装?"他问。

"对。"我说。

"那他呢?"他指着苏说,"这戏服看着倒是像真的。"

"这不是戏服,"我说,"他是一只纯种猩猩。"

"是吗?"警察说,"好吧,我跟你说,我们局里有个拍片的家伙,他会很乐意给你们两个小丑拍几张照片。所以,你们也要跟我们一起走，而且绝不能轻举妄动。"

总之，特里布尔先生又来了一趟警察局，把我保了出去。费尔德先生则带着一大群律师出现，来解救这会儿已经变得歇斯底里的拉蔻儿·薇芝。

"你给我等着！"获释后，她对我尖叫，"等我忙完这阵子，你连跑龙套的活儿都接不到！"

"这就是生活，宝贝——不过，我会给你打电话，约着一起吃午饭。"费尔德先生临走时对我说，"我们待会儿派人过来取那件怪兽装。"

"走吧，阿甘，"特里布尔先生说，"我们还有要紧的事要办。"

回到旅馆，特里布尔先生、我和苏坐在房间里开会。

"带着苏到处走，总归是个问题，"特里布尔先生说，"我的意思是，你看刚才我们只能偷偷把他带上楼。带着猩猩一起旅行非常困难，我们必须面对这个问题。"

我告诉他我对苏的感情，他如何在丛林中不止一次救过我的命。

"嗯，我想我理解你的感受，"他说，"我愿意试一试。但他必须乖乖听话，不然，我们肯定会有麻烦。"

"他会的。"我说，苏点点头，像猿猴一样咧着嘴笑。

总之，第二天是我和人称"诚实的伊凡"的国际象棋特级大师伊凡·彼得罗基维奇之间的顶尖对决。特里布尔先生带我去了一家服装店，给我租了一套燕尾服，因为这是一件时尚大事，很多大人物会到场。此外，冠军将获得一万美元奖金，而我分到的一半奖金足以让我开始做养虾生意，所以绝对不能出岔子。

好吧，我们来到即将举行国际象棋比赛的大厅，上千人在那里转悠，"诚实的伊凡"已经就座，他瞪着我，好像自己是拳王阿里似的。

"诚实的伊凡"是个身材高大的俄罗斯人，额头很高，像科学怪人，还留着一头小提琴手常留的那种黑色的长鬈发。我上去坐下后，他对我咕哝了一句什么，然后，另一个家伙说："比赛开始。"比赛就这样开始了。

"诚实的伊凡"是白方，所以先行，他采用了所谓的"蓬齐亚尼开局"。

接下来，我走棋，我采用的是"列蒂开局"。一切进展得相当顺利。我们俩又都走了两步，接着，"诚实的伊凡"尝试了一种叫"王翼弃兵"的策略，移动他的马，看能不能吃掉我的车。

但我料到他会来这么一招，于是设置了一个叫"诺亚方舟陷阱"的东西，并吃掉了他的马。"诚实的伊凡"好像不太高兴，但看上去依然从容不迫，并使用"塔拉什威胁"来威胁我的象。

但这是我无法容忍的，我设置了"后翼印度防御"，这迫使他采用了"舍维宁根变例"，他这一招又导致我使用了"别诺尼防御"。

"诚实的伊凡"似乎有点儿沮丧，他扭绞手指，咬着下唇，接着,他走了一步险棋——"煎肝攻击"——我用了"阿廖欣防御",立刻把他堵死了。

似乎暂时形成了逼和局面,可是,"诚实的伊凡"采用了"霍夫曼战术",而且脱困了!我看向特里布尔先生,他对我微微一笑,动了动嘴唇,不出声地说"现在",我立刻明白了他的意思。

是这样,大山姆在丛林里教过我两个书上没有的招数,现在是时候用上它们了——即"椰子弃兵之炖锅变例",我用我的后作诱饵,骗那个浑蛋冒着牺牲他的马的风险吃掉她。

可惜,这招没奏效。"诚实的伊凡"肯定猜到了,他迅速吃掉了我的后,这下可麻烦了!接下来,我使出"草屋策略",我冒险拿出我的最后一个车,看能不能骗到他,结果,他没上当。他吃我的车,还吃了我的另一个象,并准备用"佩特罗夫将军"消灭我,而我竭尽全力,并设下了"俾格米威胁"。

"俾格米威胁"是大山姆的绝活之一,他传授给我后,我也很擅长用这招。不过,想用这招,关键在于出其不意,利用其他几枚棋子做诱饵,一旦对手落入"俾格米威胁"的陷阱,他就可以打道回府。我非常希望这招管用,如果不管用,我就没什么好点子了,我已经快完蛋了。

"诚实的伊凡"咕哝了几句,然后拿起他的马,把它移到第八格,这意味着他就要上"俾格米威胁"的当了,再走两步,我就会将死他,而他将无力回天!

可是,"诚实的伊凡"一定是感觉到哪里不对劲了,因为他把那枚棋子从第五格移到第八格,反反复复十来次,但一直没放手,放手就意味着只能如此了。

人群静得可以听见一根针落在地上的声音,我既紧张,又兴奋,整个人都快要爆炸了。我看向特里布尔先生,他抬头望天,好像在祈祷,而那个跟"诚实的伊凡"一起来的家伙眉头紧锁,面露不悦之色。"诚实的伊凡"又把棋子移回第八格两三次,但他总是把它放回第五格。终于,他好像要做点儿别的事,但随后,他再次举起那枚棋子,它悬停在第八格上方,我屏住呼吸,房间里静得像一座坟墓。"诚实的伊凡"仍然举棋不定,我的心就像敲鼓一样,咚咚直跳,突然,他直视我——我不知道发生了什么事,大概是我太兴奋了——突然,我放了一个巨大的烤豆屁,听起来就像有人把一张床单一撕两半!

"诚实的伊凡"一脸惊讶的表情,接着,他突然放下棋子,举起双手说:"呃!"他捏住鼻子,扇风,咳嗽。站在我们周围的人开始向后退,嘴里嘟囔着,拿出手帕什么的,我的脸红得像番茄。

但是当一切平静下来后,我看了一眼棋盘,"诚实的伊凡"居然把那枚棋子放在第八格上了。于是,我伸出手,用我的马吃掉它,然后,接连吃掉他的两个兵,他的后,最后是他的王——将死!我赢得了这场比赛,并获得了五千美元奖金!"俾格米威胁"再次克敌制胜。

"诚实的伊凡"一直比比画画,大声抗议什么的,他和跟他一起来的那个人立即提交正式的投诉申请。

赛事总监一直在翻阅规则手册,直到他找到这样一条:"比赛进行期间,任何选手不得故意做出分散其他选手注意力的行为。"

特里布尔先生走上前,说:"哦,我认为您无法证明我方棋手明知故犯。他也是不由自主。"

接着,赛事总监又翻阅手册,找到这样一条:"任何选手不得有粗鲁或冒犯对手的行为。"

"听我说,"特里布尔先生说,"你难道不需要放屁吗?阿甘又没有别的意思。他在那里坐了很久。"

"我不知道,"赛事总监说,"从表面上判断,我想,我不得不取消他的比赛资格。"

"呃,你至少再给他一次机会吧?"特里布尔先生问。

赛事总监搔了搔下巴。"哦,也许吧,"他说,"但他必须控制好自己,因为我们这里不能容忍这种事,你知道吗?"

看样子,他们允许我完成这场比赛了,但忽然间,房间另一头一阵骚动,女人们惊声尖叫,我抬头一看,原来是苏来了,他抓着枝形吊灯,朝我这边荡过来。

枝形吊灯晃到我头顶时,苏一撒手,正好落到棋盘上,棋子崩得到处都是。"诚实的伊凡"向后倒在一把椅子上,倒下的过程中,一位活像珠宝店广告的胖太太被扯下半条裙子。她胡乱挥动胳膊,大喊大叫,手打到赛事总监的鼻子,苏上蹿下跳,吱哇乱叫,大家惊慌,跺脚,踉跄,大喊报警。

特里布尔先生抓住我的胳膊,说:"我们赶快离开这儿吧,阿甘——这座城市的警察,你已经见得够多的了。"

我不能否认这一点。

我们回到酒店,特里布尔先生说,我们还得再开一次会。

"阿甘,"他说,"我觉得这事成不了了。你下起棋来毫不费力,但情况变得太复杂了。今天下午发生的一切实在离奇,这还是往好听了说。"

我点点头,苏看起来也很悲伤。

"所以,我告诉你我打算怎么做。你是个好孩子,阿甘,我不能让你困在加州,所以,我要安排你和苏回亚拉巴马,或者你的家乡。我知道你需要一笔创业资金,开始你的养虾生意,你应得的奖金,扣除各种开销,总共比五千块稍微少一点。"

特里布尔先生递给我一个信封,我往里面瞅了一眼,里面装着一沓百元钞票。

"祝你的事业一帆风顺。"他说。

特里布尔先生打电话叫来出租车,把我们送到火车站。他还安排把苏装进一只柳条箱,放在行李车厢托运,他说我可以过去看苏,在他需要食物和水的时候给他送过去。他们拿出柳条箱,苏钻进去,他们把他带走了。

"哦,祝你好运,阿甘。"特里布尔先生说着,握了握我的手。

"这是我的名片——所以,保持联络,让我知道你过得怎么样,好吗?"

我接过他的名片,又握了握他的手,要离开了,我很难过,因为特里布尔先生是个很好的人,我让他失望了。我上了火车,坐在我的座位上,望着窗外,特里布尔先生仍然站在站台上。火车开动时，他抬起手，向我挥手告别。

于是，我又出发了，那天晚上，我做了很长时间的梦，各种各样的梦——我梦到我又回到家中，梦到我妈妈，梦到可怜的布巴，梦到养虾生意，当然，我还梦到了珍妮·柯伦。我多么希望我不是这样一个疯疯傻傻的人。

第二十四章

哦，终于，我又回到了家乡。

大约凌晨三点钟，火车驶入莫比尔站，他们取出柳条箱里的苏，把我们留在站台上。除了一个人在扫地，还有一个人在火车站的长椅上打盹，周围空荡荡的，于是，我和苏朝市中心走，最终，我们在一栋废弃的建筑里找到了一个睡觉的地方。

第二天早上，我在码头附近给苏买了几根香蕉，还找到一个小吃店，给自己买了一份丰盛的早餐——麦片糊、鸡蛋、培根、煎饼，等等，然后我想，我必须做点什么，让我们安顿下来，于是我朝安贫小姊妹会的济贫院走去。路上，我们路过我家的老房子，如今那里只剩下一片荒草和一些烧焦的木头。看到眼前这一幕景象，我心中升起一种异样的感觉，所以我们继续往前走。

到了济贫院，我让苏在院子里等着，免得吓坏这里的修女，我进去打听我妈妈的情况。

院长修女非常和善，她说她不知道我妈妈在哪儿，只知道她跟一个新教徒走了，不过，我可以去公园打听一下，因为以前我妈妈经常下午去公园，跟几个女人坐在那里聊天。所以，我带上苏，继续朝公园走去。

公园的长椅上坐着几个女人，我走上前，告诉其中一位我是谁，她看着苏，说："我猜到是你。"

不过，她说，她听说妈妈在镇子另一头的一家干洗店做裤子熨烫工，于是我和苏去了那边，可怜的妈妈还真在那儿，正在洗衣店里汗流浃背地熨裤子。

看见我，妈妈放下手里的活儿，扑进我怀里。她流着泪，扭绞双手，抽鼻子，和我记忆中一模一样。我的好妈妈。

"哦，阿甘，"她说，"你终于回来了。你走了以后，我没有一天不想你，每天晚上，我都哭着睡着。"不过，听她这么说，我并不感到惊讶，我问起那个新教徒。

"那个下流卑鄙的东西，"妈妈说，"我实在不该和新教徒私奔。还不到一个月，他就抛弃了我，跟一个十六岁的女孩好上了，他都快六十岁的人了。我告诉你，阿甘，新教徒根本没有道德观念。"

就在这时，干洗店里传来一声大喊："格拉迪斯，你是不是把蒸汽熨斗忘在谁的裤子上了？"

"我的老天！"妈妈大叫一声，跑回店里。突然，一柱黑烟从窗户里冒出来，店里的人吼叫、抱怨、谩骂，接下来我只知道，妈妈被一个高大丑陋的秃子从洗衣店里拖出来，那个家伙一边喊叫，一边粗暴地推搡她。

"滚出去！滚出去！"他喊道，"我实在受不了了！这是你烧坏的最后一条裤子！"

妈妈哭哭啼啼，我走到那个人跟前说："我觉得你最好把手从我妈妈身上拿开。"

"你谁啊?"他问。

"福瑞斯特·甘。"我回道。

他说:"呃,你也从这儿滚开,带上你妈,因为她不在这儿上班了!"

"你最好不要在我妈妈面前这样说话。"我说。

他回答说:"是吗?那么,你打算怎么做?"

于是,我做给他看。

首先,我抓住他,把他举到半空,然后把他扛到他们洗衣服的地方,那里有一台用来洗被子和地毯的超大号洗衣机,我打开洗衣机的盖子,把他塞进去,然后盖上盖,把旋钮转到"脱水"模式。我见到他的最后一眼,他的屁股正转向"漂洗"那一格。

妈妈一边哭喊,一边用手帕揩眼泪,她说:"噢,阿甘,这下子工作真丢了!"

"别担心,妈妈,"我告诉她,"一切都会好起来的,因为我有一个计划。"

"你怎么会有计划,阿甘?"她说,"你是个白痴。一个可怜的白痴怎么会有计划?"

"等着瞧吧。"我说。总之,我很高兴返乡第一天就很顺利。

我们离开那里,朝妈妈住的寄宿公寓走去。我已经把她介绍给苏认识了,她说她很高兴,至少我有朋友——尽管他是一只猿猴。

总之,妈妈和我在寄宿公寓吃了晚饭,她从厨房拿了一只橙子给苏，然后，我和苏去了长途汽车站，乘巴士去拜尤拉巴特里，布巴的家人住在那里。果然，我们离开时，我看到妈妈的最后一眼是她站在寄宿公寓的门廊上，抽抽搭搭，擦眼泪。不过，我把五千块钱分了一半给她，帮她渡过暂时的难关，付房租什么的，直到我安顿下来，所以我并没有很难过。

总之，巴士到达拜尤拉巴特里后，我们不费吹灰之力就找到了布巴家。当时大概是晚上八点钟，我敲了几下门，过了一会儿，一个老头出来，问我有什么事。我自报家门，我是因为打橄榄球认识的布巴，后来我们一起在陆军服役，他有点儿紧张，但还是请我进了屋。我让苏待在外面的院子里，别让人看见，因为这里的人可能没见过他这种动物。

总之，这个人是布巴的爸爸，他给我倒了杯冰茶，开始问我很多问题。他想知道布巴的事，布巴是怎么战死的，等等，我尽我所能告诉了他。

最后，他说："这些年，我一直想不明白一件事，阿甘——你认为布巴是为什么死的？"

"因为他中弹了。"我说，但他说："不，我不是这个意思。我的意思是，为什么？我们为什么要去越南？"

我想了一下，然后说："呃，我猜，我们只是尽力做对的事吧。我们只是奉命行事。"

他说："哦，你认为这么做值得吗？我们做的那些事？那么多孩子战死？"

我说："你看，我只是个白痴，你知道。不过，如果你想知道我的真实想法，我认为，那就是一坨狗屎。"

布巴的爸爸点点头。"我就是这么想的。"他说。

总之，我对他说明来意，告诉他，我和布巴原本打算一起做点养虾生意，以及我在医院遇到一个越南佬，教我如何养虾，他很感兴趣，问了很多问题，就在这时，院子里突然响起刺耳的咯咯声。

"有个东西在追我的鸡！"布巴的爸爸喊道，他从门后抄起一支枪，然后走到门廊上。

"有件事我必须告诉你。"我说，我告诉他苏在院子里，只是我们不知道他在哪儿。

布巴的爸爸回到屋里，拿了一只手电筒，他在院子里照来照去。他照到一棵大树下面，树下有一只山羊——一只大公羊，站在那里刨地。他又往树上照，照见了可怜的苏，他坐在树枝上，吓得半死。

"那只山羊每次都这样，"布巴的爸爸说，"走开！"他喊道，然后向山羊扔了根棍子。山羊走后，苏从树上下来，我们让他进了屋。

"这是什么东西？"布巴的爸爸问。

"猩猩。"我说。

"有点儿像大猩猩，是不是？"

"有点儿像，"我说，"但不是。"

总之，布巴的爸爸说，我们可以在他家住一宿，第二天早上，他跟我们一起出去转转，看能不能找个地方做养虾生意。河口吹来和爽的微风，耳边是青蛙和蟋蟀的叫声，甚至偶尔能听到鱼跳出水面的声音。这是一个美好、宁静的地方，当时我就下定决心，我不会在这里惹任何麻烦。

第二天一大早我们就起来了，布巴的爸爸做了一顿丰盛的早餐，有自制香肠、新鲜鸡蛋、饼干和糖蜜，吃完早饭，他带我坐上一条小船，撑篙沿河湾顺流而下。风平浪静，水面上笼罩着薄雾。不时会有一只大鸟从沼泽里飞出来。

"你看，"布巴的爸爸说，"这就是咸潮进来的地方。"他指着湿地里的一个泥沼："那里有几个相当大的池塘，如果我做你打算做的事，那就是我养虾的地方。"

他把船划进那片泥沼。"你看那边，"他说，"那是一小块高地，你可以看到那里有一个小棚屋的屋顶。"

"过去汤姆·勒法基住在那里，不过，他已经死了四五年了。那个房子不属于任何人。你想要的话，稍微整修一下，就可以住进去了。上次我来看的时候，他那两条小船就停在岸边。可能一钱不值，但是，如果你把船补好，没准它会漂起来。"

他把小船往深处划，他说："汤姆铺了一些木栈道，穿过沼泽，一直延伸到池塘。以前他还经常在那儿钓鱼、猎鸭子。你把木栈道修好，就可以在那附近活动了。"

噢，我跟你说，这里看起来很合适。布巴的爸爸，他们一年四季都能在泥沼和河口看到虾苗，用网子捞几只养起来太容易了。他还说，根据他的经验，虾吃棉粕，这种饲料挺好的，因为便宜。

我们要做的最主要的事是用护栏网把池塘围起来，把小木屋修好，住进去，再买些平时吃的东西——花生酱、果冻、面包什么的。然后，我们就可以开始养虾了。

于是，我们当天就干起来。布巴的爸爸把我带回家，我们进城买补给品。他说，在我们把我们的船修好之前，可以用他的船，那天晚上，我和苏第一次住在小棚屋。夜里下了雨，屋顶疯狂漏雨，但我并不介意。第二天早上，我就出去把房顶修好了。

我花了将近一个月的时间才把这些事情搞定——修好棚屋、小船和沼泽中的木栈道，用网子圈住其中一个池塘。准备撒虾苗的日子终于到了。我买了一张拖虾网，我和苏划船出去，拖着那张网走了大半天。到了晚上，我们的饵料舱里大概有五十磅重的虾，我们划船回去，把它们扔进池塘里。虾苗在水面上噼里啪啦地游动、舞蹈。哎呀，哎呀，多么可爱的画面。

第二天早上，我们弄来五百磅棉粕，把其中一百磅扔进池塘，给虾吃，第二天下午，我们开始用网子圈住另一个池塘。整个夏天、整个秋天、整个冬天和整个春天，我们都在干这些活儿，到了第二年春天，我们已经有四个池塘养虾了，前景一片大好。夜里，我会坐在棚屋的门廊上吹口琴，星期六晚上，我会进城，买一箱六瓶装的啤酒，和苏一起喝醉。我终于感觉自己属于某个地方，而且每天踏踏实实地工作了，我想，当我们收获并售出第一批虾后，或许我就可以去找珍妮了，看她是不是还在生我的气。

第二十五章

那是六月一个晴朗的日子，我们认为是时候收获我们的第一批虾了。天一亮，我和苏就起床了，来到池塘边，撒下网，拖着走，直到网被什么东西卡住。苏先试着拉网，然后我也试着拉了拉，然后我们俩一起拉，直到最后我们发现，网并没有被卡住，而且里面装满了虾，我们拽不动！

到了那天傍晚，我们已经拉上来大约三百磅虾，我们用一整夜的时间根据虾的个头进行分拣。第二天早上，我们把虾装进篓子，扛到我们的小船上。虾太沉了，去拜尤拉巴特里途中，我们差点儿翻船。

镇上有一家海产品包装厂，我和苏把虾从码头拖到称重室。所有收入加起来，我们拿到一张八百六十五美元的支票！这是我在裂蛋乐队吹口琴以来，第一笔正大光明的收入。

在将近两个星期的时间里，我和苏天天拉网捕虾，然后送到包装厂。最后结束时，我们总共赚了九千七百美元零二十六美分。养虾生意成功了！

哦，我告诉你吧——那可真是一个快乐的时刻。我们把一篓子虾，大概三十五升，送给了布巴的爸爸，他很开心，说他为我们感到骄傲，还说多么希望布巴也在。之后，我和苏坐巴士去莫比尔庆祝。我做的第一件事就是去寄宿公寓看望妈妈，我告诉她我赚到钱了什么的，果然，她又哭了。"噢，阿甘，"她说，"我真为你感到骄傲——你虽然智力迟钝，却这么有本事。"

总之，我把我的计划告诉了妈妈，那就是，明年，我们的虾池数量将是现在的三倍，我们需要有人保管钱财、管理收支什么的，我问她愿不愿意干这个活儿。

"你是说，让我大老远搬到拜尤拉巴特里去住吗？"妈妈说，"那个地方无聊死了。我一个人可怎么打发时间？"

"数钱啊。"我说。

那之后，我和苏去市中心，准备大吃一顿。我去码头给苏买了一大串香蕉，然后给自己安排了一顿再丰盛不过的牛排晚餐，有土豆泥和青豆什么的。然后，我决定找个地方喝杯啤酒，当我路过水边一家灯光昏暗的酒吧时，我听见有人大声叫骂，尽管过去了很多年，我依然认得那个声音。我把头探进去，果然是我的大学同学柯蒂斯！

柯蒂斯见到我很高兴，说我是浑蛋、杂种、王八羔子……所有他能想到的"好词"。原来，离开大学后，柯蒂斯继续在华盛顿红皮队打职业橄榄球，后来，在一次派对上，他咬了球队老板娘的屁股，因此被解约了。他又为另外两支球队效力过几年，但那之后，他在码头上找到了一份装卸工的差事，他说，这倒是适合他在大学受的那点儿教育。

柯蒂斯请我喝了两杯啤酒，我们聊起过去的时光。他说"毒蛇"在绿湾包装工队打过四分卫，直到后来他在与明尼苏达维京人队比赛中场休息时被逮到喝了整整一夸脱波兰伏特加。后来,"毒蛇"为纽约巨人队效力,直到他在与洛杉矶公羊队比赛的第三小节来了一个自由女神式传球。巨人队的教练说,自1931年以来,就没有人在职业比赛中使用过自由女神式传球,以后就再也没有人找"毒蛇"打球了。柯蒂斯说,其实根本不是什么自由女神式传球。根据柯蒂斯的说法,当时,"毒蛇"吸毒吸得精神恍惚,当他从中线区后退传球时,完全忘了扔球,左边锋恰好看到这个情形,于是跑到他身后,把球拿走了。总之,柯蒂斯说,现在"毒蛇"在佐治亚州某地的一支小球队做助理教练。

两杯啤酒落肚,我有了个主意,并告诉了柯蒂斯。

"你来给我帮忙怎么样?"我问。

柯蒂斯骂骂咧咧,但过了一会儿,我才明白,他想问我想让他做什么,所以我跟他讲了我做养虾生意,我们要扩大业务什么的。他又骂了一会儿,但大意是"行"。

就这样,历经夏秋冬春,我们拼命工作,我、苏、妈妈和柯蒂斯——我甚至给了布巴的爸爸一份工作。那年,我们赚了将近三万块钱,而且生意规模不断扩大。情况再好不过了——妈妈几乎不哭了,有一天,我们甚至看到柯蒂斯露出了笑容——尽管他一看到我们看他,就停下来,又开始骂我们。而我却不是很开心,因为我经常想念珍妮,惦记她过得怎么样。

一天,我决定做点儿什么。那是一个星期天,我穿戴整齐,乘坐巴士去莫比尔,然后去了珍妮妈妈家。我敲门的时候，她正坐在屋里看电视。

我告诉她我是谁后，她说："阿甘！我简直不敢相信。进来！"

我们坐下来聊了一会儿，她问我妈妈的事，问我这些年都在做什么，最后，我跟她打听珍妮的情况。

"噢，最近我真的很少听到她的消息。"柯伦太太说。

"他们好像住在北卡罗来纳什么地方。"

"她有室友还是什么？"我问。

"哦，你不知道吗，阿甘？"她说，"珍妮结婚了。"

"结婚了？"我说。

"那是两年前的事了。她以前住在印第安纳，后来去了华盛顿，接下来，我收到一张明信片，说她结婚了，他们要搬到北卡罗来纳还是什么地方去。如果我听到她的消息，你想让我告诉她什么吗？"

"不用了，"我说，"哦，也许你可以告诉她，我祝她好运什么的。"

"我一定会转告给她，"柯伦太太说，"我真高兴你来看我。"

我不知道，我以为我对这个消息早有心理准备，可是我没有。

我感觉我的心怦怦跳，手心又冷又湿，我能想到的就是去某个地方，像布巴死后那样，把自己蜷成一个球，我就是这么做的。我在一户人家后院发现了一片灌木丛，我钻到灌木丛下面，蜷缩成一团。我甚至开始吮吸大拇指，我已经好久没这么做过了，因为妈妈总是说：这是一个明确的迹象，说明这个人是白痴，除非他是婴儿。总之，我不知道我在那儿待了多久。我猜差不多一天半吧。

我不怪珍妮，她做了她该做的事。毕竟，我是个白痴，虽然很多人说他们嫁给了白痴，但他们无法想象嫁给一个真正的白痴会是什么样。我想，我主要是觉得自己可怜，因为不知怎么的，我竟然相信，总有一天，我会和珍妮在一起。所以，当我从她妈妈那里得知她已经结婚时，我感觉我的一部分死了，而且永远活不过来了，因为结婚可不像私奔。结婚是个非常严肃的事。夜里，我哭了，但哭也没什么用。

那天傍晚，我从灌木丛里爬出来，返回拜尤拉巴特里。我没告诉任何人发生了什么事，因为我觉得说出来也没有什么益处。虾塘还有活儿要干，补网之类的事，我就自己干了。干完活儿，天已经黑了，我做了一个决定——我要全身心投入到养虾生意中去，拼命工作。我只能如此。

于是，我就这么做了。

那年，不算各种开销，我们赚了七万五千美元，生意越做越大，我只好雇更多人来帮我经营。其中一个是"毒蛇"，我们大学球队的四分卫。他对目前在小橄榄球队的工作不太满意，所以我让他和柯蒂斯一起工作，负责疏浚和溢洪道。后来，我发现高中的费勒斯教练已经退休了，于是我给了他一份工作，那两个打手也退休了，我安排他们在船上和码头工作。

很快，报纸就得到消息，派一名记者过来采访我，要做一篇"本地男孩大获成功"之类的报道，周日见报，配了一张我、妈妈和苏的照片，标题是"白痴在新奇的海产实验中找到未来"。

总之，那之后不久，妈妈跟我说，我们需要找人帮她分担记账的工作，并给出一些财务方面的建议，因为我们赚了很多钱。我考虑了一段时间，然后决定联系一下特里布尔先生，因为他在退休前做生意赚了一大笔钱。他说，他很高兴我给他打电话，他将乘下一班飞机赶过来。

一个星期后，特里布尔先生说我们得坐下来谈一谈。

"阿甘，"他说，"你在这里所做的一切非常了不起，但你的生意做得这么大，已经做到了需要开始做一些严肃的财务规划的时候了。"

我问他怎么规划，他说："投资！多样化！听我说，依我看，下一个会计年度，你的利润将达到十九万美元。再下一年，将接近二十五万美元。利润这么高，你必须对它们进行再投资，否则，国税局会向你征收一大笔税。再投资是美国商业的核心！"

我们照着他说的做了。

特里布尔先生负责这一切，我们成立了几个公司，一个是"阿甘贝类公司"，一个是"苏蟹盖烩饭公司"，还有一个是"妈妈小龙虾炖菜公司"。

哦，二十五万变成了五十万，接下来的一年，一百万，依此类推，直到四年后，我们的年利润达到了五百万美元。现在我们有将近三百名员工，包括"粪球"和"蔬菜"，他们不再摔跤，我们让他们在仓库装箱。我们拼命想找到可怜的丹，但他消失得无影无踪。我们找到了摔跤比赛筹办人迈克，让他负责公关和广告。在特里布尔先生的建议下，迈克甚至请拉蔻儿·薇芝为我们拍了几支电视广告——他们把她打扮成一只螃蟹的样子，她跳来跳去，说："品尝过苏的螃蟹，才算真正吃过螃蟹！"

总之，生意做得非常成功。我们有一支冷藏车队和一支由捕虾船、牡蛎收割船和渔船组成的船队。我们有了自己的海产品包装厂和一栋办公楼，还在公寓和购物中心等房地产项目，以及石油天然气勘探开采租赁方面进行了大量投资。我们雇用了哈佛大学的英语教师奎肯布什教授，他因为猥亵一名学生被解雇了，我们让他在妈妈炖菜公司做厨师。我们还聘用了古奇中校，我那趟荣誉勋章之旅后，他就被陆军除名了。特里布尔先生让他负责"秘密活动"。

妈妈找人给我们盖了一栋大房子，因为她说，我这样的公司老板不该住棚屋。妈妈说，苏可以留在棚屋里照看东西。如今，我每天都像律师一样，西装革履，拎着个公文包。我成天开会，听一堆像俾格米语的屁话，大家都叫我"阿甘先生"什么的。在莫比尔，市长授予我城市钥匙，还让我担任医院和交响乐团的董事。

后来，有一天，几个人来到我的办公室，说他们想让我竞选美国参议员。

"你天生就是当参议员的料。"这个人说。他穿着泡泡纱西装，抽着大雪茄。"大熊"保罗·布赖恩特手下的前明星橄榄球员、战斗英雄、著名宇航员和两位总统的密友——你还想要什么？"他问。克拉克斯顿先生是他的名字。

"听我说，"我告诉他，"我只是个白痴。我对政治一窍不通。"

"那就更适合了！"克拉克斯顿先生说，"听着，我们需要你这样的好人。地球之盐，我告诉你！地球之盐！"

我不喜欢这个主意，就像我不喜欢人们给我出的很多其他主意，别人的主意总是给我惹麻烦。不过，当我把这个想法告诉妈妈时，不出所料，她泪眼汪汪、骄傲地说，看到自己的儿子成为美国参议员，她的美梦就全都实现了。

哦，宣布我参选的日子到了。克拉克斯顿先生他们在莫比尔租了一个礼堂，他们把我拖上台，面对一群观众，这些人花五十美分进来听我说屁话。很多人啰里吧唆轮流讲话，然后轮到我了。

"我的美国同胞们！"我开口道。克拉克斯顿先生他们已经给我写好了演讲稿，稍后还有观众提问环节。摄像机在转动，闪光灯闪个不停，记者们在本子上快速地做着笔记。我念了整篇演讲稿，篇幅不长，也没有多大意义，可是，我懂什么？我只是个白痴。

我讲完，记者席上一位女士站起来，眼睛盯着记事本。

"如今，我们正处于核灾难边缘，"她说，"经济萧条，我们的国家遭到全世界痛斥，犯罪分子在城市里横行霸道，每天都有人挨饿，宗教从家庭中消失，贪婪之风泛滥成灾，农民破产，外国人入侵我们的国家，并抢走我们的饭碗。工会腐败，婴儿在贫民窟奄奄一息，工作不公平，混乱和饥荒席卷我们的校园，瘟疫和战争如乌云般笼罩着我们——有鉴于这一切，阿甘先生，在您看来，眼下最紧迫的问题是什么？"礼堂里安静极了，连根针掉在地上的声音都能听见。

"我要尿尿。"我说。

听到这话，人们疯狂了！开始喊叫，欢呼，挥舞双手。礼堂后面有人开始呐喊，很快，整个礼堂的人齐声呐喊：

"我们要尿尿！我们要尿尿！我们要尿尿！"他们叫喊着。

我妈妈一直坐在台上，在我身后。这时，她站起来，把我从麦克风前面拖走。

"你应该为自己感到羞耻，"她说，"竟然在公共场合说这种话。"

"不，不！"克拉克斯顿先生说，"说得太好了！大家喜欢。这将是我们的竞选口号！"

"什么口号？"妈妈说着，眼睛眯成一条缝。

"我们要尿尿！"克拉克斯顿先生说，"听听他们都在喊什么！从来没有哪个人与民众有过如此融洽的关系！"

但是妈妈根本不接受。"谁听说过有人用这种竞选口号！"她说，"粗俗，恶心——再说了，这又有什么意义？"

"这是一种象征，"克拉克斯顿先生说，"试想一下，我们会制作相关的广告牌、标语牌和保险杠贴纸，再做成电视和广播广告。毫无疑问，这是神来之笔。'我们要尿尿'象征着摆脱政府压迫的枷锁——清除这个国家所有的错误……意味着沮丧和即将到来的解脱！"

"什么！"妈妈狐疑地问,"你疯了吗？"

"阿甘,"克拉克斯顿先生说,"你已经在去华盛顿的路上了。"

看起来情况是这样的。竞选活动进行得相当顺利,人们把"我们要尿尿"挂在嘴边。人们在大街上,在汽车和巴士上喊这句口号。电视评论员和报纸专栏作家花很多时间跟大家解释这句话的含义。传教士在讲坛上高声宣讲,孩子们在学校里齐声高呼。看样子,我稳操胜券,事实上,我的竞争对手已经绝望到把自己的口号改成了"我也要尿尿",并在全州各地张贴。

然后,就像我担心的那样,一切分崩离析。

"我要尿尿"这件事引起了全国性媒体的注意,很快,《华盛顿邮报》和《纽约时报》就派出记者调查此事。他们问了我很多问题,态度亲切友善,但一回去就开始挖我的历史。一天,关于我的报道登上了全国所有报纸的头版。"参议员候选人坎坷的职业生涯",头条标题这样写道。

首先,他们写道,我大学一年级就被学校开除了。接着,他们挖出来我和珍妮看电影,警察把我从电影院里拖出去的鸟事。接下来,他们找出我在玫瑰园给约翰逊总统看我屁股的照片。他们四处打听我在波士顿和裂蛋乐队一起演出的经历,并引述旁人的话,说我吸大麻,还提到我在哈佛大学涉及一起"可能的纵火事件"。

最糟糕的是,他们竟然查出我曾朝国会大厦投掷勋章,并因此受到刑事指控,被判关进疯人院。此外,他们对我曾经摔跤的经历也了如指掌,知道我的绰号是"呆瓜"。他们甚至登出一张我被"教授"绑起来的照片。最后,他们用了几个"未具名的消息来源",称我曾卷入一桩"与好莱坞某知名女演员的性丑闻"。

这下可糟了。克拉克斯顿先生冲进竞选总部,尖叫着"我们被毁了!有人从背后捅了我们一刀!"之类的屁话。但一切都结束了。我别无选择,只能退出选举。第二天,妈妈、我和特里布尔先生坐下来长谈。

"阿甘,"特里布尔先生说,"我觉得最近你最好保持低调。"

我知道他说得对。此外,还有一些事困扰了我很久,只是我从来没提起过。

养虾生意刚启动时,我还挺喜欢这份工作的,天一亮就起床,去池塘边,建网,补虾什么的,夜里,我和苏坐在棚屋的门廊上吹口琴,星期六,我们买六瓶装的啤酒,喝个酩酊大醉。

现在情况变了,我要出席各种晚宴,端上桌的菜肴看上去神秘兮兮的,女人们戴着巨大的耳环。电话整天响个不停,天底下的事都要问我。在参议院,情况会更糟。如今我根本没有时间自己待着,但不知怎么的,很多东西从我身边溜走了。

还有,现在我照镜子,脸上有皱纹了,鬓角发白,体力也不如从前了。我知道生意越做越大,但就我自己而言,我感觉我只是在原地打转。我一直纳闷儿我做这一切是为了什么?很久以前，我和布巴有个计划，现在早就梦想成真了，甚至超出了想象，可是，那又怎样？我从中得到的快乐远远比不上我在橘子碗与内布拉斯加大学剥玉米人队对抗，或者在波士顿和裂蛋乐队一起演出时来一段口琴独奏，或者，就这一点而言，与约翰逊总统一起看《贝弗利山乡巴佬》。

我想，珍妮·柯伦也和这种心情有关，但既然谁也帮不上忙，还是忘了的好。

总之，我意识到我必须离开。妈妈哭哭啼啼，用手帕抹泪，我料到她会这么做，但特里布尔先生完全理解我的想法。

"我们何不告诉大家你要休个长假，阿甘，"他说，"当然，只要你愿意，你随时可以拿走你的股份。"

于是，我就这么做了。几天后的一个早上，我拿了一点儿现金，往旅行袋里扔了点东西，然后来到工厂。我向妈妈和特里布尔先生道别，然后去和其他人握手——迈克、奎肯布什教授、"粪球"、"蔬菜"、"毒蛇"、费勒斯教练和他的两个打手，布巴的爸爸和其他所有人。然后我去了棚屋，找到苏。

"你打算怎么做？"我问。

苏抓住我的手，拎起我的包，出了门。我们坐上小船，划向拜尤拉巴特里，然后乘巴士去莫比尔。售票小姐问："你们要去哪儿？"我耸了耸肩，她说："何不去萨凡纳？我去过那儿一次，那个地方很漂亮。"

于是，我们去了萨凡纳。

第二十六章

我们在萨凡纳下了车，那里正在下瓢泼大雨。我和苏走进车站，我买了一杯咖啡，站在屋檐下，琢磨接下来做什么。

我没有计划，所以，喝完咖啡，我掏出口琴，吹了起来。吹了两首歌，瞧啊，一个路过的家伙把二十五美分扔进我的咖啡杯。我又吹了几首歌，过了一会儿，咖啡杯里装了半杯零钱。

雨停了，苏和我继续走，过了一会儿，我们就来到了市中心的一个公园。我坐在长椅上，又吹了一会儿口琴，果然，人们开始往咖啡杯里丢二十五美分、十分和五分的硬币。后来，苏明白是怎么回事了，有人路过时，他就拿起咖啡杯，走到人家跟前。一天下来，我赚了将近五美元。

那天晚上，我们睡在公园的一张长椅上，那是一个晴朗的夜晚，星星月亮都出来了。早上，我们吃了早饭，人们纷纷出门上班后，我又开始吹口琴。那天，我们赚了八块钱，第二天，我赚了九块钱，一个星期下来，总的来说，我们的收入还挺不错的。过了周末，我发现了一家乐器店，店面不大，我进去看看能不能再找到一把 G 调口琴，因为一直用 C 调口琴吹，感觉越来越单调。我在一个角落里看到一架在售的二手电子琴，特别像乔治在裂蛋乐队弹的那个，他还用那架琴教过我几个和弦。

我问老板要多少钱，那家伙说两百块，但他会给我便宜点。所以，我买下了那架电子琴，那家伙甚至在上面安了个支架，这样，我也可以吹口琴了。这么一来，我们的受欢迎程度明显提高了。下个星期结束时，我们每天赚将近十美元，所以，我回到那家乐器店，又买了一组二手鼓。练了几天，我就打得挺像样了。我丢掉那个一次性泡沫咖啡杯，买了一个漂亮的锡杯让苏拿着，我们的收入相当不错。我吹各种曲子，有《那晚他们击溃了南方军》，还有《慢慢走起来，亲爱的马车》，我还找到一个可以带着苏入住，并且提供早餐和晚餐的寄宿公寓。

一天早上，我正要和苏去公园，天又突然下起雨来。萨凡纳有个特点——每隔一天就会下一场倾盆大雨，至少看起来是这样。我们沿街走到一栋办公楼前，突然，我看到一个有点儿眼熟的东西。

有个穿西装的男人，撑着伞，站在人行道上，他正站在一个很大的塑料垃圾袋前。有个人在垃圾袋下面躲雨，只看到一双手从袋子下面伸出来，给那个西装革履的男人擦鞋。我走到马路对面，仔细看，瞧啊，我认出了袋子下面露出来的手推车的小轮子。我高兴极了，上去一把掀开垃圾袋，果然是丹，他现在以擦鞋为生！

"把袋子还给我，你这个大笨蛋！"丹说，"我都快浇成落汤鸡了。"说完，他看见了苏。"你终于结婚了，哈？"丹说。

"他是公的,"我告诉丹,"你还记得吧——我上太空的时候认识的。"

"你还给不给我擦鞋了?"穿西装的人说。

"滚开,"丹说,"别等我把你的脚掌咬成两半。"那个家伙走开了。

"你在这儿干什么,丹?"我问,"为什么给人擦鞋?"

"为了羞辱那帮帝国主义的走狗,"他回答说,"我是这么想的,皮鞋擦得锃亮的人全都一文不值,所以,我擦的皮鞋越多,我送进地狱的废物也就越多。"

"好吧,如果你要这么说。"我说,丹扔下擦鞋布,自己推车回篷子下面躲雨。

"见鬼,阿甘,我不是羞辱那帮帝国主义的走狗,"他说,"其实是他们不愿意要我这种人。"

"他们当然愿意,丹,"我说,"过去你经常跟我说,我可以成为任何我想成为的人,做任何我想做的事——你也可以。"

"你还相信这种屁话?"他问。

"我看见拉蔻儿·薇芝光屁股了。"我说。

"真的吗?"丹说,"什么样?"

从那以后,我和丹、苏开始合作。丹不想住寄宿公寓,所以,晚上他睡在外面的垃圾袋下面。"塑造性格。"用他的话说。他给我讲了他离开印第安纳波利斯后都做了什么。首先,他把摔跤赚来的钱在赛狗场上输了个精光,剩下的钱拿去喝了酒。然后,他在一家汽修厂找到一份差事,在车底下干活,他坐在小推车上，钻进去很容易，但他说，他讨厌油垢一直滴在身上。"我也许是个没腿、没用、酗酒的流浪汉，"他说，"但我从来不是一个浑身油乎乎的人。"

接下来，他回到华盛顿，他们要为我们这些参加过越战的人建造的纪念碑举行一场盛大的落成典礼，他们看到他，并得知他的身份后，请他发表演讲。但他在某个招待会上喝醉了，忘了要说什么。于是，他从他们安排他住下的旅馆偷了一本《圣经》，到他讲话的时候，他给他们读了整篇《创世记》，他正准备从《民数记》中再摘录一些句子时，他们关掉了他的麦克风，把他拖走了。那之后，他试过乞讨，但过了一阵子，他觉得"太没尊严"，就放弃了。

我告诉他我和特里布尔先生下过棋，养虾生意做得很成功，我还竞选过美国参议员什么的，但他似乎对拉蔻儿·薇芝更感兴趣。

"你认为她的奶子是真的吗？"他问。

我们在萨凡纳大概待了一个月，收入相当不赖。我做我的单人乐队表演，苏收钱，丹在人群中擦鞋。一天，有个报社记者拍了我们的照片，登在报纸头版。

标题是"流浪汉滞留公园"。

一天下午，我坐在那儿吹口琴，心想，也许接下来我们应该北上去查尔斯顿，这时，我注意到一个小男孩站在鼓前面，盯着我看。

我正在吹《在新奥尔良兜风》，但那个小家伙一直看着我，脸上一点笑容都没有,但他眼中有某种东西闪着光,隐约让我想起了什么。我抬起头,看到人群边上站着一位女士,一看到她,我差点儿昏过去。

天哪,竟然是珍妮·柯伦。

她卷了头发,看上去也有点儿老了,而且面带一丝倦容,但没错,就是珍妮。我很震惊,一不小心吹出一个刺耳的音符,但还是吹完了这首歌,珍妮走过来,拉起那个小男孩的手。

她的眼睛闪闪发光,她说:"哦,阿甘,我听到口琴声,就知道是你。没有人会像你这样吹口琴。"

"你在这儿干什么?"我问。

"我们就住在这儿,"她说,"唐纳德在一家生产屋面瓦的公司做销售部副经理。我们已经在这儿生活差不多三年了。"

我不吹口琴了,于是人群渐渐散去,珍妮挨着我坐在长椅上。小男孩和苏一起玩闹,苏翻起跟头来,逗得小男孩哈哈笑。

"你怎么搞起单人乐队来了?"珍妮问道,"妈妈写信跟我说,你在拜尤拉巴特里的养虾生意做得很大,都是百万富翁了。"

"说来话长。"我说。

"你不会又惹上什么麻烦了吧,阿甘?"她说。

"没有,这次没有,"我说,"你呢?你还好吗?"

"哦,还行,"她说,"我想,我得到了我想要的东西。"

"那是你儿子?"我问。

"对，"她说，"他是不是很可爱？"

"当然——他叫什么名字？"

"福瑞斯特。"

"福瑞斯特？"我说，"你用我的名字给他取名？"

"应该的，"她轻声说，"毕竟，他有一半是你的。"

"一半什么！"

"他是你的儿子，阿甘。"

"我的什么！"

"你的儿子。小阿甘。"我看过去，他在那儿，拍着巴掌，咯咯笑，因为苏正在倒立。

"我想，我早就该告诉你，"珍妮说，"但我离开印第安纳波利斯的时候，你知道，我怀孕了。我什么都不想说，我也不知道为什么。我觉得，嗯，你当时自称'呆瓜'什么的，我要生下这个孩子。我有点儿担心他会是什么样。"

"你是说，担心他会不会是个白痴？"

"是，差不多吧，"她说，"不过，你看，阿甘，难道你看不出来吗！他一点儿都不傻！他很聪明——他今年就要上二年级了。去年他门门功课都是 A。你能相信吗！"

"你确定他是我的？"我问。

"毫无疑问，"她说，"他长大后想成为一名橄榄球运动员，或者宇航员。"

我又望向那个小家伙——他是个强壮漂亮的男孩。他的眼神很清澈，看起来什么都不怕。他和苏正蹲在地上下井字棋。

"呃，"我说，"那么，啊，你的……"

"唐纳德？"珍妮说，"哦，他不知道有你这么一个人。是这样，我刚离开印第安纳波利斯就遇到了他。当时，我快显怀了，不知道该怎么办。他是一个善良可亲的人，细心照顾我和小阿甘。我们买了一栋房子和两辆车，每周六，他会带我们去海边或乡下什么的。礼拜日，我们去教堂，唐纳德正在攒钱，打算将来送小阿甘上大学。"

"我能看看他吗——我是说，就一会儿？"我问。

"当然可以。"珍妮说，她把那个小家伙叫过来。

"阿甘，"她说，"你来认识一下另一个阿甘。他是我的老朋友，你的名字就是随他取的。"

小家伙走过来，在我身旁坐下，说："你的猴子真好玩。"

"那是只猩猩，"我说，"他叫苏。"

"既然他是公的，你为什么叫他苏？"

我立刻明白，我儿子不是白痴。"你妈妈说，你想长大以后成为一名橄榄球运动员，或者宇航员。"我说。

"没错，"他说，"你知道橄榄球或者宇航员是怎么回事吗？"

"知道，"我说，"知道一点点，不过，你最好问你爸爸。我相信他懂的比我多得多。"

然后，他抱了我一下，不是那种热烈的拥抱，但已经足够了。"我还想再跟苏玩一会儿。"他说着从长椅上跳下来，苏想出一个玩法，小阿甘把硬币往锡杯里扔，苏在半空中接住。

珍妮走过来，坐在我旁边，叹了口气，拍拍我的腿。

"有时候，我简直不敢相信，"她说，"我们已经认识快三十年了——从小学一年级就认识。"

阳光穿过树林，正好照在珍妮脸上，她眼中好像有一滴泪，不过一直没有流下来，但那里确实有点儿什么，也许是情感，但我真的说不好是什么，即使我知道它就在那里。

"我只是不敢相信，仅此而已。"她说着，凑过来，亲了一下我的额头。

"这是什么意思？"我问。

"白痴，"珍妮说，她的嘴唇在颤抖，"谁又不是白痴呢？"说完，她就走了。她起身走到小阿甘身边，拉着他的手，他们就这样走了。

苏走过来，坐在我面前，在我脚边的地上画了一个井字。我在右上角画了一个X，苏在中间画了一个O，我立刻明白，没有人会赢。

哦，从那之后，我做了两件事。首先，我打电话给特里布尔先生，告诉他，无论我在养虾生意上赚到多少钱，把其中的百分之十给我妈妈，百分之十给布巴的爸爸，其余的全都寄到珍妮那儿，给小阿甘。

吃过晚饭，我整宿没睡，一直都在思考，尽管这并不是我特别擅长的事。但我当时想的是：过了这么久，我又找到珍妮了。她有了我们的儿子，也许，我们还能以某种方式和好如初。

但我越想这件事就越明白，这是行不通的。而且，我不能理所当然地把这归咎为我是个白痴——尽管那样再好不过。不，这只是命中注定。有时就是这样，此外，归根结底，我认为这个小男孩最好跟珍妮和她丈夫一起生活，他们会给他一个幸福的家，把他抚养成人，这样他就不会有一个傻瓜爸爸。

几天后，我跟苏和丹离开萨瓦纳，继续往前走。我们去了查尔斯顿，接下来又去了里士满、亚特兰大、查塔努加、孟菲斯、纳什维尔，最后到了新奥尔良。

如今，新奥尔良人根本不在乎你做什么，我们仨玩得很开心，每天在杰克逊广场表演，看其他疯子做他们想做的事。

我买了一辆摩托车，两侧带有两个小挎斗，苏和丹可以坐在里面，每个星期天，我们都会开车去河边，坐在岸上，钓鲶鱼。珍妮大概每个月给我写一封信，同时寄来小阿甘的照片。在我收到的最后一张照片上，他穿着一套小橄榄球服。这里有一个女孩在一家脱衣舞俱乐部当女招待，我们偶尔聚聚，玩玩。她叫旺达。很多时候，我、苏和丹只是在法国区兜风、观光，相信我，除了我们，还有一些模样滑稽的人——像俄国革命什么的留下来的东西。

一天，当地报纸的一名记者过来，说想做一篇关于我的报道，因为我是他听说过的"最棒的单人乐队"。那个家伙问了我很多问题，打听我的经历，于是我一五一十地讲给他听，但还没等我说到一半，他就走了，说这种故事不能登报，因为没有人会信。

但我跟你说吧，有时，夜里，当我仰望星空，看到整个天空展现在我眼前，你觉得我会忘掉一切吗？我还是会像其他人一样做梦，我时常会想，如果不是这样，生活还会是什么样。

然后，突然，我四十岁了，五十岁了，六十岁了，你知道吗？

哦，那又怎样？我也许是个白痴，但大多数时候，无论怎样，我都会尽力做对的事——梦想终归是梦想，不是吗？因此，无论发生了什么其他的事，我都在想：我总可以回顾过去，说至少我这一生没有碌碌无为。

你明白我的意思吗？

阿甘正传

作者 _ [美] 温斯顿 · 葛鲁姆   译者 _ 赵文伟

产品经理 _ 赵鹏　　装帧设计 _ 所以设计馆　　产品总监 _ 陈亮
技术编辑 _ 丁占旭　　执行印制 _ 梁拥军　　策划人 _ 毛婷

营销统筹 _ 毛婷　魏洋
营销经理 _ 马莹玉　张艺千　成芸姣

果麦
www.guomai.cn

以　微　小　的　力　量　推　动　文　明

FORREST GUMP By WINSTON GROOM
Copyright: © 1986 BY PERCH CREEK REALTY AND INVESTMENTS CORP.
This edition arranged with RAINES & RAINES
Through Big Apple Agency,Inc.,Labuan, Malaysia
Simplified Chinese edition copyright:
2023 BEIJING ALPHA BOOKS.CO.,INC
All rights reserved.

版贸核渝字（2023）第175号
图书在版编目（CIP）数据

阿甘正传：汉、英／（美）温斯顿·葛鲁姆著；赵文伟译. -- 重庆：重庆出版社，2025.3. -- ISBN 978-7-229-19456-7

Ⅰ．H319.4
中国国家版本馆CIP数据核字第20254W0F92号

阿甘正传（中英双语版）
AGAN ZHENGZHUAN（ZHONGYING SHUANGYUBAN）
［美］温斯顿·葛鲁姆 著 赵文伟 译

出　　品：	华章同人
出版监制：	徐宪江　连　果
责任编辑：	王昌凤
特约编辑：	赵　鹏
营销编辑：	史青苗
责任校对：	彭圆琦
责任印制：	梁善池
封面设计：	所以工作室

重庆出版集团
重庆出版社 出版
（重庆市南岸区南滨路162号1幢）
北京盛通印刷股份有限公司　印刷
重庆出版集团图书发行有限公司 发行
邮购电话：010-85869375

开本：787 mm×1092mm　1/32　印张：15.25　字数：268千
2025年3月第1版　2025年3月第1次印刷
定价：65.00元

如有印装质量问题，请致电023-61520678
版权所有 侵权必究

FORREST GUMP

by
Winston Groom

Chongqing Publishing Group
Chongqing Publishing House

果麦文化 出品

出版说明

本书以第一人称视角,讲述了阿甘的传奇故事。

英文原版有一些拼写、语法错误,乃作者有意为之,以体现主角阿甘的智力水平。

例如:文中 interestin、probly 等词,正确拼写应为 interesting、probably……

本版为保留原汁原味,故不予订正,请读者理解。

For Jimbo Meador and George Radcliff—
who have always made a point of being
kind to Forrest and his friends.

1

LET ME SAT THIS: BEIN A IDIOT IS NO BOX OF CHOCOLATES. People laugh, lose patience, treat you shabby. Now they says folks sposed to be kind to the afflicted, but let me tell you—it ain't always that way. Even so, I got no complaints, cause I reckon I done live a pretty interestin life, so to speak.

I been a idiot since I was born. My IQ is near 70, which qualifies me, so they say. Probly, tho, I'm closer to bein a imbecile or maybe even a moron, but personally, I'd rather think of myself as like a *halfwit*, or somethin—an not no idiot—cause when people think of a idiot, more'n likely they be thinkin of one of them *Mongolian idiots*—the ones with they eyes too close together an drool a lot an play with theyselfs.

Now I'm slow—I'll grant you that, but I'm probly a lot brighter than folks think, cause what goes on in my mind is a sight different than what folks see. For instance, I can *think* things pretty good, but when I got to try sayin or writin them, it kinda come out like jello or somethin. I'll show you what I mean.

The other day, I'm walkin down the street an this man was out workin in his yard. He'd got hissef a bunch of shrubs to plant an he say to me,"Forrest, you wanna earn some money?"an I says,"Uh-huh,"an so he sets me to movin dirt. Damn near ten or twelve wheelbarrows of dirt, in the heat of the day, truckin it all over creation. When I'm thru he reach in his pocket for a dollar. What I shoulda done was raised Cain about the low wages, but instead, I took the damn dollar an all I could say was"thanks"or somethin dumb-soundin like that, an I went on down the street, waddin an unwaddin that dollar in my hand, feelin like a idiot.

You see what I mean?

Now I *know* somethin bout idiots. Probly the only thing I do know bout, but I done read up on em—all the way from that Doy-chee-eveskie guy's idiot, to King Lear's fool, an Faulkner's idiot, Benjie, an even ole Boo Radley in *To Kill a Mockingbird*—now he was a *serious* idiot. The one I like best tho is ole Lennie in *Of Mice an Men*. Mos of them writer fellers got it straight—cause their idiots always smarter than people give em credit for. Hell, I'd agree with that. Any idiot would. Hee Hee.

When I was born, my mama name me Forrest, cause of General Nathan Bedford Forrest who fought in the Civil War. Mama always said we was kin to General Forrest's fambly someways. An he was a great man, she say, cept'n he started up the Ku Klux Klan after the war was over an even my grandmama say they's a bunch of no-goods. Which I would tend to agree with, cause down here, the Grand Exalted Pishposh, or whatever he calls hissef, he operate a gun store in town an once, when I was maybe twelve year ole, I were walkin by there and lookin in the winder an he got a big hangman's noose strung up inside. When he seen me watchin, he done thowed it around his own neck an jerk it up like he was hanged an let his tongue stick out an all so's to scare me. I done run off and hid in a parkin lot behin some cars til somebody call the police an they come an take me home to my mama. So whatever else ole General Forrest done, startin up that Klan thing was not a good idea—any idiot could tell you that. Nonetheless, that's how I got my name.

My mama is a real fine person. Everbody says that. My daddy, he got kilt just after I's born, so I never known him. He worked down to the docks as a longshoreman an one day a crane was takin a big net load of bananas off one of them United Fruit Company boats an somethin broke an the bananas fell down on my daddy an squashed him flat as a pancake. One time I heard some men talkin bout the accident—say it was a helluva mess, half ton of all them bananas an my daddy squished underneath. I don't care for bananas much myself, cept for banana puddin. I like that all right.

My mama got a little pension from the United Fruit people an she took in boarders at our house, so we got by okay. When I was little, she kep me inside a lot, so as the other kids wouldn't bother me. In the summer afternoons, when it was real hot, she used to put me down in the parlor an pull the shades so it was dark an cool an fix me a pitcher of limeade. Then she'd set there an talk to me, jus talk on an on bout nothin in particular, like a person'll talk to a dog or cat, but I got used to it an liked it cause her voice made me feel real safe an nice.

At first, when I's growin up, she'd let me go out an play with everbody, but then she foun out they's teasing me an all, an one day a boy hit me in the back with a stick wile they was chasin me an it raised some fearsome welt. After that, she tole me not to play with them boys anymore. I started tryin to play with the girls but that weren't much better, cause they all run away from me.

Mama thought it would be good for me to go to the public school cause maybe it would hep me to be like everbody else, but after I been there a little wile they come an told Mama I ought'n to be in there with everbody else. They let me finish out first grade tho. Sometimes I'd set there wile the teacher was talkin an I don't know what was going on in my mind, but I'd start lookin out the winder at the birds an squirrels an things that was climbin an settin in a big ole oak tree outside, an then the teacher'd come over an fuss at me. Sometimes, I'd just get this real strange thing come over me an start shoutin an all, an then she'd make me go out an set on a bench in the hall. An the other kids, they'd never play with me or nothin, cept'n to chase me or get me to start hollerin so's they could laugh at me—all cept Jenny Curran, who at least didn't run away from me an sometimes she'd let me walk nex to her goin home after class.

But the next year, they put me in another sort of school, an let me tell you, it was wierd. It was like they'd gone aroun collectin all the funny fellers they coud find an put em all together, rangin from my age an younger to big ole boys bout sixteen or seventeen. They was retards of all kinds an spasmos an kids that couldn't even eat or go to the toilet by theyselfs. I was probly the best of the lot.

They was one big fat boy, musta been fourteen or so, an he was afflicted with some kinda thing made him shake like he's in the electric chair or somethin. Miss Margaret, our teacher, made me go in the bathroom with him when he had to go, so's he wouldn't do nothin wierd. He done it anyway, tho. I didn't know no way of stoppin him, so I'd just lock mysef in one of the stalls and stay there till he's thru, an walk him back to the class.

I stayed in that school for about five or six years. It wadn't all bad tho. They'd let us paint with our fingers an make little things, but mostly, it jus teachin us how to do stuff like tie up our shoes an not slobber food or get wild an yell an holler an thow shit aroun. They wadn't no book learnin to speak of—cept to show us how to read street signs an things like the difference between the Men's an the Ladies' rooms. With all them serious nuts in there, it woulda been impossible to conduct anythin more'n that anyway. Also, I think it was for the purpose of keepin us out of everbody else's hair. Who the hell wants a bunch of retards runnin aroun loose? Even I could understand that.

When I got to be thirteen, some pretty unusual things begun to happen. First off, I started to grow. I grew six inches in six months, an my mama was all the time havin to let out my pants. Also, I commenced to grow *out*. By the time I was sixteen I was six foot six an weighed two hundrit forty-two pounds. I know that cause they took me in an weighed me. Said they jus couldn't believe it.

What happen nex caused a real change in my life. One day I'm strollin down the street on the way home from nut school, an a car stop longside of me. This guy call me over an axed my name. I tole him, an then he axed what school I go to, an how come he ain't seen me aroun. When I tell him bout the nut school, he axed if I'd ever played football. I shook my head. I guess I mighta tole him I'd seen kids playin it, but they'd never let me play. But like I said, I ain't too good at long conversation, an so I jus shook my head. That was about two weeks after school begun again.

Three days or so later, they come an got me outta the nut school. My mama was there, an so was the guy in the car an two other people what look like goons—who I guess was present in case I was to start somethin. They took all the stuff outta my desk an put it in a brown paper bag an tole me to say goodbye to Miss Margaret, an alls of a sudden she commence to start cryin an give me a big ole hug. Then I got to say goodbye to all the other nuts, an they was droolin an spasmoin an beatin on the desks with they fists. An then I was gone.

Mama rode up in the front seat with the guy an I set in back in between them goons, jus like police done in them ole movies when they took you "downtown." Cept we didn't go downtown. We went to the new highschool they had built. When we got there they took me inside to the principal's office an Mama an me an the guy went in wile the two goons waited in the hall. The principal was an ole gray-haired man with a stain on his tie an baggy pants who look like he coulda come outta the nut school hissef. We all sat down an he begun splainin things an axein me questions, an I just nodded my head, but what they wanted was for me to play football. That much I figgered out on my own.

Turns out the guy in the car was the football coach, name of Fellers. An that day I didn't go to no class or nothin, but Coach Fellers, he took me back to the locker room an one of the goons rounded me up a football suit with all them pads an stuff an a real nice plastic helmet with a thing in front to keep my face from gettin squished in. The only thing was, they couldn't find no shoes to fit me, so's I had to use my sneakers till they could order the shoes.

Coach Fellers an the goons got me dressed up in the football suit, an then they made me undress again, an then do it all over again, ten or twenty times, till I could do it by mysef. One thing I had trouble with for a wile was that jockstrap thing—cause I couldn't see no real good reason for wearing it. Well, they tried splainin it to me, an then one of the goons says to the other that I'm a"dummy"or somethin like that, an I guess he thought I wouldn't understand him, but I did, on account of I pay special attention to that kind of shit. Not that it hurt my feelins. Hell, I been called a sight worse than that. But I took notice of it, nonetheless.

After a wile a bunch of kids started comin into the locker room an takin out they football stuff and gettin into it. Then we all went outside an Coach Fellers got everbody together an he stood me up in front of them an introduced me. He was sayin a bunch of shit that I wadn't followin real close cause I was haf scared to death, on account of nobody had ever introduced me before to a bunch of strangers. But afterward some of the others come up an shook my hand an say they is glad I am here an all. Then Coach Fellers blowed a whistle, what like to make me leap outta my skin an everbody started jumpin around to get exercise.

It's a kind of long story what all happened nex, but anyway, I begun to play football. Coach Fellers an one of the goons hepped me out special since I didn't know how to play. We had this thing where you sposed to block people an they were tryin to splain it all, but when we tried it a bunch of times everbody seemed to be gettin disgusted cause I couldn't remember what I was sposed to do.

Then they tried this other thing they call the *defense*, where they put three guys in front of me an I am sposed to get thru them an grap the guy with the football. The first part was easier, cause I could just shove the other guys' heads down, but they were unhappy with the way I grapped the guy with the ball, an finally they made me go an tackle a big oak tree about fifteen or twenty times—to get the feel of it, I spose. But after a wile, when they figgered I had learnt somethin from the oak tree, they put me back with the three guys an the ball carrier an then got mad I didn't jump on him real vicious-like after I moved the others out of the way. I took a lot of abuse that afternoon, but when we quit practicin I went in to see Coach Fellers an tole him I didn't want to jump on the ball guy cause I was afraid of hurtin him. Coach, he say that it wouldn't hurt him, cause he was in his football suit an was protected. The truth is, I wasn't so much afraid of hurtin him as I was that he'd get mad at me an they'd start chasin me again if I wadn't real nice to everbody. To make a long story short, it took me a wile to get the hang of it all.

Meantime I got to go to class. In the nut school, we really didn't have that much to do, but here they was far more serious about things. Somehow, they had worked it out so's I had three homeroom classes where you jus set there an did whatever you wanted, an then three other classes where there was a lady who was teachin me how to read. Jus the two of us. She was real nice an pretty and more'n once or twice I had nasty thoughts about her. Miss Henderson was her name.

About the only class I liked was lunch, but I guess you couldn't call that a class. At the nut school, my mama would fix me a sambwich an a cookie an a piece of fruit—cept no bananas—an I'd take it to school with me. But in this school they was a cafeteria with nine or ten different things to eat an I'd have trouble makin up my mind what I wanted. I think somebody must of said somethin, cause after a week or so Coach Fellers come up to me an say to just go ahead an eat all I wanted cause it been "taken care of." Hot damn!

Guess who should be in my homeroom class but Jenny Curran. She come up to me in the hall an say she remember me from first grade. She was all growed up now, with pretty black hair an she was long-legged an had a beautiful face, an they was other things too, I dare not mention.

The football was not goin exactly to the likin of Coach Fellers. He seemed displeased a lot an was always shoutin at people. He shouted at me too. They tried to figger out some way for me to just stay put an keep other folks from grappin our guy carryin the ball, but that didn't work cept when they ran the ball right up the middle of the line. Coach was not too happy with my tacklin neither, an let me tell you, I spent a lot of time at that oak tree. But I just couldn't get to where I would thow mysef at the ball guy like they wanted me to do. Somethin kep me from it.

Then one day a event happen that changed all that too. In the cafeteria I had started gettin my food and goin over to set nex to Jenny Curran. I wouldn't say nothin, but she was jus bout the only person in the school I knew halfways, an it felt good setting there with her. Most of the time she didn't pay me no attention, an talked with other people. At first I'd been settin with some of the football players, but they acted like I was invisible or somethin. At least Jenny Curran acted like I was there. But after a wile of this, I started to notice this other guy was there a lot too, an he starts makin wisecracks bout me. Sayin shit like"How's Dumbo?"an all. And this gone on for a week or two, an I was sayin nothin, but finally I says—I can't hardly believe I said it even now—but I says,"I ain't no Dumbo,"an the guy jus looked at me an starts laughin. An Jenny Curran, she say to the guy to keep quiet, but he takes a carton of milk an pours it in my lap an I jump up an run out cause it scares me.

A day or so later, that guy come up to me in the hall an says he's gonna"get"me. All day I was afraid terribily, an later that afternoon, when I was leaving to go to the gym, there he is, with a bunch of his friends. I tried to go the other way, but he come up to me an start pushin me on the shoulders. An he's sayin all kinds of bad things, callin me a"stupo"an all, an then he hit me in the stomach. It didn't hurt so much, but I was startin to cry and I turned an begun to run, an heard him behind me an the others was runnin after me too. I jus run as fast as I could toward the gym, across the practice football field an suddenly I seen Coach Fellers, settin up in the bleachers watchin me. The guys who was chasin me stop and go away, an Coach Fellers, he has got this real peculiar look on his face, an tell me to get suited up right away. A wile later, he come in the locker room with these plays drawn on a piece of paper—three of them—an say for me to memorize them best I can.

That afternoon at the football practice, he line everbody up in two teams an suddenly the quarterback give *me* the ball an I'm sposed to run outside the right end of the line to the goalpost. When they all start chasin me, I run fast as I can—it was seven or eight of them before they could drag me down. Coach Fellers is mighty happy; jumpin up and down an yellin an slappin everbody on the back. We'd run a lot of races before, to see how fast we could run, but I get a lot faster when I'm bein chased, I guess. What idiot wouldn't?

Anyway, I become a lot more popular after that, an the other guys on the team started bein nicer to me. We had our first game an I was scared to death, but they give me the ball an I run over the goal line two or three times an people never been kinder to me after that. That highschool certainly begun to change things in my life. It even got to where I *liked* to run with the football, cept it was mostly that they made me run aroun the sides cause I still couldn't get to where I liked to just run over people like you do in the middle. One of the goons comments that I am the largest highschool *halfback* in the entire world. I do not think he mean it as a compliment.

Otherwise, I was learnin to read a lot better with Miss Henderson. She give me *Tom Sawyer* an two other books I can't remember, an I took them home an read em all, but then she give me a test where I don't do so hot. But I sure enjoyed them books.

After a wile, I went back to settin nex to Jenny Curran in the cafeteria, an there weren't no more trouble for a long time, but then one day in the springtime I was walkin home from school and who should appear but the boy that poured that milk in my lap an chased me that day. He got hissef a stick an start callin me things like"moron"and"stupo."

Some other people was watchin an then along comes Jenny Curran, an I'm bout to take off again—but then, for no reason I know, I jus didn't do it. That feller take his stick an poke me in the stomach with it, an I says to mysef, the hell with this, an I grapped a holt to his arm an with my other hand I knock him upside the head an that was the end of that, more or less.

That night my mama get a phone call from the boy's parents, say if I lay a han on their son again they is goin to call the authorities an have me"put away."I tried to splain it to my mama an she say she understand, but I could tell she was worried. She tell me that since I am so huge now, I got to watch mysef, cause I might hurt somebody. An I nodded an promised her I wouldn't hurt nobody else. That night when I lyin in bed I heard her cryin to hersef in her room.

But what that did for me, knockin that boy upside the head, put a definate new light on my football playin. Next day, I axed Coach Fellers to let me run the ball straight on and he say okay, an I run over maybe four or five guys till I'm in the clear an they all had to start chasin me again. That year I made the All State Football team. I couldn't hardly believe it. My mama give me two pair of socks an a new shirt on my birthday. An she done saved up an bought me a new suit that I wore to get the All State Football award. First suit I ever had. Mama tied my tie for me an off I went.

2

THE ALL STATE FOOTBALL BANQUET WAS TO BE HELT IN A little town called Flomaton, what Coach Fellers described as a "switch up the railroad tracks." We was put on a bus—they was five or six of us from this area who won the prize—an we was trucked up there. It was a hour or two before we arrived, an the bus didn't have no toilet, an I had drank two Slurpees fore we lef, so when we get to Flomaton, I really got to go bad.

The thing was helt at the Flomaton Highschool auditorium, an when we git inside, me and some of the others find the toilet. Somehow, tho, when I go to unzip my pants, the zipper is stuck in my shirttail an won't come down. After a bit of this, a nice little guy from a rival school goes out and finds Coach Fellers an he come in with the two goons an they be tryin to get my pants open. One of the goons say the only way to git it down is jus rip it apart. At this, Coach Fellers put his hans on his hips an say, "I spose you expect me to send this boy out there with his fly unzipped an his thing hangin out—now what kind of a impression do you think that would make?" Then he turn to me an say, "Forrest, you jus got to keep a lid on it till this thing's over, an then we get it open for you—okay?" An I nod, cause I don't know what else to do, but I figgerin I be in for a long evenin.

When we get out to the auditorium there's a million people all settin there at tables, smilin an clappin as we come out. We is put up at a big long table on the stage in front of everbody an my worst fears was realized about the long evenin. Seem like ever soul in the room got up to make a speech—even the waiters an janitor. I wished my mama coulda been there, cause she'd of hepped me, but she back at home in bed with the grippe. Finally it come time to get handed our prizes, which was little gold-colored footballs, an when our names was called we was sposed to go up to the microphone an take the prize an say "thank you," an they also tole us if anybody has anythin else he wants to say, to keep it short on account of we want to be gettin out of there before the turn of the century.

Most everbody had got they prize an said "thank you," an then it come my turn. Somebody on the microphone call out "Forrest Gump," which, if I hadn't tole you before, is my last name, an I stand up an go over an they han me the prize. I lean over to the mike an say, "Thank you," an everbody starts to cheer an clap an stand up in they seats. I spose somebody tole them aforehan I'm some kind of idiot, an they makin a special effort to be nice. But I'm so surprised by all this, I don't know what to do, so I jus kep standin there. Then everbody hush up, an the man at the mike he lean over and axe me if I got anythin else I want to say. So I says, "I got to pee."

Everbody in the audience didn't say nothin for a few moments, an jus started lookin funny at each other, an then they begun a sort of low mumblin, an Coach Fellers come up an grap me by the arm and haul me back to my seat. Rest of the night he be glarin at me, but after the banquet is over, Coach an the goons done take me back to the bathroom an rip open my pants an I done peed a bucket!

"Gump," Coach say after I am finished, "you sure got a way with words."

Now nex year wadn't too eventful, cept somebody put out the word that a idiot got hissef on the All State Football team an a bunch of letters start comin in from all round the country. Mama collect them all and start keepin a scrapbook. One day a package come from New Yawk City that contain a official baseball signed by the entire New Yawk Yankees baseball team. It was the best thing ever happen to me! I treasure that ball like a goldbrick, till one day when I was tossin it aroun in the yard, a big ole dog come up an grap it outta the air an chewed it up. Things like that always happenin to me.

One day Coach Fellers call me in an take me into the principal's office. They was a man there from up to the University who shook my han an axe me whether I ever thought bout playin football in college. He say they been "watchin" me. I shook my head, cause I hadn't.

Everbody seemed to be in awe of this man, bowin an scrapin an callin him "Mister Bryant." But he say for me to call him "Bear," which I thought was a funny name, cept he do look similar to a bear in some respects.

Coach Fellers point out that I am not the brightest person, but the Bear, he say that is plenty true of most of his players, an that he figgers to get me special hep in my studies. A week later they give me a test with all sorts of screwy questions the like of which I am not familiar with. After a wile I get bored and stop takin the test.

Two days afterward, the Bear come back again and I get hauled into the principal's office by Coach Fellers. Bear lookin distressed, but he still bein nice; he axe me have I done tried my best on that test. I nod my head, but the principal be rollin his eyes, an the Bear say,"Well, this is unfortunate then, cause the score appears to indicate that this boy is a idiot."

The principal be noddin his head now, an Coach Fellers is standin there with his hands in his pockets lookin sour. It seem to be the end of my college football prospects.

The fact that I were too dumb to play college football did not seem to impress the United States Army none. It were my last year at highschool an in the springtime everbody else graduated. They let me set up on the stage tho, an even give me a black robe to put on, an when it come time, the principal announce they was gonna give me a"special"diploma. I got up to go to the microphone an the two goons stan up an go with me— I spose so's I don't make no remarks like I did at the All State Football thing. My mama is down in the front row cryin and wringin her hans an I really feel good, like I actually done accomplish somethin.

But when we git back home, I finally realize why she bawlin an carryin on—they was a letter come from the Army say I got to report to the local daft board or somesuch. I didn't know what the deal was, but my mama did—it was 1968 an they was all sorts of shit fixin to hoppen.

Mama give me a letter from the school principal to han to the daftboard people, but somehow I lost it on the way there. It was a loony scene. They was a big colored guy in a Army suit yellin at people an dividin them up into bunches. We was all standin there and he come up an shout,"All right, I want half of you to go over there an half of you to go over here, an the other half of you to stay put!"Everbody millin aroun an lookin bewildered an even I could figger out this guy's a moron.

They took me in a room and line us up an tell us to remove our clothes. I ain't much for that, but everbody else done it an so I did too. They lookin at us everplace—eyes, noses, mouths, ears—even our private parts. At one point they tell me,"Bend over,"an when I do, somebody jam his finger up my ass.

That's it!

I turn an grapped that bastid an knock him upside the head. They was suddenly a big commotion an a bunch of people run up an jump on top of me. However, I am used to that treatment. I thowed them off an run out the door. When I get home an tell my mama what happen, she all upset, but she say,"Don't worry, Forrest—everthin gonna be okay."

It ain't. Next week, a van pull up at our house and a number of men in Army suits an shiny black helmets come up to the door be axin for me. I'm hidin up in my room, but Mama come up an say they jus wanta give me a ride back down to the daft board. All the way there, they be watchin me real close, like I'm some kinda maniac.

They was a door that lead to a big office where there's a older man all dressed up in a shiny uniform an he eyein me pretty careful too. They set me down an shove another test in front of me, an wile it's one hell of a lot easier than the college football test, it still ain't no piece of cake.

When I'm done, they take me to another room where they's four or five guys settin at a long table what start axin me questions an passin around what looked like the test I took. Then they all git into a huddle and when they finish one of em sign a paper an han it to me. When I take it home, Mama read it an begin pullin at her hair an weepin an praisin the Lord, cause it say I am"Temporarily Deferred,"on account of I am a numbnuts.

Somethin else occurred durin that week that was a major event in my life. There was this lady boarder livin with us that worked down to the telephone company as a operator. Miss French was her name. She was a real nice lady, what kep mostly to hersef, but one night when it was terribily hot, an they was thunderstorms, she stuck her head out the door to her room as I was walkin by an say,"Forrest, I just got a box of nice divinity this afternoon—would you like a piece?"

An I say"yes,"an she bring me into her room an there on the dresser is the divinity. She give me a piece of it, then she axe if I want another, an she points for me to set down on the bed. I must of ate ten or fifteen pieces of the divinity an lightnin was flashin outside an thunder an the curtains was blowin an Miss French kinda pushes me an makes me lie back on the bed. She commences to start strokin me in a personal way."Jus keep your eyes closed,"she say,"an everthing will be all right."Nex thing you know there is somethin happenin that had not happen before. I cannot say what it was, because I was keepin my eyes closed, an also because my mama woulda kilt me, but let me tell you this—it give me an entirely new outlook on things for the future.

The problem was that wile Miss French was a nice kind lady, the things that she done to me that night was the kinds of things I'd have preferred to have done to me by Jenny Curran. An yet, there was no way I could see to even begin gettin that accomplished cause what with the way I am, it is not so easy to ask anyone for a date. That is to put it mildly.

But on account of my new experience, I got up the courage to axe my mama what to do about Jenny, tho I certainly didn't say nothin bout me an Miss French. Mama said she'll take care of it for me, an she call up Jenny Curran's mama an splain the situation to her, an the nex evenin, lo an behole, who should appear at our door but Jenny Curran hersef!

She is all dressed up in a white dress an a pink flower in her hair an she look like nothin I have ever dreamt of. She come inside an Mama took her to the parlor an give her a icecream float an call for me to come down from my room, where I had run to as soon as I seen Jenny Curran comin up the walk. I'd of rather had five thousand people chasin me than to come out of my room jus then, but Mama come up an take me by the han an lead me down an give me a ice-cream float too. That made it better.

Mama said we can go to the movies an she give Jenny three dollars as we walk out of the house. Jenny ain't never been nicer, talkin an laughin an I am noddin an grinnin like a idiot. The movie was jus four or five blocks from our house, an Jenny went up an got some tickets an we went in an set down. She axed me if I want some popcorn an when she come back from gettin it, the picture done started.

It is a movie about two people, a man an a lady called Bonnie an Clyde that robbed banks an they was some interestin other people in it also. But it was a lot of killin an shootin an shit like that, too. It seemed to me funny that folks would be shootin an killin one another that way, so's I laughed a lot when that went on, an whenever I did, Jenny Curran seemed to squnch down in her seat a lot. Halfway thru the movie, she was almost squnched down to the floor. I suddenly saw this an figgered she had somehow felled out of her seat, so I reached over an grapped her by the shoulder to lif her up again.

As I did this, I heard somethin tear, an I look down an Jenny Curran's dress is ripped completely open an everthing is hangin out. I took my other han to try to cover her up, but she start makin noises an flail about wild-like, an me, I'm tryin to hole onto her so's she don't fall down again or come undone an there's people around us lookin back tryin to see what all the commotion is about. Suddenly a fellow come down the aisle an shine a bright light right on Jenny an me, but bein exposed an all, she commenced to shriek an wail an then she jump up an run out of the show.

Nex thing I know, two men come an tell me to get up an I follow them to a office. A few minutes later, four policemen arrive an axe me to come with them. They show me to a police car an two get in front an two get in back with me, jus like it was with Coach Fellers' goons, cept'n this time we *do* go "downtown," an they escort me to a room an jab my fingers onto a pad an I get my picture taken an they thowed me in jail. It was a horrible experience. I was worried all the time bout Jenny, but after a bit my mama showed up an come in wipin her eyes with a handkerchief an twistin her fingers an I knowed I'm in the doghouse again.

There was some kind of ceremony a few days later down to the courthouse. My mama dressed me in my suit an took me there, an we met a nice man with a moustache carrying a big purse who tole the judge a bunch of things an then some other people, includin my mama, say some other shit an finally it was my turn.

The man with the moustache took me by the arm so's I'd stand up, an the judge axed me how all this done happen? I couldn't figger out what to say, so I jus shrugged my shoulders an then he axes if there's anything else I want to add, an so I says, "I got to pee," cause we'd been settin there almost haf a day an I'm about to bust! The judge, he lean forward from behind his big ole desk an peer at me like I am a Marsman or somethin. Then the feller with the moustache speaks up and followin this the judge tells him to take me to the toilet, which he does. I look back as we leavin the room an see po ole Mama holdin her head an daubin at her eyes with the handkerchief.

Anyhow, when I get back, the judge be scratchin his chin an he say the whole deal is "very peculiar," but that he think I ought to go in the Army or somethin which might hep straighten me out. My mama inform him that the United States Army won't have me, account of I am a idiot, but that this very mornin a letter done come from up to the University sayin that if

I will play football for them, I can go to school there scot free.

The judge say that sounds kinda peculiar too, but it's okay with him so long as I get my big ass out of town.

The nex mornin I am all packed up an Mama, she take me to the bus station an put me on the bus. I is lookin out the winder an there is Mama, cryin an wipin her eyes with her handkerchief. That is gettin to be a scene I know too well. It is stamped permanant into my memory. Anyhow, they started up the bus, an away I went.

3

WHEN WE GIT UP TO THE UNIVERSITY, COACH BRYANT HE come out to the gym where we all settin in our shorts and sweatshirts an begin makin a speech. It bout the same kind of speech Coach Fellers would make, cept even a simpleton like mysef could tell this man mean bidness! His speech short an sweet, an conclude with the statement that the last man on the bus to the practice field will get a ride there not on the bus, but on Coach Bryant's shoe instead. Yessiree. We do not doubt his word, an stack ourselfs into the bus like flapjacks.

All this was durin the month of August, which in the state of Alabama is somewhat hotter than it is elsewhere. That is to say, that if you put a egg on top of your football helmet it would be fried sunnyside up in about ten seconds. Of course nobody ever try that on account of it might get Coach Bryant angry. That was the one thing nobody wish to do, because life was almost intolerable as it was.

Coach Bryant have his own goons to show me around. They take me to where I is gonna stay, which is a nice brick building on the campus that somebody says is called the "Ape Dorm." Them goons escort me over there in a car an lead me upstairs to my room. Unfortunately, what might of looked nice from the outside was not true for the inside. At first, it appear that nobody had lived in this building for a long time, they was so much dirt an shit aroun, an most of the doors had been torn off they hinges an bashed in, an most of the winders are busted out too.

A few of the fellers is lyin on they cots inside, wearin very little cause it about 110 degrees hot in there, an flies an things be hummin an buzzin. In the hall they is a big stack of newspapers, which at first I afraid they gonna make us read, it being college an all, but soon I learn they are for puttin down on the floor so's you don't have to step on all the dirt an shit when you walk aroun.

The goons take me to my room an say they be hopin to find my roomate there, whose name is Curtis somebody, but he nowhere to be foun. So they get my stuff unpacked an show me where the bathroom is, which look worse than what you might expect to find at a one-pump gasoline station, an they be on they way. But before they go, one of the goons say Curtis an me should get on fine cause both of us have about as much brains as a eggplant. I look real hard at the goon what said that, cause I be tired of hearin all that shit, but he tell me to drop down and give him fifty pushups. After that, I just be doin what I'm tole.

I went to sleep on my cot after spreadin a sheet over it to cover up the dirt, an was havin a dream bout settin down in the parlor with my mama like we use to do when it was hot, an she'd fix me a limeade an talk to me hour after hour—an then suddenly the door of the room done crashed in flat an scare me haf to death! A feller be standin there in the doorway with a wild look on his face, eyes all bugged out, no teeth in front, nose look like a yeller squash an his hair standin straight up like he done stuck his thing in a lightsocket. I figger this be Curtis.

He come inside the room like he expectin somebody to pounce on him, lookin from side to side, an walk right over the door that he just caved in. Curtis ain't very tall, but he look like an icebox otherwise. First thing he axe me is where I'm from. When I say Mobile, he say that is a"candyass"town, an informs me he's from Opp, where they make peanut butter, an if I don't like it, he gonna open up a jar hissef an butter my butt with it! That were the extent of our conversation for a day or so.

That afternoon at football practice it be about ten thousan degrees hot on the field, an all Coach Bryant's goons runnin roun scowlin an yellin at us an makin us exercise. My tongue hangin down like it was a necktie or somethin, but I tryin to do the right thing. Finally they divides up everbody an puts me with backs an we start to run pass patterns.

Now before I come up to the University, they done sent me a package which contain about a million different football plays, an I done axed Coach Fellers what I'm spose to do with it an he jus shake his head sadly an say not to try to do nothin—jus to wait till I get to the University an let them figger somethin out.

I wish I had not taken Coach Fellers' advice now, cause when I run out for my first pass I done turned the wrong way an the head goon come rushin up hollerin an shoutin at me an when he stop shoutin he axed me don't I study the plays they send me? When I says,"Uh, uh,"he commence to jump up an down an flail his arms like hornets is upon him, an when he calm down he tell me to go run five laps aroun the field wile he consult with Coach Bryant bout me.

Coach Bryant be settin up in a great big tower lookin down on us like the Great Gawd Bud, I'm runnin the laps and watchin the goon clime up there, an when he get to the top an say his piece, Coach Bryant crane his neck forward an I feel his eyes burnin hot on my big stupid ass. Suddenly a voice come over a megaphone for everbody to hear, say,"Forrest Gump, report to the coachin tower,"an I seen Coach Bryant an the goon climin down. All the time I be runnin over there I am wishin I were runnin backwards instead.

But imagine my surprise when I see Coach Bryant smilin. He motion me over to some bleachers an we set down an he axed me again if I'd not learnt them plays they send me. I begin to splain what Coach Fellers had tole me, but Coach Bryant he stop me an say for me to git back in the line an start catchin passes, an then I tole him somethin else I guess he didn't want to hear, which was that I had never even caught a pass at highschool, cause they figgered it hard enough to get me to remember where our own goaline is, let alone runnin aroun tryin to grap the ball outta the air too.

At this news, Coach Bryant get a real odd squint in his eyes, an he look off in the distance, as if he was lookin all the way to the moon or somethin. Then he tell the goon to go fetch a football an when the football come, Coach Bryant hissef tell me to run out a little ways an turn aroun. When I do, he thowed the football at me. I see it comin almost like slow-motion but it bounce off my fingers an fall on the ground. Coach Bryant be noddin his head up an down like he should of figgered this out earlier, but somehow I get the idea he is not pleased.

From the time I'm little, ever time I do somethin wrong, my mama, she'd say, "Forrest, you got to be careful, cause they gonna put you away." I was so scairt of bein put in this "away" place I'd always try to be better, but I'm damned if there's a worst place they could of sent me than this Ape Dorm thing I'm livin in.

People be doin shit they wouldn't of tolerated even in the nut school—rippin out the toilets, for instance, so's you'd go to the bathroom an wouldn't fine nothin but a hole in the floor to shit in, an they'd have heaved the toilet out the winder onto the top of somebody's car drivin past. One night some big ole goofball what played in the line got out a rifle an commence to shoot out all the winders in somebody's fraternity house across the street. The campus cops come rushin over, but the feller drop a big outboard motor he found someplace out the winder onto the top of the cop car. Coach Bryant make him run a bunch of extra laps for doing that.

Curtis an me ain't gettin along so hot, an I never been so lonely. I miss my mama, an wanta go back home. Trouble with Curtis is, I don't understand him. Everthing he say got so many cusswords in it, time I get to figgerin out what they are, I miss his point. Most of the time, I gather his point is that he ain't happy bout somethin.

Curtis had a car an he used to give me a ride to practice, but one day I go to meet him an he cussin an growlin an bent over a big drain grate in the street. Seems he's got a flat tire an when he go to change it he put the lug nuts in his hubcap and accidentally knock em down into the drain. We fixin to be late to practice which was not real good to do, so's I say to Curtis,"Why don't you take one lug nut off each of them three other tires an that way you will have three nuts on each tire, which ought to be enough to get us to practice?"

Curtis stop cussin for a moment an look up at me an say,"You supposed to be a *idiot*, how you figure that out?"An I say,"Maybe I am a idiot, but at least I ain't *stupid*,"an at this, Curtis jump up an commence chasin me with the tire tool, callin me ever terrible thing he can think up, an that pretty much ruin our relationship.

After that, I decide I got to find another place to stay, so when we git off from practice I gone down into the basement of the Ape Dorm an spen the rest of the night there. It wadn't no dirtier than the upstairs rooms an there was an electric lightbulb. Nex day I moved my cot down there an from then on, it was where I lived.

Meantime, school is done started an they got to figger out what to do with me. They was a guy with the atheletic department that seemed to do nothin but figger out how to get dummos to where they could pass a class. Some of the classes was sposed to be easy, such as Physical Education, an they enroll me in that. But also I have got to take one English course an one science or math, an there is no gettin aroun that. What I learnt later was that there was certain teachers that would give a football player a sort of break, meanin that they'd appreciate he is consumed with playin football an cannot spend much of his time on school. They was one of these teachers in the science department, but unfortunately, the only class he taught was somethin called"Intermediate Light,"which was apparently for graduate physics majors or something. But they put me in there anyhow, even though I didn't know physics from phys-ed.

I was not so lucky in English. They apparently did not have no sympathetic people over in that department, so's they tole me just to go ahead an take the class an fail it, an they'd figger out somethin else later.

In Intermediate Light, they provide me with a textbook that weigh five pounds an look like a Chinaman wrote it. But ever night I take it down to the basement an set on my cot under the lightbulb, an after a wile, for some peculiar reason, it begun to make sense. What did not make sense was why we was sposed to be doin it in the first place, but figgerin out them equations was easy as pie. Professor Hooks was my teacher's name, an after the first test, he axed me to come to his office after class. He say,"Forrest, I want you to tell me the truth, did somebody provide you the answers to these questions?"An I shake my head, an then he han me a sheet of paper with a problem written on it and says for me to set down an figger it out. When I'm thru, Professor Hooks look at what I done an shake his head an say,"Greatgodamighty."

English class was another deal entirely. The teacher is a Mister Boone, an he a very stern person who talk a lot. At the end of the first day, he say for us to set down that night an write a short autobiography of ourselfs for him. It's jus bout the most difficult thing I ever try to do, but I stay up most of the night, thinkin an writin, an I just say whatever come to mine on account of they tole me to fail the class anyhow.

A few days later, Mister Boone start handin back our papers an he criticism an makin fun of everbody's autobiography. Then he come to what I done, an I figger I'm in the doghouse for sure. But he hold up my paper an start readin it out loud to everbody an he commences laughin an everbody else is too. I had tole bout bein in the nut school, an playin football for Coach Fellers an goin to the All State Football banquet, an about the daft board, an Jenny Curran an the movie an all. When he's thru, Mr. Boone, he say,"Now here is *originality*! Here is what I *want*,"an everbody turn an look at me, an he says,"Mister Gump, you ought to think about gettin into the creative writing department—how did you think this up?"An I says,"I got to pee."

Mister Boone kinda jump back for a secont, an then he bust out laughin an so does everbody else, an he says,"Mister Gump, you are a very amusing feller."

An so I am surprised again.

The first football game was on a Saturday a few weeks later. Most of the time practice had been pretty bad, till Coach Bryant figgered out what to do with me, which was bout what Coach Fellers had done at highschool. They jus give me the ball an let me run. I run good that day, an score four touchdowns, an we whip the University of Georgia 35 to

3 an everbody slappin me on the back till it hurt. After I get cleaned up I phoned my mama an she done listened to the game over the radio an is so happy she can bust! That night, everbody goin to parties an shit, but nobody axed me to any, so I go on down to the basement. I'm there a wile when I hear this kind of music comin from someplace upstairs and it's real pretty-like, an, I don't know why, but I went on up there to find out what it was.

There was this guy, Bubba, settin in his room playin a mouth organ. He'd broke his foot in practice an couldn't play an didn't have nowhere to go either. He let me set on a cot an listen to him, we didn't talk or nothing, he jus settin on one cot an me on the other, an he's playing his harmonica. An after bout a hour I axed him if I could try it an he says, "Okay." Little did I know that it would change my life forever.

After I'd played aroun on the thing for a wile, I got to where's I could play pretty good, an Bubba was goin crazy, sayin he's never heard such good shit. After it got late, Bubba says for me to take the harmonica with me, an I did, an played it a long time, till I got sleepy and went to bed.

Next day, Sunday, I went to take the harmonica back to Bubba but he say for me to keep it, cause he got another one, an I was real happy, an went for a walk an set down under a tree an played all day long, till I run out of things to play.

It was late in the afternoon, an the sun was almost gone when I begun to walk back to the Ape Dorm. I was goin across the Quadrangle when suddenly I hear this girl's voice shout out, "Forrest!"

I turn aroun an who should be behin me but Jenny Curran.

She has a big smile on her face and she come up and took me by the han, an says she saw me play football yesterday and how good I was an all. It turns out she ain't mad or anythin bout what happen in the movie, an says it ain't my fault, it was jus one of them things. She axe if I want to have a Co'Cola with her.

It was too nice to believe, settin there with Jenny Curran, an she say she takin classes in music an drama an that she plannin on bein a actress or a singer. She also playin in a little band that do folk music stuff, an tells me they gonna be at the Student Union buildin tomorrow night an for me to come by. Let me tell you, I can hardly wait.

4

NOW THERE IS A SECRET THING THAT COACH BRYANT AN them done figgered out, an nobody sposed to mention it, even to ourselfs. They been teachin me how to catch a football pass. Ever day after practice I been workin with two goons an a quarterback, runnin out an catchin passes, runnin out an catchin passes, till I'm so exhausted my tongue hangin down to my navel. But I gettin to where I can catch em, an Coach Bryant, he say this gonna be our "secret weapon"—like a "Adam Bomb," or somethin, cause after a wile them other teams gonna figger out they ain't thowin me the ball an will not be watchin for it.

"Then," Coach Bryant say, "we is gonna turn your big ass loose—six foot six, two hundrit forty pounds—an run the hundrit yards in 9. 5 seconds flat. It is gonna be a sight!"

Bubba an me is real good friends by now, an he heped me learn some new songs on the harmonica. Sometimes he come down to the basement and we set aroun an play along together, but Bubba say I am far better than he ever will be. I got to tell you, that if it weren't for that harmonica music, I might of jus packed up an gone home, but it made me feel so good, I can hardly describe it. Sort of like my whole body is the harmonica an the music give me goosebumps when I play it. Mostly the trick is in the tongue, lips, fingers and how you move your neck. I think perhaps runnin after all them passes has caused my tongue to hang out longer, which is a hell of a note, so to speak.

Nex Friday, I git all slicked up an Bubba lend me some hair tonic an shavin lotion an I go on over to the Student Union building. They is a big crowd there an sure enough, Jenny Curran an three or four other people is up on stage. Jenny is wearin a long dress an playin the guitar, an somebody else has a banjo an there is a guy with a bull fiddle, pluckin it with his fingers.

They sound real good, an Jenny seen me back in the crowd, an smiles an points with her eyes for me to come up an set in the front. It is just beautiful, settin there on the floor listenin an watchin Jenny Curran. I was kinda thinkin that later, I would buy some divinity an see if she wanted some too.

They had played for an hour or so, an everbody seemed happy an feelin good. They was playin Joan Baez music, an Bob Dylan an Peter, Paul an Mary. I was lying back with my eyes closed, listenin, an all of a sudden, I ain't sure what happen, but I had pulled out my harmonica an was jus playin along with them.

It was the strangest thing. Jenny was singin"Blowin in the Wind"an when I begun to play, she stopped for a secont, an the banjo player, he stopped too, an they get this very suprised looks on they faces, an then Jenny give a big grin an she commence to pick up the song again, an the banjo player, he stop an give me a chance to ride my harmonica for a wile, an everbody in the crowd begun to clap an cheer when I was done.

Jenny come down from the stage after that an the band take a break an she say,"Forrest, what in the world? Where you learn to play that thing?"Anyhow, after that, Jenny got me to play with their band. It was ever Friday, an when there wasn't an out of town game, I made twenty-five bucks a night. It were jus like heaven till I foun out Jenny Curran been screwin the banjo player.

Unfortunately, it was not goin so good in English class. Mister Boone had called me in bout a week or so after he read my autobiography to the class and he say,"Mister Gump, I believe it is time for you to stop tryin to be amusin and start gettin serious."He han me back an assignment I had writ on the poet Wordsworth.

"The Romantic Period,"he say,"did not follow a bunch of 'classic bullshit. ' Nor were the poets Pope and Dryden a couple of 'turds. ' "

He tell me to do the thing over again, an I'm beginnin to realize Mister Boone don't understand I'm a idiot, but he was bout to find out.

Meantime, somebody must of said somethin to somebody, cause one day my guidance counselor at the athelitic department call me in an tells me I'm excused from other classes an to report the next mornin to a

Doctor Mills at the University Medical Center. Bright an early I go over there an Doctor Mills got a big stack of papers in front of him, lookin through them, an he tell me to sit down and start axin me questions. When he finished, he tell me to take off my clothes—all but my undershorts, which I breathed easier after hearin cause of what happen the last time with the Army doctors—an he commenced to studyin me real hard, lookin in my eyes an all, an bongin me on the kneecaps with a little rubber hammer.

Afterward, Doctor Mills axed if I would mine comin back that afternoon an axed if I would bring my harmonica with me, cause he had heard bout it, an would I mine playin a tune for one of his medical classes? I said I would, although it seemed peculiar, even to somebody dumb as me.

They was about a hundrit people in the medical class all wearin green aprons an takin notes. Doctor Mills put me up on the stage in a chair with a pitcher an a glass of water in front of me.

He's sayin a whole bunch of crap I don't follow, but after a wile I get the feelin he's talkin bout *me*.

"*Idiot savant*," he say loudly, an everbody be starin my way.

"A person who cannot tie a necktie, who can barely lace up his shoes, who has the mental capacity of perhaps a six- to ten-year-old, and—in this case—the body of, well, an *Adonis*." Doctor Mills be smilin at me in a way I don't like, but I'm stuck, I guess.

"But the mind," he says, "the mind of the idiot savant has rare pockets of brilliance, so that Forrest here can solve advanced mathematical equations that would stump any of you, and he can pick up complex musical themes with the ease of Liszt or Beethoven. Idiot *savant*," he says again, sweepin his han in my direction.

I ain't sure what I'm sposed to do, but he had said for me to play somethin, so I pull out the harmonica an start playin "Puff, the Magic Dragon." Everbody settin there watchin me like I'm a bug or somethin, an when the song's over they still jus settin there lookin at me— don't even clap or nothin. I figgered they don't like it, so I stood up an said, "Thanks," an I lef. Shit on them people.

They is only two more things the rest of that school term that was even halfway important. The first was when we won the National College Football Championship an went to the Orange Bowl, an the second was when I found out Jenny Curran was screwin the banjo player.

It was the night we was sposed to play at a fraternity house party at the University. We had had a terribily hard practice that afternoon, an I was so thirsty I coulda drank out of the toilet like a dog. But they was this little stow five or six blocks from the Ape Dorm an after practice I walked on up there fixin to git me some limes and some sugar an fix me a limeade like my mama used to make for me. They is a ole cross-eyed woman behin the counter an she look at me like I'm a holdup man or somethin. I'm lookin for the limes an after a wile she says, "Kin I hep you?" an I says, "I want some limes," an she tells me they ain't got no limes. So I axed her if they got any lemons, cause I's thinkin a lemonade would do, but they ain't got none of them either, or oranges or nothin. It ain't that kind of stow. I musta look aroun maybe an hour or mo, an the woman be gettin nervous, an finally she say, "Ain't you gonna buy nothin?" so I get a can of peaches off the shef, an some sugar, thinkin if I can't have anythin else I can maybe make me a *peachade*—or somethin, I bout dyin of thirst. When I git back to my basement I open the can with a knife an squash the peaches up inside one of my socks an strain it into a jar. Then I put in some water an sugar an get it stirred up, but I'll tell you what—it don't taste nothin like a limeade—matter of fact, it taste more than anythin else like hot socks.

Anyhow, I sposed to be at the fraternity house at seven o'clock an when I get there some of the fellers is settin up the stuff an all, but Jenny and the banjo guy are nowhere to be found. I assed aroun for a wile, an then I went out to get mysef some fresh air in the parkin lot. I saw Jenny's car, an thought maybe she just get here.

All the winders in the car is steamed up, so's you can't see inside. Well, all of a sudden I think maybe she's in there an can't git out, an maybe gettin that exhaust poison or somethin, so I open the door an look in. When I do, the light come on.

There she is, lying on the back seat, the top of her dress pulled down an the bottom pulled up. Banjo player there too, on top of her. Jenny seen me an start screamin an flailin jus like she done in the pitcher show, an it suddenly occur to me that maybe she bein *molested*, so's I grapped the banjo player by his shirt, which was all he's got on anyhow, an snatched his ass off her.

Well, it did not take no idiot to figger out that I gone an done the wrong thing again. Jesus Christ, you can't imagine such carryin on. He cussin me, she cussin me an tryin to git her dress pulled up an down, an finally Jenny say,"Oh Forrest—how *could* you!"an walk off. Banjo player pick up his banjo an leave too.

Anyhow, after that, it were apparent I was not welcome to play in the little band no more, an I went on back to the basement. I still couldn't understan exactly what had been goin on, but later that night Bubba seen my light on an he stop down an when I tell him bout the thing, he say,"Good grief, Forrest, them people was makin love!"Well, I reckon I might have figgered that out mysef, but to be honest, it was not somethin I wanted to know. Sometimes, however, a man got to look at the facts.

It is probly a good thing I was kep busy playin football, cause it was such a awful feelin, realizin Jenny was doin that with the banjo player, an that she probly hadn't even a thought bout me in that regard. But by this time we was undefeated the entire season an was goin to play for the National Championship at the Orange Bowl against them corn shuckers from Nebraska. It was always a big thing when we played a team from up North cause for sure they would have colored on their side, an that be a reason for a lot of consternation from some of the guys—like my ex-roomate Curtis, for example—altho I never worried bout it mysef, on account of most of the colored I ever met be nicer to me than white people.

Anyhow, we gone on down to the Orange Bowl in Miami, an come game time, we is some kind of stirred up. Coach Bryant come in the locker room an don't say much, cept that if we want to win, we got to play hard, or somesuch, an then we be out on the field an they kicked off to us. The ball come directly to me an I grap it outta the air an run straight into a pile of Nebraska corn shucker niggers an big ole white boys that weigh about 500 pounds apiece.

It were that way the whole afternoon. At halftime, they was ahead 28 to 7 an we was a forelorn an sorry lot of guys. Coach Bryant come into the dressing room an he be shakin his head like he expected all along that we was goin to let him down. Then he start drawin on the chalk board and talkin to Snake, the quarterback, an some of the others, an then he call out my name an axe me to come with him into the hallway.

"Forrest," he says, "this shit has got to stop." His face right up against mine, an I feel his breath hot on my cheeks. "Forrest," he say, "all year long we been runnin them pass patterns to you in secret, an you been doin great. Now we is gonna do it against them Nebraska corn jackoffs this second half, an they will be so faked out, they jockstraps gonna be danglin roun they ankles. But it is up to you, boy—so go out there an run like a wild animal is after you."

I nod my head, an then it be time to get back on the field. Everbody be hollerin an cheerin, but I sort of feel they is a unfair burden on my shoulders. What the hell, tho—that's jus the way it is sometimes.

First play when we git the ball, Snake, the quarterback, say in the huddle, "Okay, we gonna run the *Forrest Series* now," an he says to me, "You jus run out twenty yards an look back, an the ball be there." An damn if it wadn't! Score is 28 to 14 all of a sudden.

We play real good after that, cept them Nebraska corn jerkoff niggers an big ole dumb white boys, they ain't jus settin there observin the scene. They has got some tricks of they own—mainly like runnin all over us as if we was made of cardboard or somethin.

But they is still somewhat suprised that I can catch the ball, an after I catch it four or five more times, an the score is 28 to 21, they begin to put two fellers to chasin after me. However, that leave Gwinn, the end, with nobody much to chase him aroun, an he catch Snake's pass an put us on the fifteen yard line. Weasel, the place kicker, get a field goal an the score now be 28 to 24.

On the sideline, Coach Bryant come up to me an say,"Forrest, you may be a shit-for-brains, but you has got to pull this thing out for us. I will personally see that you are made President of the United States or whatever else you want, if you can jus haul that football over the goal line one more time."He pat me on the head then, like I was a dog, an back in the game I go.

The Snake, he get caught behin the line right at the first play, an the clock is runnin out fast. On the second play, he try to fake em out by handin me the ball, sted of thowin it, but bout two tons of Nebraska corn jackoff beef, black an white, fall on top of me right away. I lying there, flat on my back, thinkin what it must of been like when that netload of bananas fall on my daddy, an then I gone back in the huddle again.

"Forrest,"Snake says,"I gonna fake a pass to Gwinn, but I am gonna thow the ball to you, so I want you to run down there to the cornerback an then turn right an the ball be right there."Snake's eyes are wild as a tiger's. I nod my head, an do as I am tole.

Sure enough, Snake heaves the ball into my hans an I be tearin toward the middle of the field with the goalposts straight ahead. But all of a sudden a giant man come flyin into me and slow me down, an then all the Nebraska corn jerkoff niggers an big ole dumb white boys in the world start grappin an gougin an stompin on me an I fall down. Damn! We ain't got but a few yards to go fore winnin the game. When I git off my back, I see Snake got everbody line up already for the last play, on accounta we got no more timeouts. Soon as I git to my place, he calls for the snap an I run out, but he suddenly thowed the ball bout 20 feet over my head, outta bounds on purpose—to stop the clock I guess, which only has 2 or 3 seconts lef on it.

Unfortunately tho, Snake done got confused about things, I spose he's thinkin it third down an we got one more play lef, but in fact it were *forth* down, an so we lose the ball an also, of course, we lose the game. It sound like somethin I woulda done.

Anyhow, it was extra sad for me, cause I kinda figgered Jenny Curran was probly watchin the game an maybe if I done got the ball and win the game, she try to forgive me for doin what I done to her. But that were not to be. Coach Bryant were mighty unhappy over what happen, but he suck it up an say, "Well, boys, there's always nex year."

Cept for me, that is. That was not to be either.

5

AFTER THE ORANGE BOWL, THE ATHELETIC DEPARTMENT get my grades for the first term, an it ain't long before Coach Bryant send for me to come to his office. When I get there, he lookin bleak.

"Forrest," he say, "I can understan how you flunked remedial English, but it will mystify me to the end of my days how you managed to get an A in something called Intermediate Light, an then an F in phys-ed class—when you is jus been named the Most Valuable College Back in the Southeastern Conference!"

It was a long story that I did not want to bore Coach Bryant with, but why in hell do I need to know the distance between goalposts on a soccer field anyway? Well, Coach Bryant lookin at me with a terrible sad expression on his face. "Forrest," he say, "I regret awfully havin to tell you this, but you is done flunked out of school, an there is nothin I can do."

I jus stood there, twistin my hands, till it suddenly come to me what he is sayin—I ain't gonna get to play no more football. I got to leave the University. Maybe I never see any of the other guys no more. Maybe I never see Jenny Curran no more either. I got to move outta my basement, an I won't get to take Advanced Light nex term, like Professor Hooks have said I would. I didn't realize it, but tears begun comin to my eyes. I ain't sayin nothin. I jus standin there, head hangin down.

Then Coach, he stand up hissef, an come over to me an he put his arm aroun me.

He say, "Forrest, it okay, son. When you first come here, I expect somethin like this would happen. But I tole em then, I said, just give me that boy for one season—that is all I ask. Well, Forrest, we has had ourselfs one hell of a season. That is for sure. An it certainly weren't your fault that Snake thowed the ball out of bounds on forth down. . ."

I look up then, an they is little tears in Coach's eyes, too, an he is lookin at me real hard.

"Forrest," he say, "there has never been nobody like you ever played ball at this school, an there won't be never again. You was very fine."

Then Coach go over an stand lookin out the winder, an he say, "Good luck, boy—now git your big dumb ass outta here."

An so I had to leave the University.

I gone back an pack up my shit in the basement. Bubba come down an he done brought two beers an give one to me. I ain't never drank a beer, but I can see how a feller could acquire a taste for it.

Bubba walk with me outside the Ape Dorm, an lo an behole, who should be standin there but the entire football team.

They is very quiet, an Snake, he come up an shake my han an say,"Forrest, I am very sorry about that pass, okay?"An I says,"Sure Snake, okay."An then they all come up, one by one, an shake my han, even ole Curtis, who is wearin a body brace from his neck down on accounta bashin down one door too many in the Ape Dorm.

Bubba say he'd hep me carry my shit down to the bus depot, but I say I'd rather go alone."Keep in touch,"he say. Anyhow, on the way to the bus station, I pass by the Student Union store, but it ain't Friday night, an Jenny Curran's band is not playin, so I say, the hell with it, an catch the bus on home.

It was late at night when the bus got to Mobile. I had not tole my mama what had happened, cause I knew she'd be upset, so I walk on home, but they is a light on up in her room an when I get inside, they she is, crying and bawling jus like I remember. What had happen, she tell me, is that the United States Army has already heard bout me not makin my grades, an that very day a notice done come for me to report to the U. S. Army Induction Center. If I had known then what I know now, I would never had done it.

My mama take me down there a few days later. She has packed me a box lunch in case I get hungry on the way to wherever we is going. They is about a hundrit guys standin aroun an four or five busses waiting. A big ole sergeant be hollerin an yellin at everbody, an Mama goes up to him an says,"I don't see how you can take my boy—cause he's a idiot,"but the sergeant jus look back at her an say,"Well, lady, what do you think all these other people is? Einsteins?"an he gone on back to hollerin an yellin. Pretty soon he yell at me, too, an I git on the bus an away we went.

Ever since I lef the nut school people been shoutin at me—Coach Fellers, Coach Bryant an the goons, an now the people in the Army. But let me say this: them people in the Army yell longer an louder an nastier than anybody else. They is never happy. An furthermore, they do not complain that you is dumb or stupid like coaches do—they is more interested in your private parts or bowel movements, an so always precede they yellin with somethin like"dickhead"or"asshole."Someti-mes I wonder if Curtis had been in the Army before he went to play football.

Anyhow, after about a hundrit hours on the bus we get to Fort Benning, Georgia, an all I'm thinkin is 35 to 3, the score when we whupped them Georgia Dogs. The conditions in the barracks is actually a little better than they was in the Ape Dorm, but the food is not—it is terrible, altho there is a lot of it.

Other than that, it was just doin what they tole us an gettin yelled at in the months to come. They taught us to shoot guns, thow hand grenades an crawl aroun on our bellies. When we wadn't doin that we was either runnin someplace or cleanin toilets an things. The one thing I remember from Fort Benning is that they didn't seem to be nobody much smarter than I was, which was certainly a relief.

Not too long after I arrive, I get put on KP, on account of I have accidentally shot a hole in the water tower when we was down at the rifle range. When I get to the kitchen, it seems the cook is took sick or somethin, an somebody point to me an say,"Gump, you is gonna be the cook today."

"What I'm gonna cook?"I axed."I ain't never cooked before."

"Who cares,"somebody say."This ain't the Sans Souci, y'know."

"Why don't you make a stew?"somebody else say."It's easier."

"What of?"I axed.

"Look in the icebox an the pantry,"the feller say."Just thow in everthin you see an boil it up."

"What if it don't taste good?"I axed.

"Who gives a shit. You ever eat anythin around here that did?"

In this, he is correct.

Well, I commenced to get everthin I could from the iceboxes an the pantry. They was cans of tomatos an beans an peaches an bacon an rice an bags of flour an sacks of potatoes an I don't know what all else. I gathered it all together an say to one of the guys,"What I'm gonna cook it in?"

"They is some pots in the closet,"he say, but when I looked in the closet, they is jus small pots, an certainly not large enough to cook a stew for two hundrit men in the company.

"Why don't you axe the lieutenant?"somebody say.

"He's out in the field on maneuvers,"come the reply.

"I don't know,"say one feller,"but when them guys get back here today, they gonna be damn hungry, so you better think of somethin."

"What about this?"I axed. They was an enormous iron thing bout six feet high an five feet aroun settin in the corner.

"That? That's the goddamn steam boiler. You can't cook nothin in there."

"How come,"I say.

"Well, I dunno. I jus wouldn do it if I was you."

"It's hot. It's got water in it,"I says.

"Do what you want,"somebody say,"we got other shit to do."

An so I used the steam boiler. I opened all the cans an peeled all the potatoes an thowed in whatever meat I could find an onions an carrots an poured in ten or twenty bottles of catsup an mustard an all. After bout a hour, you could begin to smell the stew cookin.

"How's the dinner comin?"somebody axed after a wile.

"I'll go taste it,"I say.

I unfastened the lid to the boiler an there it was, you could see all the shit bubblin an boilin up, an ever so often a onion or a potato woud come to the top an float aroun.

"Let me taste it,"a feller axed. He took a tin cup an dip out some stew.

"Say, this shit ain't near done yet,"he says."You better turn up the heat. Them fellers'll be here any minute."

So I turned up the heat on the boiler an sure enough, the company begun comin in from the field. You could hear them in the barracks takin showers an gettin dressed for the evenin meal, an it weren't long afterward that they begun arrivin in the mess hall.

But the stew still wadnt ready. I tasted it again an some things was still raw. Out in the mess hall they begun a kind of disgruntled mumblin that soon turned to chantin an so I turned the boiler up again.

After a haf hour or so, they was beatin on the tables with they knives an forks like in a prison riot, an I knowed I had to do somethin fast, so I turned the boiler up high as it could go.

I'm settin there watchin it, so nervous I didn't know what to do, when all of a sudden the first sergeant come bustin thru the door.

"What in hell is goin on here?"he axed."Where is these men's food?"

"It is almost ready, Sergeant,"I say, an jus about then, the boiler commenced to rumble an shake. Steam begun to come out of the sides an one of the legs on the boiler tore loose from the floor.

"What is that?"the sergeant axed."Is you cookin somethin in that *boiler*!"

"That is the supper,"I says, an the sergeant got this real amazed look on his face, an a secont later, he got a real frightened look, like you might get jus before an automobile wreck, an then the boiler blew up.

I am not exactly sure what happened nex. I do remember that it blowed the roof off the mess hall an blowed all the winders out an the doors too.

It blowed the dishwasher guy right thru a wall, an the guy what was stackin plates jus took off up in the air, sort of like Rocket Man.

Sergeant an me, we is miraculously spared somehow, like they say will happen when you are so close to a han grenade that you aren't hurt by it. But somehow it blowed both our clothes off, cept for the big chef's hat I was wearin at the time. An it blowed stew all over us, so's we looked like—well, I don't know what we looked like—but man, it was strange.

Incredibly, it didn't do nothin to all them guys settin out there in the mess hall neither. Jus lef em settin at they tables, covered with stew, actin kinda shell-shocked or somethin—but it sure did shut their asses up about when they food is gonna be ready.

Suddenly the company commander come runnin into the buildin.

"What was that!" he shouted. "What happen?" He look at the two of us, an then holler, "Sergeant Kranz, is that you?"

"Gump—Boiler—Stew!" the sergeant say, an then he kind of git holt of hissef an grapped a meat cleaver off the wall.

"Gump—Boiler—Stew!" he scream, an come after me with the cleaver. I done run out the door, an he be chasin me all over the parade grounds, an even thru the Officer's Club an the Motorpool. I outrunned him tho, cause that is my specialty, but let me say this: they ain't no question in my mind that I am up the creek for sure.

One night, the next fall, the phone rung in the barracks an it was Bubba. He say they done dropped his atheletic scholarship cause his foot broke worst than they thought, an so he's leavin school too. But he axed if I can git off to come up to Birmingham to watch the University play them geeks from Mississippi. But I am confined to quarters that Saturday, as I have been ever weekend since the stew blowed up and that's nearly a year. Anyway, I cannot do it, so I listen to the game on the radio while I'm scrubbin out the latrine.

The score is very close at the end of the third quarter, an Snake is having hissef a big day. It is 38 to 37 our way, but the geeks from Mississippi score a touchdown with only one minute to go. Suddenly, its forth down an no more time-outs for us. I prayin silently that Snake don't do what he done at the Orange Bowl, which is to thow the ball out of bounds on fourth down an lose the game again, but that is *exactly* what he done.

My heart sunk low, but suddenly they is all sorts of cheering so's you can't hear the radio announcer an when it is all quieted down, what happened was this: the Snake done *faked* an out of bounds pass on fourth down to stop the clock, but he *actually* give the ball to Curtis who run it in for the winning touchdown. That will give you some idea of jus how crafty Coach Bryant is. He done already figgered them geeks from Mississippi is so dumb they will assume *we* is stupid enough to make the same mistake twice.

I'm real happy bout the game, but I'm wonderin if Jenny Curran is watchin, an if she is thinkin of me.

As it turned out, it don't matter anyhow, cause a month later we is shipped out. For nearly a year we has been trained like robots an are going to somewhere 10, 000 miles away, an that is no exaggeration. We is going to Vietnam, but they says it is not nearly as bad as what we has gone thru this past year. As it turn out, tho, that is an exaggeration.

We got there in February an was trucked on cattle cars from Qui Nhon on the South China Sea coast up to Pleiku in the highlands. It wadnt a bad ride an the scenery was nice an interestin, with banana trees an palms an rice paddies with little gooks plowin in them. Everbody on our side is real friendly, too, wavin at us an all.

We could see Pleiku almost haf a day away on account of a humongus cloud of red dust that hovered over it. On its outskirts was sad little shanties that is worst than anythin I seen back in Alabama, with folks huddled neath cloth lean-to's an they ain't got no teeth an they children ain't got no clothes an basically, they is beggars. When we get to the Brigade Headquarters an Firebase, it don't look real bad either, cept for all that red dust. Ain't nothin much going on that we can see, an the place is all neat an clean with tents stretched far as you can see in rows an the dirt an sand aroun them raked up nice an tidy. Don't hardly look like a war going on at all. We might as well of been back at Fort Benning.

Anyhow, they says it is real quiet cause it is the beginning of the gook new years—Tet, or somesuch—an they is a truce goin on. All of us is tremendously relieved, because we is frightened enough as it is. The peace and quiet, however, did not last very long.

After we get squared away in our area, they tell us to go down to Brigade Showers an clean ourselfs. Brigade Showers is just a shallow pit in the groun where they has put three or four big water tank trucks an we tole to fold our uniforms up on the edge of the pit an then get down in there an they will squirt us with water.

Even so, it ain't haf bad, account of we been for nearly a week without a bath, an was beginnin to smell pretty ripe. We is assin aroun in the pit, gettin hosed down an all, an it is jus bout gettin dark, an all of a sudden there is this funny soun in the air an some jackoff who is squirting us with the hose holler,"*Incomin*,"and everbody on the edge of the pit vanish into thin air. We standin there butt neckid, lookin at each other, an then they is a big explosion close by an then another one, an everbody start shoutin and cussin an tryin to get to they clothes. Them incomin explosions fallin all aroun us, an somebody shoutin, "Hit the dirt!" which was kind of rediculous since we was all press so flat in the bottom of the pit by now we resemble worms rather than people.

One of them explosions send a bunch of shit flyin into our pit an them boys on the far side get hit with it an start screamin an yellin an bleedin an grappin at theyselfs. It were all too apparent that the pit was not a safe place to be hidin. Sergeant Kranz suddenly appear over the edge of the pit, an he holler for all us to get the hell out of there an follow him. There is a little break between explosions an we haul ass out of the pit. I come over the top an look down an godamighty! Lyin there is four or five of the fellers who was squirtin the hose on us. They is hardly recognizable as people—all mangled up like they has been stuffed thru a cotton baler or somethin. I ain't never seen nobody dead, an it is the most horrible and scary thing ever happen to me, afore or since!

Sergeant Kranz motion for us to crawl after him, which we do. If you could of looked down on it from above, we must of made a sight! A hundrit fifty or so fellers all butt neckid squirmin along the groun in a long line.

They was a bunch of foxholes dug in a row an Sergeant Kranz put three or four of us in each hole. But soon as we get in em, I realize I'd of almost rather stayed back in the pit. Them foxholes was filled waist stinkin deep with slimy ole water from the rain, an they was all sorts of frawgs an snakes and bugs crawlin an leapin an squirmin aroun in them.

It went on the entire night, an we had to stay in them foxholes an didn't get no supper. Jus afore dawn, the shellin eased up, an we was tole to haul our asses outta the foxholes an get our clothes an weapons an prepare for the attack.

Since we was relatively new, they was really not much we could do—they didn't even know where to put us, so they tole us to go guard the south perimeter, which is where the officers' latrine was located. But it were nearly worse than the foxholes, account of one of the bombs has hit the latrine an blowed up about five hundrit pounds of officer shit all over the area.

We had to stay there all that day, no breakfast, no lunch; an then at sundown they commenced shellin us again so we had to lie there in all that shit. My, my, it were repulsive.

Finally somebody remember we might be gettin hungry, an had a bunch of c-ration cases brought over. I got the cold ham an eggs that was dated 1951 on the can. They was all kinds of rumors goin on. Somebody said the gooks was runnin over the town of Pleiku. Somebody else says the gooks got a atomic bomb an is just shellin us with mortars to soften us up. Somebody else says it ain't the gooks shellin us at all, but Austrailians, or maybe the Dutch or the Norwegians. I figger it don't matter who it is. Shit on rumors.

Anyhow, after the first day, we begun tryin to make ourselfs a livable place on the south perimeter. We dug us foxholes an used the boards an tin from the officers' latrine to make us little hooches. The attack never come tho, an we never saw no gooks to shoot at. I figger maybe they smart enough not to attack a shithouse anyway. Ever night for about three or four days they shellin us tho, an finally one mornin when the shellin stops, Major Balls, the battalion executive officer, come crawlin up to our company commander an say we has got to go up north to help out another brigade that is catchin hell in the jungle.

After a wile, Lieutenant Hooper say for us to "saddle up," an everbody stuffin as many c-rations an han grenades in his pockets as he can—which actually present sort of a dilemma, since you can't eat a han grenade but you might nevertheless come to need it. Anyway, they load us on the heliocopters an off we flew.

You could see the shit Third Brigade had stepped into even fore the heliocopters landed. They was all sorts of smoke an stuff risin up outta the jungle an huge chunks had been blown outta the groun. We had not even got to earth afore they commenced shootin at us. They blowed up one of our heliocopters in the air, an it was a dreadful sight, people set on fire an all, an nothin we could do.

I am the machine gun ammo bearer, cause they figger I can carry a lot of shit on account of my size. Before we lef, a couple of other fellers axed if I would mind carryin some of their han grenades so's they could carry more orations, an I agreed. It didn't hurt me none. Also, Sergeant Kranz made me carry a ten-gallon water can that weighed about fifty pounds. Then jus fore we lef, Daniels, who carries the tri-pod for the machine gun, he gets the runs an he can't go, so's I got to tote the tri-pod too. When it all added up, I might as well of been toting aroun one a them Nebraska corn shucker jackoffs as well. But this ain't no football game.

It is gettin to be dusk an we is tole to go up to a ridge an relieve Charlie Company which is either pinned down by the gooks or has got the gooks pinned down, dependin on whether you get your news from the *Stars an Stripes* or by just lookin aroun at what the hell is goin on.

In any event, when we get up there, all sorts of crap is flyin aroun an they is about a dozen fellers badly hurt an moanin and cryin an they is so much noise from all quarters that nobody can hardly hear nothin. I be crouchin down real low an tryin to get all that ammo an the water can an the tri-pod plus all my own shit up to where Charlie Company is, an I'm strugglin past a slit trench when this guy down in it pipe up an say to the other,"Lookit that big Bozo—he look like the Frankenstein Monster or somethin,"and I'm bout to say somethin back, cause things seem bad enough already without nobody pokin fun at you—but then, I'll be damned! The other guy in the slit trench suddenly jump up an cry out,"Forrest—Forrest Gump!"

Lo an behole, it were Bubba.

Briefly, what had happen was that even if Bubba's foot was hurt too bad to play football, it were not bad enough to keep from gettin him sent halfway roun the earth on behalf of the United States Army. Anyhow, I drag my sorry butt an everthin else up to where I sposed to be, an after a wile Bubba come up there an in between the shellin (which stop ever time our airplanes appear) Bubba an me caught up with each other.

He tells me he hear Jenny Curran done quit school an gone off with a bunch of war protesters or somethin. He also say that Curtis done beat up a campus policeman one day for givin him a parkin ticket, an was in the process of drop-kickin his official ass aroun the campus when the authorities show up an thowed a big net over Curtis an drug him off. Bubba say Coach Bryant make Curtis run fifty extra laps after practice as punishment.

Good ole Curtis.

6

THAT NIGHT WAS LONG AN UNCOMFORTABLE. WE couldn't fly our airplanes, so's they got to shell us most of the evenin for free. They was a little saddle between two ridges, an they was on one ridge an we on the other, an down in the saddle was where the dispute were takin place—tho what anybody would want with that piece of mud an dirt, I do not know. However, Sergeant Kranz have said to us time an again that we was not brought over here to understand what is goin on, only to do what we is tole.

Pretty soon, Sergeant Kranz come up an start tellin us what to do. He says we has got to move the machine gun about fifty meters aroun to the lef of a big ole tree stickin up in the middle of the saddle, an fine a good safe place to put it so's we is not all blowed away. From what I can see an hear, anyplace, includin where we presently are, is not safe, but to go down in that saddle is goddamn absurd. However, I am tryin to do the right thing.

Me an Bones, the machine gunner, an Doyle, another ammo bearer, an two other guys crawl out of our holes an start to moving down the little slope. Halfway down, the gooks see us an commence to shootin with they own machine gun. Fore anything bad happens, tho, we has scrambled down the slope an into the jungle. I cannot remember how far a meter is exactly, but it almost the same as a yard, so when we get near the big tree, I say to Doyle, "Maybe we better move lef," an he look at me real hard-like, an growl, "Shut you ass, Forrest, they is gooks here." Sure nuf, they was six or eight gooks squattin under the big ole tree, havin they lunch. Doyle take a han grenade an pull the pin an sort of lob it into the air toward the tree. It blowed up fore it hit the groun an they is all sorts of wild chatterin from where the gooks is—then Bones open up with the machine gun an me an the two other guys heave in a couple more han grenades for good measure. All of that gone down in just a minute or so, an when it come quiet again, we be on our way.

We foun a place to put the gun an stayed there till it got dark—an all night long, too, but nothin happen. We could hear all sorts of shit goin on everplace else, but we be lef to ourselfs. Sunup come, an we hungry an tired, but there we is. Then a runner come from Sergeant Kranz who say Charlie Company is goin to start movin into the saddle soon as our airplanes have totally wiped out the gooks there, which is to be in a few minutes. Sure enough, the planes come an drop they shit an everthin get exploded an wipe out all the gooks.

We can see Charlie Company movin off the ridge line, comin down into the saddle, but no sooner does they get over the edge of the ridge an start strugglin along the slope, than all the weapons in the world commence to shootin at Charlie Company an droppin mortars an all, an it is terrible confusion. From where we is, we cannot see any gooks, on account of the jungle is thick as bonfire brush, but *somebody* sure be in there shootin at Charlie Company. Maybe it the Dutch—or even the Norwegians—who knows?

Bones, the machine gunner, lookin extremely nervous durin all this, on accounta he's already figgered out that the shootin is comin from in *front* of us, meanin that the gooks is in between us an our own position. In other words, we is out here alone. Sooner or later, he says, if the gooks do not overrun Charlie Company, they will come back this way, an if they find us here, they will not like it one bit. Point is, we got to move our asses.

We get our shit together an begin to work back towards the ridge, but as we do, Doyle suddenly look down off our right to the bottom of the saddle an he see an entire busload of new gooks, armed to the teeth, movin up the hill towards Charlie Company. Best thing we coulda done then was to try an make friends with em an forget all this other shit, but that were not in the cards. So we jus hunkered down in some big ole shrubs an waited till they got to the top of the hill. Then Bones let loose with the machine gun and he must of kilt ten or fifteen of them gooks right off. Doyle an me an the other two guys is thowin grenades, an things is goin our way until Bones runs out of ammo an need a fresh belt. I feed one in for him, but just as he bout to sqeeze the trigger, a gook bullet hit him square in the head an blowed it inside out. He lyin on the ground, han still holdin to the gun for dear life, which he does not have any more of now.

Oh God, it were awful—an gettin worst. No tellin what them gooks would of done if they caught us. I call out to Doyle to come here, but they is no answer. I jerk the machine gun from po ole Bones' fingers an squirm over to Doyle, but he an the two other guys layin there shot. They dead, but Doyle still breathin, so's I grap him up an thow him over my shoulder like a flour sack an start runnin thru the brush towards Charlie Company, cause I scared outta my wits. I runnin for maybe twenty yards an bullets wizzin all aroun me from behin, an I figger I be shot in the ass for sure. But then I crash thru a canebreak an come upon a area with low grass an to my surprise it is filled with gooks, lyin down, lookin the other way, an shootin at Charlie Company—I guess.

Now what do I do? I got gooks behin me, gooks in front of me an gooks right under my feet. I don't know what else to do, so I charge up full speed an start to bellowin an howlin an all. I sort of lose my head, I guess, cause I don't remember what happen nex cept I still be bellowin an hollerin loud as I can an runnin for dear life. Everthin were completely confused, an then all of a sudden I am in the middle of Charlie Company an everbody be slappin me on the back jus like I made a touchdown.

It seem like I done frightened off the gooks an they hightail it back to wherever they live. I put down Doyle on the groun an the medics come an start fixin him up, an pretty soon the Charlie Company commander come up to me an start pumpin my han an tellin me what a good fellow I am. Then he say, "How in hell did you do that, Gump?" He be waitin for a answer, but I don't know how I done it mysef, so I says,"I got to pee"—which I did. The company commander look at me real strange, an then look at Sergeant Kranz, who had also come up, an Sergeant Kranz say,"Oh, for Chrissakes Gump, come with me,"an he take me behin a tree.

That night Bubba an me meet up an share a foxhole an eat our C-rations for supper. Afterward, I get out my harmonica Bubba had gave me an we play a few tunes. It sound real eerie, there in the jungle, playin"Oh Suzanna"an"Home on the Range."Bubba got a little box of candy his mama have sent him—pralines an divinity—an we both ate some. An let me tell you this—that divinity sure brung back some memories.

Later on, Sergeant Kranz come over an axe me where is the ten-gallon can of drinkin water. I tole him I done lef it out in the jungle when I was tryin to carry in Doyle an the machine gun. For a minute I think he gonna make me go back out there an get it, but he don't. He jus nod, an say that since Doyle is hurt an Bones is kilt, now I got to be the machine gunner. I axe him who gonna carry the tri-pod an the ammo an all, an he say I got to do that too, cause nobody else lef to do it. Then Bubba say he'll do it, if he can get transferred to our company. Sergeant Kranz think bout that for a minute, an then he say it can probly be arranged, since there is not enough lef of Charlie Company to clean a latrine anyway. An so it was, Bubba an me is together again.

The weeks go by so slow I almost think time passin backwards. Up one hill, down the other. Sometimes they be gooks on the hills, sometimes not. Sergeant Kranz say everthing okay tho, cause actually we be marchin back to the United States. He say we gonna march outta Vietnam, thru Laos an then up across China an Russia, up to the North Pole an across the ice to Alaska where our mamas can come pick us up. Bubba says don't pay no attention to him cause he's a idiot.

Things is very primitive in the jungle—no place to shit, sleep on the groun like a animal, eat outta cans, no place to take a bath or nothin, clothes is all rottin off too. I get a letter once a week from my mama. She say everthing fine at home, but that the highschool ain't won no more championships since I done lef. I write her back too, when I can, but what I'm gonna tell her that won't start her to bawlin again? So I jus say we is havin a nice time an everbody treatin us fine. One thing I done tho, was I wrote a letter to Jenny Curran in care of my mama an axe if she can get Jenny's folks to send it to her—wherever she is. But I ain't heard nothin back.

Meantime, Bubba an me, we has got us a plan for when we get outta the Army. We gonna go back home an get us a srimp boat an get in the srimpin bidness. Bubba come from Bayou La Batre, an work on srimp boats all his life. He say maybe we can get us a loan an we can take turns bein captain an all, an we can live on the boat an will have somethin to do. Bubba's got it all figgered out. So many pounds of srimp to pay off the loan on the boat, so much to pay for gas, so much for what we eat an such, an all the rest is left for us to ass aroun with. I be picherin it in my head, standin at the wheel of the srimp boat—or even better, settin there on the back of the boat eatin srimp! But when I tell Bubba bout that, he say,"Goddamn, Forrest, your big ass'll eat us outta house an home. We don't be eatin none of the srimp afore we start makin a profit."Okay, that make sense—it all right with me.

It commenced rainin one day an did not stop for two months. We went thru ever different kind of rain they is, cep'n maybe sleet or hail. It was little tiny stingin rain sometimes, an big ole fat rain at others. It came sidewise an straight down an sometimes even seem to come up from the groun. Nevertheless, we was expected to do our shit, which was mainly walkin up an down the hills an stuff lookin for gooks.

One day we foun them. They must of been holdin a gook convention or somethin, cause it seem like the same sort of deal as when you step on a anthill and they all come swarmin aroun. We cannot fly our planes in this kind of stuff either, so in about two minutes or so, we is back in trouble again.

This time they has caught us with our pants down. We is crossin this rice paddy an all of a sudden from everwhere they start thowin shit at us. People is shoutin and screamin an gettin shot an somebody says,"Fall back!"Well, I pick up my machine gun an start running alongside everbody else for some palm trees which at least look like they might keep the rain offen us. We has formed a perimeter of sorts an is gettin ready to start preparin for another long night when I lookaroun for Bubba an he ain't there.

Somebody say Bubba was out in the rice paddy an he is hurt, an I say,"Goddamn,"an Sergeant Kranz, he hear me, an say,"Gump, you can't go out there."But shit on that—I leave the machine gun behind cause it jus be extra weight, an start pumpin hard for where I last seen Bubba. But halfway out I nearly step on a feller from 2nd platoon who is mighty hurt, an he look up at me with his han out, an so I think, shit, what can I do? so I grap him up an run back with him fast as I can. Bullets an stuff be flyin all over. It is somethin I simply cannot understand—why in hell is we doin all this, anyway? Playin football is one thing. But this, I do not know why. Goddamn.

I brung that boy back an run out again an damn if I don't come across somebody else. So I reach down to pick him up an bring him back, too, but when I do, his brains fall out on the paddy groun, cause the back of his head blowed off. Shit.

So I drop his ass an kep on goin an sure enough, there is Bubba, who is been hit twice in the chest, an I say,"Bubba, it gonna be okay, you hear, cause we gotta get that srimp boat an all,"an I carry him back to where we is set up an layed him on the groun. When I catch my breath, I look down an my shirt all covered with blood an bluish yeller goo from where Bubba is hurt, an Bubba is lookin up at me, an he say,"Fuck it, Forrest, why this happen?"Well, what in hell am I gonna say?

Then Bubba axe me,"Forrest, you play me a song on the harmonica?"So I get it out, an start playin somethin—I don't even know what, an then Bubba say,"Forrest, would you please play 'Way Down Upon the Swanee River'?"an I say,"Sure, Bubba."I have to wipe off the mouthpiece, an then I start to play an there is still a terrible lot of shootin goin on, an I know I ought to be with my machine gun, but what the hell, I played that song.

I hadn't noticed it, but it had quit rainin an the sky done turned a awful pinkish color. It made everbody's face look like death itsef, an for some reason, the gooks done quit shootin for a wile, an so had we. I played "Way Down Upon the Swanee River" over an over again, kneelin nex to Bubba wile the medic give him a shot an tend to him best he could. Bubba done grapped a holt to my leg an his eyes got all cloudy an that terrible pink sky seem to drain all the color in his face.

He was tryin to say somethin, an so I bent over real close to hear what it was. But I never coud make it out. So I axed the medic, "You hear what he say?"

An the medic say, "Home. He said, *home*."

Bubba, he died, an that's all I got to say bout that.

The rest of the night was the worst I have ever known. They was no way they could get any hep to us, since it begun stormin again. Them gooks was so close we could hear them talkin with each other, an at one point it was han to han fightin in the 1st platoon. At dawn, they call in a napalm airplane, but it drop the shit damn near right on top of *us*. Our own fellers be all singed an burnt up—come runnin out into the open, eyes big as biscuits, everbody cussin an sweatin an scared, woods set on fire, damn near put the rain out!

Somewhere in all this, I got mysef shot, an, as luck would have it, I was hit in the ass. I can't even remember it. We was all in awful shape. I don't know what happened. Everthing all fouled up. I jus left the machine gun. I didn't give a shit no more. I went to a place back of a tree an jus curl up an start cryin. Bubba gone, srimp boat gone; an he the only friend I ever had—cept maybe Jenny Curran, an I done mess that up too. Wadn't for my mama, I might as well of jus died right there—of ole age or somethin, whatever—it didn't matter.

After a wile, they start landin some relief in heliocopters, and I guess the napalm bomb have frightened away the gooks. They must of figgered that if we was willing to do that to ourselfs, then what the hell would we of done to *them*?

They takin the wounded outta there, when along come Sergeant Kranz, hair all singed off, clothes burnt up, looking like he jus got shot out of a cannon. He say,"Gump, you done real good yesterday, boy,"an then he axe me if I want a cigarette.

I say I don't smoke, an he nod."Gump,"he says,"you are not the smartest feller I have ever had, but you is one hell of a soldier. I wish I had a hundrit like you."

He axe me if it hurt, an I say no, but that ain't the truth. "Gump," he say,"you is goin home, I guess you know that."

I axe him where is Bubba, an Sergeant Kranz look at me kind of funny."He be along directly,"he says. I axed if I can ride on the same heliocopter with Bubba, an Sergeant Kranz say, no, Bubba got to go out last, cause he got kilt.

They had stuck me with a big needle full of some kind of shit that made me feel better, but I remember, I reached up an grapped Sergeant Kranz by the arm, an I say,"I ain't never axed no favors afore, but would you put Bubba on the heliocopter yoursef, an make sure he get there okay?"

"Sure, Gump,"he say."What the hell—we will even get him accommodations in first class."

7

I WAS AT THE HOSPITAL AT DANANG FOR MOST OF TWO months. So far as a hospital went, it were not much, but we slep on cots with mosquito nets, an they was wooden plank floors that was swep clean twice a day, which was more than you can say for the kind of livin I'd got used to.

They was some people hurt far worst than I was in that hospital, let me tell you. Po ole boys with arms an legs an feet an hans an who knows what else missin. Boys what had been shot in they stomachs an chests an faces. At night the place sound like a torture chamber—them fellers be howlin and cryin an callin for they mamas.

They was a guy nex to my cot name of Dan, who had been blowed up inside a tank. He was all burnt an had tubes goin in an out of him everplace, but I never heard him holler. He talk real low an quiet, an after a day or so, him an me got to be friends. Dan come from the state of Connecticut, an he were a teacher of history when they grapped him up an thowed him into the Army. But cause he was smart, they sent him to officer school an made him a lieutenant. Most of the lieutenants I knowed was bout as simple-minded as me, but Dan were different. He have his own philosophy bout why we was there, which was that we was doin maybe the wrong thing for the right reasons, or visa-versa, but whatever it is, we ain't doin it right. Him bein a tank officer an all, he say it rediculous for us to be wagin a war in a place where we can't hardly use our tanks on account of the land is mostly swamp or mountains. I tole him bout Bubba an all, an he nod his head very sadly an say they will be a lot more Bubbas to die afore this thing is over.

After bout a week or so, they move me to another part of the hospital where everbody be put so's they can get well, but ever day I gone back to the tensive care ward an set for a wile with Dan. Sometimes I played him a tune on my harmonica, which he like very much. My mama had sent me a package of Hershey bars which finally catch up to me at the hospital an I wanted to share them with Dan, cept he can't eat nothin but what goin into him thru the tubes.

I think that settin there talkin to Dan was a thing that had a great impression on my life. I know that bein a idiot an all, I ain't sposed to have no philosophy of my own, but maybe it's just because nobody never took the time to talk to me bout it. It were Dan's philosophy that everythin that happen to us, or for that matter, to anythin anywhere, is controlled by natural laws that govern the universe. His views on the subject was extremely complicated, but the gist of what he say begun to change my whole outlook on things.

All my own life, I ain't understood shit about what was goin on. A thing jus happen, then somethin else happen, then somethin else, an so on, an haf the time nothin makin any sense. But Dan say it is all part of a scheme of some sort, an the best way we can get along is figger out how we fits into the scheme, an then try to stick to our place. Somehow knowin this, things get a good bit clearer for me.

Anyhow, I's gettin much better in the next weeks, an my ass heal up real nice. Doctor say I got a hide like a "rhinoceros" or somethin. They got a rec room at the hospital an since they wadn't much else to do, I wandered over there one day an they was a couple of guys playin ping-pong. After a wile, I axed if I could play, an they let me. I lost the first couple of points, but after a wile, I beat both them fellers. "You shore is quick for such a big guy," one of them say. I jus nod. I tried to play some ever day an got quite good, believe it or not.

In the afternoons I'd go see Dan, but in the mornins I was on my own. They let me leave the hospital if I wanted, an they was a bus what took fellers like me into the town so's we could walk aroun an buy some of the shit they sold in the gook shops in Danang. But I don't need any of that, so I jus walk aroun, taking in the sights.

They is a little market down by the waterfront where folks sells fish an srimp an stuff, an one day I went down there an bought me some srimp an one of the cooks at the hospital boil em for me an they sure was good. I wished ole Dan could of ate some. He say maybe if I squash em up they could put em down his tube. He say he gonna axe the nurse about it, but I know he jus kiddin.

That night I be lyin on my cot thinkin of Bubba an how much he might of liked them srimp too, an about our srimp boat an all. Po ole Bubba. So the next day I axed Dan how is it that Bubba can get kilt, an what kind of haf-assed nature law would allow that. He think bout it for a wile, an say,"Well, I'll tell you, Forrest, all of these laws are not specially pleasing to us. But they is laws nonetheless. Like when a tiger pounce on a monkey in the jungle—bad for the monkey, but good for the tiger. That is jus the way it is."

Couple of days later I gone on back to the fish market an they is a little gook sellin a big bag of srimp there. I axed him where he got them srimp, an he start jabberin away at me, count of he don't understan English. Anyway, I make sign language like a Indian or somethin, an after a wile he catch on, an motion for me to follow him. I be kind of leary at first, but he smilin an all, an so's I do.

We must of walked a mile or so, past all the boats on the beach an everthin, but he don't take me to a boat. It is a little place in a swamp by the water, kind of a pond or somethin, an he got wire nets laid down where the water from the China Sea come in at high tide. That sumbitch be *growin* srimp in there! He took a little net an scoop up some water an sure enough, ten or twelve srimp in it. He give me some in a little bag, an I give him a Hershey bar. He so happy he could shit.

That night they is a movie outdoors near Field Force Headquarters an I go on over there, cep'n some fellers in the front row start a great big fight over somethin an somebody get hissef heaved through the screen an that be the end of the movie. So afterwards, I be layin on my cot, thinkin, an suddenly it come to me. I know what I gotta do when they let me out of the Army! I goin home an find me a little pond near the Gulf an raise me some srimp! So maybe I can't get me a srimp boat now that Bubba is gone, but I sure can go up in one of them marshes an get me some wire nets an that's what I'll do. Bubba would of like that.

Ever day for the next few weeks I go down in the mornin to the place where the little gook is growin his srimp. Mister Chi is his name. I jus set there an watched him an after a wile he showed me how he was doin it. He'd catched some baby srimps aroun the marshes in a little han net, an dump them in his pond. Then when the tide come in he thowed all sorts of shit in there—scraps and stuff, which cause little teensey slimy things to grow an the srimps eat them an get big an fat. It was so simple even a imbecile could do it.

A few days later some muckity-mucks from Field Force Headquarters come over to the hospital all excited an say,"Private Gump, you is been awarded the Congressional Medal of Honor for extreme heroism, an is bein flown back to the U. S. A. day after tomorrow to be decorated by the President of the United States."Now that was early in the mornin an I had jus been lyin there, thinkin about going to the bathroom, but here they are, expectin me to say somethin, I guess, an I'm bout to bust my britches. But this time I jus say,"Thanks,"an keep my big mouth shut. Perhaps it be in the natural scheme of things.

Anyhow, after they is gone, I go on over to the tensive care ward to see Dan, but when I git there, his cot is empty, an the mattress all folded up an he is gone. I am so scant somethin has happen to him, an I run to fine the orderly, but he ain't there either. I seen a nurse down the hall an I axed her, "What happen to Dan," an she say he "gone." An I say, "Gone where?" an she say, "I don't know, it didn't happen on my shif." I foun the head nurse an axe her, an she say Dan been flown back to America on account of they can take better care of him there. I axed her if he is okay, an she say, "Yeah, if you can call two punctured lungs, a severed intestin, spinal separation, a missing foot, a truncated leg, an third degree burns over haf the body *okay*, then he is jus fine." I thanked her, an went on my way.

I didn't play no ping-pong that afternoon, cause I was so worried bout Dan. It come to me that maybe he went an died, an nobody want to say so, cause of that bidness bout notifying nex of kin first, or somethin. Who knows? But I am down in the dumps, an go wanderin aroun by mysef, kickin rocks an tin cans an shit.

When I finally get back to my ward, there is some mail lef on my bed for me that finally catch up with me here. My mama have sent a letter sayin that our house done caught on fire, an is totally burnt up, an there is no insurance or nothin an she is gonna have to go to the po house. She say the fire begun when Miss French had washed her cat an was dryin it with a hair dryer, an either the cat or the hair dryer caught afire, an that was that. From now on, she say, I am to send my letters to her in care of the "Little Sisters of the Po." I figger there will be many tears in the years to come.

They is another letter addressed to me which say, "Dear Mister Gump: You has been chosen to win a bran new Pontiac GTO, if only you will send back the enclosed card promising to buy a set of these wonderful encyclopedias an a updated yearbook every year for the rest of your life at a $75 per year." I thowed that letter in the trash. What the hell would a idiot like me want with encyclopedias anyway, an besides, I can't drive.

But the third letter is personally writ to me an on the back of the envelope it say, "J. Curran, General Delivery, Cambridge, Mass." My hans is shakin so bad, I can hardly open it.

"Dear Forrest," it say, "My mama has forwarded your letter to me that your mama gave to her, and I am so sorry to hear that you have to fight in that terrible immoral war." She say she know how horrible it must be, with all the killin an maimin goin on an all. "It must tax your conscience to be involved, although I know you are being made to do it against your will." She write that it must of been awful not to have no clean clothes an no fresh food, an all, but that she do not understand what I mean when I wrote about "havin to lie face-down in officer shit for two days."

"It is hard to believe," she say, "that even *they* would make you do such a vulgar thing as that." I think I could of explained that part a little better.

Anyhow, Jenny say that "We are organizing large demonstrations against the fascist pigs in order to stop the terrible immoral war and let the people be heard." She go on bout that for a page or so, an it all soundin sort of the same. But I read it very carefully anyway, for jus to see her hanwritin is enough to make my stomach turn flip-flops.

"At least," she say at the end, "you have met up with Bubba, and I know you are glad to have a friend in your misery."She say to give Bubba her best, an add in a p. s. that she is earnin a little money by playin in a little musical band a couple of nights a week at a coffeehouse near the Harvard University, an if ever I get up that way to look her up. The group, she say, is called The Cracked Eggs. From then on, I be lookin for some excuse to get to Harvard University.

That night I am packin up my shit to go back home to get my Medal of Honor an meet the President of the United States. However, I do not have nothin to pack cept my pajaymas an the toothbrush an razor they have gave me at the hospital, cause everthin else I own is back at the firebase at Pleiku. But there is this nice lieutenant colonel that has been sent over from Field Force, an he say,"Forgit all that shit, Gump—we is gonna have a bran new tailor-made uniform sewn up for you this very night by two dozen gooks in Saigon, on account of you cannot meet the President wearin your pajaymas."The colonel say he is gonna accompany me all the way to Washington, an see to it that I have got a place to stay an food to eat an a ride to wherever we is going an also will tell me how to behave an all.

Colonel Gooch is his name.

That night I get into one last ping-pong match with a feller from the headquarters company of Field Force, who is sposed to be the best ping-pong player in the Army or somesuch as that. He is a little wiry feller who refuse to look me in the eye, an also, he bring his own paddle in a leather case. When I be whippin his ass he stop an say the ping-pong balls ain't no good cause the humidity done ruint them. Then he pack up his paddle an go on home, which be okay with me, cause he lef the ping-pong balls he brung, an they could really use them at the hospital rec room.

The morning I was to leave, a nurse come in an lef a envelope with my name written on it. I open it up, an it was a note from Dan, who is okay after all, an had this to say:

Dear Forrest,

I am sorry there was no time for us to see each other before I left. The doctors made their decision quickly, and before I knew it, I was being taken away, but I asked if I could stop long enough to write you this note, because you have been so kind to me while I was here.

I sense, Forrest, that you are on the verge of something very significant in your life, some change, or event that will move you in a different direction, and you must seize the moment, and not let it pass. When I think back on it now, there is something in your eyes, some tiny flash of fire that comes now and then, mostly when you smile, and, on those infrequent occasions, I believe what I saw was almost a Genesis of our ability as humans to think, to create, to *be*.

This war is not for you, old pal—nor me—and I am well out of it as I'm sure you will be in time. The crucial question is, what will you do? I don't think you're an idiot at all. Perhaps by the measure of tests or the judgment of fools, you might fall into some category or other, but deep down, Forrest, I have seen that glowing sparkle of curiosity burning deep in your mind. Take the tide, my friend, and as you are carried along, make it work for you, fight the shallows and the snags and never give in, never give up. You are a good fellow, Forrest, and you have a big heart.

Your Pal,

DAN

I read over Dan's letter ten or twenty times, an there is things in it I do not understand. I mean, I *think* I see what he is gettin at, but there is sentences an words that I cannot figger out. Next morning Colonel Gooch come in an say we got to go now, first to Saigon to get me the new uniform that done been sewn up by the twenty gooks last night, then right off to the United States an all that. I shown him Dan's letter an axed him to tell me what exactly it means, an Colonel Gooch look it over an han it back an say, "Well, Gump, it is pretty plain to me he means that you had better the hell not fuck up when the President pins the medal on you."

8

WE BE FLYIN HIGH OVER THE PACIFIC OCEAN, AN COLONEL Gooch is tellin me what a great hero I am going to be when we get back to the United States. He say people will turn out for parades an shit an I will not be able to buy mysef a drink or a meal on account of everbody else will be wantin to do it for me. He also say that the Army is gonna want me to go on a tour to drum up new enlistments an sell bonds an crap like that, an that I will be given the "royal treatment." In this, he is correct.

When we land at the airport at San Francisco, a big crowd is waiting for us to get off the plane. They is carryin signs an banners and all. Colonel Gooch look out the winder of the plane an say he is suprised not to see a brass band there to greet us. As it turn out, the people in the crowd is quite enough.

First thing that happen when we come off the plane is the people in the crowd commence to chantin at us, an then somebody thowed a big tomato that hit Colonel Gooch in the face. After that, all hell break loose. They is some cops there, but the crowd busted thru an come runnin towards us shoutin an hollerin all kinds of nasty things, an they is about two thousan of them, wearing beards an shit, an it was the mos frightenin thing I have seen since we was back at the rice paddy where Bubba was kilt.

Colonel Gooch is tryin to clean the tomato off his face an act dignified, but I figger, the hell with that, cause we is outnumbered a thousan to one, an ain't got no weapons to boot. So I took off runnin.

That crowd was sure as hell lookin for somethin to chase too, cause ever one of them start chasin me jus like they used to do when I was little, hollerin and shoutin and wavin they signs. I run damn near all over the airport runway, an back again an into the terminal, an it was even scarier than when them Nebraska corn shucker jackoffs was chasin me aroun the Orange Bowl. Finally, I done run into the toilet an hid up on the seat with the door shut until I figger they have give up an gone on home. I must of been there an hour or so.

When I come out I walked down to the lobby an there is Colonel Gooch surrounded by a platoon of M. P. 's an cops, an he is lookin very distressed till he seen me. "C'mon, Gump!" he say. "They is holdin a plane for us to get to Washington."

When we get on the plane to Washington they is a bunch of civilians on it too, an Colonel Gooch an me set in a seat up front. We has not even took off yet, before all the people aroun us get up an go set somewhere else in the back of the plane. I axed Colonel Gooch why that was, an he say it probly cause we smell funny or somethin. He say not to worry about it. He say things be better in Washington. I hope so, cause even a moron like me can figger out that so far, it is not like the colonel say it would be.

When the plane get to Washington I am so excited I can bust! We can see the Washington Monument an the Capitol an all from out the winder an I have only saw picures of them things, but there they are, real as rain. The Army have sent a car to pick us up an we is taken to a real nice hotel, with elevators an stuff an people to lug your shit aroun for you. I have never been in a elevator before.

After we get squared away in our rooms, Colonel Gooch come over an say we is goin out for a drink to this little bar he remembers where they is a lot of pretty girls, an he say it is a lot different here than in California on account of people in the East are civilized an shit. He is wrong again.

We set down at a table an Colonel Gooch order me a beer an somethin for hissef an he begin tellin me how I got to act at the ceremony tomorrow when the President pin the medal on me.

Bout halfway through his talk, a pretty girl come up to the table an Colonel Gooch look up an axe her to git us two more drinks cause I guess he think she is the waitress. But she look down an say, "I wouldn get you a glass of warm spit, you filthy cocksucker." Then she turn to me an say, "How many babies have you kilt today, you big ape?"

Well, we gone on back to the hotel after that, an ordered some beer from room service, an Colonel Gooch get to finish tellin me how to act tomorrow.

Nex morning we up bright an early an walk on over to the White House where the President live. It is a real pretty house with a big lawn an all that look almost as big as city hall back in Mobile. A lot of Army people be there pumpin my han an tellin me what a fine feller I am, an then it is time to get the medal.

The President is a great big ole guy who talk like he is from Texas or somethin an they has assembled a whole bunch of people some of which look like maids an cleanin men an such, but they is all out in this nice rose garden in the bright sunshine.

An Army guy commence to readin some kind of bullshit an everbody be listenin up keen, cept for me, on account of I is starvin since we has not had our breakfast yet. Finally the Army guy is thru an then the President come up to me an take the medal out of a box an pin it on my chest. Then he shake my han an all these people start takin pichers an clappin an such as that.

I figger it is over then, an we can get the hell out of there, but the President, he still standin there, lookin at me kind of funny. Finally he say, "Boy, is that your stomach that is growlin like that?"

I glance over at Colonel Gooch but he jus roll his eyes up, an so I nod, an say, "Uh, huh," an the President say, "Well, c'mon boy, lets go an git us somethin to eat!"

I foller him inside an we go into a little roun room an the President tell a guy who is dressed up like a waiter to bring me some breakfast. It jus the two of us in there, an wile we is waitin for the breakfast he start axin me questions, such as do I know why we is fightin the gooks an all, an is they treatin us right in the Army. I jus nod my head an after a wile he stop axin me questions an they is this kind of silence an then he say, "Do you want to watch some television wile we is waitin for your food?"

I nod my head again, an the President turn on a tv set behin his desk an we watch "The Beverly Hillbillies." The President is most amused an say he watches it ever day an that I sort of remin him of Jethro. After breakfast, the President axe me if I want him to show me aroun the house, an I say, "Yeah," an off we go. When we get outside, all them photographer fellers are followin us aroun an then the President decide to set down on a little bench an he say to me, "Boy, you was wounded, wasn't you?" an I nod, an then he say, "Well, look at this," an he pull up his shirt an show me a big ole scar on his stomach where he has had an operation of some kind, an he axe, "Where was you wounded?" an so I pull down my pants an show him. Well, all them photographer fellers rush up an start to take pichers, an several folks come runnin over an I am hustled away to where Colonel Gooch is waitin.

That afternoon back at our hotel, Colonel Gooch suddenly come bustin into my room with a hanful of newspapers an boy is he mad. He begun hollerin an cussin at me an flung the papers down on my bed an there I am, on the front page, showin my big ass an the President is showin his scar. One of the papers has drawn a little black mask over my eyes so they can't recognize me, like they do with dirty pitchers.

The caption say, "President Johnson and War Hero Relaxing in the Rose Garden."

"Gump, you idiot!" Colonel Gooch say. "How could you do this to me?

I am ruint. My career is probly finished!"

"I dunno," I says, "but I am tryin to do the right thing."

Anyhow, after that I be in the doghouse again, but they has not give up on me yet. The Army have decided that I will go on the recruitment tour to try to get fellers to sign up for the war, an Colonel Gooch has gotten somebody to write up a speech that they expect me to make. It is a long speech, an filled with such things as "In time of crisis, nothin is more honorable an patriotic than to serve your country in the Armed Forces," an a whole bunch of shit like that. Trouble was, I could not never get the speech learnt. Oh, I could see all the words in my head okay, but when it come time to say it, everthin get all muddled up.

Colonel Gooch is beside hissef. He make me stay up till almost midnight ever day, tryin to get the speech right, but finally he thowed up his hans an say, "I can see this is not gonna work."

Then he come up with a idea. "Gump," he say, "here's what we is gonna do. I am gonna cut this speech shorter, an so all you will have to do is say a few things. Let us try that." Well, he cut it shorter an shorter an shorter, till he is finally satisfied that I can remember the speech an not look like a idiot. In the end, all I have got to say is "Join the Army an fight for your freedom."

Our first stop on the tour is a little college an they have got some reporters an photographers there, an we is in a big auditorium up on the stage. Colonel Gooch get up an he begin givin the speech I done sposed to have made. When he is thru, he say, "An now, we will have a few remarks from the latest Congressional Medal of Honor winner, P. F. C. Forrest Gump,"an he motion for me to come forward. Some people are clappin, an when they stop, I lean forward an say,"Join the Army an fight for your freedom."

I reckon they be expectin somethin more, but that's all I been tole to say, so I jus stand there, everbody lookin at me, me lookin back at them. Then all of a sudden somebody in the front shout out,"What do you think of the war?"an I say the first thing that come into my mind, which is,"It is a bunch of shit."

Colonel Gooch come an grapped the microphone away from me an set me back down, but all the reporters be scribblin in they notebooks an the photographers be takin pichers, an everbody in the audience goin wild, jumpin up an down an cheerin. Colonel Gooch get me out of there pronto, an we be in the car drivin fast out of town, an the colonel ain't sayin nothin to me, but he is talkin to hissef an laughin this weird, nutty little laugh.

Next mornin we is in a hotel ready to give our second speech on the tour when the phone ring. It is for Colonel Gooch. Whoever on the other end of the line seem to be doin all the talkin, an the colonel is doin the listenin an sayin"Yessir"a whole lot, an ever so often he is glarin over at me. When he finally put the phone down, he be starin at his shoes an he say,"Well, Gump, now you has done it. The tour is canceled, I have been reassigned to a weather station in Iceland, an I do not know or care what is to become of your sorry ass."I axed Colonel Gooch if we could get ourselfs a Co'Cola now, an he jus look at me for a minute, then start that talkin to hissef again an laughin that weird, nutty laugh.

They sent me to Fort Dix after that, an assign me to the Steam Heat Company. All day an haf the night I be shovelin coal into the boilers that keep the barracks warm. The company commander is a kind of ole guy who don't seem to give much of a damn bout nothin, an he say when I get there I has just got two more years left in the Army before I am discharged, an to keep my nose clean an everthin will be okay. An that is what I am tryin to do. I be thinkin a lot about my mama an bout Bubba an the little srimp bidness an Jenny Curran up at Harvard, an I am playin a little ping-pong on the side.

One day next spring there is a notice that they is gonna have a post ping-pong tournament an the winner will get to go to Washington to play for the All Army championship. I signed mysef up an it was pretty easy to win on account of the only other guy that was any good had got his fingers blowed off in the war an kep droppin his paddle.

Next week I am sent to Washington an the tournament is bein helt at Walter Reed Hospital, where all the wounded fellers can set an watch us play. I won pretty easy the first roun, an the secont too, but in the third, I have drawn a little bitty feller who puts all sorts of spin on the ball an I am havin a terrible time with him, an gettin my ass whipped. He is leadin me four games to two an it look like I am gonna lose, when all of a sudden I look over in the crowd an who should be settin there in a wheelchair but Lieutenant Dan from the hospital back at Danang!

We have a little break between games an I go over to Dan an look down at him an he ain't got no legs no more.

"They had to take them off, Forrest," he say, "but other than that, I am jus fine."

They have also taken off the bandages from his face, an he is terrible scarred an burnt from where his tank caught fire. Also, he still have a tube runnin into him from a bottle hooked onto a pole on his wheelchair.

"They say they gonna leave that like it is," Dan say. "They think it looks good on me."

Anyhow, he lean forward an look me in the eye, an say, "Forrest, I believe that you can do any damn thing you want to. I have been watchin you play, an you can beat this little guy because you play a hell of a game of ping-pong an it is your destiny to be the best."

I nod an it is time to go on back out there, an after that, I did not lose a single point, an I go on to the finals an win the whole tournament.

I was there for about three days, an Dan an me got to spend some time together. I would roll him aroun in his wheelchair, sometimes out in the garden where he could get some sun, an at night I would play my harmonica for him like I did for Bubba. Mostly, he liked to talk bout things—all sorts of things—such as history and philosophy, an one day he is talkin bout Einstein's theory of relativity, an what it mean in terms of the universe. Well, I got me a piece of paper an I drawed it out for him, the whole formula, cause it was somethin we had to do in the Intermediate Light class back at the University. He look at what I have done, an he say, "Forrest, you never cease to amaze me."

One day when I was back at Fort Dix shovelin coal in the Steam Heat Company, a feller from the Pentagon showed up with a chest full of medals an a big smile on his face, an he say,"P. F. C. Gump, it is my pleasure to inform you that you is been chosen as a member of the United States Ping-Pong Team to go to Red China an play the Chinese in ping-pong. This is a special honor, because for the first time in nearly twenty-five years our country is having anything to do with the Chinamen, an it is an event far more important than any damn ping-pong game. It is diplomacy, and the future of the human race might be at stake. Do you understand what I am saying?"

I shrug my shoulders an nod my head, but somethin down in me sinkin fast. I am jus a po ole idiot, an now I have got the whole human race to look after.

9

HERE I AM, HALFWAY ROUN THE WORLD AGAIN, THIS TIME in Peking, China.

The other people that play on the ping-pong team are real nice fellers what come from ever walk of life, an they is specially nice to me. The Chinamen is nice, too, an they is very different sorts of gooks from what I seen in Vietnam. First off, they is neat an clean an very polite. Second, they is not tryin to murder me.

The American State Department have sent a feller with us who is there to tell us how to behave aroun the Chinamen, an of all I have met, he is the only one not so nice. In fact, he is a turd. Mister Wilkins is his name, an he have a little thin moustache and always carry a briefcase an worry about whether or not his shoes is shined an his pants is pressed or his shirt is clean. I bet in the mornin he get up an spit-shines his asshole.

Mister Wilkins is always on my case. "Gump," he say, "when a Chinaman bow to you, you gotta bow back. Gump, you gotta quit adjustin yoursef in public. Gump, what are them stains on your trousers? Gump, you have got the table manners of a hog."

In that last, maybe he is right. Them Chinamen eat with two little sticks an it is almost impossible to shovel any food in your mouth with em, an so a lot of it wind up on my clothes. No wonder you do not see a lot of fat Chinamen aroun.

Anyway, we is playin a whole lot of matches against the Chinamen an they has got some very good players. But we is holdin our own. At night they has almost always got somethin for us to do, such as go out for supper someplace, or listen to a concert. One night, we is all sposed to go out to a restaurant called the Peking Duck, an when I get down to the lobby of the hotel, Mister Wilkins say, "Gump, you has got to go back to your room an change that shirt. It look like you has been in a food fight or somethin." He take me over to the hotel desk an get a Chinaman who speak English to write a little note for me, saying in Chinese that I am goin to the Peking Duck restaurant, an tell me to give it to the cab driver.

"We are going ahead," Mister Wilkins say. "You give the driver the note an he will take you there." So I gone on back to my room an put on a new shirt.

Anyhow, I find a cab in front of the hotel an get in, an he drive away. I be searchin for the note to give him, but by the time I figger out I must of lef it in my dirty shirt, we is long gone in the middle of town. The driver keep jabberin back at me, I reckon he's axin me where I want to go, an I keep sayin,"Peking Duck, Peking Duck,"but he be thowin up his hans an givin me a tour of the city.

All this go on for bout a hour, an let me tell you, I have seed some sights. Finally I tap him on the shoulder an when he turn aroun, I say,"Peking Duck,"an start to flap my arms like they is ducks' wings. All of a sudden, the driver get a big ole smile, an he start noddin an drive off. Ever once in a wile he look back at me, an I start flappin my wings again. Bout a hour later, he stop an I look out the winder an damn if he ain't took me to the airport!

Well, by this time, it is gettin late, an I ain't had no dinner or nothin, an I'm gettin bout starved, so we pass this restaurant an I tole the driver to let me out. I han him a wad of this gook money they give us, an he han me some back an away he go.

I went in the restaurant an set down an I might as well of been on the moon. This lady come over an look at me real funny, an han me a menu, but it is in Chinese, so after a wile, I jus point to four or five different things an figger one of them has to be eatable. Actually, they was all pretty good. When I am thru, I paid up an went on out on the street an try to fine my way back to the hotel, but I be walkin for hours I guess, when they pick me up.

Next thing I knowed, I has been thown in police station. They is a big ole Chinaman what speak English, an he is axin me all sorts of questions an offerin me cigarettes, jus like they did in them old movies. It were the nex afternoon before they finally got me out; Mister Wilkins come down to the jail an he is talkin for bout a hour, an they let me go.

Mister Wilkins is hoppin mad."Do you realize, Gump, that they think you are a spy?"he say."Do you know what this can do to this whole effort? Are you crazy?"

I started to tell him,"No, I is jus a idiot,"but I let it go. Anyhow, after that, Mister Wilkins buy a big balloon from a street vender an tied it on my shirt button, so he can tell where I is"at all times."Also, from then on, he pinned a note on my lapel, sayin who I was an where I am stayin. It made me feel like a fool.

They sent me back to Fort Dix after that, but instead of puttin me in the Steam Heat Company, I am tole they is lettin me out of the Army early. It don't take but a day or so, an then I am gone. They give me some money for a ticket home, an I have got a few dollars mysef. Now I got to decide what to do.

I know I ought to go on home an see my mama, cause she's in the po house an all. I think maybe I ought to get started with the little srimp bidness, too, an begin to make somethin of my life, but all this time, in the back of my mind, I have been thinkin of Jenny Curran up at Harvard University. I got a bus to the train station, an all the way there I am tryin to figger what is the right thing to do. But when the time come to buy my ticket, I tole them I wanted to go to Boston. There are jus times when you can't let the right thing stand in yo way.

10

I DID NOT HAVE NO ADDRESS FOR JENNY CEPT A POST OFFICE box, but I did have her letter with the name of the little place where she said she was playin with her band, The Cracked Eggs. It was called the Hodaddy Club. I tried to walk there from the train station, but I kep gettin lost, so I finally took a taxicab. It was in the afternoon an there was nobody in there but a couple of drunk guys an bout a half inch of beer on the floor from the night before. But they was a feller behin the bar say Jenny an them will be there bout nine o'clock. I axed if I can wait, an the guy say, "Sure," so I set down for five or six hours an took a load off my feet.

Directly, the place begun to fill up. They was mostly collegelookin kids but was dressed like geeks at a sideshow. Everbody wearin dirty blue jeans an tee shirts an all the guys had beards an wore glasses an all the girls have hair that look like a bird gonna fly out of it any secont. Presently the band come out on stage an start settin up. They is three or four fellers an they has got all this huge electric stuff, pluggin it in everwhere. It certainly is a far cry from what we done in the Student Union building back at the University. Also, I do not see Jenny Curran noplace.

After they get the electric stuff set up, they start to play, an let me say this: them people was loud! All sorts of colored lights begin to flash an the music they is makin sound sort of like a jet airplane when it takin off. But the crowd lovin it an when they is done, everbody begin to cheer an yell. Then a light fall on a side of the stage an there she is—Jenny hersef!

She is changed from the way I known her. First, she is got hair down to her ass, an is wearin sunglasses inside, at *night*! She is dressed in blue jeans an a shirt with so many spangles on it she look like a telephone switchboard. The band start up again an Jenny begun to sing. She has grapped hole of the microphone an is dancin all aroun the stage, jumpin up an down an wavin her arms an tossin her hair aroun. I am tryin to understan the words to the song, but the band is playin too loud for that, beatin on the drums, bangin on the piano, swattin them electric guitars till it seem like the roof gonna cave in. I am thinkin, what the hell is this?

After a wile they take a break an so I got up an tried to get through a door that go backstage. But they is a feller standing there who say I cannot come in. When I go walkin back to my seat, I notice everbody is starin at my Army uniform."That is some costume you has got on there,"somebody says, an somebody else say,"Far out!"an another one say,"Is he for real?"

I am beginnin to feel like a idiot again, an so I gone on outside, thinkin maybe I can walk aroun an figger things out. I guess I must of walked for haf an hour or so, an when I get back to the place they is a long line of people waitin to get in. I go up to the front an try to splain to the guy that all my stuff is in there, but he say to go wait at the end of the line. I guess I stood there a hour or so, an listened to the music comin from inside, an I have to tell you, it sounded a little better when you got away from it like that.

Anyway, after a wile, I got bored an went down a alley an roun to the back of the club. They was some little steps an I sat down there an watched the rats chasin each other in the garbage. I had my harmonica in my pocket, so's to pass the time, I got it out an started to play a little. I could still hear the music from Jenny's band, an after a wile I foun mysef bein able to play along with them, sort of usin the chromatic stop to get half out of key so it would fit in with what they was playin. I don't know how long it was, but it didn't take much afore I was able to make runs of my own, way up in C major, an to my suprise, it didn't soun half bad when you was playin it—so long as you didn't have to *listen* to it too.

All of a sudden the door behin me bust open an there is Jenny standin there. I guess they had taken their break again, but I wadn't payin no attention an had kep on playin.

"Who is that out there?" she say.

"It's me," I say, but it is dark in the alley an she stick her head out the door an say, "Who is playin that harmonica?"

I stand up an I am kind of embarrassed on account of my clothes, but I say, "It's me. Forrest."

"It is *who*?"she say.

"Forrest."

"Forrest? *Forrest Gump!*"an suddenly she rush out the door an thowed herself into my arms.

Jenny an me, we set aroun backstage an caught up on things till she had to play her nex set. She had not exactly quit school, she had got thowed out when they foun her in a feller's room one night. That was a thowin-out offense in them days. The banjo player had run off to Canada rather than go in the Army, an the little band had broke up. Jenny had gone out to California for a wile, an weared flowers in her hair, but she say them people is a bunch of freaks who is stoned all the time, an so she met this guy an come with him to Boston, an they had done some peace marches an all, but he turned out to be a fairy, so she split up with him, an took up with a real serious peace marcher who was in to makin bombs an stuff, an blowin up buildins. That didn't work out neither, so she met up with this guy what teached at Harvard University, but it turned out he was married. Next, she went with a guy that had seemed real nice but one day he got both their asses arrested for shoplifting, an she decided it was time to pull herself together.

She fell in with The Cracked Eggs, an they started playin a new kind of music, an got real popular aroun Boston, an they was even gonna go to New York an make a tape for an album nex week. She say she is seein this guy that goes to Harvard University, an is a student in philosophy, but that after the show tonight, I can come home an stay with them. I am very disappointed that she has got hersef a boyfrien, but I don't have noplace else to go, so that's what I done.

Rudolph is the boyfrien's name. He is a little guy bout a hundrit pounds or so, an has hair like a dustmop an wears a lot of beads aroun his neck an is settin on the floor when we get to their apartment, meditatin like a guru.

"Rudolph," Jenny say, "this is Forrest. He is a friend of mine from home, an he is gonna be stayin with us a wile."

Rudolph don't say nothin, but he wave his hand like the Pope when he is blessin somethin.

Jenny ain't got but one bed, but she made up a little pallet for me on the floor an that is where I slept. It wadn't no worse than a lot of places I slept in the Army, an a damn sight better than some.

Next mornin I get up an there is Rudolph still settin in the middle of the room meditatin. Jenny fixed me some breakfast an we lef ole Rudolph settin there an she took me on a tour of Cambridge. First thing she says is that I have got to get mysef some new clothes, on account of people up here does not understan an will think I am tryin to put them on. So we go to a surplus store an I get me some overalls an a lumber jacket an change into them right there an take my uniform in a paper bag.

We is walkin aroun Harvard University, an who does Jenny run into but the married professor she used to date. She is still friends with him, even tho in private she like to refer to him as a "degenerate turd." Doctor Quackenbush is his name.

Anyway, he is all excited on account of he is beginnin to teach a new course next week that he thunk up all by hissef. It is called the "Role of the Idiot in World Literature."

I pipe up an say I think it sounds pretty interestin, an he say, "Well, Forrest, why don't you sit in on the class? You might enjoy it."

Jenny look at both of us kind of funny-like, but she don't say nothin. We gone on back to the apartment an Rudolph is still squattin on the floor by hissef. We was in the kitchen an I axed her real quiet if Rudolph could talk, an she say, yes, sooner or later.

That afternoon Jenny took me to meet the other guys in the band an she tell them I play the harmonica like heaven itsef, an why don't they let me set in with them at the club tonight. One of the guys axe me what I like to play best, an I say, "Dixie," an he say he don't believe he has heard what I say, an Jenny jump in an say, "It don't matter, he will be fine once he's got a ear for our stuff."

So that night I be playin with the band an everbody agree I am makin a good contribution an it is very enjoyable, gettin to set there an watch Jenny sing an thow hersef all over the stage.

That nex Monday I have decided to go ahead an set in on Doctor Quackenbush's class, "Role of the Idiot in World Literature." The title alone is enough to make me feel sort of important.

"Today," Doctor Quackenbush says to the class, "we has a visitor who is gonna be auditing this course from time to time. Please welcome Mister Forrest Gump." Everbody turn an look at me an I give a little wave, an then the class begin.

"The idiot,"Doctor Quackenbush say,"has played an important role in history an literature for many years. I suppose you has all heard of the village idiot, who was usually some retarded individual livin in a village someplace. He was often the object of scorn an mockery. Later, it become the custom of nobility to have in their presence a court jester, a sort of person that would do things to amuse the royalty. In many instances, this individual was actually an idiot or a moron, in others, he was merely a clown or jokester. . ."

He go on like this for a wile, an it begun to become apparent to me that idiots was not jus useless people, but was put here for a purpose, sort of like Dan had said, an the purpose is to make people laugh. At least that is somethin.

"The object of having a fool for most writers,"Doctor Quackenbush say,"is to employ the device of *double entendre*, permittin them to let the fool make a fool of hissef, an at the same time allow the reader the revelation of the greater meaning of the foolishness. Occasionally, a great writer like Shakespeare would let the fool make an ass out of one of his principal characters, thereby providing a twist for the readers' enlightenment."

At this point, I am becomin somewhat confused. But that is normal. Anyhow, Mister Quackenbush say that to demonstrate what he has been talkin about, we is gonna do a scene from the play, *King Lear*, where there is a fool an a madman in disguise an the king hissef is crazy. He tells this guy named Elmer Harrington III to play the part of Mad Tom o'Bedlam, an for this girl called Lucille to play The Fool. Another guy called Horace somebody was to be crazy ole King Lear. An then he say,"Forrest, why doesn't you play the role of the Earl of Gloucester?"

Mister Quackenbush say he will get a few stage props from the drama department, but he want us to get up our own costumes, just so the thing would be more"realistic."How I got into this deal, I do not know, is what I am thinkin.

Meantime, things is happenin with our band, The Cracked Eggs. A feller from New Yawk have flown up an listened to us an says he wants to get us in a recordin studio an make a tape of our music. All the fellers is excited, includin Jenny Curran, an me, of course. The feller from New Yawk, Mister Feeblestein is his name. He say if everthing go well, we could be the hottest thing since the invention of night baseball. Mister Feeblestein say all we got to do is sign a piece of paper an then start gettin rich.

George, the guy who plays keyboard for us, has been teachin me a little bit of how to play it, an Mose, the drummer, is also lettin me beat on his drums some. It is kind of fun, learnin how to play all them things, an my harmonica too. Ever day I practice some, an ever night the band play at the Hodaddy Club.

Then one afternoon I come home from class an there is Jenny settin by herself on the couch. I axed her where is Rudolph, an she say he has"split."I axed what for, an she say,"Cause he is a nogood bastid like all the rest,"an so I says,"Why don't we go out an get ourselfs some supper an talk bout it?"

Naturally, she does most of the talkin, an it is really jus a string of gripes bout men. She say we are "lazy, unresponsible, selfish, low-down lyin shits." She is goin on that way for a wile an then she start to cry. I says, "Awe, Jenny, don't do that. It ain't nothin. That ole Rudolph didn't look like the kinda feller for you no how, squattin on the floor like that an all." An she say, "Yes, Forrest, probly you is right. I'd like to go home now." An so we do.

When we get home, Jenny begun takin off her clothes. She is down to her underpants, an I am jus settin on the couch tryin not to notice, but she come up an stand in front of me an she say, "Forrest, I want you to fuck me now."

You coulda knocked me over with a feather! I jus set there an gawked up at her. Then she set down nex to me an started foolin with my britches, an nex thing I knowed, she'd got off my shirt an was huggin an kissin me an all. At first, it was jus a little odd, her doin all that. Course I had dreamed bout it all along, but I had not expected it quite this way. But then, well I guess somethin come over me, an it didn't matter what I'd expected, cause we was rollin aroun on the couch an had our clothes nearly off an then Jenny pulled down my undershorts an her eyes get big an she say, "Whooo—lookit what you got there!" an she grapped me jus like Miz French had that day, but Jenny never say nothin about me keepin my eyes closed, so I didn't.

Well, we done all sorts of things that afternoon that I never even dreamt of in my wildest imagination. Jenny shown me shit I never could of figgered out on my own—sidewise, crosswise, upside down, bottom-wise, lengthwise, dogwise, standin up, settin down, bendin over, leanin back, inside-out an outside-in—only way we didn't try it was apart! We rolled all over the livin room an into the kitchen—stove in furniture, knocked shit over, pulled down drapes, mussed up the rug an even turned the tv set on by accident. Wound up doin it in the sink, but don't axe me how. When we is finally finished, Jenny jus lie there a wile, an then she look at me an say,"Goddamn, Forrest, where is you *been* all my life?"

"I been aroun,"I says.

Naturally, things are a bit different between Jenny an me after that. We commenced to sleep in the same bed together, which was also kind of strange for me at first, but I sure got used to it. When we was doin our act at the Hodaddy Club, ever so often Jenny would pass by me an muss up my hair, or run her fingers down the back of my neck. All of a sudden things start to change for me—like my whole life jus begun, an I am the happiest feller in the world.

11

THE DAY ARRIVED WHEN WE IS TO GIVE OUR LITTLE PLAY IN Professor Quackenbush's class at Harvard. The scene we is to do is when King Lear an his fool go out onto the heath, which is like a marsh or a field back home, an a big storm done blowed up an everbody run into a shack called a "hovel."

Inside the hovel there is a guy called Mad Tom o'Bedlam who is actually a character name of Edgar disguised up as a crazy person on account of being fucked over by his brother, who is a bastid. Also, the king is gone totally nuts by this time, an Edgar is playin a nut too, an the fool, of course, is actin like one. My part is to be the Earl of Gloucester, who is Edgar's father, an sort of a straight man for them other stooges.

Professor Quackenbush have rigged up a ole blanket or somethin to resemble a hovel an he has got some kind of wind machine to sound like a storm—big electric fan with clothespins holdin pieces of paper to the blades. Anyway, here come Elmer Harrington III as King Lear, dressed in a gunnysack an wearin a colander on his head. The girl they got to play the fool has foun a fool's costume someplace, with a little cap that has bells tied to it, an them kinds of shoes that curl up in front like Arabs wear. The guy playin Tom o'Bedlam has foun hissef a Beatle wig an some clothes out of the garbage an has painted his face with dirt. They is takin it all very seriously.

I am probly the best-lookin of the bunch, tho, cause Jenny done set down an sewed me up a costume out of a sheet an a pillow case that I am wearin like a diaper, an she has also made me a cape out of a tablecloth, just like Superman wears.

Anyway, Professor Quackenbush start up his wind machine an say for us to begin at page twelve, where Mad Tom is tellin us his sad story.

"Do poor Tom some charity, whom the foul fiend vexes,"Tom say.

An King Lear say,"What? Have his daughters brought him to this pass? Couldst thou save nothing? Didst thou give them all?"

An the fool say,"Nay, he reserved a blanket, else we had all been shamed."

This shit go on for a wile, then the fool say,"This cold night will turn us all to fools and madmen."

In this, the fool is correct.

Just bout this time, I am sposed to enter into the hovel carrying a torch, which Professor Quackenbush have borrowed from the drama department. The fool call out,"Look! Here come a walking fire!"an Professor

Quackenbush light my torch an I go across the room into the hovel.

"This is the foul fiend Flibbertigibbet,"Tom o'Bedlam say.

"What's he?"the king axes.

An I say,"What are you there? Your names?"

Mad Tom say he is jus"Po Tom, that eats the swimmin frawg, the toad, the tadpole and the newt. . ."an a bunch of other shit, an then I sposed to suddenly recognize the king, an say:

"What! Hath your grace no better company?"

An Mad Tom, he answer,"The prince of darkness is a gentleman—Modo he's call'd, and Mahu."

The wind machine be blowin hard now, an I reckon Professor Quackenbush have not considered that I am six feet six inches tall when he built the hovel, cause the top of my torch is bumpin against the ceiling.

Mad Tom, he is now sposed to say,"Poor Tom's a-cold,"but instead, he say,"Watch that torch!"

I look down at my book to see where that line come from, an Elmer Harrington III say to me,"Look out for that torch, you idiot!"an I say back to him,"For once in my life I am not the idiot—*you* is!"An then all of a sudden the roof to the hovel catch on fire an fall on Mad Tom's Beatle wig an set it on fire too.

"Turn off the goddamn wind machine!"somebody shout, but it is too late. Everthing burning up!

Mad Tom is hollerin an yellin an King Lear take off his colander an jam it on Mad Tom's head to put the fire out. People is jumpin aroun an choakin an coughin an cussin an the girl playin the fool gets hysterical an commence to shriek an cry, "We will all be kilt!" For a moment or two, it actually looks that way.

I turn behin me, an damn if my cape ain't caught on fire, an so I thowed open the winder an grapped the fool aroun her waist an out we leaped. It was only from the secont story winder, an they was a bunch of shrubs down there that broke our fall, but it was also lunchtime an hundrits of people was wanderin aroun the Yard. There we was, all a-fire an smolderin.

Black smoke come pourin from up in the open winder of the class an all of a sudden there is Professor Quackenbush, leanin out an lookin aroun, shakin his fist, face all covered up with soot.

"Gump, you fuckin idiot—you stupid asshole! You will pay for this!" he shoutin.

The fool is grovelin aroun on the groun an bawlin an wringing her hans but she is okay—just singed up a bit—so I just took off—bounded across the Yard fast as I could run, cape still on fire, smoke trailin behin me. I didn't stop till I got home, an when I get into the apartment, Jenny say, "Oh, Forrest, how was it? I bet you was wonderful!" Then she get a peculiar look on her face. "Say, do you smell somethin burnin?" she axes.

"It is a long story," I say.

Anyhow, after that I did not attend the "Role of the Idiot in World Literature" no more, as I have seen quite enough. But ever night I an Jenny are playin with The Cracked Eggs an all day long we is makin love an takin walks an havin picnics on the banks of the Charles River an it is heaven.

Jenny has written a nice tender song called "Do It to Me Hard an Fast," in which I get to take bout a five-minute ride on my harmonica. It were a splendid spring an summer, an we went down to New Yawk an made the tapes for Mister Feeblestein an a few weeks later he call up to say we is gonna have a record album. Not too long after that, everbody be callin us up to play in their towns an we took the money we got from Mister Feeblestein an bought us a big bus with beds an shit in it an go on the road.

Now there is somethin else durin that period that played a great role in my life. One night after we is finished the first set at the Hodaddy Club, Mose, the drummer for The Cracked Eggs, take me aside an say, "Forrest, you is a nice clean-cut feller an all, but they is somethin I want you to try that I think will make you play that harmonica better."

I axe what it is, an Mose say, "Here," an he give me a little cigarette. I tell him I don't smoke, but thanks, an Mose say, "It is not a regular cigarette, Forrest. It have got somethin in it to expand your horizons."

I tole Mose I ain't sure I need my horizons expanded, but he sort of insisted. "At least try it," he say, an I thought for a minute, an conclude that one cigarette ain't gonna hurt none, an so I do.

Well let me say this: my horizons indeed become expanded.

Everthing seem to slow down an get rosy keen. That secont set we played that night was the best of my life, I seemed to hear all the notes a hundrit times as I was playin them, an Mose come up to me later an say, "Forrest, you think *that's* good—use it when you're screwin."

I did, an he was right bout that too. I used some of my money to buy me some of that stuff, an before you know it, I was doin it day in an day out. The only problem was, it kind of made me stupider after a wile. I just get up in the mornin an light up one of them joints, which is what they called them, an lie there all day till it was time to go an play. Jenny didn't say nothin for a wile, cause she been known to take a puff or two hersef, but then one day she say to me, "Forrest, don't you think you been doin too much of that shit?"

"I dunno," I says, "how much is too much?"

An Jenny say, "As much as you are doin is too much."

But I didn't want to stop. Somehow, it got rid of everthing I might be worried bout, tho there wadn't too much of that at that time anyway. At night I'd go out between sets at the Hodaddy Club an set in the little alley an look up at the stars. If they weren't any stars, I'd look up anyway, an one night Jenny come out an find me lookin up at the rain.

"Forrest, you has got to quit this," she say. "I am worried bout you, cause you ain't doin nothin cept playin an lyin aroun all day. It ain't healthy. I think you need to get away for a wile. We ain't got no concerts booked after tomorrow down in Provincetown, so I think maybe we ought to go someplace an take a vacation. Go up to the mountains maybe."

I jus nod my head. I ain't even sure I heard all she said.

Well, the nex night in Provincetown, I find the backstage exit an go on outside to lite up a joint. I am settin there by mysef, mindin my business, when these two girls come up. One of them say, "Hey, ain't you the harmonica player with The Cracked Eggs?"

I nod yes, an she jus plop hersef down in my lap. The other girl is grinnin an squealin an suddenly she take off her blouse. An the other girl is tryin to unzip my pants an have her skirt pulled up an I am jus settin there blowed away. Suddenly the stage door open an Jenny call out, "Forrest, it is time to. . ." an she stop for a secont an then she say, "Awe shit," an slam the door.

I jumped up then, an the girl in my lap felled on the groun an the other one is cussin an all, but I went inside an there is Jenny leaned up against the wall cryin. I went up to her but she say, "Keep away from me, you shithead! You men is all alike, jus like dogs or somethin—you got no respect for anybody!"

I ain't never felt so bad. I don't remember much bout that last set we played. Jenny went up to the front of the bus on the trip back an wouldn't speak to me none at all. That night she slep on the sofa an the nex mornin she say maybe it is time for me to find my own place. An so I packed up my shit an left. My head hangin very low. Couldn't explain it to her or nothin. Thowed out again.

Jenny, she took off someplace after that. I axed aroun, but nobody knowed where she was. Mose say I can bunk with him till I find a place, but it is a terrible lonely time. Since we ain't playin none for the moment, there ain't nothin much to do, an I be thinkin maybe it's time I go on back home an see my mama an maybe start up that little srimp bidness down where po ole Bubba used to live. Perhaps I is not cut out to be a rock an roll star. Perhaps, I think, I ain't nothin but a bumblin idiot anyhow.

But then one day Mose come back an he say he was over to a saloon on the corner watchin the tv news, an who should he see but Jenny Curran.

She is down in Washington, he say, marchin in a big demonstration against the Vietnam War, an Mose say he wonderin why she botherin with that shit when she ought to be up here makin us money.

I say I has got to go see her, an Mose say, "Well, see if you can bring her back." He say he knows where she probly is stayin, on account of they is this group from Boston that has taken an apartment in Washington to demonstrate against the war.

I packed up all my shit—everthin I own—an thanked Mose an then I am on my way. Whether I come back or not, I do not know.

When I get down to Washington, everthin is a mess. They is police everwhere an people be shoutin in the streets an thowin things like in a riot. Police be bongin folks on the head what thow things, an the situation look like it be gettin out of han.

I find the address of the place Jenny might be at, an go over there, but ain't nobody home. I waited on the steps for most of the day, then, bout nine o'clock at night, a car pull up an some folks get out an there she is!

I get up from the steps an walk towards her, but she turn away from me an run back to the car. Them other people, two guys an a girl, they didn't know what to do, or who I was, but then one of them say, "Look, I wouldn't fool with her right now—she is awful upset." I axed why, an the feller take me aside an tell me this:

Jenny has done jus got out of jail. She have been arrested the day before, an spent the night in the women's jail, an this mornin, fore anybody could get her out, the people at the jail done said she might have lice or somethin in her hair cause it so long an all, an they had all her hair shaved off. Jenny is bald.

Well, I reckon she don't want me to see her this way, cause she has done got into the back seat of the car an is lyin down. So I crawled up on my hans an knees so I couldn't see in the winder, an I say, "Jenny—it's me, Forrest."

She don't say nothing, so I start tellin her how sorry I am bout what's happened. I tell her I ain't gonna smoke no more dope, nor play in the band no more on account of all the bad temptations. An I say I'm sorry bout her hair. Then I crawled back to the steps where my shit is, an looked in my duffelbag an find a ole watch cap from the Army an crawled back to the car an stuck it on a stick an polked it thru the winder. She took it, an put it on, an come out of the car, an say, "Awe get up off the groun you big Bozo, an come into the house."

We set an talked for a wile, an them other people been smokin dope an drinkin beer, but I ain't havin none. They is all discussin what they is gonna do tomorrow, which is that they is a big demonstration at the U. S. Capitol at which a bunch of Vietnam veterans is gonna take off they medals an thow them on the steps of the Capitol.

An Jenny suddenly say, "Do you know Forrest here done won the Congressional Medal of Honor?" An everbody get completely quiet an be lookin at me, an then at each other, an one of them say, "Jesus Christ have just sent us a present!"

Well, the next mornin, Jenny come into the livin room where I is sleepin on the sofa an say, "Forrest, I want you to go with us today, an I want you to wear your Army uniform."When I axed why, she say,"Because you is gonna do somethin to stop all the sufferin over in Vietnam."An so I get into my uniform, an Jenny come back after a wile with a bunch of chains she has bought at the hardware store, an say,"Forrest, wrap these aroun you."

I axed why again, but she say,"Just do it, you will find out later. You want to make me happy, doesn't you?"

An so off we went, me in my uniform an the chains an Jenny an the other folks. It is a bright clear day an when we get to the Capitol they is a mob there with tv cameras an all the police in the world. Everbody be chantin an hollerin an givin the finger to the police. After a wile, I seen some other guys in Army uniforms an they was bunched together an then, one by one, they commenced to walk as close as they can get to the steps of the Capitol an they took off they medals an thowed them. Some of the fellers was in wheelchairs an some was lame an some was missing arms an legs. Some of them jus tossed they medal on to the steps, but others really thowed them hard. Somebody tap me on the shoulder an say it is my turn now. I look back at Jenny an she nod, so I go on up there mysef.

It get sort of quiet, then somebody on a bullhorn announce my name, an say I is gonna thow away the Congressional Medal of Honor as a token of my support for endin the Vietnam War. Everbody cheer an clap, an I can see the other medals lyin there on the steps. High above all this, up on the porch of the Capitol, is a little bunch of people standin aroun, couple of cops an some guys in suits. Well, I figger I gotta do the best I can, so I take off the medal an look at it for a secon, an I be rememberin Bubba an all, an Dan, an I dunno, somethin come over me, but I got to thow it, so I rare back an heave that medal hard as I can. Couple of seconts later, one of the guys on the porch that is wearin a suit, he jus keel over. Unfortunately, I done thowed the medal too far an knocked him in the head with it.

All hell break loose then. Police be chargin into the crowd an people be shoutin all sorts of things an tear gas bust open an suddenly five or six police pounced on me an commence knockin me with they billy sticks. A bunch more police come runnin up an nex thing you know, I am handcuffed an thowed in a police wagon an hauled off to jail.

I am in jail all night long, an in the mornin they come an take me in front of the judge. I has been there before.

Somebody tell the judge that I is accused of "assault with a dangerous weapon—a medal—an resistin arrest," an so on an han him a sheet of paper. "Mister Gump," the judge say, "do you realize that you have conked the Clerk of the U. S. Senate on the head with your medal?"

I ain't sayin nothin, but it look like I am in serious trouble this time.

"Mister Gump," the judge say, "I do not know what a man of your stature, a man what has served his country so well, is doin mixed up with a bunch of tuity-fruities that is thowin away their medals, but I will tell you what, I is gonna order you committed for psychiatric observation for thirty days to see if they can figger out why you has done such a idiotic thing."

They took me back to my cell after that, an a wile later load me on a bus an truck me off to St. Elizabeth's mental hospital.

Finally, I am "Put Away."

12

THIS PLACE IS A SERIOUS LOONY BIN. THEY PUT ME IN A room with a feller called Fred that has been here for almost a year. He begun to tell me right off what kind of nuts I got to contend with. They is one guy that poisoned six people, somebody else that used a meat cleaver on his mama. They is people who have done all sorts of shit—from murder an rape to sayin they is the King of Spain or Napoleon. Finally I axed Fred why he is in here an he say because he is a axe murderer, but they is lettin him out in another week or so.

The secont day I am there, I is tole to report to the office of my psychiatrist, Doctor Walton. Doctor Walton, it turn out, is a woman. First, she say, she is gonna give me a little test, then I is gonna have a physical examination. She set me down at a table an start showin me cards with ink blots on them, axin me what I thought they were. I kep sayin "ink blot" till she finally get mad an tell me I got to say somethin else, an so I started makin things up. Then I am handed a long test an tole to take it. When I am done, she say, "Take off your clothes."

Well, with one or two exceptions, ever time I take off my clothes, somethin bad happen to me, so I says I would rather not, an she make a note of this an then tell me either I do it mysef, or she will get the attendants to hep me. It was that kind of deal.

I go on an do it, an when I is butt neckid, she come into the room an look at me, up an down, an say, "My, my—you is a fine specimen of a man!"

Anyhow, she start bongin me on the knee with a little rubber hammer like they done back at the University, an polkin me in all sorts of places. But she ain't never said for me to "bend over," an for this I am grateful. Afterward, she say I can get dressed an go back to my room. On the way there, I past by a room with a glass door an inside it they is a bunch of little guys, settin an lyin aroun, droolin an spasmoin an beatin on the floor with they fists. I jus stood there for a wile, lookin in, an I'm feelin real sorry for them—kinda remind me of my days back at the nut school.

A couple of days later, I am tole to report to Doctor Walton's office again. When I get there, she is with two other guys dressed up as doctors, an she say they is Doctor Duke and Doctor Earl—both with the National Institute of Mental Health. An they is very interested in my case, she say.

Doctor Duke an Doctor Earl set me down an start axin me questions—all kinds of questions—an both of them took turns bongin me on the knees with the hammer. Then Doctor Duke say,"Look here, Forrest, we has got your test scores, an it is remarkable how well you is done on the math part. So we would like to give you some other tests."They produce the tests, an make me take them, an they is a lot more complicated than the first one, but I figger I done okay. Had I knowed what was gonna happen nex, I would of fucked them up.

"Forrest,"Doctor Earl say,"this is phenomenal. You is got a brain jus like a computer. I do not know how well you can reason with it—which is probly why you is in here in the first place—but I have never seen anything quite like this before."

"You know, George,"Doctor Duke say,"this man is truly remarkable. I have done some work for NASA a wile back, an I think we ought to send him down to Houston to the Aeronautics and Space Center an have them check him out. They has been lookin for just this sort of feller."

All the doctors be starin at me, an noddin they heads, an then they bonged me on the knees with a hammer one more time an it look like here I go again.

They flown me down to Houston, Texas, in a big ole plane with nobody on it but me an Doctor Duke, but it is a pleasant sort of trip cept they got me chained to my seat han an foot.

"Look here, Forrest,"Doctor Duke say,"the deal is this. Right now you is in a shitpot of trouble for thowin that medal at the Clerk of the U. S. Senate. You can go to jail for ten years for that. But if you cooperates with these people at NASA, I will personally see to it that you is released—

okay?"

I nod my head. I knowed I got to get outta jail an find Jenny again. I am missin her somethin terrible.

I am at the NASA place at Houston for about a month. They has examined me an tested me an questioned me so much I feel like I am goin on the Johnny Carson show.

I ain't.

One day they haul me into a big room an tell me what they has in mind.

"Gump," they say, "we wants to use you on a flight to outer space. As Doctor Duke has pointed out, your mind is jus like a computer-only better. If we can program it with the right stuff, you will be extremely useful to America's space program. What do you say?"

I thought for a minute, an then I says I had better axe my mama first, but they make an even stronger argument—like spendin the next ten years of my life in the slammer.

An so I says yes, which is usually what gets me in trouble ever time.

The idea they has thought up is to put me in a spaceship an shoot me up aroun the earth bout a million miles. They has already shot people up to the moon, but they didn't find nothin there worth a shit, so what they is plannin nex is a visit to Mars. Fortunately for me, Mars is not what they got in mind at the moment—instead, this is to be a sort of trainin mission in which they gonna try to figger out what kind of folks would be suited best for the Mars trip.

Besides me, they has picked a woman an a ape to go along.

The woman is a crabby-lookin lady called Major Janet Fritch, who is sposed to be America's first woman astronaut, only nobody knows bout her cause all this be pretty top secret. She is a sort of short lady with hair look like it been cut by puttin a bowl over her head, an she don't seem to have much use for either me or the ape.

The ape ain't so bad, actually. It is a big ole female orangutang called Sue, what has been captured in the jungles of Sumatra or someplace. Actually they has got a whole bunch of them apes down here, an have been shootin them up into space for a long wile, but they says Sue will be best on this trip on account of she is a female an will be friendlier than a male ape, an also, this will be her third space flight. When I find this out, I am wonderin how come they gonna send us way up there with the only experienced crew member bein a ape. Kind of makes you think, don't it?

Anyhow, we got to go thru all kinds of trainin before the flight. They puttin us in cyclotrons an spinnin us aroun, an in little rooms with no gravity an such as that. An all day long they be crammin my mind with shit they want me to remember, such as equations to figger the distance between wherever we is, an wherever they want us to go, an how to get back again; all kinds of crap like coaxiel coordinates, co sine computations, spheriod trigonometry, Boolean algebra, antilogarithms, Fourier analysis, quadrats an matrix math. They say I is to be the"backup"for the backup computer.

I have writ a bunch of letters to Jenny Curran but all of them done come back "Addressee not Known." Also I done wrote to my mama, an she send me back a long letter the gist of which is "How can you do this to your po ole mama when she is in the po house an you is all she got lef in the world?"

I dared not tell her that I am facin a jail sentence if I don't, so I jus write her back an say not to worry, on account of we has an experienced crew.

Well, the big day finally come, an let me say this: I am not jus a little bit nervous—I am scant haf to death! Even tho it was top secret, the story done leaked to the press and now we gonna be on tv an all.

That mornin, somebody brung us the newspapers to show us how famous we was. Here is some of the headlines:

"Woman, Ape and Idiot in Next U. S. Space Effort."

"America Launching Odd Messengers Toward Alien Planets."

"Girl, Goon, and Gorilla to Lift Off Today."

There was even one in the New Yawk *Post* that say, "Up They Go—But Who's in Charge?"

The only one that sounded halfway nice was the headline in the New Yawk *Times*, which say, "New Space Probe Has Varied Crew."

Well, as usual, everthing is all confusion from the minute we get up. We go to get our breakfast an somebody say, "They ain't sposed to eat no breakfast the day of the flight." Then somebody else say, "Yes we is," an then somebody else say, "No they ain't," an it go on like that for a wile till ain't nobody hungry anymore.

They get us into our space suits an take us out there to the launchin pad in a little bus with ole Sue ridin in back in a cage. The spaceship is about a hundrit stories tall an is all foamin an hissin an steamin an look like it bout to eat us alive! A elevator take us to the capsule we is to be in, an they strap us in an load ole Sue in her place in back. Then we wait.

An we wait some more.

An we wait some more.

An we wait some more.

All along, the spaceship be boilin an hissin an growlin an steamin. Somebody say a hundrit million people out there watchin us on television. I reckon they be waitin too.

Anyhow, bout noon, somebody come up an knock on the spaceship door an say, we is temporarily cancelin this mission till they get the spaceship fixed.

So we all get to go back down in the elevator again, me, Sue, an Major Fritch. She be the only one moanin an bitchin, cause Sue an me is very relieved.

Our relief was not to last long, however. Bout a hour later somebody run into the room where we is jus about to set down to lunch an say, "Get in your space suits again right now! They is fixin to shoot you up in space!"

Everbody be hollerin an shoutin again an rushin aroun. I reckon maybe a bunch of the tv viewers have called in to complain or somethin, an so they decided to lite that fire under our asses no matter what. Whatever it is, it don't matter now.

Anyhow, we is put back on the bus an taken to the spaceship an we is halfway up the elevator when somebody suddenly say,"Jesus, we forgot the goddamn ape!"an he start hollerin down to the fellers on the groun to go back an get ole Sue.

We is strapped in again an somebody is countin backwards from one hundrit when they come thru the door with Sue. We is all leaned back in our seats an the count is down to about"ten,"when I be hearin some strange growlin noises from behin us where Sue is. I sort of turned aroun, an low an behole, it ain't Sue settin there at all, it is a big ole *male* ape, what got his teeth bared an is grappin holt of his seatbelt straps like he is about to bust loose any secont!

I tell Major Fritch an she look aroun an say,"Oh my God!"an get on the radio to whoever it is in the groun control tower."Listen,"she say,"you has made a mistake an put one of them male apes in here with us, so we better call this thing off till it is straightened out."But all of a sudden the spaceship start to rumblin an quakin an the guy in the control tower says over the radio,"That's *your* problem now, sister, we got a schedule to meet."

An away we go.

13

MY FIRST IMPRESSION IS OF BEIN SQUASHED UNDER somethin, such as my daddy was when them bananas fell on him. Can't move, can't yell, can't say nothin, can't do nothin—we is strictly here for the ride. Outside, lookin thru the winder, all I can see is blue sky. The spaceship is movin out.

After a little wile, we seem to slow down some, an things ease up. Major Fritch say we can unbuckle our seatbelts now, an get on bout our bidness, whatever it is. She say we is now travelin at a speed of fifteen thousan miles a hour. I look back an sure enough, the earth is only a little ball behin us, just like it look in all them pichers from outer space. I look aroun, an there's the big ole ape, all sour-lookin, an glum, glarin at Major Fritch an me. She say maybe he want his lunch or somethin, an for me to go on back there an give him a banana afore he gets angry an does somethin bad.

They has packed a little bag of food for the ape an it contain bananas an some cereals an dried berries an leaves an shit like that. I get it open an start rummagin thru it lookin for somethin that will make the ape happy, an meantime, Major Fritch is on the radio with Houston Groun Control.

"Now listen here," she say, "we has got to do somethin bout this ape. It ain't Sue—it is a male ape, an he don't look none to glad to be here. He might even be violent."

It took a wile for the message to get there an a reply to get back to us, but some feller down there say, "Awe pooh! One ape is jus like any other."

"The hell it is," Major Fritch say. "If you was in this little bitty compartment with that big ole thing you would be singing a different tune."

An after a minute or two a voice come cracklin over the radio, say, "Look, you is ordered not to tell anybody about this, or we will all be made laughing-stocks. As far as you or anybody else is concerned, that ape is Sue—no matter what it's got between its legs."

Major Fritch look at me an shake her head. "Aye, aye, sir," she say, "but I'm gonna keep that fucker strapped in as long as I'm in here with him— you understand that?"

An from the ground control there come back one word:

"Roger."

Actually, after you get used to it, bein in outer space is kind of fun. We is without gravity, an so can float all over the spaceship, an the scenery is remarkable—moon an sun, earth an stars. I wonder where Jenny Curran is down there, an what she is doin.

Aroun an aroun the earth we go. Day an night go by ever hour or so an it sort of put a different perspective on things. I mean, here I am doin this, an when I get back—or should I say *if* I get back—what then? Go an start up my little srimp-growin bidness? Go find Jenny again? Play in The Cracked Eggs? Do somethin about my mama bein in the po house? It is all very strange.

Major Fritch be catchin a wink or two of sleep whenever she can, but when she ain't sleepin, she is bitchin. Crabbin bout the ape, crabbin bout what kind of jackoffs they is down at groun control, crabbin bout she got no place to put on her makeup, crabbin bout me eatin food when it ain't supper or lunchtime. Hell, all we got to eat is Granola bars anyway. I don't want to be complainin too much, but it seem like they might of picked a good-lookin woman or at least one that don't bitch all the time.

An furthermore, let me say this: that ape ain't no dreamboat either.

First I give it a banana—okay? It grapped the banana an started peelin it, but then it put the banana down. Banana started floatin all aroun the cabin of the spaceship an I got to go find it. I give it back to the ape an he start mushin it up an flingin the mush everplace, an I got to go clean that up. Wants attention all the time too. Evertime you leave it alone it commences to put up an enormous racket an clack its jaws together like a set of them wind-up teeth. Drive you nuts after a wile.

Finally I got out my harmonica an started playin a little somethin—"Home on the Range," I think it was. An the ape started to calm down a little. So I played some more-stuff like "The Yellow Rose of Texas" an "I Dream of Jeannie with the Light Brown Hair." Ape is lyin there lookin at me, peaceful as a baby. I forget there is a tv camera in the spaceship an they is pickin all this up down there at groun control. Nex mornin when I wake up somebody hole up a newspaper in front of the camera down in Houston for us to see. The headline say, "Idiot Plays Space Music to Soothe Ape." That is the sort of shit I has got to contend with.

Anyhow, things are goin along pretty good, but I been noticin that ole Sue is lookin at Major Fritch in a kind of strange way. Ever time she get near him, Sue sort of perk up an be reachin out like he wants to grap her or somethin, an she start bitchin at him—"Git away from me you awful thing. Keep your hans to yoursef!" But ole Sue has got somethin in mind. That much I can tell.

It ain't long before I find out what it is. I have gone behin this little partition to take a pee in a jar in private, when all of a sudden I hear this commotion. I stick my head aroun the partition an Sue has managed to grap a holt of Major Fritch an he has got his han down in her space suit. She is yellin an hollerin to beat the band an is crackin Sue over the head with the radio microphone.

Then it dawns on me what the problem is. Wile we has been up in space for nearly two days, ole Sue been strapped into his seat an ain't had a chance to take a leak or nothin! An I sure remember what that's like. He must be bout to bust! Anyhow, I go over an got him away from Major Fritch an she still hollerin an yellin, callin him a "filthy animal," an shit like that. When she get loose, Major Fritch go up to the front of the cockpit an put her head down an start sobbin. I unstrap Sue an take him behin the partition with me.

I find a empty bottle for him to pee in, but after he finished, he take the bottle an heave it into a panel of colored lights an it bust to pieces an all the pee start floatin aroun in the spaceship. I say, to hell with this, an start leadin Sue back to his seat when I seen a big glob of pee headin straight for Major Fritch. It look like it gonna hit her in the back of the head, so I turn Sue loose an try to head off the pee with a net they have give us for catchin stuff that's floatin aroun. But jus as I am bout to net the glob of pee, Major Fritch sit back up an turn aroun an it caught her right in the face.

She start hollerin an bawlin again an in the meantime, Sue has done gone an started rippin out wires from the control panel. Major Fritch is screamin, "Stop him! Stop him!" but before you know it, sparks an stuff is flyin all aroun inside the spaceship an Sue is jumpin from ceilin to floor tearin shit up. A voice come over the radio wantin to know "What in hell is goin on up there?" but by then it is too late.

The spaceship is weavin all aroun an goin end over end an me, Sue an Major Fritch is tossed aroun like corks. Can't grap holt of nothin, can't turn off nothin, can't stan up or set down. The voice of groun control come over the radio again, say, "We is noticin some kine of minor stabilization trouble with your craft. Forrest, will you manually insert the D-six program into the starboard computer?"

Shit—he got to be jokin! I'm spinnin aroun like a top an I got a wild ape loose in here to boot! Major Fritch is hollerin so loud I cannot hear or even think nothin, but the gist of what she is hollerin seem to be that we is bout to crash an burn. I managed to get a glance out of the winder, an in fact things don't look good. That earth comin up on us mighty fast.

Somehow I managed to get to where the starboard computer is, an hold on to the panel with one han an I'm puttin D-six into the machine. It is a program designed to land the spaceship in the Indian Ocean in case we get in trouble, which we certainly is now.

Major Fritch an ole Sue be holdin on for dear life, but Major Fritch holler out, "What is you doin over there?" When I tole her, she say, "Forgit that, you stupid turd—we is already done passed over the Indian Ocean. Wait till we go roun again an see if you can set us down in the South Pacific."

Believe it or not, it don't take much time to go roun the world when you is in a spaceship, an Major Fritch has grapped holt to the radio microphone an is hollerin at them people at groun control that we is headed for either a splash-down or crash-down in the South Pacific Ocean an to come get us as soon as they can. I'm punchin buttons like crazy an that big ole earth is loomin closer. We fly over somethin Major Fritch thinks look like South America an then there be only water again, with the South Pole off to our left an Australia up ahead.

Then everthing get scorchin hot, an funny little souns are comin from the outside of the spaceship an it start shakin an hissin an the earth is dead up ahead. Major Fritch shout to me, "Pull the parachute lever!" but I am pinned in my seat. An she is pressed up against the ceilin of the cabin, an so it look like it's curtains for us, since we is goin bout ten thousan miles a hour, an headed straight for a big ole green blob of land in the ocean. We hit that goin this fast, ain't even gonna be a grease spot lef.

But then all of a sudden somethin go"pop"an the spaceship slow down. I look over, an damn if ole Sue ain't pulled the parachute lever hissef an saved our asses. I remind mysef then an there to feed him a banana when all this shit is over.

Anyhow, the spaceship be swingin back an forth under the parachute, an it look like we is gonna hit the big ole green blob of land-which apparently ain't so good neither, since we is sposed only to hit water an then ships will pick us up. But ain't nothin gone right from the time we set foot in this contraption, so why should anybody expect it to now?

Major Fritch is on the radio an sayin to groun control,"We is bout to land on someplace north of Australia out in the ocean, but I ain't sure where we is."

Couple of seconts later a voice come back say,"If you ain't sure where you is, why don't you look out the winder, you dumb broad?"

So Major Fritch put the radio down an go look out the winder an she say,"Jesus—this look like Borneo or someplace,"but when she try to tell that to groun control, the radio done gone dead.

We be gettin real close to the earth now, an the spaceship still swinging under the parachute. There is nothin but jungle an mountains beneath us cept for a little bitty lake that is kind of brown. We can barely make out somethin going on nex to the lake down there. The three of us—me, Sue an Major Fritch—all got our noses pressed to the winder lookin down, an all of a sudden Major Fritch cry out, "Good God! This ain't Borneo—this is fuckin New Guinea, an all that shit on the groun must be one of them Cargo Cults or somethin!"

Sue an me lookin down hard, an there on the groun nex to the lake, lookin back at us, is about a thousan natives, all with they arms raised up towards us. They is wearin little grass skirts an has their hair all flayed out, an some is carryin shields an spears.

"Damn," I say, "what you say they is?"

"Cargo Cult," Major Fritch say. "In World War II we used to drop packages of candy an stuff like that on these jungle bunnies to keep em on our side, an they ain't never forgot it. Figgered it was God or somebody doin it, an ever since, they is waiting for us to come back. Even built crude runways an all—see down there? They has got a landin zone all marked off with them big roun black markers."

"Them things look more like cookin pots to me," I says.

"Yeah, they do, sort of," Major Fritch say curiously.

"Ain't this where cannibals come from?" I axed.

"I reckon we will soon find out," she say.

Spaceship is gently swingin towards the lake, an jus afore we hit, they start beatin they drums an movin they mouths up and down. We can't hear nothin on account of bein in the capsule, but our maginations doin just fine.

14

OUR LANDIN IN THE LITTLE LAKE WAS NOT TOO BAD. THEY was a splash an a bounce an then we is back on earth again. Everthin got real quiet, an me an Sue and Major Fritch peek out the winder.

They is a whole tribe of natives standin bout ten feet away on the shore, lookin at us, an they is bout the fiercest-looking folks imaginable—scowlin an leanin forward so's to see what we is. Major Fritch say maybe they is upset cause we didn't thow them nothin from the spaceship. Anyhow, she say she is gonna set down an try to figger out what to do now, on account of we has somehow got this far okay an she don't want to make no false moves with these spooks. Seven or eight of they biggest fellas jumps into the water and begin pushin us over to land.

Major Fritch still be settin there figgerin when there is a big knock at the door of the spaceship. We all look at each other an Major Fritch say,"Don't nobody do nothin."

An I say,"Maybe they be gettin angry if we don't let em in."

"Just be quiet,"she say,"an maybe they think nobody's in here an go away."

So we waited, but sure enough, after a wile they is another knock on the spaceship.

I say,"It ain't polite not to answer the door,"an Major Fritch hiss back at me,"Shut up your dumbfool ass—can't you see these people is dangerous?"

Then all of a sudden ole Sue go over an open the door hissef. Standin there outside is the biggest coon I has seen since we played them Nebraska corn shucker jackoffs in the Orange Bowl.

He got a bone thru his nose an is wearin a grass skirt an carryin a spear an has a lot of beads strung aroun his neck, an his hair look somethin like that Beatle wig Mad Tom o'Bedlam wore in the Shakespeare play.

This feller seem extremely startled to find Sue starin back at him from inside the spaceship door. As a matter of fact, he is so suprised that he keel over in a dead faint. Major Fritch an me is peepin out the winder again, an when all them other natives seen this feller keel over, they run off in the shrubs an hide—I guess to wait an see what's gonna happen nex.

Major Fritch say,"Hole still now—don't make a move,"but ole Sue, he grapped holt of a bottle that was settin there an he jump out on the groun an pour it in the feller's face to revive him. All of a sudden the feller set up an start sputterin an coughin an spittin an shakin his head from side to side. He was revived all right, but what Sue had grapped an poured in his face was the bottle what I used to pee in. Then the feller recognize Sue again, an he thowed his hans up an fall over on his face an begin bowin an scrapin like a Arab.

An then out from the bushes come the rest of them, movin slow an scarit-like, eyes big as saucers, ready to thow they spears. The feller on the groun stop bowin for a moment an look up an when he seen the others, he holler out somethin an they put down they spears an come up to the spaceship an gather aroun it.

"They look friendly enough now,"Major Fritch say."I spose we better go on out an identify ourselfs. The people from NASA will be here in a few minutes to pick us up."As it turns out, that is the biggest piece of bullshit I have ever heard in my life—before or since.

Anyhow, Major Fritch an me, we walk on out of the spaceship an all them natives goin"ooooh"an"ahhhh."That ole boy on the groun, he look at us real puzzled-like, but then he get up an say,"Hello—me good boy. Who you?"an he stick out his han.

I shake his han, but then Major Fritch start tryin to tell him who we is, sayin we is,"Participants in the NASA multi-orbital pre-planetary sub-gravitational inter-spheroid space-flight trainin mission."

The feller jus stan there gapin at us like we was spacemen, an so I says,"We is Americans,"an all of a sudden his eyes light up an he say,"Do tell! Americans! What a jolly fine show—I say!"

"You speak English?"Major Fritch axed.

"Why hell yes,"he say."I've been to America before. During the war.

I was recruited by the Office of Strategic Services to learn English, and then sent back here to organize our people in guerrilla warfare against the Japanese."At this, Sue's eyes get big an bright.

It seem kinda funny to me, though—a big ole boon like this speaking such good American out in the middle of noplace, so I says,"Where'd you go t'school?"

"Why, I went to Yale, old sport,"he says."Boola-Boola, an all that."When he say"boola-boola,"all them other Sambo's start chantin it too, an the drums start up again, until the big guy wave them quiet.

"My name is Sam,"he say."At least that's what they called me at Yale. My real name's quite a mouthful. What a delight you dropped in. Would you like some tea?"

Me an Major Fritch be lookin at each other. She is damn near speechless, so I says,"Yeah, that'd be good,"an then Major Fritch get her voice back an speak up kind of high-pitched,"You ain't got a phone we can use, do you?"she say.

Big Sam sort of scowl an wave his hans an the drums start up again an we be escorted into the jungle with everbody chantin"boola-boola."

They has got theyselfs a little village set up in the jungle with grass huts an shit jus like in the movies, an Big Sam's hut is the grandest of all. Out in front he got a chair look like a throne, an four or five women wearin nothin on top are doin whatever he say. One of the things he say is for them to get us some tea, an then he point to a couple of big stones for Major Fritch an me to set down on. Sue has been followin along behin us all the way, holdin on to my han, an Big Sam motion for him to set on the groun.

"That's a terrific ape you have there,"Sam says."Where'd you get him?"

"He works for NASA,"Major Fritch says. She ain't lookin none too happy bout our situation.

"You don't say?"says Big Sam."Is he paid?"

"I think he'd like a banana,"I says. Big Sam said somethin an one of the woman natives brung Sue a banana.

"I'm awfully sorry,"Big Sam say,"I think I haven't asked your names."

"Major Janet Fritch, United States Air Force. Serial number 04534573. That's all I'm going to tell you."

"Oh, my dear woman,"says Big Sam."You are not a prisoner here. We are just poor backward tribesmen. Some say we've not progressed much since the Stone Age. We mean you no harm."

"I ain't got nothin else to say till I can use the phone,"Major Fritch say.

"Very well then,"says Big Sam."And what of you, young man?"

"My name is Forrest,"I tell him.

"Really,"he say."Is that taken from your famous Civil War General Nathan Bedford Forrest?"

"Yep,"I says.

"How very interesting. I say, Forrest, where did you go to school?"

I started to say I went up to the University of Alabama for a wile, but then I decided to play it safe, an so I tole him I went to Harvard, which was not exactly a lie.

"Ah, Harvard—the old Crimson,"Big Sam says."Yes—I knew it well. Lovely bunch of fellows—even if they couldn't get into Yale,"an then he start to laugh real loud."Actually, you do look sort of like a Harvard man at that,"he say. Somehow, I figger that trouble lay ahead.

It was late in the afternoon an Big Sam tole a couple of them native women to show us where we is gonna stay. It is a grass hut with a dirt floor an a little entranceway, an it sort of remind me of the hovel where King Lear went. Two big ole fellers with spears come up an be standin guard outside our door.

All night long them natives be beatin on they drums an chantin"boola-boola,"an we could see out the entrance that they have set up a great big cauldron an built a fire under it. Me an Major Fritch don't know what to make of all this, but I reckon ole Sue does, cause he settin over in the corner by hissef, lookin glum.

Bout nine or ten o'clock they still ain't fed us no food, an Major Fritch say maybe I ought to go axe Big Sam for our supper. I start to go out the door of the hovel but them two natives cross they spears in front of me, an I get the message an go back inside. Suddenly it dawn on me how come we ain't been invited to supper—we is the supper. It is a bleak outlook.

Then the drums quit an they stop chantin"boola-boola."Outside we hear somebody squawkin an he is answered by somebody else squawkin that sound like Big Sam. That go on for a wile, an the argument get real heated up. Just as it seem like they can't shout any louder, we hear this big"conk,"which sound like somebody get hit over the head with a board or somethin. Everthing get quiet for a moment, then the drums start up again an everbody chantin"boola-boola"once more.

Next mornin, we settin there an Big Sam come thru the door an he say,"Hello—did you have a nice sleep?"

"Hell no,"Major Fritch say."How in God's name does you expect us to sleep with all that racket out there?"

Big Sam get a pained look on his face, an say,"Oh, I'm sorry about that. But you see, my people were, ah, sort of expectin a gift of some sort when they saw your vehicle drop from the sky. We have been waiting since 1945 for the return of your people an their presents to us. When they saw that you had no presents, naturally they assumed that *you* were the present, and they were prepared to cook you and eat you until I persuaded them otherwise."

"You're shittin me, buster,"Major Fritch say.

"To the contrary,"says Big Sam."You see, my people are not exactly what you would call *civilized*—at least by your standards—as they have a particular affection for human flesh. Especially white meat."

"Do you mean to tell me you people are cannibals?"Major Fritch say.

Big Sam shrug his shoulders."That's bout the size of it."

"That's disgusting,"says Major Fritch."Listen, you has got to see to it that we is not harmed, an that we get out of here an back to civilization. There is probably a search party from NASA about to arrive any minute. I demand that you treat us with the dignity you would accord any allied nation."

"Ah," Big Sam say, "that was precisely what they had in mind last night."

"Now see here!" says Major Fritch. "I demand that we be set free this instant, and allowed to make our way to the nearest city or town where there is a telephone."

"I am afraid," Big Sam say, "that would be impossible. Even if we did turn you loose, the pygmies would get you before you went a hundred yards into the jungle."

"Pygmies?" say Major Fritch.

"We have been at war with the pygmies for many generations. Somebody stole a pig once, I think—nobody remembers who or where—it is lost in legend. But we are virtually surrounded by the pygmies, and have been ever since anyone can remember."

"Well," says Major Fritch, "I'd rather us take our chances with pygmies than with a bunch of fucking cannibals—the pygmies ain't cannibals, is they?"

"No, madam," Big Sam say, "they are head-hunters."

"Terrific," Major Fritch say sourly.

"Now last night," Big Sam says, "I managed to save you from the cooking pot, but I am not sure how long I can keep my people at bay. They are determined to turn your appearance into some sort of gain."

"Is that so?" Major Fritch says. "Like what?"

"Well, for one thing, your ape. I think they would at least like to be able to eat him."

"That ape is the sole property of the United States of America," says

Major Fritch.

"Nonetheless," Big Sam says, "I think it would be a diplomatic gesture on your part."

Ole Sue be frownin an noddin his head slowly an lookin sorrowfully out the door.

"And then," Big Sam continue, "I think that wile you are here, you could perhaps do some work for us."

"What sort of work?" Major Fritch say suspiciously.

"Well," say Big Sam, "farming work. Agriculture. You see, I have been trying to improve the ignominious lot of my people for many years. And not too long ago I stumbled on an idea. If we can simply turn the fertile soil here to our advantage, and bring to it some of the modern techniques of agronomy, we might thus begin to haul ourselves out of our tribal predicament and assume a role in the world marketplace. In short, turn ourselves away from this backward and stale economy and become a viable, cultured race of peoples."

"What kind of farming?" Major Fritch axed.

"Cotton, my dear woman, cotton! King of cash crops! The plant that built an empire in your own country some years ago."

"You expectin us to grow cotton!" Major Fritch squawked.

"You bet your sweet ass I do, sister," Big Sam say. ?

15

WELL, HERE WE IS, PLANTIN COTTON. ACRES AN ACRES AN acres of it. All up an down the whole creation. If they is anythin sure in my life, it is that if we ever get our asses outta here, I don't never want to be no cotton farmer.

Several things done happened after that first day in the jungle with Big Sam an the cannibals. First, Major Fritch an me has convinced Big Sam not to make us give po ole Sue to his tribe to eat. We has persuaded him that Sue would be of a lot more use heppin us plant the cotton than he would be as a meal. An so ever day there is ole Sue out there with us, wearin a big straw hat an carryin a gunnysack, plantin cotton.

Also, bout the third or forth week we was there, Big Sam come into our hovel an say, "Look here, Forrest old boy, do you play chess?"

An I says, "No."

An he say,"Well, you're a Harvard man, you might like to learn."

An I nod my head, an that's how I learnt to play chess.

Ever evenin when we is thru work in the cotton fields, Big Sam'd get out his chess set an we'd set aroun the fire an play till late at night. He showed me all the moves, an for the first few days he taught me strategy. But after that, he quit doin it cause I beat him a game or two.

After a wile, the games get longer. Sometime they last for several days, as Big Sam can not make up his mind where to move to. He'd sit an study them chessmen an then he'd do somethin with one of them, but I always managed to beat him. Sometimes he'd get real angry with hissef, an pound on his foot with a stick or butt his head against a rock or somethin.

"For a Harvard man, you is a pretty good chess player,"he'd say, or he'd say,"See here, Forrest—why did you make that last move?"I wouldn't say nothin, or jus shrug my shoulders, an that woud send Big Sam into a rage.

One day he say,"You know, Forrest, I am surely glad you have come here, so I can have somebody to play chess with, an I am glad I have saved you from that cooking pot. Only thing is, I really would like to win jus one chess game from you."

At that, Big Sam be lickin his chops, an it didn't take no idiot to figger out that if I let him win jus one game, he was gonna be satisfied, an have me for his supper, then an there. Kinda kep me on my toes, if you know what I mean.

Meantime, a very strange thing has happened with Major Fritch.

One day she is walkin back from the cotton fields with Sue an me, when a big ole black arm poke out from a clump of bushes an beckon her over. Me an Sue stopped, an Major Fritch walk over to the clump of bushes an say, "Who's that in there?" All of a sudden, the big ole arm reached out an grapped a holt of Major Fritch an snatched her into the bush. Sue an me looked at each other an then run over to where she was. Sue got there first an I was about to leap into the bushes mysef, when Sue stop me. He start shakin his head an wavin me away, an we walked off a little bit an waited. They was all sorts of souns comin from in there, an the bushes is shakin like crazy. I finally figgered out what was goin on, but from the soun of Major Fritch's voice, it didn't appear she was in no danger or nothin, so Sue an me went on back to the village.

Bout a hour later, here come Major Fritch an this great big ole feller who is grinnin ear-to-ear. She has got him by the han, leadin him along. She bring him into the hovel an say to me, "Forrest, I want you to meet Grurck," an she lead him forward.

"Hi," I say. I had seen this feller aroun the village before. Grurck be grinnin an noddin an I nodded back. Sue, he be scratchin his balls.

"Grurck done axed me to move in with him," she say, "an I think I will, since it is sort of crowded in here for the three of us, wouldn't you say?"

I nod my head.

"Forrest. You wouldn't tell nobody bout this, would you?" Major Fritch axed.

Now who in hell was she thinkin I would tell, is what I want to know? But I just shook my head, an Major Fritch got her shit an went off with Grurck to his place. An that's the way it was.

The days an months an finally the years come an go, an ever day me an Sue an Major Fritch be workin in the cotton fields, an I am beginnin to feel like Uncle Remus or somebody. At night, after I finish wuppin Big Sam at chess, I go into the hovel with ole Sue an we set aroun for a wile. It has got to where Sue an me can sort of talk to each other, gruntin an makin faces an wavin our hans. After a long time I am able to piece together his life story, an it turn out to be bout as sorry as mine.

When he was jus a little bitty ape, Sue's mama an poppa was walkin in the jungle one day when these guys come along an thowed a net over them, an drug them off. He managed to get on with an aunt an uncle till they kicked him out for eatin too much, an then he was on his own.

He was okay, jus swingin in the trees an eatin bananas till one day he got curious bout what is goin on in the rest of the world, an he swang hissef thru tree after tree till he come on a village near the edge of the jungle. He is thirsty an come down an set by a stream to drink some water when this feller come by paddlin a canoe. Sue ain't never seen a canoe, so he set there watchin it an the feller paddle over to him. He think the feller want to give him a ride, but instead, the feller conked Sue over the head with his oar an hog-tied him an nex thing he knew, he was sold to some guy that put him in a exhibit in Paris.

There was this other orangutang in the exhibit, name of Doris, what was one of the finest-looking apes he had ever seed, an after a wile, they fell in love. The guy that had the exhibit took them aroun the world, an everplace he'd go, the main attraction was to put Doris an Sue together in a cage so's everbody could watch them screw—that was the kind of exhibit it was. Anyway, it was kinda embarrassin for ole Sue, but it were the only chance they had.

Then one time they was on exhibit in Japan, an some guy come up to the feller running the show an offer to buy Doris. So off she went, Sue knowed not where, an he was by hissef.

That caused a definate change in Sue's attitude. He got grouchy, an when they put him on display, he took to growlin an snarlin an finally he begun takin a shit an then flingin the shit thru the cage bars all over them people what had paid their good money to see what an orangutang acts like.

After a wile of this, the exhibit feller got fed up an sold Sue to the NASA people an that's how come he wind up here. I know how he feels a little, cause he's still lonesome for Doris, an I'm still lonesome for Jenny Curran, an ain't a day go by I ain't wonderin what's become of her. But here we both is, stuck out in the middle of nowhere.

The cotton farmin adventure of Big Sam's is beyon anyone's wildest dreams. We has sowed an harvested bale after bale, an they is storin it in big grass shacks built up off the groun. Finally one day, Big Sam say they is fixin to construct a big boat—a barge—to load up the cotton an fight our way thru pygmy country down to where we can sell the cotton an make a fortune.

"I have got it all figured out," Big Sam says. "First we auction off the cotton and get our money. Then we will use it to buy the kinds of things my people need."

I axed him what was that, an he say,"Oh, you know, old sport, beads and trinkets, perhaps a mirror or two—a portable radio and maybe a box of good Cuban cigars—and a case or two of booze."

So this is the kind of deal we is in.

Anyhow, the months go by, an we is harvesting the last cotton crop of the season. Big Sam has done just bout finished the river barge that is to take us thru pygmy country to the town, an the night before we is to leave, they hold a big hoedown to celebrate everthin an also ward off evil spirits.

All the tribe be settin aroun the fire chantin"boola-boola"and beatin on they drums. They has also drug out that big cauldron an got it on the fire steamin an boilin, but Big Sam say it is only a"symbolic gesture."

We is settin there playin chess, an let me tell you this—I am so excited I am bout to bust! Just let us get near a town or city, an we is long gone. Ole Sue knows the deal too, cause he's settin over there with a big grin on his face, ticklin hissef under the arms.

We has played one or two games of chess an is bout to finish another, when I suddenly look down, an damned if Big Sam ain't got me in check. He is smilin so big, all I can see in the dark is his teeth, an I figger I had better get outta this situation quick.

Only problem is, I can't. Wile I've been assin aroun countin my chickens afore they're hatched, I have put mysef in a impossible position on the chessboard. They ain't no way out.

I studied that thing for a wile, my frown lit up plain as day from the fire's reflection off Big Sam's smilin teeth, an then I says,"Ah, look here—

I got to go pee."Big Sam nod, still grinnin, an I'll tell you this, it was the first time I can remember when sayin somethin like that got me *out* of trouble instead of in it.

I went on back behin the hovel an took a pee, but then instead of goin back to the chess game, I went in an got ole Sue an splained to him what the deal was. Then I snuck up on Grurck's hut an whispered for Major Fritch. She come out, an I tole her too, an say we'd better get our butts outta here afore we is all parboiled or somethin.

Well, we all decided to make a break for it. Grurck, he say he's comin with us on account of he's in love with Major Fritch—or however he expressed it. Anyway, the four of us started creepin out of the village an we got down to the edge of the river an was just bout to get in one of the native canoes, when all of a sudden I look up an standin there over me is Big Sam with about a thousan of his natives, lookin mean an disappointed.

"Come now, old sport,"he say,"did you really think you could outsmart this old devil?"An I tell him,"Oh, we was jus goin for a canoe ride in the moonlite—you know what I mean?"

"Yeah,"he say, he knowed what I meant, an then his men grapped us up an haul us back to the village under armed guard. The cookin cauldron is bubblin an steamin to beat the band an they has got us tied to stakes in the groun an the outlook is somethin less than rosy.

"Well, old sport,"Big Sam say,"this is a unfortunate turn of events indeed. But look at it this way, you will at least be able to console yourself by the knowledge that you have fed a hungry mouth or two. And also, I must tell you this—you are without a doubt the best chess player I have ever encountered, and I was the chess champion of Yale for three of the four years I was there.

"As for you, madam," Big Sam say to Major Fritch, "I am sorry to have to bring your little *affaire d'amour* with old Grurck here to an end, but you know how it is."

"No I *don't* know how it is, you despicable savage," Major Fritch say. "Where do you get off, anyway? You oughta be ashamed of yoursef!"

"Perhaps we can serve you an Grurck on the same platter," Big Sam chuckled, "a little light an dark meat—myself, I'll take a thigh, or possibly a breast—now that would be a nice touch."

"You vile, unspeakable ass!" say Major Fritch.

"Whatever," Big Sam says. "And now, let the feast begin!"

They begun untyin us an a bunch of them jiggaboos hauled us towards the cookin pot. They lifted up po ole Sue first, cause Big Sam say he will make good "stock," an they was holdin him above the cauldron about to thow him in, when lo an behole, a arrow come out of noplace an strike one of the fellers hoistin up Sue. The feller fall down an Sue drop on top of him. Then more arrows come rainin down on us from the edge of the jungle, an everbody is in a panic.

"It is the pygmies!" shout Big Sam. "Get to your arms!" an everbody run to get they spears an knives.

Since we ain't got no spears or knives, Major Fritch, me an Sue an Grurck start runnin down towards the river again, but we ain't no more than ten feet down the path when all of a sudden we is snatched up feet first by some kind of snares set in the trees.

We is hangin there, upside down like bats, an all the blood rushin to our heads, when this little guy come out of the brush an he be laughin an gigglin at us all trussed up. All sorts of savage sounds are comin from the village, but after a wile, everthing quiet down. Then a bunch of other pygmies come an cut us down an tie our hans an feet an lead us back to the village.

It is a sight! They has captured Big Sam an all his natives an has them tied up han an foot too. Look like they is bout to thow them into the boilin pot.

"Well, old sport," Big Sam say, "seems like you were saved in the nick of time, doesn't it?"

I nod my head, but I ain't sure if we isn't jus out of the fryin pan an into the fire.

"Tell you what," says Big Sam, "looks like it's all over for me an my fellers, but maybe you have a chance. If you can get to that harmonica of yours an play a little tune or two, it might save your life. The king of the pygmies is crazy for American music."

"Thanks," I say.

"Don't mention it, old sport," Big Sam say. They lifted him up high an was holdin him over the boilin cauldron, an suddenly he call out to me, "Knight to bishop three—then rook ten to king seven—that's how I beat you!"

They was a big splash, and then all Big Sam's trussed-up natives begun chantin "boola-boola" again. Things are lookin down for us all.

16

AFTER THEY DONE FINISHED COOKIN BIG SAM'S TRIBE, AN shrinkin they heads, the pygmies slung us between long poles an carried us off like pigs into the jungle.

"What do you spose they intend to do with us?"Major Fritch call out to me.

"I don't know, an I don't give a shit,"I call back, an that were about the truth. I'm tired of all this crappola. A man can take jus so much.

Anyhow, after about a day or so we come to the village of the pygmies, an as you might expec, they has got a bunch of little tiny huts in a clearin in the jungle. They truck us up to a hut in the center of the clearin where there is a bunch of pygmies standin aroun—an one little ole feller with a long white beard an no teeth settin up in a high chair like a baby. I figger him to be the king of the pygmies.

They tumped us out onto the groun an untied us, an we stood up an dusted ourselfs off an the king of the pygmies commence jabberin some gibberish an then he get down from his chair an go straight up to Sue an kick him in the balls.

"How come he done that?"I axed Grurck, who had learnt to speak some English wile he was livin with Major Fritch.

"Him want to know if ape is boy or girl,"Grurck say.

I figger there must be a nicer way to find that out, but I ain't sayin nothin.

Then the king, he come up to me an start talkin some of that gibberish—pygmalion, or whatever it is—an I'm preparing to get kicked in the balls too, but Grurck say,"Him want to know why you livin with them awful cannibals."

"Tell him it weren't exactly our idea,"Major Fritch pipe up an say.

"I got a idea,"I says."Tell him we is American musicians."

Grurck say this to the king an he be peerin at us real hard, an then he axe Grurck somethin.

"What's he say?"Major Fritch want to know.

"Him axe what the ape plays,"say Grurck.

"Tell him the ape plays the spears,"I say, an Grurck do that, an then the king of the pygmies announce he want to hear us perform.

I get out my harmonica an start playin a little tune—"De Camptown Races."King of the pygmies listen for a minute, then he start clappin his hans an doin what look to be a clog dance.

After I'm finished, he say he wants to know what Major Fritch an

Grurck plays, an I tell Grurck to say Major Fritch plays the knives an that Grurck don't play nothin—he is the manager.

King of the pygmies look sort of puzzled an say he ain't never heard of anybody playin knives or spears before, but he tell his men to give Sue some spears an Major Fritch some knives an let's see what sort of music we come up with.

Soon as we get the spears an knives, I say,"Okay—now!"an ole Sue conk the king of the pygmies over the head with his spear an Major Fritch threatened a couple of pygmies with her knives an we run off into the jungle with the pygmies in hot pursuit.

The pygmies be thowin all sorts of rocks an shit at us from behin, an shootin they bows an arrows an darts from blowguns an such. Suddenly we come out on the bank of a river an ain't no place to go, an the pygmies are catchin up fast. We is bout to jump into the river an swim for it, when suddenly from the opposite side of the river a rifle shot ring out.

The pygmies are right on top of us, but another rifle shot ring out an they turn tail an run back into the jungle. We be lookin across the river an lo an behole on the other bank they is a couple of fellers wearin bush jackets an them white pith helmets like you used to see in *Ramar of the Jungle*. They step into a canoe an be paddlin towards us, an as they get closer, I seen one of them is got NASA stamped on his pith helmet. We is finally rescued.

When the canoe reach our shore, the guy with NASA stamped on his helmet get out an come up to us. He go right up to ole Sue an stick out his han an say,"Mister Gump, I presume?"

"Where the fuck has you assholes been?"hollared Major Fritch."We been stranded in the jungle nearly four goddamn years!"

"Sorry bout that, ma'am,"the feller say,"but we has got our priorities, too, you know."

Anyway, we is at last saved from a fate worse than death, an they loaded us up in the canoe an started paddlin us downriver. One of the fellers say,"Well folks, civilization is just aroun the corner. I reckon you'll all be able to sell your stories to a magazine an make a fortune."

"Stop the canoe!"Major Fritch suddenly call out.

The fellers look at one another, but they paddle the canoe over to the bank.

"I have made a decision,"Major Fritch say."For the first time in my life, I have found a man that truly understands me, an I am not going to let him go. For nearly four years, Grurck an I have lived happily in this land, an I have decided to stay here with him. We will go off in the jungle an make a new life for ourselfs, an raise a family an live happily ever after."

"But this man is a cannibal,"one of the fellers say.

"Eat your heart out, buster,"says Major Fritch, an she an Grurck get out of the canoe an start back into the jungle again, han in han. Jus before they disappeared, Major Fritch turn aroun an give Sue an me a little wave, an then off they go.

I looked back to the end of the canoe, an ole Sue is settin there twistin his fingers.

"Wait a minute,"I says to the fellers. I go back an set down on the seat nex to Sue an say, "What you thinkin bout?"

Sue ain't sayin nothin, but they is a little bitty tear in his eye, an I knowed then what was bout to happen. He grapped me aroun the shoulders in a big hug, an then leaped out of the boat an ran up a tree on the shore. Last we seen of him, he is swingin away thru the jungle on a vine.

The feller from NASA be shakin his head. "Well, what about you, numbnuts? You gonna follow your friends there into Bonzoland?"

I looked after them for a minute, then I said, "Uh, uh," an set back down in the canoe. Wile they was paddlin us away, don't you believe I didn't think bout it for a moment. But I jus couldn't do it. I reckon I got other weenies to roast.

They flown me back to America an tole me on the way how there was to be a big welcome home reception for me, but seems like I have heard that before.

Sure enough tho, soon as we landed in Washington bout a million people was on han, cheerin an clappin an actin like they is glad to see me. They drove me into town in the back seat of a big ole black car an said they was takin me to the White House to see the President. Yep, I been there before too.

Well, when we get to the White House, I'm expectin to see the same ole President what fed me breakfast an let me watch "The Beverly Hillbillies," but they is got a new President now—feller with his hair all slicked back, puffy little cheeks an a nose look like Pinocchio's.

"Tell me now," this President say, "did you have an exciting trip?"

A feller in a suit standin next to the President lean over an whisper somethin to him, an suddenly the President say,"Oh, ah, accually what I meant was, how great it is that you have escaped from your ordeal in the jungle."

The feller in the suit whisper somethin else to the President, an he say to me,"Er, now what about your companion?"

"Sue?"I say.

"Was that her name?"Now he be lookin at a little card in his han."Says here it was a Major Janet Fritch, and that even as you were being rescued she was dragged off into the jungle by a cannibal."

"Where it say that?"I axed.

"Right here,"the President say.

"That's not so,"I says.

"Are you suggesting I am a liar?"say the President.

"I'm jus sayin it ain't so,"I says.

"Now look here,"say the President,"I am your commander in chief. I am not a crook. I do not lie!"

"I am very sorry,"I says,"but it ain't the truth bout Major Fritch. You jus take that off a card, but—"

"Tape!"the President shout.

"Huh?"I says.

"No, no,"says the feller in the suit."He said '*take*'—not 'tape'—Mister President."

"TAPE!"scream the President."I told you never to mention that word in my presence again! You are all a bunch of disloyal Communist swines."The President be poundin hissef on the knee with his fist.

"None of you understand. I don't know anything bout anything! I never heard of anything! And if I did, I either forgot it, or it is top secret!"

"But Mister President,"say the feller in the suit,"he didn't say it. He only said—"

"Now *you* are calling me a liar!"he say."You're fired!"

"But you can't fire me,"the feller say."I am the Vice President."

"Well, pardon me for saying so,"says the President,"but you are never going to make President if you go aroun calling your commander in chief a liar."

"No, I guess you're right,"say the Vice President."I beg your pardon."

"No, I beg yours,"the President say.

"Whatever,"say the Vice President, kinda fiddlin with hissef."If you will all excuse me now, I have to go pee."

"That's the first sensible idea I have heard all day,"say the President. Then he turn to me an axe,"Say, aren't you the same fellow that played ping-pong and saved the life of old Chairman Mao?"

I says,"Yup,"an the President say,"Well what did you want to do a thing like that for?"

An I says,"Cause he was drownin,"an the President say,"You should have held him under, instead of saving him. Anyway, it's history now, because the son of a bitch died while you were away in the jungle."

"You got a tv set?"I axed.

The President look at me kind of funny."Yeah, I have one, but I don't watch it much these days. Too much bad news."

"You ever watch 'The Beverly Hillbillies'?"I say.

"It's not on yet,"he say.

"What is?"I axed.

" 'To Tell the Truth'—but you don't want to look at that—it's a bunch of shit."Then he say,"Look here, I have a meeting to go to, why don't I walk you to the door?"When we get outside on the porch, an the President say in a very low voice,"Listen, you want to buy a watch?"

I say,"Huh?"an he step over close to me an shove up the sleeve on his suit an lo an behole he must of had twenty or thirty wristwatches aroun his arm.

"I ain't got no money,"I says.

The President, he roll down his sleeve an pat me on the back."Well, you come back when you do and we'll work something out, okay?"

He shook my han an a bunch of photographers come up an start takin our picher an then I'm gone. But I'll say this, that President seem like a nice feller after all.

Anyhow, I'm wonderin what they gonna do with me now, but I don't have to wonder long.

It took bout a day or so for things to quiet down, an they had put me up in a hotel, but then a couple of fellers come in one afternoon an say,"Listen here, Gump, the free ride's over. The government ain't payin for none of this anymore—you're on your own now."

"Well, okay,"I say,"but how bout givin me a little travelin money to get home on. I'm kinda light right now."

"Forget it, Gump," they say. "You is lucky not to be in jail for conkin the Clerk of the Senate on the head with that medal. We done you a favor to get you off that rap—but we is washin our hans of your ass as of right now."

So I had to leave the hotel. Since I ain't got no things to pack, it wadn't hard, an I just went out on the street. I walked a wile, down past the White House where the President live, an to my suprise they is a whole bunch of people out front got on rubber masks of the President's face an they is carryin some kind of signs. I figger he must be pleased to be so popular with everbody.

17

EVEN THO THEY SAID THEY WOULDN'T GIVE ME NO MONEY, one of the fellers did loan me a dollar before I lef the hotel. First chance I got, I phoned home to the po house where my mama was stayin to let her know I'm okay. But one of them nuns says,"We ain't got no Mrs. Gump here no longer."

When I axed where she was, the nun say,"Dunno—she done run off with some protestant."I thanked her an hanged up the phone. In a way, I'm sort of relieved. At least mama done run off with *somebody*, an ain't in the po house no more. I figger I got to find her, but to tell the truth, I ain't in no big hurry, cause sure as it's gonna rain, she'll be bawlin an hollerin an fussin at me on account of I lef home.

It did rain. Rained cats an dogs an I foun me a awnin to stand under till some guy come out an run me off. I was soakin wet an cold an walkin past some government buildin in Washington when I seen a big ole plastic garbage bag settin in the middle of the sidewalk. Just as I get close to it, the bag commenced to move a little bit, like there is somethin in there!

I stopped an went up to the bag an nudged it a little with my toe. Suddenly the bag jump bout four feet back an a voice come out from under it, say, "Git the fuck away from me!"

"Who is that in there?" I axed, an the voice say back, "This is *my* grate—you go find your own."

"What you talkin bout?" I say.

"My grate," the voice say. "Git off my grate!"

"What grate?" I axed.

All of a sudden the bag lift up a little an a feller's head peek out, squintin up at me like I'm some kinda idiot.

"You new in town or somethin?" the feller says.

"Sort of," I answered. "I'm jus tryin to get outta the rain."

The feller under the bag is pretty sorry-lookin, half bald-headed, ain't shaved in months, eyes all red an bloodshot an most of his teeth gone.

"Well," he say, "in that case I reckon it okay for a little wile—here." He reach up an han me another garbage bag, all folded up.

"What I'm sposed to do with this?" I axed.

"Open it up an git under it, you damn fool—you said you wanted to git outta the rain." An then he pull his bag back down over hissef.

Well, I did what he said, an to tell you the truth, it wadn't so bad, really. They was some hot air comin up outta the grate an it make the bag all warm an cozy inside an kep off the rain. We be squattin side-by-side on the grate with the bags over us an after a wile the feller says over to me, "What's your name anyway?"

"Forrest," I says.

"Yeah? I knew a guy named Forrest once. Long time ago."

"What's your name?" I axed.

"Dan," he say.

"Dan? *Dan?*—hey, wait a minute," I says. I thowed off my garbage bag an went an lifted up the bag off the feller an it was him! Ain't got no legs, an he is settin on a little wood cart with roller-skate wheels on the bottom. Must of aged twenty years, an I could hardly recognize him. But it was him. It was ole Lieutenant Dan!

After he had got out of the Army hospital, Dan went back to Connecticut to try to get back his ole job teachin history. But they wadn't no history job available, so they made him teach math. He hated math, an besides, the math class was on the secont floor of the school an he had a hell of a time makin it up the stairs with no legs an all. Also, his wife done run off with a tv producer that lived in New Yawk an she sued him for divorce on grounds of "incompatibility."

He took to drinkin an lost his job an jus didn't do nothin for a wile. Thieves robbed his house of everthin he had an the artificial legs they had give him at the VA hospital were the wrong size. After a few years, he said, he jus "give up," an took to livin like a bum. There's a little money ever month from his disability pension, but most of the time he jus give it away to the other bums.

"I dunno, Forrest," he say, "I guess I'm jus waitin to die or somethin."

Dan han me a few bucks an say to go aroun the corner an git us a couple of bottles of Red Dagger wine. I jus got one bottle tho, an used the money for mine to git one of them ready-made sambwiches, cause I ain't had nothin to eat all day.

"Well, old pal," Dan say after he has polished off half his wine, "tell me what you been doin since I saw you last."

So I did. I tole him about goin to China an playin ping-pong, an findin Jenny Curran again, an playin in The Cracked Eggs band an the peace demonstration where I thowed my medal away an got put in jail.

"Yeah, I remember that one all right. I think I was still here in the hospital. I thought bout going down there mysef, but I guess I wouldn't have thowed my medals away. Look here," he say. He unbutton his jacket an inside, on his shirt, is all his medals—Purple Heart, Silver Star—must of been ten or twelve of them.

"They remind me of somethin," he said. "I'm not quite sure what—the war, of course, but that's jus a part of it. I have suffered a loss, Forrest, far greater than my legs. It's my spirit, my soul, if you will. There is only a blank there now—medals where my soul used to be."

"But what about the 'natural laws' that's in charge of everthin?" I axe him. "What about the 'scheme of things' that we has all got to fit ourself into?"

"Fuck all that," he say. "It was just a bunch of philosophic bullshit."

"But ever since you tole it to me, that's what I been goin by. I been lettin the 'tide' carry me an tryin to do my best. Do the right thing."

"Well, maybe it works for you, Forrest. I thought it was working for me too—but look at me. Just *look* at me," he say. "What good am I? I'm a goddamn legless freak. A bum. A drunkard. A thirty-five-year-old vagrant."

"It could be worse," I says.

"Oh yeah? How?" he say, an I reckon he got me there, so I finished tellin him bout mysef—gettin thowed in the loony bin an then bein shot up in the rocket an landin down with the cannibals an bout ole Sue an Major Fritch an the pygmies.

"Well my God, Forrest my boy, you sure as hell have had some adventures," Dan say. "So how come you are sittin here with me on the grates under a garbage bag?"

"I dunno," I says, "but I ain't plannin to stay here long."

"What you got in mind then?"

"Soon as this rain stops," I say, "I'm gonna get off my big fat butt an go lookin for Jenny Curran."

"Where is she?"

"Dunno that either," I says, "but I'll find out."

"Sounds like you might need some help," he say.

I look over at Dan an his eyes is gleamin from behin his beard. Somethin is tellin me *he* is the one needs some hep, but that's okay with me.

Ole Dan an me, we went to a mission flophouse that night on account of it didn't stop rainin, an Dan, he paid them fifty cents apiece for our suppers an a quarter for our beds. You could of got supper free for settin an listenin to a sermon or somesuch, but Dan say he'd sleep out in the rain afore wastin our precious time hearin a Bible-thumper give us his view of the world.

Next mornin Dan loaned me a dollar an I foun a pay phone an called up to Boston to ole Mose, that used to be the drummer for The Cracked Eggs. Sure enough, he still there in his place, an is damn suprised to hear from me.

"Forrest—I don't believe it!"Mose say."We had given your ass up for lost!"

The Cracked Eggs, he says, have broken up. All the money that Mister Feeblestein have promised them is eaten up by expenses or somethin, an after the secont record they didn't get no more contracts. Mose say people is listenin to a new kind of music nowRollin Stoned's or the Iggles or somethin—an most of the fellers in The Cracked Eggs is gone someplace an foun real jobs.

Jenny, Mose say, is not been heard of in a long wile. After she had gone down to Washington for the peace demonstration where I was arrested, she went back with The Cracked Eggs for a few months, but Mose say somethin in her jus wadn't the same. One time he say, she broke up cryin on the stage an they had to play a instrumental to get thru the set. Then she started drinkin vodka an showin up late for performances an they was bout to speak to her bout it when she jus done up an quit.

Mose say he personally feel her behavior has somethin to do with me, but she never would talk bout it. She moved out of Boston a couple of weeks later, sayin she was goin to Chicago, an that is the last he seen of her in nearly five years.

I axed if he knew any way for me to reach her, an he say maybe he have a ole number she give him jus before she lef. He leave the phone an come back a few minutes later an give the number to me. Other than that, he say, "I ain't got a clue."

I tole him to take care, an if I ever get up to Boston I will look him up.

"You still playin your harmonica?" Mose axed.

"Yeah, sometimes," I say.

I went an borrowed another dollar from Dan an called the number in Chicago.

"Jenny Curran—Jenny?" a guy's voice say. "Oh, yeah—I remember her. Nice little piece of ass. Been a long time."

"You know where she's at?"

"Indianapolis is where she say she was goin when she lef here. Who knows? Got herself a job at Temperer."

"At what?"

"Temperer—the tire factory. You know, they make tires—for cars."

I thank the guy an went back an tole Dan.

"Well," he say, "I never been to Indianapolis. Heard it's nice there in the fall."

We started tryin to thumb a ride out of Washington, but didn't have no luck to speak of. A guy gave us a ride to the city limits on the back of a brick truck, but after that, nobody didn't want to pick us up. I guess we was too funny-lookin or somethin—Dan settin on his little roller dolly an my big ole ass standin nex to him. Anyhow, Dan say why don't we take a bus, cause he's got enough money for that. To tell you the truth, I felt bad about takin his money, but somehow I figgered that he wanted to go, and it would be good to get him outta Washington too.

An so we caught a bus to Indianapolis an I put Dan in the seat nex to me an stowed his little cart in the shelf up above. All the way there he be sluggin down Red Dagger wine an sayin what a shitty place the world is to live in. Maybe he's right. I don't know. I'm just a idiot anyhow.

The bus left us off in the middle of Indianapolis an Dan an me is standin on the street tryin to figger out what to do nex when a policeman come up an say, "Ain't no loiterin on the street," an so we moved on. Dan axed a feller where is the Temperer Tire Company an it is way outside of town so we started headin in that direction. After a wile there ain't no sidewalks an Dan can't push his little cart along, so I picked him up under one arm and the cart under the other an we kep on goin.

Bout noon, we seed a big sign say "Temperer Tires," an figger this be the place. Dan say he will wait outside an I go on in an they is a woman at the desk an I axed if I could see Jenny Curran. Woman look at a list an say Jenny is workin in "re-treads," but ain't nobody allowed to go there cept'n if they works in the plant. Well, I'm just standin there, tryin to decide what to do, an the woman say, "Look, honey, they is bout to get a lunch break in a minute or so, why don't you go roun to the side of the buildin. Probly she'll come out," so that's what I did.

They was a lot of folks come out an then, all by hersef, I seen Jenny walk thru a door an go over to a little spot under a tree an pull a sambwich out of a paper bag. I went over an sort of creeped behin her, an she's settin on the groun, an I says, "That shore look like a tasty sambwich." She didn't even look up. She kep starin right ahead, an say, "Forrest, it has to be you."

18

WELL, LET ME TELL YOU—THAT WERE THE HAPPIEST reunion of my life. Jenny is cryin an huggin me an I'm doin the same an everbody else in re-treads is standin there wonderin what is goin on. Jenny say she is off work in bout three hours, an for me an Dan to go over to this little tavern across the street an have a beer or somethin an wait for her. Then she will take us to her place.

We go to the tavern an Dan is drinkin some Ripple wine on account of they got no Red Dagger, but he say Ripple is better anyhow cause it got a nicer "bouquet."

Bunch of other fellers is in there too, playin darts an drinkin an arm rasslin each other at a table. One big ole guy seem to be the bes arm rassler of the tavern, an ever once in a wile some feller would come up an try to beat him but couldn't. They be bettin on it too, five an ten dollars a whack.

After a little bit, Dan whisper over to me, "Forrest, you think you could beat that big bozo over there at arm rasslin?" An I say I dunno, an Dan say, "Well, here's five bucks, cause I'm bettin you can."

So I go up an say to the feller, "Would you mine if I set down an arm rassle with you?"

He look up at me, smilin, an say, "Long as you got money, you is welcome to try."

So I set down an we grapped each other's hans an somebody say, "Go!" an the rassle is on. Other feller be gruntin an strainin like a dog tryin to shit a peach seed, but in about ten secons I had smushed his arm down on the table an whipped him at arm rasslin. All the other fellers had come gatherin aroun the table an were goin "oooh" an "ahh" an I could hear ole Dan shoutin an cheerin.

Well, the other feller ain't none too happy but he paid me five dollars an got up from the table.

"My elbow slipped," he say, "but nex time you come back here I want to have a go at you again, hear?" I nodded an went back to the table Dan was at an give him the money.

"Forrest," he say, "we may have foun a easy way to make ourselfs some bread." I axed Dan if I could have a quarter to git me a pickled egg from the jar on the counter, an he han me a dollar an say, "You git anything you want, Forrest. We is now got a way to earn a livelyhood."

After work, Jenny come over to the tavern an take us to her place. She is livin in a little apartment not too far from the Temperer Tire Company an has got it all fixed up nice with things like stuffed animals an strings of colored beads hangin from the bedroom door. We went out to a grocery an bought some chicken an Jenny cooked supper for Dan an me an I tole her all that had happened since I seen her last.

Mostly, she is curious about Major Fritch, but when I say she run off with a cannibal, Jenny seemed more relaxed bout it. She say life has not exactly been a bowl of cherries for her either durin the past few years.

After she lef The Cracked Eggs, Jenny done gone to Chicago with this girl she met in the peace movement. They had demonstrated in the streets an got thowed in jail a bunch of times an Jenny say she is finally gettin tired of havin to appear in court an besides, she is concerned that she is developin a long police record.

Anyhow, she is livin in this house with about fifteen people an she says they is not exactly her type of persons. Didn't wear no underwear or nothin, an nobody flushed the toilets. She an this guy decided to take an apartment together, cause he didn't like where they was livin neither, but that didn't work out.

"You know, Forrest," she say, "I even tried to fall in love with him, but I jus couldn't because I was thinkin of you."

She had wrote to her mama an axed her to get in touch with my mama to try an find out where I was bein kept, but her mama write her back sayin our house done burnt up an my mama is now livin in the po house, but by the time the letter get to Jenny, Mama done already run off with the protestant.

Anyhow, Jenny said she didn't have no money an so she heard they is hirin people at the tire company an she come down to Indianapolis to get a job. Bout that time she seen on the television that I am bout to be launched into space, but they is no time for her to get down to Houston. She say she watched,"with horror,"as my spaceship crashed, an she give me up for dead. Ever since, she jus been puttin in her time makin re-treads.

I took her an hole her in my arms an we stayed like that for a wile. Dan rolled hissef into the bathroom, say he's got to take a pee. When he's in there, Jenny axe how he gonna do that, an don't he need hep? an I say,"No, I seen him do it before. He can manage."

She shake her head an say,"This is where the Vietnam War have got us."

There ain't much disputin that either. It is a sad an sorry spectacle when a no-legged man have got to pee in his hat an then dump it over into the toilet.

The three of us settle into Jenny's little apartment after that. Jenny fixed up Dan a place in a corner of the livin room with a little mattress an she kep a jar on the bathroom floor so he wouldn't have to use his hat. Ever mornin she'd go off to the tire company an Dan an me would set aroun the house an talk an then go down to the little tavern near where Jenny worked to wait till she got off.

First week we started doin that, the guy I beat arm rasslin wanted a chance to git back his five bucks an I gave it to him. He tried two or three times more an in the end lost bout twenty-five dollars an after that he didn't come back no more. But they was always some other feller wanted to try his luck an after a month or two they was guys comin from all over town an from other little towns too. Dan an me, we is pullin in bout a hundrit fifty or two hundrit dollars a week, which weren't bad, let me tell you. An the owner of the tavern, he is sayin he gonna hole a national contest, an git the tv there an everthing. But before that happen, another thing come along that changed my life for sure.

One day a feller come into the tavern that was wearin a white suit an a Hiwaian shirt an a lot of gold jewelry aroun his neck. He set up at the bar wile I was finishin off some guy at arm rasslin an then he come an set down at our table.

"Name's Mike,"he say,"an I have heard bout you."

Dan axed what has he heard, an Mike say,"That this feller here is the strongest man in the world."

"What of it?"Dan says, an the feller say,"I think I got a idea how you can make a hell of a lot more money than this nickel an dime shit you're doin here."

"How's that?"Dan say.

"Rasslin,"says Mike,"but not this piss-ant stuff—I mean the real thing. In a ring with hundrits of thousands of payin customers."

"Rasslin who?"Dan axed.

"Whoever,"says Mike."They is a circuit of professional rasslers—The Masked Marvel, The Incredible Hulk, Georgeous George, Filthy McSwine—you name em. The top guys make a hundrit, two hundrit thousand dollars a year. We's start your boy here off slow. Teach him some of the holds, show him the ropes. Why, I bet in no time he'd be a big star—make everybody a pile of money."

Dan look at me, say,"What you think, Forrest?"

"I dunno,"I says."I was kinda thinkin bout goin back home an startin a little srimp bidness."

"Shrimp!"says Mike."Why boy, you can make fifty times more money doing this than shrimpin! Don't have to do it all your life—just a few years, then you'll have something to fall back on, money in the bank, a nest egg."

"Maybe I ought to axe Jenny,"I say.

"Look,"Mike say,"I come here to offer you a chance of a lifetime. You don't want it, jus say so, an I'll be on my way."

"No, no,"Dan say. Then he turn to me."Listen, Forrest, some of what this feller say make sense. I mean, how else you gonna earn enough money to start a srimp bidness?"

"Tell you what,"Mike say,"you can even take your buddy here with you. He can be your manager. Anytime you want to quit, you're free to do it. What do you say?"

I thought bout it for a minute or so. Sounded pretty good, but usually they is some catch. Nevertheless, I open my big mouth an say the fatal word:"Yes."

Well, that's how I become a professional rassler. Mike had his office in a gymnasium in downtown Indianapolis an ever day me an Dan would catch the bus down there so's I could get taught the proper way to rassle.

In a nutshell, it was this: nobody is sposed to get hurt, but it sposed to look like they do.

They be teachin me all sorts of things—half-nelsons, the airplane spin, the Boston crab, the pile driver, hammerlocks an all such as that. Also, they taught Dan how to yell an scream at the referee, so as to cause the greatest commotion.

Jenny is not too keen on the rasslin bidness on account of she say I might git hurt, an when I say nobody gits hurt cause it's all put-on, she say, "Then what's the point of it?" It is a good question that I cannot rightly answer, but I am lookin foward to makin us some money anyhow.

One day they is tryin to show me somethin called "the belly flop," where I is sposed to go flyin thru the air to lan on top of somebody but at the last minute he rolls away. But somehow, I keep screwin it up, an two or three times I lan right on the feller afore he gits a chance to move out the way. Finally Mike come up into the ring an say, "Jesus, Forrest—you some kind of idiot or somethin! You could hurt somebody that way, a big ole moose like you!"

An I says, "Yep—I *am* a idiot," an Mike say, "What you mean?" an then Dan, he say for Mike to come over to him for a secont an he splain somethin to him, an Mike say, "Good God! Is you kiddin?" an Dan shake his head. Mike look at me an shrug his shoulders an say, "Well, I guess it takes all kinds."

Anyway, bout a hour later Mike come runnin out of his office up to the ring where Dan an me is.

"I've got it!" he shoutin.

"Got what?"Dan axed.

"His name! We have to give Forrest a name to rassle under. It just came to me what it is."

"What might that be?"Dan say.

"The Dunce!"says Mike."We will dress him up in diapers an put a big ole dunce cap on his head. The crowd will love it!"

Dan think for a minute."I dunno,"he says,"I don't much like it. Sounds like you are tryin to make a fool out of him."

"It's only for the crowd,"Mike say."He has to have a gimmick of some sort. All the big stars do it. What could be better than The Dunce!"

"How about callin him The Spaceman?"say Dan."That would be appropriate. He could wear a plastic helmet and some antennas."

"They already got somebody called The Spaceman,"Mike says.

"I still don't like it,"Dan say. He looks at me, an axed,"What you think, Forrest?"

"I don't really give a shit,"I says.

Well, that was the way it was. After all them months of trainin I am finally bout to make my debut as a rassler. Mike come in to the gym the day before the big match an he has a box with my diaper an a big ole black dunce cap. He say to be back at the gym at noon tomorrow so he can drive us to my first rasslin match which is in Muncie.

That night when Jenny get home I gone into the bathroom an put on the diaper an the dunce cap an come out into the livin room. Dan is settin on his little platform cart watchin tv an Jenny is readin a book. Both of them look up when I walk thru the door.

"Forrest, what on earth?"Jenny says.

"It's his costume,"say Dan.

"It makes you look like a fool,"she say.

"Look at it this way,"Dan says."It's like he is in a play or somethin."

"He still looks like a fool,"says Jenny."I can't believe it! You'd let them dress him up like that an go out in public?"

"It's only to make money,"Dan say."They got one guy called 'The Vegetable' that wears turnip greens for a jockstrap an puts a hollowed-out watermelon over his head with little eyes cut out for him to see thru. Another guy calls himself 'The Fairy, ' an has wings on his back an carries a wand. Sumbitch probly weighs three hundred pounds—you oughta see him."

"I don't care what the rest of them do,"Jenny says,"I don't like this one bit. Forrest, you go an get out of that outfit."

I gone on back to the bathroom an took off the costume. Maybe Jenny is right, I'm thinkin—but a feller's got to make a livin. Anyhow, it ain't near as bad as the guy I got to rassle tomorrow night in Muncie. He calls hissef"The Turd,"an dresses in a big ole body stockin that is painted to look like a piece of shit. Lord knows what he gonna smell like.

19

THE DEAL IN MUNCIE IS THIS: I AM TO GET WHUPPED BY The Turd.

Mike tell me that on our ride up there. It seem that The Turd has got "seniority" over me an therefore he is due for a win, an bein that it's my first appearance, it is necessary for me to be on the losin end. Mike say he jus want to tell me how it is from the beginnin so there won't be no hard feelins.

"That is rediculous," Jenny say, "somebody callin theyself 'The Turd.'"

"He probly is one," Dan say, tryin to cheer her up.

"Just remember, Forrest," Mike says, "it's all for show. You can't lose your temper. Nobody is to be hurt. The Turd must win."

Well, when we finally git to Muncie, they is a big ole auditorium where the rasslin is to be helt. One bout is already in progress-The

Vegetable is rasslin a guy that calls hissef "The Animal."

The Animal is hairy as a ape, an is wearin a black mask over his eyes, an the first thing he does is to snatch off the hollered-out watermelon that The Vegetable is got over his head an drop kick it into the upper bleachers. Nex, he grapped The Vegetable by his head an ram him into the ring post. Then he bite The Vegetable on the han. I was feelin kinda sorry for the po ole Vegetable, but he got a few tricks hissef—namely, he reached down into the collard green leaves he is wearin for a jockstrap an grapped a hanful of some kind of shit an rub it in The Animal's eyes.

The Animal be bellowin an staggerin all over the ring rubbin his eyes to git the stuff out, an The Vegetable come up behin him an kick him in the ass. Then he thowed The Animal into the ropes an wind them up aroun him so's he can't move an start to beatin the hell outta The Animal. The crowd be booin The Vegetable an thowin paper cups an stuff at him an The Vegetable be givin them back the finger. I was gettin kinda curious how it was gonna wind up, but then Mike come up to me an Dan an say for us to go on back into the dressin room an get into my costume cause I'm on nex against The Turd.

After I get into my diapers an the dunce cap, somebody knock on the door an axe, "Is The Dunce in there?" an Dan say, "Yes," an the feller say, "You is on now, c'mon out," an off we go.

The Turd is already in the ring when I come down the aisle with Dan pushin hissef along behin me. The Turd is runnin aroun the ring makin faces at the crowd an damn if he don't actually look somethin like a turd in that body stockin. Anyhow, I climbed up in the ring an the referee get us together an say, "Okay, boys," I want a good clean match here—no gougin eyes or hittin below the belt or bitin or scratchin or any kind of shit like that. I nod an say, "Uh-huh," an The Turd be glarin at me fiercely.

When the bell rung, me an The Turd be circlin each other an he reached out with his foot to trip me but missed an I grapped him by the shoulders an slung him into the ropes. It was then I foun out he have greased hissef up with some kinda slippery shit that make him hard to hold on to. I tried to grap him aroun his waist but he shot out from my hans like a eel. I took a holt of his arm, but he squished away from that too, an be grinnin an laughin at me.

Then he come runnin at me head on to butt me in the stomach but I stepped aside an The Turd go flyin thru the ropes an land in the front row. Everbody be booin an catcallin him, but he climbed on back up in the ring an brung with him a foldup chair. He start chasin me aroun with the chair an since I got nothin to defend mysef with, I start to run away. But The Turd, he hit me in the back with the chair, an let me tell you, that hurt. I tried to get the chair away from him, but he conked me on the head with it, an I was in a corner an there wadn't no place to hide. Then he kicked me in the shin an when I bend over to hole my shin, he kick me in the other shin.

Dan is settin on the ring apron yellin at the referee to make The Turd put down the chair, but it ain't doin no good. The Turd hit me four or five times with the chair an knock me down an get on top of me an grap my hair an start bangin my head on the floor. Then he grap holt to my arm an begun twistin my fingers. I look over at Dan an say, "What the hell is this?" an Dan be tryin to get thru the ring ropes but Mike, he stand up an pull Dan back by his shirt collar. Then all of a sudden the bell rung, an I get to go to my corner.

"Listen," I says, "this bastid is tryin to kill me, beatin me on the head with a chair an all. I is gonna have to do somethin bout it."

"What you is gonna do is *lose*," Mike say. "He ain't tryin to hurt you—he is just tryin to make it look good."

"It sure don't *feel* good," I say.

"Jus stay in there for a few more minutes an then let him pin you down," Mike says. "Remember, you is makin five hundrit dollars for comin here an losin—not winnin."

"He hits me with that chair again, I don't know what I'm gonna do," I says. I am lookin out in the audience an there is Jenny lookin upset an embarrassed. I am beginnin to think this is not the right thing to do.

Anyhow, the bell rung again an out I go. The Turd try to grap me by the hair but I flung him off an he go spinnin into the ropes like a top. Then I picked him up aroun the waist an lif him up but he slid out of my grip an land on his ass an be moanin an complainin an rubbin his ass, an the nex thing I knew, his manager done handed him one of them "plumber's helpers" with the rubber thing on the end an he commence to beat me on the head with that. Well, I grapped it away from him an busted it in two over my knee an start goin after him, but I see Mike there, shakin his head, an so I let The Turd come an take holt of my arm an twist it in a hammerlock.

The sumbitch damn near broke my arm. Then he shoved me down on the canvas an begun to hit me in the back of the head with his elbow. I coud see Mike over there, noddin an smilin his approval. The Turd get off me an commenced to kickin me in the ribs an stomach, then he got his chair again an wacked me over the head with it eight or nine times an finally he kneed me in the back an there wadn't a thing I coud do bout it.

I jus lay there, an he set on my head an the referee counted to three an it was sposed to be over. The Turd get up an look down at me an he spit in my face. It was awful an I didn't know what else to do, an I jus couldn't hep it, an I started to cry.

The Turd was prancin aroun the ring an then Dan come up an rolled himsef over to me an started wipin my face with a towel, an nex thing I knew, Jenny had come up in the ring too an was huggin me an cryin hersef an the crowd was hollerin an yellin an throwin stuff into the ring.

"C'mon, let's get outta here,"Dan say, an I got to my feet an The Turd be stickin out his tongue at me an makin faces.

"You is certainly correctly named,"Jenny says to The Turd as we was leavin the ring."That was disgraceful."

She could of said it bout both of us. I ain't never felt so humiliated in my life.

The ride back to Indianapolis was pretty awkward. Dan an Jenny ain't sayin nothin much an I am in the back seat all sore an skint up.

"That was a damn good performance you put on out there tonight, Forrest,"Mike says,"especially the cryin at the end—crowd loved it!"

"It wadn't no performance," Dan says.

"Oh, shucks," Mike say. "Look—somebody's always got to lose. I'll tell you what—nex time, I will make sure Forrest wins. How's that make you feel?"

"Ought not to be any 'nex time, '" Jenny says.

"He made good money tonight, didn't he?" Mike say.

"Five hundrit dollars for gettin the shit beat out of him ain't so good," Jenny says.

"Well it was his first match. Tell you what—nex time, I'll make it six hundrit."

"How about twelve hundrit?" Dan axed.

"Nine hundrit," Mike says.

"How bout lettin him wear a bathin suit instead of that dunce cap an diapers?" says Jenny.

"They loved it," Mike says. "It's part of his appeal."

"How would you like to have to dress up in somethin like that?" Dan says.

"I ain't a idiot," says Mike.

"You shut the fuck up bout that," Dan say.

Well, Mike was good for his word. Nex time I rassled, it was against a feller called "The Human Fly." He was dressed up in somethin with a big pointed snout like a fly have, an a mask with big ole bugged-out eyes. I got to thow him bout the ring an finally set on his head an I collected my nine hundrit dollars. Furthermore, everbody in the crowd cheered wildly an kep hollerin, "We want The Dunce! We want The Dunce!" It wadn't such a bad deal.

Nex, I got to rassle The Fairy, an they even let me bust his wand over his head. After that, they was a hole bunch of guys I come up against, an Dan an me had managed to save up about five thousan dollars for the srimp bidness. But also let me say this: I was gettin very popular with the crowds. Women was writin me letters an they even begun to sell dunce caps like mine as souvenirs. Sometimes I'd go into the ring an they would be fifty or a hundrit people settin there in the audience wearin dunce caps, all clappin an cheerin an callin out my name. Kinda made me feel good, you know?

Meantime, me an Jenny is gettin along fairly good cept for my rasslin career. Ever night when she get back to the apartment we cook ourselfs some supper an her an me an Dan set aroun in the livin room an plan bout how we gonna start the srimp bidness. The way we figger it, we is gonna go down to Bayou La Batre, where po ole Bubba come from, an get us some marsh land off the Gulf of Mexico someplace. We has got to buy us some mesh wire an nets an a little rowboat an somethin to feed the srimp wile they growin, an they will be other things too. Dan say we has also got to be able to have us a place to live an buy groceries an stuff wile we wait for our first profits an also have some way to git them to the market. All tole, he figgers it is gonna take bout five thousan dollars to set everthing up for the first year—after that, we will be on our own.

The problem I got now is with Jenny. She say we already got the five thousan an so why don't we jus go ahead an pack up an go down there?

Well, she have a point there, but to be perfectly truthful, I jus ain't quite ready to leave.

You see, it ain't really been since we played them Nebraska corn shucker jackoffs at the Orange Bowl that I has really felt like I done accomplished somethin. Maybe for a little bit durin the ping-pong games in Red China, but that lasted just for a few weeks. But now, you see, ever Saturday night ever week, I am goin out there an hearin them cheer. An they is cheerin *me*—idiot or not.

You should of heard them cheer when I whupped The Grosse Pointe Grinder, who come into the ring with hundrit dollar bills glued to his body. An then they was "Awesome Al from Amarillo," that I done put a Boston Crab hold on an won mysef the Eastern Division champeenship belt. After that, I got to rassle Juno the Giant, who weighed four hundrit pounds an dressed in a leopard skin an carried a papier-maché club.

But one day when Jenny come home from work she say, "Forrest, you an me has got to have a talk."

We went outside an took a walk near a little creek an Jenny foun a place to set down, an then she say, "Forrest, I think this rasslin business is gone far enough."

"What you mean?" I axed, even though I kind of knew.

"I mean we have got nearly ten thousan dollars now, which is more than twice what Dan says we need to start the srimp business. And I am beginnin to wonder jus why you are continuin to go up there ever Saturday night an make a fool of yoursef."

"I ain't makin no fool of mysef," I says, "I has got my fans to think of. I am a very popular person. Cain't jus up an leave like that."

"Bullshit,"Jenny say."What you callin a 'fan', an what you mean by 'popular'? Them people is a bunch of screwballs to be payin money to watch all that shit. Bunch of grown men gettin up there in they jockstraps an pretendin to hurt each other. An whoever heard of people callin theyselfs 'The Vegetable, ' or 'The Turd, ' an such as that-an you, callin yourself 'The Dunce'!"

"What's wrong with that?"I axed.

"Well how do you think it makes me feel, the feller I'm in love with bein known far an wide as 'The Dunce', an makin a spectacle of hissef ever week—an on television, too!"

"We get extra money for the television,"I says.

"Screw the extra money,"Jenny says."We don't need no extra money!"

"Whoever heard of nobody didn't need any extra money?"I say.

"We don't need it that bad,"Jenny say."I mean, what I want is to find a little quiet place for us to be in an for you to get a respectable job, like the srimp business—for us to get us a little house maybe an have a garden an maybe a dog or somethin—maybe even kids. I done had my share of fame with The Cracked Eggs, an it didn't get me nowhere. I wadn't happy. I'm damned near thirty-five years old. I want to settle down. . ."

"Look,"I says,"it seem to me that *I* oughta be the one what say if I quit or not. I ain't gonna do this forever—jus till it is the right time."

"Well I ain't gonna wait aroun forever, neither,"Jenny say, but I didn't believe she meant it.

20

I HAD A COUPLE OF MATCHES AFTER THAT AN WON BOTH OF them, naturally, an then Mike call Dan an me in his office one day an says,"Look here, this week you are gonna rassle The Professor."

"Who is that?"Dan axed.

"He comes from California,"says Mike,"an is pretty hot stuff out there. He is runner up to the Western Division champion."

"Okay by me,"I say.

"But there is just one other thing,"say Mike."This time, Forrest, you got to lose."

"Lose?"I says.

"Lose,"say Mike."Look, you been winnin ever week for months an months. Don't you see you got to lose ever once in a wile to keep up your popularity?"

"How you figger that?"

"Simple. People like a underdog. Makes you look better the nex time."

"I don't like it," I say.

"How much you payin?" Dan axed.

"Two thousan."

"I don't like it," I says again.

"Two thousan's a lot of money," Dan say.

"I still don't like it," I says.

But I took the deal.

Jenny is been actin sort of peculiar lately, but I put it down to nerves or somethin. Then one day she come home an say, "Forrest, I'm at the end of my rope. Please don't go out there an do this."

"I got to," I says. "Anyhow, I is gonna lose."

"Lose?" she say. I splain it to her jus like Mike splain it to me, an she say, "Awe shit, Forrest, this is too much."

"It's my life," I says—whatever that meant.

Anyway, a day or so later, Dan come back from someplace an says him an me got to have a talk.

"Forrest, I think I got the solution to our problems."

I axed what it was.

"I think," says Dan, "we better be bailin out of this business pretty soon. I know Jenny don't like it, an if we are gonna start our srimp thing, we best be on bout it. But," he say, "I think I got a way to bail out an clean up at the same time."

"How's that?"I axed.

"I been talkin to a feller downtown. He runs a bookie operation an the word is out you gonna lose to The Professor this Saturday."

"So?"I says.

"So what if you win?"

"Win?"

"Kick his ass."

"I get in trouble with Mike,"I says.

"Screw Mike,"Dan say."Look, here's the deal. Spose we take the ten thousan we got an bet it on you to *win*? Two-to-one odds. Then you kick his ass an we got *twenty* grand."

"But I'll be in all sorts of trouble,"I says.

"We take the twenty grand an blow this town,"Dan say."You know what we can do with twenty grand? We can start one hell of a srimp business an have a pile left over for ourselves. I'm thinkin maybe it's time to get out of this rasslin stuff anyway."

Well, I'm thinkin Dan is the manager, an also that Jenny has said I gotta get out of rasslin too, an twenty grand ain't a bad deal.

"What you think?"Dan says.

"Okay,"I say."Okay."

The day come for me to rassle The Professor. The bout is to be helt up at Fort Wayne, an Mike come by to pick us up an is blowin the horn outside, an I axed Jenny if she is ready.

"I ain't goin,"she say."I'll watch it on television."

"But you got to go,"I says, an then I axed Dan to splain why.

Dan tole Jenny what the plan was, an that she had to go, on account of we needed somebody to drive us back to Indianapolis after I done whupped The Professor.

"Neither of us can drive,"he say,"an we gonna have to have a fast car right outside the arena when it's over to get us back here to collect the twenty grand from the bookie an then hightail it out of town."

"Well, I ain't havin nothin to do with a deal like that,"Jenny say.

"But it's twenty grand,"I says.

"Yeah, an it's dishonest too,"she says.

"Well, it's dishonest what he's been doin all the time,"Dan says,"winnin an losin all planned out beforehand."

"I ain't gonna do it,"Jenny said, an Mike was blowin his horn again, an Dan say,"Well, we gotta go. We'll see you back here sometime after it's over—one way or the other."

"You fellers oughta be ashamed of yourselfs,"Jenny say.

"You won't be so high-falutin when we come back with twenty thousan smackeroos in our pocket,"Dan says.

Anyhow, off we go.

On the ride to Fort Wayne, I ain't sayin much on account of I'm kinda embarrassed bout what I'm fixin to do to ole Mike. He ain't treated me so badly, but on the other han, as Dan have splained, I has made a lot of money for him too, so it gonna come out aroun even.

We get to the arena an the first bout is already on—Juno the Giant is gettin the hell kicked out of him by The Fairy. An nex up is a tag team match between lady midgets. We gone on into the dressin room an I put on my diapers an dunce cap. Dan, he get somebody to dial the number of the taxicab company an arrange for a cab to be there outside with its motor runnin after my match.

They beat on my door an it's time to go on. Me an The Professor is the feature bout of the evenin.

He is already there in the ring when I come out. The Professor is a little wiry guy with a beard an wearin spectacles an he have on a black robe an morter-board hat. Damn if he don't look like a professor at that. I decided right then to make him eat that hat.

Well, I climb on up in the ring an the announcer say, "Ladies an Gentlemen." At this there be a lot of boos, an then he say, "We is proud tonight to have as our main attraction for the North American Professional Rasslin Association title bout two of the top contenders in the country— The Professor versus The Dunce!"

At this, they is so much booin an cheerin that it is impossible to say if the crowd is happy or angry. It don't matter nohow, cause then the bell ring an the match is on.

The Professor has taken off his robe, glasses, an the morter-board hat an is circlin me, shakin his finger at me like I'm bein scolded. I be tryin to grap a holt of him, but ever time, he jump out of the way an keep shakin his finger. This go on for a minute or two an then he make a mistake. He run aroun behin me an try to kick me in the ass, but I done snatched a holt of him by the arm an slung him into the ropes. He come boundin off the ropes like a slingshot ball an as he go past me I trip him up an was bout to pounce on him with the Bellybuster maneuver, but he done scrambled out of the way to his corner an when I look up, he is got a big ole ruler in his han.

He be whoppin the ruler in his palm like he gonna spank me with it, but instead, when I grapped for him this time, he done jam the ruler in my eye, like to gouge it out. I'll tell you this—it hurt, an I was stumblin aroun tryin to get my sight back when he run up behin me an put somethin down my diapers. Didn't take long to find out what it was—it was ants! Where he got them, lord knows, but the ants commence to bitin me an I was in a awful fix.

Dan is there, hollerin for me to finish him off, but it ain't no easy thing with ants in your pants. Anyhow, the bell rung an that was the end of the roun an I go on back to my corner an Dan be tryin to get the ants out.

"That was a dirty trick," I say.

"Just finish him," Dan says, "we can't afford no screwups."

The Professor come out for the secont round an be makin faces at me. Then he get close enough for me to snatch him up an I lifted him over my head an begun doin the Airplane Spin.

I spinned him aroun bout forty or fifty times till I was pretty sure he was dizzy an then heaved him hard as I could over the ropes into the audience. He land up in bout the fifth row of bleachers in the lap of a ole woman who is knittin a sweater, an she start beatin him with a umbrella.

Trouble is, the Airplane Spin have taken its toll on me too. Everthin spinnin aroun but I figger it don't matter cause it'll stop pretty soon, an

The Professor, he is finished anyway. In this, I am wrong.

I am almost recovered from the spinnin when all of a sudden somethin got me by the ankles. I look down, an damn if The Professor ain't climbed back in the ring an brought with him the ball of yarn the ole lady was knittin with, an now he done rapped it aroun my feet.

I started tryin to wriggle out, but The Professor be runnin circles aroun me with the yarn, rappin me up like a mummy. Pretty soon, I am tied up han an foot an cain't move or nothin. The Professor stop an tie the yarn up in a little fancy knot an stand in front of me an take a bow—like he is a magician just done some trick or somethin.

Then he saunter over to his corner an get a big ole book—look like a dictionary—an come back an take another bow. An then he crack me on the head with the book. Ain't nothin I can do. He must of cracked me ten or twelve times before I gone down. I am helpless an I am hearin everbody cheer as The Professor set on my shoulders an pin me—an win the match.

Mike an Dan, they come in the ring an unraveled the yarn off me an heped me up.

"Terrific!" Mike say, "Just terrific! I couldn't of planned it better mysef!"

"Oh shut up," Dan say. An then he turn to me. "Well," he say, "this is a fine state of affairs—gettin yoursef outsmarted by The Professor."

I ain't sayin nothin. I am miserable. Everthin is lost an the one thing I know for sure is that I ain't gonna rassle never again.

We didn't need the getaway cab after that, so Dan an me rode back to

Indianapolis with Mike. All the drive back, he be sayin how great it was that I lost to The Professor that way, an how nex time I gonna get to win an make everbody thousans of dollars.

When he pull up in front of the apartment, Mike reach back an han Dan a envelope with the two thousan dollars he was gonna pay me for the match.

"Don't take it," I says.

"What?" says Mike.

"Listen," I say. "I got to tell you somethin."

Dan cut in. "What he wants to say is, he ain't gonna be rasslin no more."

"You kiddin?" Mike say.

"Ain't kiddin," says Dan.

"Well how come?" Mike axed. "What's wrong, Forrest?"

Before I could say anythin, Dan say, "He don't want to talk about it now."

"Well," says Mike, "I understan, I guess. You go get a good night's sleep. I'll be back first thing in the mornin an we can talk bout it, okay?"

"Okay," Dan says, an we get out of the car. When Mike is gone, I says, "You shouldn't of took the money."

"Well it's all the hell we got left now," he say. Everthin else is gone. I didn't realize till a few minutes later how right he was.

We get to the apartment an lo an behole, Jenny is gone too. All her things is gone, cept she lef us some clean sheets an towels an some pots an pans an stuff. On the table in the livin room is a note. Dan foun it first, an he read it out loud to me.

Dear Forrest, [it says]

I am just not able to take this anymore. I have tried to talk to you about my feelings, and you don't seem to care. There is something particularly bad about what you are gonna do tonight, because it isn't honest, and I am afraid I cannot go on with you any longer.

Maybe it is my fault, partly, because I have gotten to an age where I need to settle down. I think about having a house and a family and goin to church and things like that. I have known you since the first grade, Forrest—nearly thirty years—and have watched you grow up big and strong and fine. And when I finally realized how much I cared for you—when you came up to Boston—I was the happiest girl in the world.

And then you took to smoking too much dope, and you fooled with those girls down in Provincetown, an even after that, I missed you, and was glad you came to Washington during the peace demonstration to see me.

But when you got shot up in the spaceship and were lost in the jungle nearly four years, I think maybe I changed. I am not as hopeful as I used to be, and think I would be satisfied with just a simple life somewhere. So, now I must go an find it.

Something is changed in you, too, dear Forrest. I don't think you can help it exactly, for you were always a"special"person, but we no longer seem to think the same way.

I am in tears as I write this, but we must part now. Please don't try to find me. I wish you well, my darling—good-bye.

love,
Jenny

Dan handed the note to me but I let it drop on the floor an just stood there, realizin for the first time in my life what it is truly like to be a idiot.

21

WELL, AFTER THAT I WAS ONE SORRY BASTID.

Dan an me stayed at the apartment that nite, but the nex mornin started packin up our shit an all, cause there wadn't no reason to be in Indianapolis no longer. Dan, he come to me an say,"Here, Forrest, take this money,"an helt out the two thousand dollars Mike had give us for rasslin The Professor.

"I don't want it,"I says.

"Well you better take it,"says Dan,"cause it's all we got."

"You keep it,"I says.

"At least take haf of it,"he say."Look, you gotta have some travelin money. Get you to wherever your goin."

"Ain't you goin with me?"I axed.

"I'm afraid not, Forrest,"he says."I think I done enough damage already. I didn't sleep none last night. I'm thinkin about how I got you to agree to bet all our money, an how I got you to keep on rasslin when it oughta have been apparent Jenny was about to freak out on us. An it wadn't your fault you got whupped by The Professor. You did what you could. I am the one to blame. I jus ain't no good."

"Awe, Dan, it wadn't your fault neither,"I says."If I hadn't of got the big head bout bein The Dunce, an begun to believe all that shit they was sayin bout me, I wouldn't of got in this fix in the first place."

"Whatever it is,"Dan say,"I jus don't feel right taggin along anymore. You got other fish to fry now. Go an fry em. Forget about me. I ain't no good."

Well, me an Dan talked for a long time, but there wadn't no convincin him, an after a wile, he got his shit an I hepped him down the steps, an the last I seen of him, he was pushin hissef down the street on his little cart, with all his clothes an shit piled in his lap.

I went down to the bus station an bought a ticket to Mobile. It was sposed to be a two day an two nite trip, down thru Louisville, to Nashville, to Birmingham an then Mobile, an I was one miserable idiot, settin there wile the bus rolled along.

We passed thru Louisville durin the nite, an the nex day we stopped in Nashville an had to change busses. It was about a three hour wait, so I decided to walk aroun town for a wile. I got me a sambwich at a lunch counter an a glass of iced tea an was walkin down the street when I seen a big sign in front of a hotel say,"Welcome Grandmaster's Invitational

Chess Tournament."

It sort of got my curiosity up, on account of I had played all that chess back in the jungle with Big Sam, an so I went on into the hotel. They was playin the chess game in the ballroom an had a big mob of people watchin, but a sign say, "Five dollars admission," and I didn't want to spend none of my money, but I looked in thru the door for a wile, an then jus went an set down in the lobby by mysef.

They was a chair across from me with a little ole man settin in it. He was all shriveled up an grumpy-lookin an had on a black suit with spats an a bow tie an he had a chessboard set out on a table in front of him.

As I set there, ever once in a wile he would move one of the chessmen, an it begun to dawn on me that he was playin by hissef. I figgered I had bout another hour or so fore the bus lef, so I axed him if he wanted somebody to play with. He jus looked at me an then looked back down at his chessboard an didn't say nothin.

A little bit later, the ole feller'd been studyin the chessboard for most of a half hour an then he moved his white bishop over to black square seven an was jus bout to take his han off it when I says," 'scuse me."

The feller jumped like he'd set on a tack, an be glarin across the table at me.

"You make that move," I says, "an you be leavin yoursef wide open to lose your knight an then your queen an put your ass in a fix."

He look down at his chessboard, never takin his han off the bishop, an then he move it back an say to me, "Possibly you are right."

Well, he go on back to studyin the chessboard an I figger it's time to get back to the bus station, but jus as I start to leave, the ole man say,"Pardon me, but that was a very shrewd observation you made."

I nod my head, an then he say,"Look, you've obviously played the game, why don't you sit down an finish this one with me? Just take over the white in their positions now."

"I cain't,"I says, cause I got to catch the bus an all. So he jus nods an gives me a little salute with his han an I went on back to the bus station.

Time I get there, the damn bus done lef anyway, an here I am an ain't no other bus till tomorrow. I jus cain't do nothin right. Well, I got a day to kill, so I walked on back to the hotel an there is the little ole man still playin against hissef, an he seems to be winnin. I went on up to him an he look up an motion for me to set down. The situation I have come into is pretty miserable-haf my pawns gone an I ain't got but one bishop an no rooks an my queen is about to be captured nex.

It took me most of a hour to git mysef back in a even position, an the ole man be kinda gruntin an shakin his head evertime I improve my situation. Finally, I dangle a gambit in front of him. He took it, an three moves later I got him in check.

"I will be damned,"he say."Just who *are* you, anyway?"

I tole him my name, an he say,"No, I mean, where have you played? I don't even recognize you."

When I tole him I learnt to play in New Guinea, an he say,"Good heavens! An you mean to say you haven't even been in regional competition?"

I shook my head an he says,"Well whether you know it or not, I am a former international grand master, and you have just stepped into a game you couldn't possibily have won, and totally annihilated me!"

I axed how come he wadn't playin in the room with the other people, an he says,"Oh, I played earlier. I'm nearly eighty years old now, an there is a sort of senior tournament. The real glory is to the younger fellows now—their minds are jus sharper."

I nodded my head an thanked him for the game an got up to go, but he says,"Listen, have you had your supper yet?"

I tole him I had a sambwich a few hours ago, an he say,"Well how about letting me buy you dinner? After all, you gave me a superb game."

I said that woud be okay, an we went into the hotel dinin room. He was a nice man. Mister Tribble was his name.

"Look,"Mister Tribble say wile we is havin dinner,"I'd have to play you a few more games to be sure, but unless your playing this evening was a total fluke, you are perhaps one of the brightest unrecognized talents in the game. I would like to sponsor you in a tournament or two, and see what happens."

I tole him about headin home an wantin to get into the srimp bidness and all, but he say,"Well, this could be the opportunity of a lifetime for you, Forrest. You could make a lot of money in this game, you know."He said for me to think it over tonight, an let him know somethin in the mornin. So me an Mister Tribble shook hans, an I went on out in the street.

I done wandered aroun for a wile, but they ain't a lot to see in

Nashville, an finally I wound up settin on a bench in a park. I was tryin to think, which don't exactly come easy to me, an figger out what to do now. My mind was mostly on Jenny an where she is. She say not to try to find her or nothin, but they is a feelin down deep in me someplace that she ain't forgot me. I done made a fool of mysef in Indianapolis, an I know it. I think it was that I wadn't tryin to do the right thing. An now, I ain't sure what the right thing is. I mean, here I am, ain't got no money to speak of, an I got to have some to start up the srimp bidness, an Mister Tribble say I can win a good bit on the chess circuit. But it seem like ever time I do somethin besides tryin to get home an get the srimp bidness started, I get my big ass in hot water—so here I am again, wonderin what to do.

I ain't been wonderin long when up come a policeman an axe me what I'm doin.

I says I'm jus settin here thinkin, an he say ain't nobody allowed to set an think in the park at night an for me to move along. I go on down the street, an the policeman be followin me. I didn't know where to go, so after a wile I saw an alley an walked on back in it an foun a place to set down an rest my feet. I ain't been settin there more'n a minute when the same ole policeman come by an see me there.

"All right," he say, "come on outta there." When I get out to the street, he say, "What you doin in there?"

I says, "Nothin," an he say, "That's exactly what I thought—you is under arrest for loiterin."

Well, he take me to the jail an lock me up an then in the mornin they say I can make one phone call if I want. Course I didn't know nobody to phone but Mister Tribble, so that's what I did. Bout haf a hour later, he shows up at the police station an springs me out of jail.

Then he buys me a big ole breakfast at the hotel an says, "Listen, why don't you let me enter you in the interzonal championships next week in Los Angeles? First prize is ten thousan dollars. I will pay for all your expenses an we will split any money you win. Seems to me you need a stake of some sort, and, to tell you the truth, I would enjoy it immensely mysef. I will be your coach and adviser. How bout it?"

I still had some doubts, but I figgered it wouldn't hurt to try. So I said I woud do it for a wile. Till I got enough money to start the srimp thing. An me an Mister Tribble shook hans an become partners.

Los Angeles was quite a sight. We got there a week early an Mister Tribble would spend most of the day coachin me an honin down my game, but after a wile of this, he jus shook his head an say there ain't no sense in tryin to coach me, cause I got "every move in the book" already. So what we did was, we went out on the town.

Mister Tribble took me to Disneyland an let me go on some rides an then he arranged to get us a tour of a movie lot. They is got all sorts of movies goin on, an people is runnin aroun shoutin "take one," an "cut," an "action," an shit like that. One of the movies they was doin was a Western an we seen a feller get hissef thowed thru a plate glass winder about ten times—till he got it right.

Anyway, we was jus standin there watchin this, when some guy walk up an says, "I beg your pardon, are you an actor?"

I says,"Huh?"An Mister Tribble, he says,"No, we are chess players."

An the feller say,"Well that's kind of a shame, because the big guy here, he looks ideal for a role in a movie I'm doing."And then he turn to me an feel of my arm an say,"My, my, you *are* a big strong feller—are you sure you don't act?"

"I did once,"I says.

"Really!"the feller says."What in?"

"*King Lear.*"

"Marvelous, baby,"he says,"that's just marvelous—do you have your SAG card?"

"My what?"

"Screen Actors Guild—oh, no matter,"he say."Listen, baby, we can get that, no trouble. What I want to know is, where have they been hiding you? I mean, just look at you! A perfect big strong silent type—another John Wayne."

"He is no John Wayne,"Mister Tribble say sourly,"he is a world-class chess player."

"Well all the better,"the feller say,"a *smart* big, strong, silent type. Very unusual."

"Ain't as smart as I look,"I says, tryin to be honest, but the feller say none of that matters anyhow, cause actors ain't sposed to be smart *or* honest or nothin like that—just be able to get up there an say they lines.

"My name's Felder,"he says,"an I make movies. I want you to take a screen test."

"He has to play in a chess tournament tomorrow,"Mister Tribble say."He has no time for acting or screen tests."

"Well, you could squeeze it in, couldn't you? After all, it might be the break you've been looking for. Why don't you come along, too, Tribble, we'll give you a screen test as well."

"We'll try,"Mister Tribble say."Now come along, Forrest, we have a little more work to do."

"See you later, baby,"say Mister Felder,"don't forget now."

An off we go.

22

THE NEX MORNIN IS WHEN THE CHESS TOURNAMENT IS BEIN helt out at the Beverly Hills Hotel. Me an Mister Tribble is there early an he has me signed up for matches all day.

Basically, it ain't no big deal. It took me about seven minutes to whup the first guy, who was a regional master an also a professor in some college, which made me secretly feel kind of good. I had beat a professor after all.

Nex was a kid about seventeen, an I wiped him out in less than half a hour. He thowed a tantrum an then commenced to bawlin an cryin an his mama had to come drag him off.

They was all sorts of people I played that day an the nex, but I beat em all pretty fast, which was a relief since when I played against Big Sam I had to keep settin there an not go to the bathroom or nothin, cause if I got up from the chessboard he would move the pieces aroun an try to cheat.

Anyhow, by that time I had got my way into the finals an they was a day's rest in between. I gone on back to the hotel with Mister Tribble an found a message to us from Mister Felder, the movie guy. It say,"Please call my office this afternoon an arrange for a screen test tomorrow morning,"an it give a telephone number to call.

"Well, Forrest,"Mister Tribble say,"I don't know bout this. What do you think?"

"I dunno either,"I says, but to tell the truth, it soun sort of excitin, bein in the movies an all. Maybe I even get to meet Raquel Welch or somebody.

"Oh, I don't suppose it would hurt anything,"Mister Tribble say."I guess I'll call an set up an appointment."So he call Mister Felder's office an be findin out when an where for us to go an all of a sudden he cup his hand over the phone an say to me,"Forrest, can you swim?"An I say,"Yup,"an he say back into the phone,"Yes, he can."

After he done hung up, I axed why they want to know if I can swim, an Mister Tribble say he don't know, but he recon we will find out when we get there.

The movie lot we gone to is a different place than the other one, an we was met at the gate by a guard that took us to where the screen test is bein helt. Mister Felder is there arguin with a lady that actually look somethin like Raquel Welch, but when he seen me, he is all smiles.

"Ah, Forrest,"he say,"terrific you came. Now what I want you to do is go thru that door to Makeup and Costuming, and then they will send you back out when they are finished."

So I gone on thru the door an there is a couple of ladies standin there an one of em say, "Okay, take off your clothes." Here I go again, but I do as I am tole. When I get thru takin off my clothes, the other lady han me this big blob of rubber-lookin clothes with scales an shit all over it an funny-lookin webbed feet an hans. She say to put it on. It take the three of us to get me in the thing but after bout a hour we manage. Then they point me in the direction of Makeup an I is tole to set in a chair wile a lady an a feller commence to jam down this big rubber mask over my head an fit it to the costume an start paintin over the lines where it showed. When they is thru, they say for me to go back out to the movie set.

I can hardly walk on account of the webbed feet an it is hard to get the door open with a webbed han, but finally I do an I suddenly find myself in a outdoor place with a big lake an all sorts of banana trees an tropical-lookin shit. Mister Felder is there an when he seen me, he jump back an say, "Terrific, baby! You is perfect for the part!"

"What part is that?" I axed, an he say, "Oh, didn't I tell you? I am doing a remake of *The Creature from the Black Lagoon*." Even a idiot like me could guess what part he have in mind for me to play.

Mister Felder motion for the lady he had been arguin with to come over. "Forrest," he say, "I want you to meet Raquel Welch."

Well, you coudda knocked me over with a feather! There she were, all dressed up in a low-cut gown an all. "Please to meet you," I says thru the mask, but Raquel Welch turn to Mister Felder lookin mad as a hornet.

"What'd he say? Something about my tits, wasn't it!"

"No, baby, no," say Mister Felder. "He just said he was glad to meet you. You can't hear him too well because of that mask he's got on."

I stuck out my webbed han to shake hans with her, but she jump back about a foot, an say, "Uggh! Let's get this goddamn thing over with."

Anyhow, Mister Felder say the deal is this: Raquel Welch is to be flounderin in the water an then she faints, an then I am to come up from under her an pick her up an carry her outta the water. But when she revives, she looks up at me an is scared an commences to scream, "Put me down! Help! Rape!" an all that shit.

But, Mister Felder say, I am not to put her down, cause some crooks is sposed to be chasin us; instead, I am to carry her off into the jungle.

Well, we tried the scene, an the first time we done it, I thought it come off pretty well, an it is really excitin to actually be holdin Raquel Welch in my arms, even tho she be hollerin, "Put me down! Help, police!" an so on.

But Mister Felder say that ain't good enough, an for us to do it again. An that wadn't good enough either, so we be doin that same scene bout ten or fifteen times. In between doin the scene, Raquel Welch is crabbin an bitchin an cussin at Mister Felder, but he just kep on sayin, "Beautiful, baby, beautiful!" an that sort of thing.

Mysef, I'm startin to have a real problem tho. On account of I been in the creature suit nearly five hours now, an they ain't no zipper or nothin to pee thru, an I'm bout to bust. But I don't wanta say nothin bout that, cause this is a real movie an everthin, an I don't want to make nobody mad.

But I gotta do *somethin*, so's I decide that the nex time I get in the water, I will jus pee in the suit, an it will run out my leg or somethin into the lagoon. Well, Mister Felder, he say, "Action!" an I go in the water an start to pee. Raquel Welch be flounderin aroun an then she faints, an I dive under an grap her an haul her onto shore.

She wakes up an start to beatin on me an hollerin, "Help! Murder! Put me down!" an all, but then she suddenly stop hollerin an she say, "What is that smell?"

Mister Felder holler, "Cut!" an he stand up an say, "What was that you said, baby? That ain't in the script."

An Raquel Welch say, "Shit on the script! Somethin stinks aroun here!" Then she suddenly look at me an say, "Hey, you—whoever you are—did you take a leak?"

I was so embarrassed, I did not know what to do. I just stood there for a secont, holdin her in my arms, an then I shake my head an say, "Uh uh."

It was the first lie I ever tole in my life.

"Well somebody sure did," she say, "cause I know pee when I smell it! An it wadn't me! So it *has* to be you! How dare you pee on me, you big oaf!" Then she start beatin on me with her fists an hollerin to "Put me down!" and "Get away from me!" an all, but I jus figgered the scene is startin up again an so I begun to carry her back into the jungle.

Mister Felder shout, "*Action!*" The movie cameras begun to rollin once more, an Raquel Welch is beatin an clawin an yellin like she never done before. Mister Felder is back there hollerin, "That's it, baby—terrific! Keep it up!" I coud see Mister Tribble back there too, settin in a chair, kinda shakin his head an tryin to look the other way.

Well, when I get back in the jungle a little ways, I stopped an turned aroun to see if that's where Mister Felder is fixin to yell"Cut,"like he had before, but he was jumpin aroun like a wild man, motionin to keep on goin, an shoutin,"Perfect, baby! That's what I want! Carry her off into the jungle!"

Raquel Welch is still scratchin an flailin at me an screamin,"Get away from me you vulgar animal!"an such as that, but I kep on goin like I'm tole.

All of a sudden she screech,"Oh my god! My dress!"

I ain't noticed it till now, but when I look down, damn if her dress ain't caught on some bush back there an done totally unravel itself, Raquel Welch is butt neckid in my arms!

I stopped an said,"Uh oh,"an started to turn aroun to carry her back, but she begin shriekin,"No, no! You idiot! I can't go back there like this!"

I axed what she wanted me to do, an she say we gotta find someplace to hide till she gets things figgered out. So I keep on goin deeper into the jungle when all of a sudden out of noplace come a big object thru the trees, swingin towards us on a vine. The object swung past us once an I could tell it was a ape of some sort, an then it swung back again an dropped off the vine at our feet. I almost fainted dead away. It was ole Sue, hissef!

Raquel Welch begun to bawlin an hollerin again an Sue has grapped me aroun the legs an is huggin me. I don't know how he recognized me in my creature suit, cept I guess he smelt me or somethin. Anyhow, Raquel

Welch, she finally say, "Do you *know* this fucking baboon?"

"He ain't no baboon," I says, "he's a orangutang. Name's Sue."

She look at me kinda funny an say, "Well if it's a *he*, then how come its name is Sue?"

"That is a long story," I say.

Anyhow, Raquel Welch is tryin to cover herself up with her hans, but ole Sue, he knows what to do. He grapped holt of a couple of big leaves off one of them banana trees an han them up to her an she partly covered herself up.

What I find out later is that we have gone across our jungle location onto another set where they is filmin a Tarzan movie, an Sue is being used as a extra. Not long after I got rescued from the pygmies in New Guinea, white hunters come along an captured ole Sue an shipped his ass to some animal trainer in Los Angeles. They been usin him in movies ever since.

Anyway, we ain't got time to jack aroun now, on account of Raquel Welch is screechin an bitchin again, say, "You gotta take me someplace where I can get me some clothes!" Well, I don't know where you can find no clothes in the jungle, even if it *is* a movie set, so we jus keep movin along, hopin somethin will happen.

It does. We suddenly come to a big fence, an I figger there probly be someplace on the other side of it to get her some clothes. Sue finds a loose board in the fence an lifts it up so's we can get thru, but as soon as I step on the other side, ain't nothin to step on, an me an Raquel go tumblin head over heels down the side of this hill. We finally rolled all the way to the bottom an when I look aroun, damn if we ain't landed right on the side of a big ole road.

"Oh my God!"Raquel Welch yell."We're on the Santa Monica Freeway!"

I look up, an here come ole Sue, lopin down the hillside. He finally get down to us, an the three of us be standin there. Raquel Welch is movin the banana leaves up an down, tryin to cover herself up.

"What we gonna do now?"I axed. Cars are wizzin by, an even tho we must of been a odd-lookin sight, ain't nobody even payin us the slightest attention.

"You gotta take me someplace!"she hollers."I got to get some clothes on!"

"Where?"I says.

"Anywhere!"she screams, an so we started off down the Santa Monica Freeway.

After a wile, up in the distance, we seen a big white sign up in some hills say"HOLLYWOOD,"an Raquel Welch say,"We got to get off this damn freeway and get to Rodeo Drive, where I can buy me some clothes."She is keepin pretty busy tryin to cover herself up—ever time a car come towards us, she put the banana leaves in front, an when a car come up from behin, she move em back there to cover her ass. In mixed traffic, it is quite a spectacular sight—look like one of them fan dancers or somethin.

So we got off the freeway an went across a big field."Has that fuckin monkey got to keep followin us?"Raquel Welch say."We look rediculous enough as it is!"I ain't sayin nothin, but I look back, an ole Sue, he got a pained look on his face. He ain't never met Raquel Welch before, neither, an I think his feelins is hurt.

Anyhow, we kep goin along an they still ain't nobody payin us much mind. Finally we come to a big ole busy street an Raquel Welch say,"Goodgodamighty—this is Sunset Boulevard! How am I gonna explain goin across Sunset Boulevard butt neckid in broad daylight!"In this, I tend to see her point, an I am sort of glad I got on the creature suit so's nobody will recognize me-even if I *am* with Raquel Welch.

We come to a traffic light an when it turn green, the three of us walked on across the street, Raquel Welch doin her fan dance to beat the band an smilin at people in cars an stuff like she was on stage."I am totally humiliated!"she hisses at me under her breath."I am violated! Just wait till we get outta this. I am gonna have your big ass, you goddamn idiot!"

Some of the people waitin in their cars at the traffic light commence to honkin they horns and wavin, on account of they must of recognized Raquel Welch, an when we get across the street, a few cars turn our way an start to followin after us. By the time we get to Wilshire Boulevard we have attracted quite a sizable crowd; people come out of they houses an stores an all to follow us—look like the Pied Piper or somethin—an Raquel Welch's face is red as a beet.

"You'll never work in this town again!"she say to me, flashin a smile to the crowd, but her teeth is clenched tight.

We gone on a bit further, an then she say,"Ah—finally—here is Rodeo Drive."I look over at a corner an, sure enough, there is a woman's clothing store. I tap her on the shoulder an point at it, but Raquel Welch say, "Uggh—that's Popagallo. Nobody would be caught dead these days wearing a Popagallo dress."

So we walked some more an then she say, "There—Giani's—they got some nice things in there," an so we go inside.

They is a sales feller at the door with a little moustache an a white suit with a handkerchief stickin out of the coat pocket, an he is eyein us pretty carefully as we come thru the door.

"May I help you, madam?" he axed.

"I want to buy a dress," Raquel Welch say.

"What did you have in mind?" say the feller.

"Anything, you fool—can't you see what's going on!"

Well, the sales feller point to a couple of racks of dresses an say there might be somethin in there her size, so Raquel Welch go over an begin to look thru the dresses.

"An is there somethin I can do for you gentlemen?" the feller says to me an Sue.

"We is just with her," I say. I look back, an the crowd is all gathered outside, noses pressed to the winder.

Raquel Welch took about eight or nine dresses into the back an tried them on. After a wile she come out an say, "What do you think about this one?" It is a sort of brown lookin dress with a bunch of belts an loops all over it an a low neckline.

"Oh, I'm not so sure, dear," say the salesman, "somehow it—it just isn't *you*." So she go back an try on another one an the salesman say, "Oh, wonderful! You look absolutely precious."

"I'll take it,"say Raquel Welch, an the salesman say,"Fine—how would you like to pay for it?"

"What do you mean?"she axed.

"Well, cash, check, credit card?"he say.

"Look you bozo—can't you see I don't have anything like that with me? Where the hell do you think I'd *put* it?"

"Please, madam—don't let's be vulgar,"the salesman say."I am Raquel Welch,"she tell the man."I will send somebody around here to pay you later."

"I am terribly sorry, lady,"he say,"but we don't do business that way."

"But I'm *Raquel Welch*!"she shout."Don't you recognize me?"

"Listen lady,"the man say,"half the people that come in here say they are Raquel Welch or Farrah Fawcett or Sophia Loren or somebody. You got any ID?"

"ID!"she shout."Where do you think I would keep ID?"

"No ID, no credit card, no money—no dress,"say the salesman.

"I'll prove who the hell I am,"Raquel Welch say, an all of a sudden she pull down the top of the dress."Who else is got tits like these in this one-horse town!"she screech. Outside, the crowd all be beatin on the winders an hollerin an cheerin. But the salesman, he punched a little button an some big guy what was the security detective come over an he say,"Okay, your asses is all under arrest. Come along quietly an there won't be no trouble."

23

SO HERE I AM, THOWED IN JAIL AGAIN.

After the security feller corralled us at Giani's, two carloads of cops come screamin up an this one cop come up to the salesman an say, "Well, what we got here?"

"This one says she's Raquel Welch," the salesman say. "Come in here wearin a bunch of banana leaves an wouldn't pay for the dress. I don't know bout these other two—but they look pretty suspicious to me."

"I *am* Raquel Welch!" she shout.

"Sure, lady," the cop say. "An I am Clint Eastwood. Why don't you go along with these two nice fellers here." He point to a couple of other cops.

"Now," says the head cop, an he be lookin at me an Sue, "what's your story?" "We was in a pitcher," I says.

"That why you're wearin that creature suit?" he axe.

"Yup,"I says.

"An what bout him?"he say, pointin to Sue."That's a pretty realistic costume, if I say so myself."

"Ain't no costume,"I says."He's a purebread orangutang."

"Is that so?"the cop say."Well I'll tell you what. We got a feller down to the station who makes pitchers, too, an he would love to get a couple of shots of you clowns. So you jus come along too—an don't make no sudden moves."

Anyhow, Mister Tribble has got to come down an bail me out again. An Mister Felder showed up with a whole platoon of lawyers to git out Raquel Welch, who by this time is hysterical.

"You jus wait!"she shriek back at me as they turnin her loose."When I git finished, you won't be able to find a job as a spear carrier in a nightmare!"

In this, she is probly correct. It look like my movie career is over.

"That's life, baby—but I'll call you for lunch sometime,"Mister Felder says to me as he is leavin."We'll send somebody by later to pick up the creature suit."

"C'mon, Forrest,"say Mister Tribble."You and I have got other fish to fry."

Back at the hotel, Mister Tribble an me an Sue is settin in our room havin a conference.

"It is going to pose a problem, with Sue here,"Mister Tribble says."I mean, look how we had to sneak him up the stairs and everthin. It is very difficult to travel with an orangutan, we have to face that."

I tole him how I felt bout Sue, bout how he saved my ass more than once in the jungle an all.

"Well, I think I understand your feelings," he says. "And I'm willing to give it a try. But he's going to have to behave himself, or we'll be in trouble for sure."

"He will," I say, an ole Sue be noddin an grinnin like a ape.

Anyhow, nex day is the big chess match between me an the International Grand Master Ivan Petrokivitch, also known as Honest Ivan. Mister Tribble have taken me to a clothes store an rented me a tuxedo on account of this is to be a big fashionable deal, an a lot of muckity-mucks will be on han. Furthermore, the winner will get ten thousan dollars, an my haf of that ought to be enough to get me started in the srimp bidness, so I cannot afford to make no mistakes.

Well, we get to the hall where the chess game is to take place an there is bout a thousan people millin aroun an already settin at the table is Honest Ivan, glarin at me like he's Muhammad Ali or somebody.

Honest Ivan is a big ole Russian feller with a high forehead, jus like the Frankenstein monster, an long black curly hair such as you might see on a violin player. When I go up an set down, he grunt somethin at me an then another feller say, "Let the match begin," an that was it.

Honest Ivan is got the white team an he get to make the first move, startin with somethin call The Ponziani Opening.

I move nex, using The Reti Opening, an everthin is goin pretty smooth. Each of us make a couple of more moves, then Honest Ivan try somethin known as The Falkbeer Gambit, movin his knight aroun to see if he can take my rook.

But I seed that comin, an set up somethin called The Noah's Ark Trap, an got his knight instead. Honest Ivan ain't lookin none too happy but he seem to take it in stride an employed The Tarrasch Threat to menace my bishop.

I ain't havin none of that, tho, an I thowed up The Queen's Indian Defense an that force him to use The Schevenigen Variation, which lead me to utilize The Benoni Counter.

Honest Ivan appear to be somewhat frustrated, an was twistin his fingers an bitin on his lower lip, an then he done tried a desperation move—The Fried Liver Attack—to which I applied Alekhine's Defense an stopped his ass cold.

It look for a wile like it gonna be a stalemate, but Honest Ivan, he went an applied The Hoffman Maneuver an broke out! I look over at Mister Tribble, an he sort of smile at me, an he move his lips an mouth the word"*Now*,"an I knowed what he mean.

You see, they was a couple of tricks Big Sam taught me in the jungle that was not in the book an now was the time to use them—namely, The Cookin Pot Variation of The Coconut Gambit, in which I use my queen as bait an sucker that bastid into riskin his knight to take her.

Unfortunately, it didn't work. Honest Ivan must of seen that comin an he snapped up my queen an now my ass is in trouble! Nex I pull somethin called The Grass Hut Ploy, in which I stick my last rook out on a limb to fool him, but he wadn't fooled. Took my rook an my other bishop too, an was ready to finish me off with The Petroff Check, when I pulled out all the stops an set up The Pygmie Threat.

Now the Pygmie Threat was one of Big Sam's specialties, an he had taught it to me real good. It depends a lot on suprise an usin several other pieces as bait, but if a feller falls victim to The Pygmie Threat, he might as well hang up his jockstrap an go on home. I was hopin an prayin it woud work, cause if it didn't, I ain't got no more bright ideas an I'm just about done for already.

Well, Honest Ivan, he grunt a couple of times an pick up his knight to move it to square eight, which meant that he would be suckered in by The Pygmie Threat an in two more moves I would have him in check an he would be powerless to do anythin about it!

But Honest Ivan must of smelt somethin fishy, cause he moved that piece from square five to square eight an back again nine or ten times, never takin his han off it, which would have meant the move was final.

The crowd was so quiet you coulda heard a pin drop, an I am so nervous an excited I am bout to bust. I look over an Mister Tribble is rollin his eyes up in the air like he's prayin an a feller what come with Honest Ivan is scowlin an lookin sour. Honest Ivan move the piece back to square eight two or three more times, but always he put it back on square five. Finally, it look like he gonna do somethin else, but then he lif up the piece one more time an have it hoverin above square eight an I be holdin my breath an the room is quiet as a tomb. Honest Ivan still be hoverin with the piece an my heart is beatin like a drum, an all of a sudden he look straight at me—an I don't know what happened, I guess I was so excited an all—

but suddenly I cut a humongus baked-bean fart that sound like somebody is rippin a bedsheet in haf!

Honest Ivan get a look of suprise on his face, an then he suddenly drop his chess piece an thowed up his hans an say,"Uggh!"an start fannin the air an coughin an holdin his nose. Folks standin aroun us begun to move back an was mumblin an takin out they handkerchiefs an all, an I am so red in the face I look like a tomato.

But when it all settle down again, I look at the chessboard an damn if Honest Ivan ain't lef his piece right on square eight. So I reached out an snap it up with my knight, an then I grapped two of his pawns an his queen an finally his king—checkmate! I done won the match an the five thousan dollars! The Pygmie Threat done come thru again.

All the wile, Honest Ivan be makin loud gestures an protestin an all an him an the feller that come with him immediately file a formal complaint against me.

The guy in charge of the tournament be thumbin thru his rule book till he come to where it say,"No player shall knowingly engage in conduct that is distractive to another player while a game is in progress."

Mister Tribble step up an say,"Well, I don't think you can prove that my man did what he did *knowingly*. It was a sort of involuntary thing."

Then the tournament director thumb thru his book some more, an come to where it say,"No player shall behave in a manner that is rude or offensive to his opponent."

"Listen,"Mister Tribble say,"haven't you ever had the need to break wind? Forrest didn't mean anything by it. He's been sitting there a long time."

"I don't know," the tournament director say, "on the face of it, I think I'm going to have to disqualify him."

"Well can't you give him another chance at least?" Mister Tribble axed.

The tournament director scratched his chin for a minute. "Well, perhaps," he say, "but he is gonna have to contain hissef because we cannot tolerate this sort of thing here, you know?"

An so it was beginnin to look like I might be allowed to finish the game, but all of a sudden they is a big commotion at one end of the room, an ladies are screaming an shrieking an all an then I look up an here come ole Sue, swingin towards me on a chandelier.

Jus as the chandelier got overhead Sue let go an dropped right on top of the chessboard, scatterin all the pieces in a dozen directions. Honest Ivan fell over backwards across a chair an on the way down ripped haf the dress off a fat lady that looked like a advertisement for a jewelry store. She commenced to flailin an hollerin an smacked the tournament director in the nose an Sue was jumpin up an down an chatterin an everbody is in a panic, stompin an stumblin an shoutin to call the police.

Mister Tribble grapped me by the arm an say, "Let's get out of here, Forrest—you have already seen enough of the police in this town."

This I coud not deny.

Well, we get on back to the hotel, an Mister Tribble say we got to have another conference.

"Forrest," he say, "I just do not believe this is going to work out anymore. You can play chess like a dream, but things have gotten too complicated otherwise. All that stuff that went on this afternoon was, well, to put it mildly, it was bizarre."

I am noddin an ole Sue is lookin pretty sorrowful too.

"So, I'll tell you what I'm going to do. You're a good boy, Forrest, and I can't leave you stranded out here in California, so I am going to arrange for you and Sue to get back to Alabama or wherever it is you came from. I know you need a little grubstake to start your shrimp business, and your share of the winnings, after I deduct expenses, comes to a little under five thousand dollars."

Mister Tribble hand me a envelope an when I look inside it, there is a bunch of hundrit dollar bills.

"I wish you all the best in your venture," he say.

Mister Tribble phone for a taxicab an got us to the railroad station. He has also arranged for Sue to ride in the baggage car in a crate, and says I can go back there an visit with him an take him food an water when I want. They brung out the crate an Sue got on inside it an they took him off.

"Well, good luck, Forrest," Mister Tribble say, an he shake my han. "Here's my card—so stay in touch and let me know how it's going, okay?"

I took the card an shook his han again an was sorry to be leavin cause Mister Tribble was a very nice man, an I had let him down. I was settin in my seat on the train, lookin out the winder, an Mister Tribble was still standin on the platform. Jus as the train pulled out, he raised up his han at me an waved goodbye.

So off I went again, an for a long time that night my head was full of dreams—of going back home again, of my mama, of po ole Bubba an of the srimp bidness an, of course, of Jenny Curran too. More than anythin in the world, I wished I were not such a loony tune.

24

WELL, FINALLY, I DONE COME HOME AGAIN.

The train got into the Mobile station bout three o'clock in the mornin an they took off ole Sue in his crate an lef us standin on the platform. Ain't nobody else aroun cept some feller sweepin the floor an a guy snoozin on a bench in the depot, so Sue an me walked on downtown an finally foun a place to sleep in a abandoned buildin.

Nex mornin, I got Sue some bananas down by the wharf an found a little lunch counter where I bought a great big breakfast with grits an eggs an bacon an pancakes an all, an then I figgered I had to do *somethin* to get us squared away, so I begun to walk out to where the Little Sisters of the Poor home was located. On the way, we passed by where our ole house used to be, an it wadn't nothin lef but a field of weeds an some burnt up wood. It was a very strange feelin, seein that, an so we kep on goin.

When I got to the po house, I tole Sue to wait in the yard so as not to startle them sisters none, an I went in an axed about my mama.

The head sister, she was real nice, an she say she don't know where Mama is, cept she went off with the protestant, but that I might try axin aroun in the park cause mama use to go an set there in the afternoons with some other ladies. So I got Sue an we gone on over there.

They was some ladies settin on the benches an I went up an tole one of them who I was, an she looked at ole Sue, an say, "I reckon I might of guess it."

But then she say she has heard that Mama was workin as a pants presser in a dry cleanin store on the other side of town, an so me an Sue went over there an sho enough, there is po ole Mama, sweatin over a pair of pants in the laundry.

When she seen me, Mama drop everthin an thowed herself into my arms. She is cryin an twistin her hans an snifflin just like I remembered. Good ole Mama.

"Oh, Forrest," she say. "You have come home at last. There wadn't a day gone by I didn't think bout you, an I done cried mysef to sleep ever night since you been gone." That didn't suprise me none tho, an I axed her bout the protestant.

"That low-down polecat," Mama say. "I should of knowed better than to run off with a protestant. Wadn't a month went by before he chucked me for a sixteen-year-ole girl—an him bein nearly sixty. Let me tell you, Forrest, protestants ain't got no morals."

Just then a loud voice come from inside the dry cleanin stow, say, "Gladys, have you done lef the steam press on somebody's pants?"

"Oh my God!" Mama shout, an run back inside. All of a sudden a big column of black smoke blowed out thru the winder an people inside is bawlin an hollerin an cussin an nex thing I knowed, Mama is bein hauled out of the stow by a big old ugly bald-headed guy that is shoutin an manhandlin her.

"Git out! Git out!" he holler. "This is the last straw! You done burnt up your last pair of pants!"

Mama be cryin an weepin an I stepped up to the feller an say, "I think you better be takin your hans off my mama."

"Who the hell is you?" he axed.

"Forrest Gump," I says back, an he say, "Well you git your ass outta here too, an take your mama with you, cause she don't work here no more!"

"You best not be talkin that way aroun my mama," I says, an he say back, "Yeah? What you gonna do about it?"

So I showed him.

First, I grapped him an picked him up in the air. Then I carried him into where they was washin all these clothes in a big ole oversize laundry machine they use for quilts and rugs, an I open the top an stuff him in an close the lid shut an turned the dial to "Spin." Last I seen of him, his ass were headed for the "Rinse" cycle.

Mama is bawlin an dawbin at her eyes with a handkerchief an say, "Oh, Forrest, now I done lost my job!"

"Don't worry none, Mama," I tole her, "everthin gonna be okay, cause I have got a plan."

"How you gonna have a plan, Forrest?" she say. "You is a idiot. How is a po idiot gonna have a plan?"

"Jus wait an see," I says. Anyhow, I am glad to have got off on the right foot my first day home.

We got outta there, an started walkin towards the roomin house where Mama stayin. I had done introduced her to Sue an she say she was pleased that at least I have got *some* kinda friend—even if he is a ape.

Anyhow, Mama an me ate supper at the roomin house an she got Sue a orange from the kitchen, an afterwards, me an Sue went down to the bus station an got the bus to Bayou La Batre, where Bubba's folks lived. Sure as rain, last thing I saw of Mama she was standin on the porch of the roomin house wipin her eyes an sobbin as we lef. But I had give her haf the five thousan dollars to sort of tide her over an pay her rent an all till I could get mysef established, so I didn't feel so bad.

Anyhow, when the bus get to Bayou La Batre we didn't have no trouble findin Bubba's place. It's about eight o'clock at night an I knocked on the door an after a wile an ole feller appears an axed what I want. I tole him who I was an that I knowed Bubba from playin football an from the Army, an he got kinda nervous but he invited me inside. I had tole ole Sue to stay out in the yard an kinda keep outta sight since they probly hasn't seen nothin look like him down here.

Anyhow, it was Bubba's daddy, an he got me a glass of iced tea an started axin me a lot of questions. Wanted to know bout Bubba, bout how he got kilt an all, an I tole him the best I could.

Finally, he say, "There's somethin I been wonderin all these years, Forrest—what do you think Bubba died for?"

"Cause he got shot," I says, but he say, "No, that ain't what I mean. What I mean is, why? Why was we over there?"

I thought for a minute, an say, "Well, we was tryin to do the right thing, I guess. We was jus doin what we was tole."

An he say, "Well, do you think it was worth it? What we did? All them boys gettin kilt that way?"

An I says, "Look, I am jus a idiot, see. But if you want my real opinion, I think it was a bunch of shit."

Bubba's daddy nod his head. "That's what I figgered," he say.

Anyhow, I tole him why I had come there. Tole him bout me an Bubba's plan to open up a little srimp bidness, an how I had met the ole gook when I was in the hospital an he showed me how to grow srimp, an he was gettin real interested an axin a lot of questions, when all of a sudden they is a tremendous squawkin set up out in the yard.

"Somethin's after my chickens!" Bubba's daddy shout, an he went an got a gun from behin the door an go out on the porch.

"They is somethin I got to tell you," I says, an I tole him bout Sue bein there, cept we don't see hide nor hair of him.

Bubba's daddy go back in the house an get a flashlight an shine it aroun in the yard. He shine it under a big tree an down at the bottom is a goat—big ole billy goat, standin there pawin the groun. He shine it up in the tree an there is po Sue, settin on a limb, scared haf to death.

"That goat'll do it ever time," say Bubba's daddy. "Git on away from there!" he shout, an he thow a stick at the goat. After the goat was gone, Sue come down from the tree an we let him inside the house.

"What is that thing?" Bubba's daddy axed.

"He is a orangutang," I says.

"Looks kinda like a gorilla, don't he?"

"A little bit," I says, "but he ain't."

Anyway, Bubba's daddy say we can sleep there that night, an in the mornin, he will go aroun with us an see if we can find some place to start the srimp bidness. They was a nice breeze blowin off the bayou an you coud hear frawgs an crickets an even the soun of a fish jumpin ever once in a wile. It was a nice, peaceful place, an I made up my mind then an there that I was not gonna get into no trouble here.

Nex mornin brite an early we get up an Bubba's daddy done fixed a big breakfast with homemade sausage an fresh yard eggs an biscuits an molasses, an then he take me an Sue in a little boat an pole us down the Bayou. It is calm an they is a bit of mist on the water. Ever once in a wile a big ole bird would take off outta the marsh.

"Now," say Bubba's daddy, "here is where the salt tide comes in," an he point to a slew that runs up in the marsh. "There's some pretty big ponds up in there, an if I was gonna do what you plannin to do, that's where I'd do it."

He pole us up into the slew. "Now you see there," he say, "that is a little piece of high groun an you can jus see the roof of a little shack in there.

"It used to be lived in by ole Tom LeFarge, but he been dead four or five years now. Ain't nobody own it. You wanted, you could fix it up a little an stay there. Last time I looked, he had a couple of ole rowboats pulled up on the bank. Probly ain't worth a damn, but you caulk em up, they'd probly float."

He pole us in further, an say,"Ole Tom used to have some duckboards runnin thru the marsh down to the ponds. Used to fish an shoot ducks in there. You could probly fix em up. It'd be a way of gettin aroun in there."

Well, let me tell you, it looked ideal. Bubba's daddy say they get seed srimp up in them slews an bayous all the time, an it wouldn't be no trouble to net a bunch of em to start off the bidness with. Another thing he say is that in his experience, a srimp will eat cottonseed meal, which is good on account of it is cheap.

The main thing we got to do is block off them ponds with mesh nets an get the little cabin fixed up to live in an get some supplies like peanut butter an jelly an bread an all that kind of shit. Then we be ready to start growin our srimp.

So we got started that very day. Bubba's daddy took me back to the house an we gone into town an begun buyin supplies. He say we can use his boat till we get ours fixed up, an that night me an Sue stayed in the little fishin shack for the first time. It rained some an the roof leaked like crazy, but I didn't mind. Nex mornin I jus went out an fixed it up.

It took almost a month to get things goin—makin the shack nice an fixin up the rowboats an the duckboards in the marsh an layin the mesh nets aroun one of them ponds. Finally the day come when we is ready to put in some srimp. I have bought a srimp net an me an Sue went on out in the rowboat an dragged it aroun for most of the day. By that night, we had probly fifty pounds of srimp in the bait well an we rowed up an dumped em into the pond. They be crackin an swimmin aroun an dancin on top of the water. My, my, it was a lovely site.

Nex mornin we got us five hundrit pounds of cottonseed meal an thowed a hundrit pounds of it in the pond for the srimp to eat an the nex afternoon we set about nettin-in another pond. We done that all summer an all fall an all winter an all spring an by that time we has got four ponds operatin an everthin is lookin rosy. At night I would set out on the porch of the shack an play my harmonica an on Saturday night I would go into town an buy a six-pack of beer an me an Sue would get drunk. I finally feel like I belong someplace, an am doin a honest day's work, an I figger that when we get the first srimp harvested an sold, maybe then it will be all right to try to find Jenny again, an see if she is still mad at me.

25

IT WAS A VERY NICE DAY IN JUNE WHEN WE FIGGERED IT WAS time to start our first srimp harvest. Me an Sue got up with the sun an went down to the pond an dragged a net acrost it till it got stuck on somethin. Sue tried to pull it loose first, then I tried, then we tried together till we finally figgered out the net wadn't stuck—it was jus so full of srimp we couldn't move it!

By that evenin we had pulled in about three hundrit pouns of srimp, an we spent the night sortin em out in various sizes. Nex mornin we put the srimp in baskets an took em down to our little rowboat. They weighed so much we damn near tumped over on the way up to Bayou La Batre.

They was a seafood packin house there an Sue an me hauled the srimp from the dock to the weighin room. After everthin is toted up, we got ourselfs a check for eight hundrit, sixty-five dollars! It is about the first honest money I ever made since I played harmonica for The Cracked Eggs.

Ever day for nearly two weeks Sue an me harvested srimp an brought em in to the packin house. When it was finally over, we had made a total of nine thousand, seven hundrit dollars an twenty-six cents. The srimp bidness was a success!

Well, let me tell you—it were a happy occasion. We took up a bushel basket of srimp to Bubba's daddy an he was real happy an say he is proud of us an that he wished Bubba were there too. Then me an Sue caught the bus up to Mobile to celebrate. First thing I done was gone to see my mama at the roomin house, an when I tole her about the money an all, sure enough, she be cloudin up again. "Oh, Forrest," she say, "I am so proud of you—doin so good an all for bein retarded."

Anyhow, I tole Mama about my plan, which was that nex year we was gonna have three times as many srimp ponds, an that we needed somebody to watch over the money an look after our expenses an all, an I axed if she would do that.

"You mean I gotta move all the way down to Bayou La Batre?" Mama say. "Ain't nothin goin on down there. What am I gonna do with mysef?"

"Count money," I says.

After that, me an Sue went downtown an got ourselfs a big meal. I gone down to the docks an bought Sue a big bunch of bananas, an then went an got mysef the biggest steak dinner I could find, with mashed potatoes an green peas an everthin. Then I decided to go drink me a beer someplace an jus as I am walkin by this dark ole saloon near the waterfront, I hear all this loud cussin an shoutin an even after all these years, I knowed that voice. I stuck my head in the door, an sure enough, it were ole Curtis from the University!

Curtis were very happy to see me, callin me a asshole an a cocksucker an a motherfucker an everthin else nice he could think of. As it turns out, Curtis had gone on to play pro football with the Washington Redskins after he lef the University, an then he done got put on waivers after bitin the team owner's wife on the ass at a party. He played for a couple of other teams for a few years, but after that he got hissef a job on the docks as a longshoreman which, he say, was suitable for the amount of education he got at the University.

Anyway, Curtis bought me a couple of beers an we talked about ole times. The Snake, he say, had played quarterback for the Green Bay Packers till he got caught drinkin a entire quart of Polish vodka durin halftime in the Minnesota Vikings game. Then Snake went an played for the New Yawk Giants till he called a Statue-of-Liberty play in the third quarter of the Rams game. The Giants' coach say ain't nobody used a Statue-ofLiberty play in pro ball since nineteen hundrit thirty-one, an that Snake ain't got no bidness callin one now. But actually, Curtis say, it wadn't no Statue-of-Liberty play at all. The truth, accordin to Curtis, was that Snake was so spaced out on dope that when he faded back for a pass he done completely forgot to thow the ball, an the lef end jus happen to see what is goin on, an run aroun behin him an take the ball away. Anyhow, Curtis say the Snake is now assistant coach for a tinymight team someplace in Georgia.

After a couple of beers, I got a idea, an tole Curtis about it.

"How'd you like to come work for me?" I axed.

Curtis be cussin an hollerin but after a minute or two I figger out he is tryin to axe me what I want him to do, so I tole him about the srimp bidness an that we was gonna expand our operation. He cuss an holler some more, but the gist of what he is sayin is "yes."

So all thru that summer an fall an the next spring we be workin hard, me an Sue an Mama an Curtis—an I even had a job for Bubba's daddy. That year we made nearly thirty thousan dollars an are gettin bigger all the time. Things couldn't of been goin better—Mama ain't bawlin hardly at all, an one day we even seen Curtis smile once—altho he stopped an started cussin again soon as he saw us watchin. For me, tho, it ain't quite as happy as it might be, cause I am thinkin a lot about Jenny an what has become of her.

One day, I jus decided to do somethin bout it. It was a Sunday, an I got dressed up an caught the bus up to Mobile an went over to Jenny's mama's house. She was settin inside, watchin tv, when I knocked on the door.

When I tole her who I was, she say, "Forrest Gump! I jus can't believe it. C'mon in!"

Well, we set there a wile an she axed bout Mama an what I'd been doin an everthin, an finally I axed about Jenny.

"Oh, I really don't hear from her much these days," Mrs. Curran say. "I think they livin someplace in North Carolina."

"She got a roomate or somethin?" I axed.

"Oh, didn't you know, Forrest?" she say. "Jenny got married."

"Married?" I say.

"It was a couple of years ago. She'd been livin in Indiana. Then she went to Washington an nex thing I knew, I got a postcard sayin she was married, an they was movin to North Carolina or someplace. You want me to tell her anythin if I hear from her?"

"No'm," I says, "not really. Maybe jus tell her I wish her good luck an all."

"I sure will," Mrs. Curran say, "an I'm so glad you came by."

I dunno, I reckon I ought to of been ready for that news, but I wadn't.

I could feel my heart poundin, an my hans got cold an damp an all I coud think of was goin someplace an curlin up into a ball the way I had that time after Bubba got kilt, an so that's what I did. I foun some shrubs in back of somebody's yard an I crawled under there an jus got mysef into a ball. I think I even commenced to suck my thumb, which I ain't done in a long wile since my mama always said it was a sure sign that somebody's a idiot, unless they are a baby. Anyhow, I don't know how long I stayed there. It was most of a day an a haf I guess.

I didn't feel no blame for Jenny, she done what she had to. After all, I am a idiot, an wile a lot of people say they is married to idiots, they couldn't never imagine what would be in store if they ever married a real one. Mostly, I guess, I am jus feelin sorry for mysef, because somehow I had actually got to where I *believed* that Jenny an me would be together someday. An so when I learnt from her mama that she is married, it was like a part of me has died an will never be again, for gettin married is not like runnin away. Gettin married is a very serious deal. Sometime durin the night I cried, but it did not hep much.

It was later that afternoon when I crawled out of the shrubs an gone on back to Bayou La Batre. I didn't tell nobody what had happened, cause I figgered it wouldn't of done no good. They was some work I needed to do aroun the ponds, mendin nets an such, an I went on out by mysef an done it. By the time I get finished it is dark, an I done made a decision—I am gonna thow mysef into the srimp bidness an work my ass off. It is all I can do.

An so I did.

That year we made seventy-five thousan dollars before expenses an the bidness is gettin so big I got to hire more people to hep me run it. One person I get is ole Snake, the quarterback from the University. He is not too happy with his present job with the tinymight football team an so I put him to work with Curtis in charge of dredgin an spillway duties. Then I find out that Coach Fellers from the highschool is done retired an so I give him a job, along with his two goons who has also retired, workin on boats an docks.

Pretty soon the newspapers get wind of what is goin on an send a reporter down to interview me for a sort of "local boy makes good" story. It appears the nex Sunday, with a photo of me an Mama an Sue, an the headline say, "Certifiable Idiot Finds Future in Novel Marine Experiment."

Anyhow, not too long after that, Mama say to me that we need to get somebody to hep her with the bookkeepin part of the bidness an give some kind of advice on financial things on account of we is makin so much money. I done thought bout it a wile, an then I decided to get in touch with Mister Tribble, cause he had made a bunch of money in bidness before he retired. He was delighted I had called, he say, an will be on the nex plane down.

A week after he gets here, Mister Tribble say we got to set down an talk.

"Forrest," he say, "what you have done here is nothing short of remarkable, but you are at a point where you need to begin some serious financial planning."

I axed him what bout, an he say this: "Investments! Diversification! Look, as I see it, this next fiscal year you are going to have profits at about a hundred and ninety thousand dollars. The following year it will bear near a quarter of a million. With such profits you must reinvest them or the IRS will tax you into oblivion. Reinvestment is the very heart of American business!"

An so that's what we did.

Mister Tribble took charge of all that, an we formed a couple of corporations. One was "Gump's Shellfish Company." Another was called "Sue's Stuffed Crabs, Inc.," an another was "Mama's Crawfish Étouffée, Ltd."

Well, the quarter of a million become haf a million an the year followin that, a million, an so on, till after four more years we done become a five million dollar a year bidness. We got nearly three hundred employees now, includin The Turd an The Vegetable, whose rasslin days were over, an we got them loadin crates at the warehouse. We tried like hell to find po Dan, but he done vanished without a trace. We did find ole Mike, the rasslin promoter, an put him in charge of public relations an advertisin. At Mister Tribble's suggestion, Mike done even hired Raquel Welch to do some television ads for us—they dressed her up to look like a crab, an she dance aroun an say, "You ain't never had crabs till you try Sue's!"

Anyhow, things has gotten real big-time. We got a fleet of refrigerator trucks an a fleet of srimp, oyster an fishin boats. We got our own packin house, an a office buildin, an have invested heavily in real estate such as condominiums an shoppin centers an in oil an gas leases. We done hired ole Professor Quackenbush, the English teacher from up at Harvard University, who have been fired from his job for molestin a student, an made him a cook in Mama's étouffée operation. We also hired Colonel Gooch, who got drummed out of the Army after my Medal of Honor tour. Mister Tribble put him in charge of "covert activities."

Mama has gone an had us a big ole house built cause she say it ain't right for a corporate executive like me to be livin in no shack. Mama say Sue can stay on in the shack an keep an eye on things. Ever day now, I got to wear a suit an carry a briefcase like a lawyer. I got to go to meetins all the time an listen to a bunch of shit that sound like pygmie talk, an people be callin me "Mister Gump," an all. In Mobile, they done give me the keys to the city an axed me to be on the board of directors of the hospital an the symphony orchestra.

An then one day some people come by the office an say they want to run me for the United States Senate.

"You're an absolute natural,"this one feller say. He is wearing a searsucker suit an smokin a big cigar."A former star football player for Bear Bryant, a war hero, a famous astronaut and the confidant of Presidents—what more can you ask? !"he axe. Mister Claxton is his name.

"Look,"I tell him,"I am just a idiot. I don't know nothin bout politics."

"Then you will fit in perfectly!"Mister Claxton say."Listen, we need good men like you. Salt of the earth, I tell you! Salt of the earth!"

I did not like this idea any more than I like a lot of the other ideas people have for me, on account of other people's ideas are usually what get me into trouble. But sure enough, when I tole my mama, she get all teary-eyed an proud an say it would be the answer to all her dreams to see her boy be a United States Senator.

Well, the day come when we is to announce my candidacy. Mister Claxton an them others hired the auditorium up in Mobile an hauled me out on the stage in front of a crowd that paid fifty cents apiece to come listen to my shit. They begin with a lot of long-winded speeches an then it come my turn.

"My feller Americans,"I begin. Mister Claxton an the others have writ me a speech to give an later they will be questions from the audience. TV cameras are rollin an flashbulbs are poppin an reporters are scribblin in their notebooks. I read the whole speech, which ain't very long an don't make much sense—but what do I know? I am jus a idiot.

When I am finished talkin, a lady from the newspaper stand up an look at her notepad.

"We are currently on the brink of nuclear disaster," she say, "the economy is in ruins, our nation is reviled throughout the world, lawlessness prevails in our cities, people starve of hunger every day, religion is gone from our homes, greed and avarice is rampant everywhere, our farmers are going broke, foreigners are invading our country and taking our jobs, our unions are corrupt, babies are dying in the ghettos, taxes are unfair, our schools are in chaos and famine, pestilence and war hang over us like a cloud—in view of all this, Mister Gump," she axe, "what, in your mind, is the most pressing issue of the moment?" The place was so quiet you coulda heard a pin drop.

"I got to pee," I says.

At this, the crowd went wile! People begun hollerin an cheerin an shoutin an wavin they hands in the air. From the back of the room somebody started chantin an pretty soon the whole auditorium was doin it.

"WE GOT TO PEE! WE GOT TO PEE! WE GOT TO PEE!" they was yellin.

My mama had been settin there behind me on the stage an she got up an come drug me away from the speaker's stand.

"You ought to be ashamed of yoursef," she say, "talkin like that in public."

"No, no!" Mister Claxton says. "It's perfect! They love it. This will be our campaign slogan!"

"What will?" Mama axed. Her eyes narrowed down to little beads.

"*We Got to Pee*!" Mister Claxton say. "Just listen to them! No one has ever had such a rapport with the common people!"

But mama ain't buyin none of it. "Whoever heard of anybody usin a campaign slogan like that!" she says. "It's vulgar an disgusting—besides, what does it mean?"

"It's a symbol," Mister Claxton says. "Just think, we'll have billboards and placards and bumper stickers made up. Take out television and radio ads. It's a stroke of genius, that's what it is. *We Got to Pee* is a symbol of riddance of the yoke of government oppression—of evacuation of all that is wrong with this country... It signifies frustration and impending relief!"

"What!" Mama axed suspiciously. "Is you lost your mind?"

"Forrest," Mister Claxton says, "you are on your way to Washington."

An so it seemed. The campaign was goin along pretty good an "We Got to Pee" had become the byword of the day. People shouted it on the street an from cars an busses. Television commentators an newspaper columnists spent a lot of time trying to tell folks what it meant. Preachers yelled it from their pulpits an children chanted it in school. It was beginnin to look like I was a shoo-in for the election, an, in fact, the candidate runnin against me, he got so desperate he made up his own slogan, "*I Got to Pee, Too*," an plastered it all over the state.

Then it all fell apart, jus like I was afraid it would.

The "I Got to Pee" deal done come to the attention of the national media an pretty soon the Washington *Post* an the New Yawk *Times* sent down their investigating reporters to look into the matter. They axed me a lot of questions an was real nice an friendlysounding, but then they went back an begun to dig up my past. One day the stories broke on the front page of ever newspaper in the country. "Senatorial Candidate Has Checkered Career," say the headlines.

First, they write that I done flunked out of the University my first year. Then they dug up that shit about me an Jenny when the cops hauled me in from the movie theater. Next they drag out the photograph of me showin my ass to President Johnson in the Rose Garden. They axed aroun about my days in Boston with The Cracked Eggs an quote people sayin that I done smoked marijuana an also mention "a possible arson incident" at Harvard University.

Worst—they done find out about the criminal charges I got for thowin my medal at the U. S. Capitol an that I been sentenced by a judge to a loony asylum. Also, they knew all about my rasslin career, too, an that I was called The Dunce. They even ran a photo of me being tied up by The Professor. Finally, they mention several "unnamed sources" sayin I was involved in a "Hollywood sex scandal with a well-known actress."

That did it. Mister Claxton come rushin into campaign headquarters screamin, "We are ruint! We have been stabbed in the back!" an shit like that. But it was over. I had no choice cept to withdraw from the race, an the next day Mama an me an Mister Tribble set down for a talk.

"Forrest," Mister Tribble say, "I think it might be good for you to lay low for a while."

I knowed he was right. An besides, there is other things that been naggin at my mind for a long time now, though I ain't said nothin about them before.

When the srimp bidness first started up, I kind of enjoyed the work, gettin up at dawn an goin down to the ponds an puttin up the nets an then harvestin the srimp an all, an me an Sue settin at night on the porch of the fishin shack playin the harmonica, an gettin a six-pack of beer on Saturday an gettin drunk.

Now it ain't nothing like that. I got to go to all sorts of dinner parties where people servin a lot of mysterious-lookin food an the ladies wearin big ole earrings an shit. All day long the phone don't never stop ringin an people be wantin to axe me bout everthin under the sun. In the Senate, it would have jus been worse. Now I ain't got no time to mysef as it is, an somehow, things are slippin past me.

Furthermore, I look in the mirror now an I got wrinkles on my face, an my hair is turnin gray at the edges an I ain't got as much energy as I used to. I know things are movin along with the bidness, but mysef, I feel like I'm jus spinnin in place. I'm wonderin jus why am I doin all this for? A long time ago, me an Bubba had a plan, which has now gone beyon our wildest dreams, but so what? It ain't haf as much fun as the time I played against them Nebraska corn shucker jackoffs in the Orange Bowl, or took a ride on my harmonica up at Boston with The Cracked Eggs, or, for that matter, watched"The Beverly Hillbillies"with ole President Johnson.

An I spose Jenny Curran has somethin to do with it, too, but since ain't nobody can do nothin bout that, I might as well forget it.

Anyhow, I realize I got to get away. Mama be weepin an bawlin an daubbin at her eyes with the handkerchief like I figgered she woud, but Mister Tribble understan completely.

"Why don't we jus tell everbody you are taking a long vacation, Forrest," he say. "An of course your share of the bidness will be here whenever you want it."

So that's what I done. One mornin a few days later I got a little cash, an thowed a few things in a dufflebag an then gone down to the plant. I tole Mama an Mister Tribble goodbye an then went aroun an shook hans with everbody else—Mike an Professor Quackenbush an The Turd an The Vegetable an Snake an Coach Fellers an his goons an Bubba's daddy an all the rest.

Then I gone to the shack an foun ole Sue.

"What you gonna do?" I axed.

Sue grapped holt of my han an then he picked up my bag an carried it out the door. We got in the little rowboat an paddled up to Bayou La Batre an caught the bus to Mobile. A lady in the ticket office there say, "Where you want to go?" an I shrugged my shoulders, so she say, "Why don't you go to Savannah? I been there once an it is a real nice town."

So that's what we did.

26

WE GOT OFF THE BUS AT SAVANNAH, WHERE IT WAS RAININ to beat the band. Sue an me went in the depot an I got a cup of coffee an took it out under the eaves an tried to figger out what we gonna do nex.

I ain't got no plan, really, so after I finish my coffee I took out my harmonica an begun to play. I played a couple of songs, an lo an behole, a feller that was walkin by, he thowed a quarter in my coffee cup. I played a couple of more songs, an after a wile the coffee cup is bout haf full of change.

It done quit rainin so Sue an me walked on off an in a little bit come to a park in the middle of town. I set down on a bench an played some more an sure enough, people begun to drop quarters an dimes an nickels in the coffee cup. Then ole Sue, he caught on, an when folks would pass by, he'd take the coffee cup an go up to them with it. At the end of the day, I'd got nearly five dollars.

We slep in the park that night on a bench an it was a fine, clear night an the stars an moon was out. In the mornin we got some breakfast an I begun to play the harmonica again as folks started showin up for work. We made eight bucks that day an nine the nex, an by the end of the week we had done pretty good, considerin. After the weekend, I foun a little music shop an went in there to see if I could find another harmonica in the key of G on account of playing in C all the time was gettin monotonous. Over in a corner I seen that the feller had a used keyboard for sale. It look pretty much like the one ole George used to play with The Cracked Eggs an that he had taught me a few chords on.

I axed how much he wanted for it, an the feller say two hundrit dollars, but he will make me a deal. So I bought the keyboard an the feller even rigged up a stand on it so's I could play my harmonica too. It definately improved our popularity with the people. By the end of the nex week we was makin almost ten bucks a day, so I gone on back to the music shop an bought a set of used drums. After a few days practice, I got to where I could play them drums pretty good too. I chucked out the ole Styrofoam coffee cup an got a nice tin cup for Sue to pass aroun an we was doin pretty good for ourselfs. I was playin everthing from"The Night They Drove Ole Dixie Down"to"Swing Lo, Sweet Chariot,"and I had also foun a roomin house that let ole Sue stay there, an served breakfast an supper too.

One morning Sue an me is going to the park when it started to rain again. One thing about Savannah—it rains buckets ever other day there, or so it seems. We was walking down the street in front of a office building when suddenly I seen something that looked vaguely familiar.

There is a man in a business suit standing on the sidewalk with a unbrella an he is standin right in front of a big plastic garbage bag. Somebody is under the garbage bag, keepin out of the rain, an all you can see is a pair of hands reachin out from under the bag, shinin the shoes of the man in the suit. I gone acrost the street and looked closer, an lo and behol, I can just make out the little wheels of one of them dolly-wagons stickin out from under the bag too. I was so happy I could of just about bust, an I went up an thowed the garbage bag off an sure enough, it was ole Dan hissef, shinin shoes for a livin!

"Gimme that bag back you big oaf,"Dan say,"I'm gettin soakin wet out here."Then he saw Sue."So you finally got married, huh?"Dan say.

"It's a *he*,"I tole him."You remember—from when I went to space."

"You gonna shine my shoes, or what?"say the feller in the suit.

"Fuck off,"Dan says,"before I chew your soles in half."The feller, he walked away.

"What you doin here, Dan?"I axed,"What you shinin shoes for?"

"To shame the imperialist lackeys,"he answers."The way I got it figured, nobody with shined shoes is worth a shit, so the more shoes I shine, the more I'll send to hell in a handbasket."

"Well, if you say so,"I says, an then Dan thowed down his rag an wheel himself back under the awnin to git outta the rain.

"Awe hell, Forrest, I ain't shame the imperialist lackeys,"he say."They wouldn't want nobody like me anyhow, way I am."

"Sure they would, Dan," I says. "You always tole me I could be anythin I wanted to be an do anythin I want to do—an so can you."

"You still believin that shit?" he axed.

"I got to see Raquel Welch butt neckit," I says.

"Really?" Dan say, "what was it like?"

Well, after that, Dan an Sue an me kinda teamed up. Dan didn't want to stay in the boardin house, so he slep outside at night under his garbage bag. "Builds character," was how he put it. He tole bout what he'd been doin since he left Indianapolis. First, he'd lost all the money from the rasslin business at the dog track an what was lef he drank up. Then he got a job at a auto shop working under cars cause it was easy for him with the little dolly-wagon an all, but he said he got tired of oil an grease bein dripped on him all the time. "I may be a no-legged, no-good, drunken bum," he say, "but I ain't never been no greaseball."

Nex, he gone back to Washington where they's havin a big dedication for some monument for us what went to the Vietnam War, an when they seen him, an foun out who he was, they axed him to make a speech. But he got good an drunk at some reception, an forgot what he was gonna say. So he stole a Bible from the hotel they put him up in, an when it come his time to speak, he read them the entire book of Genesis an was fixin to do some excerpts from Numbers when they turned off his mike an hauled his ass away. After that, he tried beggin for a wile, but quit because it was "undignified."

I tole him about playin chess with Mister Tribble an about the srimp bidness bein so successful an all, an about runnin for the United States Senate, but he seemed more interested in Raquel Welch.

"You think them tits of hers are real?"he axed.

We had been in Savannah about a month, I guess, an was doin pretty good. I done my one-man band act an Sue collected the money an Dan shined people's shoes in the crowd. One day a guy come from the newspaper an took our pitchers an ran them on the front page.

"Derelicts Loitering in Public Park,"says the caption.

One afternoon I'm settin there playin an thinkin maybe we outta go on up to Charleston when I notice a little boy standin right in front of the drums, jus starin at me.

I was playin"Ridin on the City of New Orleans,"but the little feller kep lookin at me, not smilin or nothin, but they was somethin in his eyes that kinda shined an glowed an in a wierd way reminded me of somethin. An then I look up, an standin there at the edge of the crowd was a lady, an when I saw her, I like to fainted.

Lo an behole, it was Jenny Curran.

She done got her hair up in rollers an she looked a bit older, too, an sort of tired, but it is Jenny all right. I am so surprised, I blowed a sour note on my harmonica by mistake, but I finished the song, an Jenny come up an take the little boy by the han.

Her eyes was beamin, an she say,"Oh, Forrest, I knew it was you when I heard the harmonica. Nobody plays the harmonica like you do."

"What you doin here?"I axed.

"We live here now," she say. "Donald is assistant sales manager with some people make roofin tiles. We been here bout three years now."

Cause I quit playin, the crowd done drifted off an Jenny set down on the bench nex to me. The little boy be foolin aroun with Sue, an Sue, he done started turnin cartwheels so's the boy would laugh.

"How come you playin in a one-man band?" Jenny axed. "Mama wrote me you had started a great big ole srimp bidness down at Bayou La Batre an was a millionaire."

"It's a long story," I says.

"You didn't get in trouble again, did you, Forrest?" she say.

"Nope, not this time," I says. "How bout you? You doin okay?"

"Oh, I reckon I am," she say. "I spose I got what I wanted."

"That your little boy?" I axed.

"Yep," she say, "ain't he cute?"

"Shore is—what you call him?"

"Forrest."

"Forrest?" I say. "You name him after me?"

"I ought to," she say sort of quietly. "After all, he's haf yours."

"Hafwhat!"

"He's your son, Forrest."

"My what!"

"Your son. Little Forrest." I looked over an there he was, gigglin an clappin cause Sue was now doin han-stands.

"I guess I should of tole you," Jenny say, "but when I lef Indianapolis, you see, I was pregnant. I didn't want to say anything, I don't know just why. I felt like, well, there you was, callin yourself 'The Dunce' an all, an I was gonna have this baby. An I was worried, sort of, bout how he'd turn out."

"You mean, was he gonna be a idiot?"

"Yeah, sort of," she say. "But look, Forrest, can't you see! He ain't no idiot at all! He's smart as a whip—gonna go into second grade this year. He made all 'A's' last year. Can you believe it!"

"You sure he's mine?" I axed.

"Ain't no question of it," she say. "He wants to be a football player when he grows up—or a astronaut."

I look over at the little feller again an he is a strong, fine-lookin boy. His eyes is clear an he don't look like he afraid of nothin. Him an Sue is playin tic-tac-toe in the dirt.

"Well," I says, "now what about, ah, your. . ."

"Donald?" Jenny says. "Well, he don't know bout you. You see, I met him just after I left Indianapolis. An I was bout to start showin an all, an I didn't know what to do. He's a nice, kind man. He takes good care of me an little Forrest. We got us a house an two cars an ever Saturday he takes us someplace like the beach or out in the country. We go to church on Sunday, an Donald is savin up to send little Forrest to college an all."

"Coud I see him—I mean, jus for a minute or two?" I axed.

"Sure," Jenny say, an she call the little feller over.

"Forrest," she says, "I want you to meet another Forrest. He's a ole friend of mine—an he is who you are named after."

The little guy come an set down by me an say, "What a funny monkey you got."

"That is a orangutang," I say. "His name is Sue."

"How come you call him Sue, if it's a *he*?"

I knowed right then that I didn't have no idiot for a son. "Your mama say you want to grow up to be a football player, or a astronaut," I says.

"I sure would," he say. "You know anything about football or astronauts?"

"Yep," I say, "a little bit, but maybe you ought to axe your daddy bout that. I'm sure he knows a lot more than me."

Then he give me a hug. It weren't a big hug, but it was enough. "I want to play with Sue some more," he say, an jump down from the bench, an ole Sue, he done organized a game where little Forrest could thow a coin into the tin cup an Sue would catch it in the air.

Jenny come over an set nex to me an sighed, an she pat me on the leg.

"I can't believe it sometimes," she say. "We've knowed each other nearly thirty years now—ever since first grade."

The sun is shinin thru the trees, right on Jenny's face, an they might of been a tear in her eyes, but it never come, an yet they is somethin there, a heartbeat maybe, but I really couldn't say what it was, even tho I knowed it was there.

"I just can't believe it, that's all," she say, an then she lean over an kiss me on the forehead.

"What's that?" I axed.

"Idiots," Jenny says, an her lips is tremblin. "Who ain't a idiot?" An then she is gone. She got up an fetched little Forrest an took him by the

250

han an they walked on off.

Sue come over an set down in front of me an drawed a tic-tac-toe thing in the dirt at my feet. I put a *X* to the upper right corner, an Sue put a *O* in the middle, an I knowed right then an there ain't nobody gonna win.

Well, after that, I done a couple of things. First, I called Mister Tribble an tole him that anything I got comin in the srimp bidness, to give ten percent of my share to my mama an ten percent to Bubba's daddy, an the rest, send it all to Jenny for little Forrest.

After supper, I set up all night thinkin, altho that is not somethin I am sposed to be particularly good at. But what I was thinkin was this: here I have done foun Jenny again after all this time. An she have got our son, an maybe, somehow, we can fix things up.

But the more I think about this, the more I finally understan it cannot work. And also, I cannot rightly blame it on my bein a idiot—tho that would be nice. Nope, it is jus one of them things. Jus the way it is sometimes, an besides, when all is said an done, I figger the little boy be better off with Jenny an her husband to give him a good home an raise him right so's he won't have no peabrain for a daddy.

Well, a few days later, I gone on off with ole Sue an Dan. We went to Charleston an then Richmond an then Atlanta an then Chattanooga an then Memphis an then Nashville an finally down to New Orleans.

Now they don't give a shit what you do in New Orleans, an the three of us is havin the time of our lifes, playin ever day in Jackson Square an watchin the other fruitcakes do they thing.

I done bought a bicycle with two little sidecars for Sue an Dan to ride in, an ever Sunday we peddle down to the river an set on the bank an go catfishin. Jenny writes me once ever month or so, an sends me pictures of Little Forrest. Last one I got showed him dressed up in a tinymight football suit. They is a girl here that works as a waitress in one of the strip joints an ever once in a wile we get together an ass aroun. Wanda is her name. A lot of times, me an ole Sue an Dan jus cruise aroun the French Quarter an see the sights, an believe me, they is some odd-lookin people there besides us—look like they might be lef over from the Russian Revolution or somethin.

A guy from the local newspaper come by one day an say he want to do a story on me, cause I am the "best one-man band" he ever heard. The feller begun axin me a lot of questions bout my life, an so I begun to tell him the whole story. But even before I got haf thru, he done walked off; say he can't print nothin like that cause nobody would'n ever believe it.

But let me tell you this: sometimes at night, when I look up at the stars, an see the whole sky jus laid out there, don't you think I ain't rememberin it all. I still got dreams like anybody else, an ever so often, I am thinkin about how things might of been. An then, all of a sudden, I'm forty, fifty, sixty years ole, you know?

Well, so what? I may be a idiot, but most of the time, anyway, I tried to do the right thing—an dreams is jus dreams, ain't they? So whatever else has happened, I am figgerin this: I can always look back an say, at least I ain't led no hum-drum life.

You know what I mean?

252